# experience

*Psychology Series under the editorship of H. Philip Zeigler*

# experience:
## an introduction to a personal psychology

JOSEPH LYONS
University of California, Davis

Harper & Row, Publishers
New York, Evanston, San Francisco, London

Experience: An Introduction to a Personal Psychology

Standard Book Number: 06-044138-0

Library of Congress Catalog Card Number: 72-11492

# acknowledgments

Page 7: From Eugene Gendlin, *Experiencing and the Creation of Meaning: A Philosophical and Psychological Approach to the Subjective*. Copyright © 1962 by The Free Press of Glencoe, a division of The Macmillan Company. Reprinted by permission.

Page 15: Reprinted by permission of G. P. Putnam's Sons from *Invitation to a Beheading* by Vladimir Nabokov. Copyright © 1959 by Vladimir Nabokov. All rights reserved. Published by permission of the author.

Page 24: From Marguerite Sechehaye, *Autobiography of a Schizophrenic Girl*. English translation copyright © 1951 by Grune & Stratton, Inc. Reprinted by permission.

Page 49: William Hogarth, "Scene in Bedlam," from *The Rake's Progress*. Courtesy of the Metropolitan Museum of Art, Harris Brisbane Dick Fund, 1932.

Page 51: From Thomas Szasz, "The Myth of Mental Illness," *American Psychologist*, 15 (1960), 113-118. Copyright © 1960 by the American Psychological Association, and reproduced by permission.

Pages 52-54, 56-57. From Thomas Szasz, *The Manufacture of Madness*. Copyright © 1970 by Thomas S. Szasz, Trustee. By permission of Harper & Row, Publishers, Inc., and Routledge & Kegan Paul Ltd.

Pages 54-56: From Thomas Szasz, "Science and Public Policy," *Medical Opinion and Review*, 4 (May 1968), 25-35. Reprinted by permission of the publisher.

Page 68: From "Mrs. Robinson" by Paul Simon. Copyright © 1968 by Paul Simon. Used with permission of the publisher.

Pages 71-72: From Erving Goffman, "Asylums," in Donald Cressey, ed., *Prison: Studies in Institutional Organization and Change*. Copyright © 1961 by Erving Goffman. Reprinted by permission.

Pages 77-78: From Jay Haley, *Strategies of Psychotherapy*. Copyright © 1963 by Grune & Stratton, Inc. Reprinted by permission.

Pages 95, 190: Archibald MacLeish, "The End of the World," and "The Hamlet of A. MacLeish" in *Collected Poems 1917-1952*. Reprinted by permission of Houghton Mifflin Company.

Pages 98, 99, 100, 101, 102, 105, 106, 107-108, 110, 115: From Romola Nijinsky, *Nijinsky*. Copyright © 1941 by Romola Nijinsky. Reprinted by kind permission of the author and her agent. Eric Glass Ltd.

Pages 108, 112, 116-117, 121, 122: From Romola Nijinsky, ed., *The Diary of Nijinsky*. Copyright © 1968 by the University of California Press, Berkeley and Los Angeles. Reprinted by permission of the author and the publisher.

Pages 131-132: From Jean Genet, *The Thief's Journal*. Copyright © 1964 by Grove Press, Inc. Reprinted by permission of Grove Press, Inc. and, for British rights, by the author's agent, Rosica Colin Ltd.

Page 133: "The Crimeless Criminal." Reprinted by permission of *The Davis Enterprise*, Davis, California.

Pages 145-146: From T. V. Smith, ed., *From Thales to Plato* (2nd ed., 1956), pp. 313-316. Copyright © 1956. Reprinted by permission of the University of Chicago Press.

Page 153: Cartoon by Al Johns. Reprinted by permission from *The Saturday Evening Post*. Copyright © 1953 The Curtis Publishing Company.

Page 159: From Baba Ram Dass, "From Bindu to Ojas." Reprinted by permission of the Lama Foundation, San Cristobal, New Mexico.

Pages 159-160: From Leo M. Davidoff, "Migraine," in Max Pinner and Benjamin F. Miller, eds., *When Doctors Are Patients*. By permission of Mrs. Benjamin F. Miller, Executrix of the estate of Dr. Benjamin F. Miller.

Pages 165-166: From *Three Faces of Being: Toward an Existential Clinical Psychology*, by Ernest Keen. Copyright © 1970. By permission of Appleton-Century-Crofts, Educational Division, Meredith Corporation.

Page 173: "Richard Cory" is reprinted by permission of Charles Scribners' Sons from *The Children of the Night* by Edward Arlington Robinson (1897).

49955

Page 177: Letter in the *San Francisco Chronicle*. Reprinted by permission of Eugene Schoenfeld, M. D.

Page 193: From O. H. Mowrer, "Sin—The Lesser of Two Evils," *American Psychologist,* 15 (1960), 301-304. Copyright © 1960 by the American Psychological Association and reproduced by permission.

Page 204: From Werner M. Mendel, "The Phenomenon of Interpretation," *The American Journal of Psychoanalysis,* 24 (1964), 188-189. Reprinted by permission of the Editor of *The American Journal of Psychoanalysis.*

Page 206: From Carl R. Rogers, "The Necessary and Sufficient Conditions of Therapeutic Personality Change," *Journal of Consulting Psychology,* 21 (1957), 95-103. Copyright © 1957 by the American Psychological Association, and reproduced by permission.

Page 209: From Jean Genet, *The Balcony*. Reprinted by permission of Faber and Faber Ltd.

Page 210: "Peanuts" cartoon by Charles M. Schultz. Copyright © 1961 United King Features Syndicate, Inc. Reprinted by permission.

Pages 212-214: Joseph Wolpe, "Desensitization for Phobia." Excerpted from pp. 8-10 of script accompanying Tape No. 30 of the American Academy of Psychotherapists Tape Library, 6420 City Line Avenue, Philadelphia, Pa. 19151. Reprinted by permission.

Pages 212-214: From George Devereux, *Reality and Dream*. Copyright © 1951, 1969 by George Devereux. Reprinted by permission of Doubleday & Company, Inc.

Pages 225-226: From *Learning Foundations of Behavior Therapy* by Frederick H. Kanfer and Jeanne S. Phillips. Copyright © 1970 by John Wiley & Sons, Inc. By permission.

Page 226: From M. H. Klein, A. T. Dittmann, M. B. Parloff, and M. B. Gill, "Behavior Therapy: Observations and Reflections," *Journal of Consulting and Clinical Psychology,* 33 (1969), 259-266. Copyright © 1969 by the American Psychological Association, and reproduced by permission.

Pages 235-236: From Carl R. Rogers, "Persons or Science? A Philosophical Question," *American Psychologist,* 10 (1955), 267-268. Copyright © 1955 by the American Psychological Association, and reproduced by permission.

Pages 238, 239-240, 287-288, 288-289, 290, 293: From F. S. Perls, *Gestalt Therapy Verbatim*. Copyright © 1969 by Real People Press. Reprinted by permission.

Pages 255-256: From William H. Gass, "The Stylization of Desire," *New York Review of Books* (Feb. 25, 1971), pp. 33-37. Copyright © 1971 by William H. Gass. Reprinted by permission of International Famous Agency.

Pages 257-258: From Charlotte Selver, "Report on Work in Sensory Awareness," in Herbert A. Otto, ed., *Explorations in Human Potentialities*. Courtesy of Charles C. Thomas, Publisher, Springfield, Illinois.

Pages 260-261: From Ida Rolf, "Structural Integration," *Journal of the Institute for the Comparative Study of History, Philosophy, and the Sciences,* 1 (1963), 3-20. Reprinted by permission.

Pages 266, 267, 268, 269, 270, 272, 273-274: From Wilhelm Reich, *The Function of the Orgasm*. Copyright © 1961, 1973 by Mary Boyd Higgins as Trustee of the Wilhelm Reich Infant Trust Fund. Reprinted by permission of Farrar, Straus & Giroux, Inc.

Pages 267, 270, 272-273: From Wilhelm Reich, *Character Analysis*. Copyright © 1949 by the Wilhelm Reich Infant Trust Fund. Reprinted by permission of Farrar, Straus & Giroux, Inc.

Page 268: From R. Wallen, "Gestalt Theory and Gestalt Psychology"; pages 286-287: from R. C. Cohn, "Theory in Groups: Psychoanalytic, Experiential, and Gestalt"; in Joen Fagan and Irma L. Shepherd, eds., *Gestalt Therapy Now: Theory, Techniques, Application*. Copyright © 1970 by Science and Behavior Books, Inc. Reprinted by permission.

Page 271: From Carney Landis and William A. Hunt, *The Startle Pattern*. Copyright © 1939 by Carney Landis and William A. Hunt. Reprinted by permission.

Pages 276-277: From Alexander Lowen, *Physical Dynamics of Character Structure* (later titled *The Language of the Body* [Collier, 1971]). Copyright © 1958 by Grune & Stratton, Inc. Reprinted by permission.

*To Stan. Thanks.*

*Beloved Pan, and all ye other gods who haunt this place, give me beauty in the inward soul; and may the outward and the inward man be at one.*
                                                                        —*Socrates*

*It's all in the mind, y'know.*
                    —*George Harrison*

*Some day, after mastering the winds, the waves, the tides, and gravity, we shall harness for God the energies of love and then, for a second time in the history of the world, Man will have discovered fire.*
                                                        —*Teilhard de Chardin*

# contents

# experience

# part one
# in search of experience

# chapter
# 1
# experiencing
# and
# sensing

Picture a lively marketplace in the center of a village. From the time the stalls open at dawn until they close in the evening, the area hums with activity as the villagers move around, buying, selling, bargaining, and trading. What would we see if, at the end of a day of this activity, we could survey in one panoramic view all the transactions that had taken place? The weaver of silk, we would note, now has some fish for his dinner, and the fisherman has gotten a bit of cloth for his wife. The peddler of ironware carries home two loaves of bread and some fresh fruit. The baker, in turn, has a new pair of shoes, while the shoemaker has bought a new pot to heat his glue in.

And so it goes. A round of activity, hour after hour, has resulted in these transactions—for everyone in the marketplace is a seller but also a buyer, and so everyone is a potential customer of every other seller. The total amount of money among all these buyers and sellers remains the same, of course. It has served as the energy to carry the flow of the transactions.

Viewing all this, we would be entitled to draw some general conclusions about the overall patterning of village life, particularly its economic aspects. We might decide that what happened here on this day was a good thing and ought to be continued, say, on the first Wednesday of every month. Or we might conclude that it was wasteful and inefficient and that a better way could surely be found to satisfy the villagers' needs. But then we might also begin to think about this day's events in a distinctively different way. We might think of the individuals, not as anonymous members of groups or as nameless representatives of occupational roles—a fish peddler, a baker, a wife, or a husband—but as persons in whose unique lives we are interested.

As soon as we shift our emphasis from considering the village's activity as a whole to looking at its individual parts, we become aware that there were really two levels of activity going on all the time. Together with the *over-life* of market-place activity there was an *under-life* of individual behavior, of trials and efforts, successes and failures, comings and goings. In its own way the under-life was just as organized as the over-life and certainly just as significant—and it was clearly just as busy—but it proceeded in such a way that a panoramic view of the day's activities might easily overlook it. Here, evidently, are two interdependent levels or modes of activity going on side by side—or perhaps above and below, or possibly even intermixed—but as we look first at one and then at another it becomes clear that which one we become aware of depends on what we are looking for. If our interest is in the patterning of village life, especially its economic aspects, no amount of knowledge about marketplace activity will help us get in touch with the equally busy level of personal activity. Indeed, quite likely the one will interfere with the other.

In order to gain access to the under-life of the marketplace we would have to agree to give up a panoramic view, with all its advantages for the tourist or the economist. In place of this external approach we would have to take up a position, so to speak, that is inside the situation we want to observe. We would then spend some time in the marketplace, preferably participating in what is going on—or, if this were not feasible, at least taking an interest in the individuals as persons. Because our approach and stance are now different, as well as our relation to what we observe, the data we obtain will be different in many ways. Of these, the most significant change will result from our participant position. In this arrangement, observer and observed form an indissoluble unit, and no finding that refers to only one of the pair will be of any significance at all. This is the price paid and also the advantage gained by an observer who undertakes to insert himself into a situation in order to deal with its inner life.

## AN INTRODUCTION TO MY-EXPERIENCE

The preceding is only an example; my interest here is not in observing villages or their marketplaces, but people. Yet the example serves, I think, as a useful analogy to the problem of observing people. Here too the observer can choose between the over-life and the under-life as targets, between taking up an external position for considering the outer aspects of the person or assuming a participative stance to get at the inner aspects. The differences between these two views are great; the consequences of choosing one or the other are profound. Thus it is imperative that I make clear at the outset which stance I will be taking in this book. In addition to a factual view from the outside of the person I propose to explore a personal view from the inside. The general term I will use for the inner life of persons, and therefore the general heading under which I will expound a personal view, is *experience*—hence the title of this book. To begin, I will have to spend some time on the term itself, my reasons for using it, and what I mean by it.

### A New Term

Even before I have defined the way I will be using the term *experience*, it will be clear that there are many other, related terms from which it will have to be distinguished; that it may be taken in many senses; and that other writers have used it before me for their own, often quite different, purposes. I might have used the familiar terms *awareness* or *consciousness*, which certainly have long and even honorable histories in that gray area where psychology meets philosophy. I have not done so in order to stay clear of all the quarrels that these words bring to mind. For this reason I have chosen to bring back into psychology, as a foundational term, the reasonably neutral word, *experience*. It needs bringing back and dusting off, as is now becoming apparent, after a half-century of its being kept in the shadows like something either unmentionable or unthinkable. A growing interest in cognition, in so-called inner states, in consciousness, and in imagery and fantasy all testify to a recent change in the intellectual climate of psychology with its growing promise of a hesitant but well-meant welcome for a serious examination of experience.

To begin on a negative note, I can say what I do not mean by experience. I do not mean the term to refer to that vaguely useful philosopher's abstraction called mind, which can never be made concrete enough to help in an examination of significant problems in everyday living. Nor do I mean the sum total of the contents of the mind, or the brain, or the system of the person. This is the definition that we imply when we talk, as even the behaviorists do, about the person's "past experience." It refers to some collection of impressions that the person, having accumulated, now carries around with him, either in his nervous system or in some less specifically identified place in his head. Carl Rogers' definition of experience, for all its usefulness as a starting point for a theory of personality, is really only a sophisticated form of this version. He says:

> *This term is used to include all that is going on within the envelope of the organism at any given moment which is potentially available to awareness. It includes events of which the individual is unaware, as well as all the phenomena which are in consciousness. . . . I have in the past used such phrases as "sensory and visceral experiences" and "organic experiences" in the attempt to convey something of the total quality of this concept.[1]*

These distinctions are straightforward enough. However, one other distinction is more subtle and more difficult to make with confidence. A number of recent works have claimed to deal with experience, in the sense that the authors have considered as legitimate objects of scientific study such topics as perception, thinking, dreams, imagery, fantasy, hallucinations, and memory. An excellent example of this trend toward broadening the range of permissible topics is Peter McKellar's *Experience and Behavior.*[2] It represents a step beyond a purely behavioristic approach because the topics of perception and thinking and so on are not treated as modes of behavior, admissible only if an experimenter can observe them under his imposed conditions, but as phenomena in their own right to be studied by whatever means and with whatever data seem relevant. Similarly, Jerome Singer's recent study of daydreaming is directed exclusively at "inner processes" and at such phenomena as "the unrolling of a sequence of events, memories, or creatively constructed images of future events"; in his research Singer feels free to use introspective material, including a lengthy study of his own fantasies, as well as questionnaires and experimental investigations.[3]

The problem here, unfortunately clouded over by these authors' legitimate aim of broadening the range of topics permissible in a psychological science, is that no distinction is made between experience as experienced and experience as observed. They may not be the same phenomena; they may demand different approaches; and perhaps they do not even belong in the same discipline. The question remains to be explored and it should at least remain open. In this respect, then, my definition of experience is not to be settled in advance but will have to be developed as I examine the issues. All that can be offered at this point is a general and introductory statement: I will take the term *experience* to refer to what happens with me when I direct myself at what is happening. My definition is as general as that of Eugene Gendlin, although his view is somewhat more process-oriented: "that partly unformed stream of feeling that we have every moment . . . the flow of feeling, concretely, to which you can every moment attend inwardly, if you wish."[4]

Given this general statement about experience, I can offer for discussion a wide range of more specific statements—for example, that I experience my breathing, but not in the same way that I experience my anger or joy; that *my-experience* is mine alone and that no one else has access to my-experience unless I choose to display it or communicate about it; that no two persons can be possessed of the same totality of experience; that the aspect of me that we call my expression—of my face, or my posture, or my voice—refers to some of my-experience as it is grasped in your experience; that the ways in which experience

---

## ON EXPERIENCING

It is something so simple, so easily available to every person. . . . Let me give a few very simple examples, just to point your attention toward experiencing. In each example I will be using symbols that will specify some specific aspect of experiencing. Yet I would like you not so much to think of the specific aspect I refer to as to notice where you are inwardly looking.

First, feel your body. Your body can, of course, be looked at from the outside, but I am asking you to feel it from the inside. There you are. There, as simply put as possible, is your experiencing of this moment, now. . . .

Perhaps you feel some tension, or perhaps you feel at ease. . . . Let us fashion another, different sort of aspect: how

does your chest feel when you inhale?
. . . Nor need we remain with entirely
present descriptions. . . . I ask you: how
do you generally feel before a meal
when you haven't eaten for a long time?
(You feel hunger—using that word to
refer to your inward sense of it.) Or recall the way you feel after you have
filled your stomach, the heavy satiation.
Boredom, that strained impatient deadness which hurts in quite an alive way,
often is another aspect you can specify
in experiencing. . . .

Notice, it is always there for you. It
may not always be clearly definable . . .
[but] always it is concretely and defi-

nitely there, present for you, an inward
sensing. . . .

Perhaps now you know where I wish
to point your attention when I say "experiencing." Perhaps you can appreciate
the ubiquity, the constant presence, to
you, to me, and to anyone, of this concrete feeling datum: experiencing. . . .
Experiencing is a constant, ever present,
underlying phenomenon of inwardly sen-
tient living, and therefore there is an
experiential side of anything, no matter
how specifically detailed and finely specified, no matter whether it is a concept,
an observed act, an inwardly felt behavior, or a sense of a situation.[5]

---

is shared can become one of the major topics in the social sciences; that no two
persons even when seeming to share experience totally are ever collaborating to
the same degree or in the same way—except, perhaps, in love.

### Experience: Direct and Mediate

A first problem is that there seem to be three "parts" of this event; if I have
the experience of some target—for example, I experience my own breathing—
there is the *I*, there is the *experiencing*, and there is the *target*. Up to this point
I have used the term experience to refer loosely to the second and third of these,
to what I am doing as well as what my doing is directed at. To clarify the
matter, I would now like to restrict the term experience simply to the second
part, to the process carried on by me. (As for the first part, a definition and
analysis of the *I* are not my concern in this book. I will just take for granted
that every sentence that I make about my-experience refers to the *I* as subject.
Experience is always mine; never yours; never no one's; therefore it is always
I who experience.)

A second problem is this: What complicates any talk about experience, any
attempt to introduce and discuss it, is that experience seems to shift uncertainly

---

THE "PURE" EXPERIENCE
I suddenly realize that at last after
more than seventy years of looking I see
things as they are—what a phrase, "as
they are"—and not, as in all past years,
wrapped in concepts, e.g., man, woman,
flowers, trees. I see them now as islands
of black and white that move, or spots of

color making an herbaceous border, or a
garden of flowers.[6]

. . . the effort to establish relation
comes first—the hand of the child arched
out so that what is over against him may
nestle under it; second is the actual relation, a saying of THOU without words, in

the state preceding the word-form; the thing, like the I, is produced late, arising after the original experiences have been split asunder and the connected partners separated. In the beginning is relation— as category of being, readiness, grasping form, mould for the soul; it is the A PRIORI of relation, the INBORN THOU.[7]

. . . if the adult . . . gives himself over to the pure sensation himself, then he experiences a fusion of pleasure and sensory quality which probably approximates the infantile experience. . . . The emphasis is not on any object but entirely on feeling or sensation.[8]

May 11. 12:15 a.m. It is late, but I've just had an experience which I wish to record. At midnight I went topside to have a last look at the aurora, but found only a spotty glow on the horizon extending from north to northeast. I had been playing the victrola while I waited for the midnight hour. I was using my homemade repeater and was playing one of the records of Beethoven's Fifth Symphony. The night was calm and clear. I left the door to my shack open and also my trapdoor. I stood there in the darkness to look around at some of my favorite constellations, which were as bright as I had ever seen them.

Presently I began to have the illusion that what I was seeing was also what I was hearing, so perfectly did the music seem to blend with what was happening in the sky. As the notes swelled, the dull aurora on the horizon pulsed and quick-

ened and draped itself into arches and fanning beams which reached across the sky until at my zenith the display attained its crescendo. The music and the night became one; and I told myself that all beauty was akin and sprang from the same substance. I recalled a gallant, unselfish act that was of the same essence as the music of the aurora.[9]

. . . an attempt to accept all sense impressions in the form in which they are received by the senses, and to avoid all interpretation of them by the mind. . . . To accept the impression as it was received meant that one had to try to leave the sound simply as sound and not allow the mind to start on its sequence of interpretations. This could be done by fixing the attention on the sound IN THE EAR and following it until it faded into silence. . . . [And] now I became far more intensely aware of the characteristically golden-toned singing of the temple bells that lingered on the air until it was a gossamer thread of sound. It filled the whole of my awareness, and became a part of me; until, as it finally faded in the ear, I felt that I was losing a cherished possession.[10]

It's a wonder to discover the basic self, to discover the sweetness of it, for that is what it is, a sweetness so intensely vivid that one is overwhelmed by it, unable to handle it out of one's wits . . . the ego realizes it has a friend, a friend in the depths, it is not alone; not alone with its ideas or words.[11]

---

between two levels. There are times when I am sure that my experience has a direct and immediate quality. It seems pure; it seems to have grasped its object directly; its effect is striking enough to be described in many different ways. But at other times experience seems mediate, less direct, more like sensing or knowing or judging than pure experiencing. It is a subtle distinction to grasp, but anyone who has ever had both experiences will be able to testify as to the difference. On the one hand, I am angry (which equals, I experience my anger), and on the other hand, I am aware of my hostility. Or, on the one hand, I experience my body presence, and on the other hand, I know that my body is here. It is the difference between having-a-sense-of in place of having-an-experience-of; it is what happens to direct experience when knowing, judging, or interpreting is interposed between the I and its experience.

An example will help to point up the difference. There is a series of volumes for which prominent psychologists have been invited to write their autobiographies, for the enlightenment of colleagues and students as well as, one presumes, for the edification of future generations. One of the requests made of those asked to contribute was that they discuss their "feelings, personal motives, and aspirations." Leonard Carmichael, in the course of his autobiography, responded to this request as follows:

> *I do not know how to do this, so the following description will have to suffice. A Rorschach test was given to me some years ago and scored by one of the great authorities in this field. The results of this test showed that I did especially well in my ability to organize relations not commonly seen and in grasping connections between elements. On the Z factor my total was 145.5, which is among the highest scores that had been recorded. The range at that time for the healthy superior was said to be 50-85. I am not quite sure how to interpret this, but it is as close to a formal psychological analysis of my personality as anything that I know of.*[12]

He does not, he says, know how to make any reference—that is, any direct reference—to his own feelings, motives, or aspirations. In place of this, which would constitute a report of his own experience, he offers a set of impersonally known data, a judgment or interpretation, to describe himself. Now, I do not mean to imply here that Carmichael was not capable of having a direct experience of himself. I have no basis for making such a statement, and it would be impertinent of me to attempt it. But he has, in any case, given us a very clear example of the distinction between reporting an experience (in this instance, an experience of himself) and reporting a piece of knowledge about the target of that experience.

One way to get at the differences between direct and mediate reports of experience—or, to introduce the terms that I will be using, between *experience* and *sensing*—is to consider the various emotions. They provide convenient examples of two characteristics of experience: that experience is essentially irreducible and so must be accepted as such, and that experience is always mine. My joy, my sadness are simply known to me; that is all. I cannot tell you how I know this, and most of the time I could not even tell you what it is that I know. All that I can report, regardless of how I am pressed, is that on various occasions I have certain experiences, that I call these by their common names—sadness, joy, anger, love—that I know what the names refer to, and that I am fairly certain that much the same thing happens with you and with most other people. For the mind intent on precision, this is a messy state of affairs, but there is little that any of us can do beyond accepting it as a starting point and proceeding from there.

We can, for instance, go in the direction of science—that is, we identify my common experiences as a recurring fact; we associate that fact with similar, observed facts in other persons; and we attempt to find ties between these facts and some others such as changes in skin temperature, or quantity of tears shed, or scores on an adjective checklist. In the other direction, we can—as I will try to do in these pages—explore in organized fashion the characteristics of these experiences in me, raise the question of their fit with your similar experiences, and attempt to find out how these experiences find a place in the scheme of things that I call my world. One convenient starting place is simply a trip through the list of normal emotions to see how they appear in one's body-experience. When I do this, I find, for example, that the difference between sadness and anger appears clearly with respect to my breathing, my muscle tensions, my skin, my movements. To discover this all I need to do is give myself permission to have the emotions. They're mine, they're all I have, and I am in some way the responsible author of them, so I must begin by accepting them and not putting value judgments on them.

I stress the matter of accepting my emotions because it is also easy for me to discover the consequences of not fully accepting them. What then happens is that my direct experience of the emotion gets transmuted into a sensing of it; here the difference shows up very sharply. I am pretty sure that this is what usually happens with me, for example, under circumstances when many people would have the direct experience of fear. In my own case I will not permit myself this experience; under circumstances in which other people usually report something like, "You know, I'm really scared right now," I will say, if asked, "No, I don't feel scared at all." As far as I can say, I am being honest when I do this. I am not experiencing fear and then publicly denying it. Rather, I am engaged in denying it to myself first of all, and my public report is then a truthful account of what I do experience.

Mine is an extreme case, perhaps, but it does provide a useful instance to explore. When I report that I feel no fear, do I mean that I experience nothing in there, an emptiness where some familiar experience ought to be found? No, my experience is not one of nothing at all, but rather of—and now we begin to get more deeply into the matter—a substitute that is almost a feeling in itself. It is a near-feeling of calmness, effectiveness, almost of dismissal, with a little pleasurable superiority mixed in. What I can also report is that this complex emotional state does not have, for me, the feeling of immediacy that characterizes, say, my moments of joy or contentment. I can almost, but not quite, penetrate it to discover its shaky, almost rigid status: something held, and held to, rather than simply occurring. And so I now try to explore the body-experience associated with the state. I find immediately that most commonly the holding takes place across my chest, a band of stiffness and constraint that is centered quite neatly at the base of my throat. I find, in other words, that in the subtlest of ways I am holding my breath against the experience of fear.

This containment can be broken and in fact it was in a memorable session in a therapist's office. I was helped to breathe through the block, and so I found myself (and that is literally the correct expression) screaming in terror. I do not know what the object of my expressed fear was at that moment; I was not then afraid of anything or anyone. I was purely and simply experiencing fear and so expressing it—not sensing my own fear, and not merely knowing about it, and certainly in no way interpreting it or passing judgment on it. There is therefore nothing I can tell anyone about my experience in that session except that it was, and that it was mine.

This is, admittedly, a very special kind of evidence I am offering here. It is almost anecdotal, biased to an extreme degree, and so dramatically imprecise as to make it hardly comparable with an experience that might be reported by any other person or about a group of others. Yet it is evidence, and somehow we are going to have to find ways to integrate evidence of this sort with the kind that we are more accustomed to offer in regard to psychological problems; or if integration turns out to be impossible, then to offer at least a scheme on which we can agree for segregation into separate but equal categories of evidence.

### Areas of Experience: My Head

In the course of preliminary exploration of experience from the inside it will be useful to see if it comprises distinctive areas. My own attempts in this direction immediately suggest a tripartite breakdown into experience of my body, of my head, and of the world and its people. The first of these seems to me, on various grounds, to be the most fundamental as well as the most complex; I have therefore reserved consideration of it until the last chapter. The second, my head-experience, is, for me, very close to my usual state, and therefore offers an appropriate place to begin a more detailed exploration of the differences between what I have called experience and sensing.

When I revert to my usual state, by getting back up into my head, I become aware immediately that the ordinary me, or the way in which I experience myself most of the time, unthinkingly and nonreflectively, is that complex of ever-present thoughts and images, ideas and bodiless sensations, fantasies and memories and plans and unspoken words that churn around in my head. In this respect my findings about the ordinary me are similar to those of William James. When he attempted to track down "precisely in what the feeling of this central active self consists[13] . . . this self of all the other selves,"[14] he found on introspective examination that it was up in his head: ". . . it is difficult for me to detect in the activity any purely spiritual element at all. Whenever my introspective glance succeeds in turning round quickly enough to catch one of these manifestations of spontaneity in the act, all it can ever feel distinctly is some bodily process, for the most part taking place within the head."[15]

I notice on spinning around to catch the experience on the wing that my head is a busier place than I had ever imagined, but busy in a special way of its own. For me, at least, what goes on in my head usually pushes forward to take the stage of attention without any effort on my part. Unless I try to empty my mind of them, as I might do at the beginning of a body "trip," the head-experiences tend to take over, and if you were to ask me suddenly this is often all that I am able to report. Either an effort of attention or a situation which makes a direct demand on my body is needed to get me down out of my head.

What goes on up there is a collection of varied experiences, some of them not easy to categorize or even to describe. Here I would guess there are sharp differences between persons. For me, the contents of my head range from fairly well-organized fantasies that I usually spell out in words, in a kind of subvocal action-experience, to scattered, rapidly shifting bits of imagery and sound. And very often threading through it all or faintly in the background will be repetitive snatches of melody, so ever-present that I hardly realize they are there.

It is not too easy to turn inward in this way toward my own head-experience, but when I do I am struck with a clearly defined split between the fact that this is all going on and the targets to which the goings-on are directed. It is a split that is not at all as evident if I were to explore my body-experience. One difference here has to do with time. The targets to which my head-experience is directed are almost never in the present; they refer to the past or the future, as either memory or expectation. The experience itself, however, goes on right now. This is not a very startling discovery, but it is most curious because it points up the split between the not-now time of my targets of experience and the very evident now time of the experience itself. If my fantasy has to do with a plan for tomorrow, it is right now that I experience the fantasy. I really need an additional thought to remind myself that this moment's experience has to do with tomorrow's activity. The same is true with memories. I may think, how could I have made such a stupid remark; if I had only kept quiet, he would have respected me as a man of dignity and self-control. But caught up as I am in the shame, it is at this moment that I experience the shame and the memory, though both may refer to what is already past. Tomorrow's plan and yesterday's memory belong not to then but to now.

There are persons whose perverseness it is to take advantage of this dual aspect of head-experience. They are the ones who are so immersed in planning for some other time that they avoid the present entirely. They keep doing Tuesday's work on Monday, and so in the end Monday passes them by without happening and Tuesday never comes, and they lose both ways.

The difference between the now and the not-now is similar to the distinction between pure and indirect experience, or between experience and sensing. There is a kind of head-experience or awareness that is grounded in ongoing behavior; it is, as Enright puts it, "simply there, flowing along with behavior"[16]—and there is, by contrast, the busy work of the head, in which I indulge so often, that uses up energy by carrying on a separate and parallel life of its own. There is direct and naive perception and there is perceptual judgment; there is concentrated thought that is rooted in what I am doing and how I am doing it and there is thinking that takes me, quite literally, out of my body and out of my physical situation and transports me to ideal realms of imagining, planning, daydreaming. An example: Wolfgang Köhler, one of the founders of Gestalt psychology, once posed a question about everyday perception. "Why is it," he asked, "that when I look out my window, I see that building against the sky instead of the sky against the building?"[17]

This is a remarkable kind of question. My first reaction to it is not to look for an answer but to marvel at the question itself. I am simply astonished that someone could have, in one sentence, forced me to look at a familiar scene with entirely fresh eyes. Now that he has helped me, I am able to view this kind of familiar sight not already limited by what I am accustomed to and not pre-determined by what I may know about the scene, but with a special kind of freshness. I now see the view out my own window from the stance of someone who is inquiring, not verifying. What a contrast between the world as con-tinually discovered in this way and the "predigested information"[18] that passes for most of our everyday reality!

Grasping the world in this way is perception, to be sure, but in some im-portant way it seems to differ from perception that takes place entirely within prearranged categories. It is—at the moment I have no other term for it—a kind of pure perception, uncontaminated by the known and not yet debased by the contempt which familiarity is supposed to breed. It is perception as direct as some sensation can be, sensation that has been described by one scientist as the very basis of science itself: "Intelligent, meaningful science gradually develops with the observable world around us. This is the world of visible, audible, smell-able, touchable, dissectible organisms, rocks, and minerals, the visible stars and clouds, and the feelable atmosphere."[19] The reference here, as in Köhler's question, is simply to a direct experience, not with any implication that either experience or sensing is better or closer to some ideal, but rather as a way of emphasizing a mode of experience that is too often hidden behind another, more organized one that the world demands.

Another example, this one a matter of the senses rather than perception: If you hold in your hand a solid piece of lead in the form of a cube three or four inches square, you will have a peculiar experience. The cube will, of course, seem very heavy. More, it will seem much heavier than it ought to, so much heavier, in fact, that you will find that you must resolve the discrepancy between a felt object whose weight is very much and a seen object whose weight ought not to be very much.[20] One way that you may make this resolution is to have the curious experience that the block of lead is willfully pressing down on your palm, in the way that a person might. For many persons, the illusory experience is quite compelling and it provides a good instance of the almost pure experience of what-is-heavy. It is easy to conclude that the converse might also happen. When I hold in my palm a large, empty cardboard box I should be aware of a dis-crepancy between seeing a large box that ought to be heavy and feeling a box that is quite light. I should then have an illusory experience of the box lifting my hand or at least holding it up. No one, as far as I know, reports such an experience. Why not?

Since we are talking here about different kinds of experiences, the only way to answer the question of why we have one experience but not the other is to take a closer look at the experiences themselves. When I look at the experiences without preconceptions, I make the discovery that I can have the direct experience of something being heavy but not of something being light. My direct experience is always of what is, not of what is not; of a presence, not of an absence nor even a relative absence. Heaviness is a concretely and directly experienced phenomenon—a way that things can be in the world—whereas lightness is a fact that I may know about some of the things in the world. Therefore, there is no discrepancy to be resolved in my experience when I hold a box that feels lighter than it looks, because both the feeling and the looking are not direct but mediated, not experiencing but sensing. With the piece of lead, however, I have a true discrepancy to resolve between the lightness that I sense and the heaviness that I directly experience. What this suggests in general is worth exploring further: that illusions are situations in which we are forced to resolve discrepancies between experiencing and sensing.

### Areas of Experience: the World

There is a world of people and things about me and it is obvious that this constitutes a second distinctive area of experience. The world is, in fact, so inescapably there that I must work hard to get it out of my awareness. But in doing so, as I now discover, I do not put the world away, so to speak. That is not ever what happens in experience, for experience is always concretely of something and so I cannot dismiss something by trying to put it away. What I must do, rather, is turn to something else, and then the world recedes. But even when my world-experience is very much out of attention, it does not seem to have gone. For me at least, it remains as a fairly close and encompassing horizon. From this inner point of view, then, it is not at all a world out there, but an inescapably continuing part of me. The world is a functional part of my experience.

In addition, two characteristics of my world-experience of people seem to stand out. The first is that my experience of them is exactly equivalent to their experiencing me; the second is that the most salient dimension of my experience of them is the distance between us. These two characteristics merit a brief discussion.

I noted above that for me the presence of the world, and particularly of other persons, is constant, self-evident, and ever-present rather than doubtful— that it is almost always central rather than peripheral. I must add to this that I do not merely experience others as there, as a kind of collective target for my sensibilities. What I experience, rather, is that they and I are present to each other: they are there for me, but just as strongly I am here for them. I do not know exactly what this implies or even whether this is unique to me. It may be that I have more than an ordinary sense of constantly being onstage and that for other persons the balance between they-for-me and I-for-them would not ordinarily be equal but weighted much more toward the former. Another term for the I-for-them aspect of my experience would be *paranoia*, which is usually defined as an overdeveloped and unjustified sense of being in another's spotlight.

What I am describing here may be my own paranoid tendencies. Like so many of the other issues that are uncovered in attempting an honest account of one's experience, this will have to be compared extensively with the experiences of other persons before I can evaluate it.

For the second characteristic of my experience of people—their felt distance from me—I have a little more confidence that it is not completely idiosyncratic, but some justification and support may still be in order. What I am referring to here is the experience that another person is like me or unlike me, close to what I am or not, near the central core of my being or distant. This dimension, it seems to me, enters immediately, naturally, and inescapably into every experience I can have of another person as person. If that man is human to me, then he is myself in another guise; I could be him, I could be in his situation. I am potentially brother to every living person with whom I come together in a shared situation. When I need to stay clear of this agonizing kinship, as is most often the case, I must either declare him to be nonhuman or I must refuse to share the situation with him. Then I am free to sense him rather than experience him. With my knowledge well mediated by a lifetime of learned interpretations and judgments, I can shake my head sympathetically and say with all solemnity, "Ah, yes, there but for the grace of God . . ."

---

THE MOMENT

In Vladimir Nabokov's novel INVITATION TO A BEHEADING, the victim/hero Cincinnatus, condemned to be executed and awaiting his fate in a cell, is visited by his mother, Cecilia C. She babbles on foolishly, avoiding him and avoiding the situation they are in. His irritated question, interrupting her, provokes a moment of . . . but see how you would characterize it:

"Why do you tell me all this?" asked Cincinnatus.

She was silent.

"What's the point of all this? Don't you know that one of these days, perhaps tomorrow . . ."

He suddenly noticed the expression in Cecilia C.'s eyes—just for an instant, an instant—but it was as if something real, unquestionable (in this world, where everything was subject to question), had passed through, as if a corner of this horrible life had curled up, and there was a glimpse of the lining. In his mother's gaze, Cincinnatus suddenly saw that ultimate, secure, all-explaining and from-all-protecting spark that he knew how to discern in himself also. What was this spark so piercingly expressing now? It does not matter what—call it horror, or pity . . . But rather let us say this: the spark proclaimed such a tumult of truth that Cincinnatus's soul could not help leaping for joy. The instant flashed and was gone.[21]

---

In one very crucial respect my experience of the world and of its people is different from, say, my head-experience. It is only in regard to the world that the question of reality usually enters, whereas when the experience belongs to my body or my head, where it is all mine, the question usually cannot arise as to whether it refers to what is real.[22] My thoughts, my sensations, or my feelings when I experience them, are real, at least to me; perhaps it would be more exact to say that the question of their reality is irrelevant and so never arises. But when my experience is of the world and in particular of its people—a world and a people who can go their own ways—I must always be faced with the question of what might be there independently of my experience. Here, if anywhere, I badly need a test of reality.

It is the world's independence from my experience that gives rise to my own basic test of what is real. Suppose a child wakes at night frightened by a dream and in the dim light of his bedroom sees—or thinks he sees—a shadowy white figure peering at him over the foot of the bed. Instead of crying out, however, he first tries something. He wiggles his toes under the sheet and immediately discovers that the figure that he thought he saw was really nothing but the blanket sticking up over his toes. He laughs with relief at the discovery that what he saw was real. How did he know this? By a simple test—that he could make it go away. What is real is what can disappear. If no act by the child could change what he saw, if it remained the frightening image that it was as long as he remained in his frightened state, if it did not change either of itself or as a result of his action, then he would have known that it was not real, not a part of the world, but a part of him, that is, a figment of his imagination.

This is a good test, at least for the most fundamental aspect of the world, its presence or absence. But the test is not subtle enough to help with all the other aspects of the world and its people. Is my boss really more curt with me than with the other people in my department or is it just my imagination? Does that girl really like this boy or does his eagerness to have her like him make every little gesture on her part seem to him like a promise or an invitation? How is one ever to know for certain? Certain knowledge is a form of direct experience and most welcome when it occurs, but what is the more common experience falling short of this? The curious thing is that this is not an experience of uncertainty—for that is a direct experience in and of itself. Rather, falling short of the desired experience of other people seems to consist in something like shoring up a wall that is caving in. What is experienced is the resulting activity of shoring up rather than the condition of the wall that led to the activity. Thus when I fail to get my message across and I say to myself, "He certainly is hard to talk to," I am in this way reconstructing him, in my experience, along the lines needed to keep up my own self-confidence.

The mechanism has been called projection; its extreme case is paranoia. In its milder forms, however, it is the sum of all the games that we play because we cannot or will not meet the other person in direct experience. When the risks are too great to take we fall back on the fact of the world's independence, and we then reorder its reality status so that we can reconstruct it in terms more comfortable for us. We are all philosophers playing with the metaphysics of our experiences—unless we take up the challenge of acting in a world that can never be certain. This is the alternative: to join fully in situations and to experience ourselves directly as part of them, as children and animals must do. The gain would be the surety of direct and pure experience, but what of the great peaks and troughs when experience swings wildly at the mercy of events and people?

## THE CHARACTERISTICS OF HUMAN EXPERIENCE

Thus far I have discussed either my-experience, the singular and unique case, or experience in the convenient plural, that is, our experience insofar as it resembles my own. For convenience I chose to begin the treatment of the topic of experience by considering it as qualified by the adjective *my*. If I were to stick to this restricted view of experience, I might argue that experience is always my-experience; that your experience, so-called, is not experience at all except as I experience your expression of it; and that if for some reason I do not do this your experience reduces, for me, to a series of guesses on my part or else a known set of facts. I would then argue that experience in general is nothing but an abstraction.

But all this runs quite counter to a proposition that I—and I think most other persons as well—hold as a matter of faith. It is to the effect that I am not alone in the world as an experiencing being; that other persons also have their unique experiences; and that the separate my-experience belonging to other persons bears some general similarity to my own. Because I take this multiple proposition as self-evident, I can properly talk about some of the common or general characteristics of human experience.

### The Range of Experience

The first and most general characteristic of experience might be its range or limits. I think it can be said of the totality of my experience that at any one time it has a certain range, that it extends out to or reaches certain limits. The spectrum may be very wide or very narrow for each individual; it may contain many possibilities or few; it may be expressed in a myriad of ways or just barely. No matter which of these attributes holds true at any one time, however, the notion of range seems applicable.

We know very little in a systematic way about the range of human experience or its characteristics except in regard to some of its more exotic forms. How might we describe the experience, for example, in terms of range, of a dying person totally overcome with pain?

Does the range of my experience vary with my mood? For example, is the range contracted in depression, expanded in joy? What about the relation between range and emotion? Is what is beyond my range associated, for me, with fear or perhaps anxiety? What about affect-laden life states such as loneliness?[23]

I think of such an expression as, "It was just like a whole new world opening up for me," and what this might say in regard to the way a range of experience will alter with changes in one's life pattern. Think of moving away from home to begin college, or being released from prison, or having a religious conversion, or undergoing successful psychotherapy, or even reading a single great book.

How might the range of experience vary with so many of the conditions of life—with age, or sex, or historical era, with individual variations in intelligence or ability, or even with changes in the condition of one's body?

On this subject of range I can only raise questions and suggest problems for study. Much work remains to be done.

### The Structure of Experience

By the term *structure* I mean that inner articulation of one's experience when it is considered as a whole. Speaking for myself, I know that I do not simply have an experience in an undifferentiated sense. Every moment of experience is structured in some way.

Consider, first, that my experience seems to be structured differently depending on whether it is a body-experience or head-experience. If I deliberately shift back and forth between my body and my head, trying to compare the two areas of experience, I very soon discover that my body-experience is limited internally, my head-experience externally. I mean by this that my body appears to me as a shifting kaleidoscope of attention areas marked off by a rather diffuse boundary; the limits and the portions that are for the moment off limits seem to lie within the boundaries of my total body-experience. In regard to my head-experience, on the other hand, I very soon become aware of rather hard edges to my experience, limits beyond which I seem not to be able to push. But within these limits everything is available, nothing blocked out. Thus, I need my attention in order to bring one or another aspect of my body's functioning into focus, but the more attention I bring to bear on my head-experience, the more frustratingly clear it becomes that I am up against limits. If I begin a fantasy about eating, for example, I very easily reach a limit in regard to what I might eat. I try very hard to be rational, to talk myself into it, to tell myself firmly that this is only a fantasy—but there is no way I can imagine myself eating live worms. And the strange part is that I can't imagine why, and so the limit itself is off limits; in a very real sense, I can't think about it.

One aspect of the structuring of experience, then, is that it differs from one area to another. A second aspect is that some experiences, or some experiencing occasions, are more richly detailed and particularized than others; and I would guess that this is a highly individual matter. There is evidence, for example, that the field of experience, particularly in regard to visual perception, is more highly articulated in anger than in sadness. My own experience of colors, of my body, and of other persons, has become more finely structured as the result of some changes brought about in me through psychotherapy. Painters, I would suspect, have rather richly articulated experiences of certain visual aspects of the world, but not necessarily of other areas, such as themselves.

An even more interesting aspect of the structure of experience—perhaps, clinically, its most significant aspect—refers to areas within the totality that are in some way blocked out. A number of different terms have been associated with this blocking, since it is a phenomenon that plays an important role in the socialization process in all cultures. The blocking-out has been called dissociation, forgetting, repression, proscription, or taboo, depending on who applies the term and what the supposed conditions are for its occurrence. The taboo may be that aspect of experience so basic that, as Georges Bataille argues,[24] it gave rise to socialization itself. Man, he says, is the only living creature capable of denying himself the privilege of doing something. Or it may be, as Freud argued when he incorporated it in his theory under the name of *superego*, the individual's personal basis for morality: a rigid and unarguable parental proscription. It may take the form of a society's law; eight of the original Ten Commandments begin with "Thou shalt not," and all laws have taken the same form, as descriptions of what must not be done. What is taboo, then, is that part of my experience that is off limits to me. Either I dare not allow myself to enter that area or, if perchance I blunder in, my experience is likely to be one of shame or guilt or, at the very least, acute embarrassment as though at a ritual contamination. We experience this in milder fashion, though much more commonly, in our use of the euphemism, a kind of verbal small-coin of taboos, useful for most everyday transactions.

Since the taboo is off limits as experience, its very existence is unspeakable. This in turn gives rise to its very special characteristic: both the content of the taboo and its taboo status as such are not to be discussed or mentioned or thought about. In brief, because the taboo is a no-no whose tabooness is itself unthinkable it can only be described as a *meta-no-no*.

Taboos persist in spite of all our claims to sophistication and freedom of thought; thus it is not at all difficult to make up a new set of commandments

---

SOME COMMANDMENTS FOR TODAY

You may, on reading this list, be offended by some of it. This is unfortunate, but it will at least prove that these are genuine taboos. One of the marks of a true taboo is that those who hear it are offended to have it mentioned, even if the mention is for the purpose of reminding the hearers that it is a taboo.

1. Do not spit on other persons' food.
2. Do not touch yourself in the genital area in public.
3. Do not say the following words out loud in public.*
4. Do not do anything that will in-crease the amount of odor around you.
5. Do not eat the flesh of human beings.
6. Do not enter a public restroom of the opposite sex.
7. Do not have sexual intercourse with a member of your immediate family.

This list is merely representative. Any adult and most children could easily add to the list or make up another one.

* The power of this taboo requires me to refrain from listing these words; but that does not matter since every reader knows what they would be.

---

appropriate to contemporary standards. An even more glaring instance of the taboo as an off-limits area of experience is the existence of words whose use is forbidden.[25] To refrain from using a word, especially when the word is well known even if not familiar, is of course not the same as having the experience itself blocked out. There are apparently complex and subtle relations between the level of experience and the level of overt expression, as was revealed some years back in the course of experimental studies of subliminal perception.[26] But in any case it seems clear that the two levels are closely interrelated, so that, for example, to be unable to say a certain word out loud, and to persist in this inability, inevitably affects the experience itself. Even thinking about the word or just hearing someone else say it produces a special reaction, a thrill of excitement, or shame, or distress, or whatever.

### The Flux of Experience

A third general characteristic of experience, in addition to its range and its internal structure, is that it is in constant flux. It would be interesting to try to track down, if one could, the sources of all the changes that take place almost moment to moment in every area of experience. I don't at all mean by this suggestion to imply the kind of determinism of which Freud, for one, was so enamored; he was convinced that every single item and element of psychic experience could, if we only knew how, be tracked down to its ultimate source in some tremor in one's reservoir of surging biological energies. What I mean to suggest here is a possible search for the preconditions (rather than causes) of identifiable experiences—a flash of anxiety, a joyous mood on awakening, a clever idea, an urge to play golf. It may very well be that the sources and preconditions are far too general to be tied to such specific experiences. Perhaps only complex patterns of experiencing can be traced back in this way. The sources may be, as one hypothesis, exclusively in bodily changes—a real possibility, especially in regard to emotional states. Or they may begin in an act of will, as when I say to myself, "Well let's see, what kind of fantasy do I want to have now?" But can everyone do this? There are some preliterate tribes whose members make a practice, a rather commonplace and matter-of-fact practice, of dreaming the kind of dream they want to and thus using their dreams for practical purposes such as to solve problems or to get through personal crises.[27]

In any case, I seem now to have distinguished two major, general sources of change in my experience. For one thing, I can will to do or experience something. Does the spontaneous decision itself come from some other source? I am tempted to say that the answer is irrelevant, that the experience of willing to do something presents itself as a kind of starting point, that it does not permit the question of where it came from. Such a question would change the experience of willing to a quite different experience of being influenced. A second general source of changes in experience, as I mentioned, is in my body and in the usual case this would, I think, occur in terms of some state that arises without my willing it to be so. Perhaps this change in bodily state might also have been influenced—some would say it had been caused—by still other events either outside my skin or within it. But the pursuit of these causal chains down some reductionistic path toward the universal ultimate seems to me a tedious and time-wasting activity and quite irrelevant to the understanding I am trying to develop here.

As far as my own experience is concerned, I seem either to create a new and original event by way of a spontaneous decision or else I discover an event in my body and then come to terms with it as best I can.[28]

---

RECOGNIZING THE NEW EVENT

The objection that they are not crazy enough applies to all the attempts which have so far been launched at a radically new theory of elementary particles. It applies especially to crackpots. Most of the crackpot papers which are submitted to THE PHYSICAL REVIEW are rejected, not because it is impossible to understand them, but because it is possible. Those which are impossible to understand are usually published. When the great innovation appears, it will almost certainly be in a muddled, incomplete and confusing form. To the discoverer himself it will be only half-understood; to everybody else it will be a mystery. For any speculation which does not at first glance look crazy, there is no hope.[29]

---

This characteristic of experience, that it is always in a state of continuing change, has the very important consequence that I am then constantly at work in the world, actively making and remaking it for myself. Every change in my experience necessarily goes along with a change in the world as I exist in it. And these changes, because they are sensible to me, are necessarily irreversible. It is only in the external, mechanical world that what is done can be undone. My own world of experience, because it is embedded in my ongoing history, cannot ever reverse its direction. What is done is done, forever—or at least for as long as I remember it, for my memory is the repository of my history, and so what I do is always consequential for me, and I bear responsibility for it.

To take an example, suppose I start to write this book. I sit down at the typewriter, insert a sheet of paper and boldly type "Chapter One" at the top. Then I find that I have nothing to say this day, so I pull out the paper in discouragement, crumple it up, and leave the typewriter. The next day, at exactly the same time, with all external conditions the same, I sit down to make another try. Again, I take a fresh sheet, insert it, and once more type "Chapter One" at the top. Now, am I today directed at the same perceptual target as yesterday? Not quite. As far as I am concerned, today's sheet of paper may be identical to yesterday's, but it is the second in a sequence. In my experience, today's target would be the same as yesterday's only if I could wipe out of my memory any recollection of having made a prior attempt at this spot one day before. Since I cannot usually do this the change that took place in my world, when I typed a few words yesterday, is irreversible. Either my act, and the consequent change in my world, escapes my notice, or else it is meaningful to me and so brings me to a new place. Whatever I do is done, forever, so long as I retain any memory of it. For someone who longs for stability the prospect is indeed frightening. For this reason, much of the busy work that occupies us consists of ways to get things done while still preserving a semblance of sameness in a constantly changing personal world.

### Experience as Directed and Significant

Two interconnected characteristics of experience, both of which have been implied in much of the foregoing discussion, need now to be made explicit. The first of these is that what I experience always has some meaning and significance for me; and the second is that all experience must have a target, must be directed at something, or be an experience of something.

Whatever my experience is directed to has some meaning for me; and perhaps vice versa as well. I seem to care about what goes on in my world, and so for me it is not a screen crowded with neutral events but a patterning of situations in which I, myself, am caught up. I can only dismiss the world by means of an effort. Admittedly, my caring does not always take appropriate or consensual forms; that in fact may be the major source of differences between people—that individual commitments to unique worlds take odd and diverse forms. But in any case, I think that here is the essence of what I mean by experience: What is experienced has meaning, makes sense, and so requires caring. For me, the world is well meant.

The other, correlative characteristic is that experience is always about something. Suppose that I try, by stopping for an instant, to catch my own experience on the wing. I try to find out, right now, at this instant, what is going on with me. I very soon discover that there is no way to stop completely because I go on experiencing even as I work away at what was going on in the just-past moment of stopping. But what little I can grasp, like a fleeting glance at something whizzing by my shoulder, goes something like this: I was feeling this, moving that, thinking one thing or imagining another. You will notice that each of these verbs has its object. I was not just in a feeling state without content, but feeling something; and I was not just thinking or imagining in the abstract, so to speak, but literally and concretely in regard to some object of thought or imagining. It is always a matter of thinking something, imagining something. The world appears to me in experience as a changing field of intended objects (with perhaps an I intuited dimly at the center), and so I find a noun for every one of my verbs, without exception.

Easily discoverable as this is, I cannot dismiss it on grounds of triviality, for it turns out to be a general principle of experience or, as Franz Brentano said, and then Edmund Husserl, the basic principle of the mental life and of all psychic activity.[30] Yet pointing out this general principle will lead most persons to nod, if not to yawn, and then to say something like, "So what?" Once the characteristic of experience—that it is always directed at some object—has been noted, it seems almost absurdly self-evident; so why should one stress the obvious? But the principle that is involved here may be more than a self-evident and trivial truth that remains unnoticed until pointed out, like the key piece in a puzzle. What it implies when it is traced out in all its implications is that it does make some difference whether or not experience is treated as a series of isolated systems. True, such systems can be mechanically or structurally isolated, as, for example, is done by specialists in regard to the visual apparatus. But this is feasible only when organismic processes are considered in their external aspects in the same way that one might examine and analyze a piece of machinery. Viewed from the inside, as it were, from the standpoint of experience, every process or system is revealed as functionally tied to its target. Thought and thought's object are one; the system is not just an "empty" process but always filled with its contents. In short, it makes no sense to speak of a visual experience in the abstract, only of the concrete seeing of something.

It might not be very difficult in the near future to build into a robot a small facsimile of one of the processes that presumably goes on in a person's head. It might even be possible to build in a mechanism approximating "awareness" of an approaching target in the sense that when the appropriate stimulus energy impinged on the proper receptor organ, energy fields would be triggered, internal parts would be energized, and information would then be sent around the network. But one characteristic of experience would still be missing. The poor robot might be busily engaged in thinking (I suppose the term is appropriate here) but it would not necessarily—that is, inevitably—be thinking *of* anything. Its internal mechanism would be energized and functioning, but that is all. Process without target, experience without object—this defines the machine in contrast with the living creature with its sensory equipment. For these sensory receptors, so-called, which are found on the surface of the living creature are far more than mere bodily organs placed for convenience on the outside of the skin; they can only be understood as true functional parts of the surround. Does this notion seem far-fetched? It should not, for it has its parallel in familiar instances in nature—for example, the foraging honey bee. In a very real sense, it can be said that functionally the flower is part of the bee's anatomy. Similarly, whenever my sense organs clue me into a situation in which I can potentially take a meaningful part, my sensory apparatus and its target together form a functional unit.[31] The link is broken when or if I give up the possibility of participating in the situation with the target. For this reason the barnacle, in that portion of its life cycle when it becomes attached to a fixed object and loses its organs of mobility, also gives up its external sense organs.

If my experience is, by its nature, always directed at its target, and if I have at any one time an ongoing field of experience, there should be at any time a concurrent target field. What is this latter field? It is my world, of course. What I am saying here is that my experience occurs in my world and is directed to it. But I am also saying that this is a necessary consequence of experience; that it is not possible for me to get out of my world; that as long as my ongoing experience continues (and I can think of no way that it can stop in a living person), it will be directed actively toward my world; that to be in-my-body, as I necessarily am, is to be in-my-world, as I must be. I am in a situation whatever I do, not in the existential vacuum postulated by behavioral theorists; a robot may suffer the ultimate *angst* of being worldless, never I.

Hence the curious expression *in-the-world*. The hyphens are necessary, at least in the English language, to emphasize that this is not a case in which one independent thing, an I, is inserted into a place separate from it called the world. Rather, to be in-the-world defines me and my-experience as an adjective defines a noun.

And because I am always in a world that is meaningful to me my world is always peopled. I can imagine stripping it of any of the elements that make it up—the objects, kinds of feelings, possible situations or events, anything at all—but not of eliminating the very possibility of people. That there may be no one out there is the most terrifying of all possibilities, the one fear that lies behind every other fear. I cannot imagine what my life would be like if I could not possibly care for anyone or if I could not even hope that anyone would care whether I lived or died.

## THE UNREAL AND THE REAL

One day, while I was in the principal's office, suddenly the room became enormous, illuminated by a dreadful electric light that cast false shadows. Everything was exact, smooth, artificial, extremely tense; the chairs and tables seemed models placed here and there. Pupils and teachers were puppets revolving without cause, without objective. I recognized nothing, nobody. It was as though reality, attenuated, had slipped away from all these things and these people. Profound dread overwhelmed me, and as though lost, I looked around desperately for help. I heard people talking but I did not grasp the meaning of the words. The voices were metallic, without warmth or color. From time to time, a word detached itself from the rest. It repeated itself over and over in my head, absurd, as though cut off by a knife. . . . During class, in the quiet of the work period, I heard the street noises—a trolley passing, people talking, a horse neighing, a horn sounding, each detached, immovable, separated from its source, without meaning. Around me, the other children, heads bent over their work, were robots or puppets, moved by an invisible mechanism. On the platform, the teacher, too, talking, gesticulating, rising to write on the blackboard, was a grotesque jack-in-the-box. . . . On the way to school in the morning at seven-thirty, sometimes the same thing happened. Suddenly the street became infinite, white under the brilliant sun; people ran about like ants on an ant-hill; automobiles circled in all directions aimlessly; in the distance a bell pealed.[32]

. . . things had completely changed. Instead of infinite space, unreal, where everything was cut off, naked, and isolated, I saw Reality, marvelous Reality, for the first time. The people whom we encountered were no longer automatons, phantoms revolving around, gesticulating without meaning; they were men and women with their own individual characteristics, their own individuality. It was the same with things. They were useful things, having sense, capable of giving pleasure. Here was an automobile to take me to the hospital, cushions I could rest on. . . . As I entered my room after arriving at the hospital, it was no longer my room but living, sympathetic, real, warm. And to the stupefaction of the nurse, for the first time I dared to handle the chairs, to change the arrangement of the furniture. What unknown joy, to have an influence on things; to do with them what I liked and especially to have the pleasure of wanting the change.[33]

So I fill my world with other persons; my energy is devoted to peopling the world. Some are real, some remembered or imagined, some known to be present, others long gone into the world's history, some appearing to me as they might appear to others, perhaps some not—but all of them, I proudly boast, my own creations, my million Adams and million Eves. I value some more and others less; I seek out one and tend to avoid another; I need this one far more than that. But they are there in an increasingly more populated world, for none are ever completely gone and new ones keep arriving. My mother is dead, but she surely belongs there. My daughter is now grown up, but my-daughter-as-child-aged-four lives on, side by side with a much bigger girl whom in some ways she resembles. The president of the United States lives in my world, a man something like but something unlike the well-known president who, I believe, resides in yours. And a friend who works with great competence with his hands is here very close—a much bigger person in my world than (I'm sorry to say) in his own. The actual world has a relatively small population, only four-plus billion. My world not only has far more people, it is far less crowded.

The meaning that my world has for me is tied, inescapably, to those who people it. They provide its significance and most of its possibilities. They are my targets. They are where I invest my caring. I can't help this. I am not only situated in my world with all these people of my creating, I am also caught with them in value-laden circles of reciprocal meanings. The intricate minuet of our relations is always to the tune of things mattering between us, of my caring and being convinced that others do also, of their then acting toward me as though they cared about what happened, and of my reacting in turn. In such a charged arena things at times can turn out wondrously right, but perhaps just as often they can go wrong, even disastrously wrong.

## THREE REGIONS OF EXPERIENCE

The survey of experience that I have presented thus far suggests that each person is composed of many regions of experience, not all of which are available to him in the same way. It is possible to distinguish three regions of experience—central, mediate, and peripheral:[34] (1) some regions of experience are *central* to the person, in the sense that they refer to him as a specific and unique individual, to his own past and his history, to the body that is his alone, or to the individual life situation that no one but he can occupy; (2) other regions are *mediate*, in the sense that they refer to the person as one among others, as one man or one woman in company with others of the same kind, or as a member of a known group; (3) and still other regions are *peripheral*, in the sense that they refer to the person as situated in certain historical and cultural contexts, such as an American of the professional middle class in the last half of the twentieth century.

Let me return to the first person singular in order to explore some of the consequences of this division. In general, I would say that at any moment I fully experience only the region that is closest to my own center. If I want to go beyond this central and personal knowing I have to turn to the experience that is to be found in more peripheral regions. Thus, my personal association to a picture of my father might be a groundless and irrational fear. Unless I can find some other, less central region of experience on which to take a stand, I might stay trapped and ineffective in this fear. But if I have available a more mediate region of experience referring to my age—let us say that I am middle-aged and therefore not a child in the presence of his father—I may be able to take a stand in that region, so to speak, and come to the conclusion that I have no reasonable basis for my fear. In general terms, in order to avoid being caught in an experience belonging to some region, I need to get a grip on the experience by having available a region that is less central, more peripheral, further from my immediate, vital center—in a word, more distant and impersonal. A full awareness of myself as a historically and culturally conditioned being will therefore save me a lot of personal bewilderment or anguish. I will then be able to place my personal experiences in a proper perspective.

An example is the leper. The condition itself is no longer a thing of horror, yet the word still evokes, uncontrollably, some response of aversion in the twentieth-century citizen. My own experience is that the word *leper* calls back, over the span of five centuries, a faint reminder of what it meant to citizens of another age.[35] I seem to have no control over this; it is as though the experience associated with hearing this word lies in a region for which I have no corrective. Whatever experience I have in regard to this word, it cannot be handled by reference to another region; there are none, and I am caught by what the word signifies for me. It is like the more familiar experience that is evoked when we suggest to some persons that they eat a live worm. There is no rational stance they can be persuaded to take that will change their response. I mean here not simply the response of saying, "No, thanks, I'd rather not," but the total reaction, with all its associated affect. For most persons, there is no region that is more peripheral, less central, more impersonal, on which they can base a reasoned awareness of the pros and cons of the matter; there are no such regions, and they are caught by the total signification. They can neither change their position nor even talk about why they can't change their position.

For each of us there are individual experiences that trap us with some laden significance and for which we have neither recourse nor explanation. In addition, every culture shares certain experiences among its members, and they will usually respond in similar ways, just as most of us in our culture will respond predictably to the word *leper*. Finally, there may be experiences so general that they run through all the history of human civilization, or perhaps even antedate it. In short, there seem to be experiences within each of the three regions—central, mediate, and peripheral—which the individual cannot handle by finding a more impersonal stance.

Some examples may make clear how powerful is the grip that these nether regions of experience have on us, the regions closer to our individual centers having proportionately greater power. Least central, but still moving, are collective images such as those related to rising or sweeping up versus falling or sinking down. We are all moved in the same way toward visions of hope in one case and despair or loss in the other, yet our response is as inexplicable as it is unarguable. In the median range of such regions there is the phenomenon that gave rise to our word *panic*. To the ancient Greeks, the term referred to the terrifying possibility that Pan, god of lustful animality in the dark forests, might suddenly appear in a public square in the bright sunlight of noon. The image, the possibility by which the Greek citizen was (truly) possessed, was of proud reason overcome by brute passion, of order collapsing in the face of unreason, or, in a word, panic. Finally, there is a personal and individual region, exemplified by certain kind of possibilities that I sense, but can never know, within myself. The madman is one such possibility. If I were to look in the mirror there is no way that I could ever see a woman or a leper, but if I chance to look at just the proper angle I might catch a terrifying glimpse of that region of Me forever hidden from myself. It is no more than a shadow at the corner of my gaze, a secret given only to me, and to you, and you, and you. It is a secret that all of us may sense and none can share. The name of the watchman at the gate to this region is Fear.

### The Public Secret

In every region of experience, then, the individual can be trapped in a reaction for which he has no answer; it is as though he is overcome. The concept behind this class of experiences has been of interest to most thinkers who have concerned themselves with problems of experience and awareness. Freud, in particular, made the phenomenon into a central pillar of his theoretical system, under the name of the *Unconscious*, although he restricted his use of the term to central and mediate regions of experience. Jung added the concept of *collective unconscious*, with its archetypal experiences in the third, peripheral region. For both these thinkers, and to others as well who have thought about such uncontrollable experiences, the phenomenon can be summed up in this way: There are always some regions of experience that are outside awareness; the totality of the person as an experiencing being is greater than can be summed up in his current awareness and report.

One appropriate term for this phenomenon, I suggest, is *the public secret*,[36] that reverberating set of presences that each person both hides from the world and shares with his fellows. My term is meant to refer to a person's whole life— to the general fact that each one of us comprises a great congeries of possibilities that can profitably be viewed from a thousand different angles and to the general fact that each of us, like a great, unique diamond, can be turned this way and that by the world and by history in an endlessly changing patterning of meanings. Each life among us, even the meanest and smallest, is many lives, every one significant in its own way; there is almost no limit to the number of biographies that might be written about anyone at all. Were we only a collection of facts this could not be said, but the first great consequence of our nonfactual status is just this: as persons we are experience incarnate, experience actualized in the world, therefore inexhaustibly rich in meaning to ourselves and to others.

Within the totality of the public secret that defines each of us there is an area of individual meanings that is closely tied to personal functioning and has most probably come out of the vicissitudes of one's personal history. A fear of swimming, a special joy in seeing a fire flame up, an inability to control a tightening of the throat muscles when frustrated, shallow breathing, easy blushing, talking too fast or too low or too loud, a strong temptation to eat when depressed— these are all familiar indicators that almost define individual persons. They are often integral aspects of total functioning as well, their meanings intertwined with the person's total public secret, but they are special in that they are written into everyday behavior and might be traced to specific events or sequences in a developmental history. They are, in short, just the kinds of material that clinicians work with, and they closely resemble the data that gave evidence for Freud's first hypothesizing of unconscious processes.

What Freud and other pioneer psychoanalytic clinicians sensed as they began to deal intimately with their patients—for we have to keep in mind that theirs was the first true psychotherapy, in the sense of a personal encounter charged with import for change—was that each individual lived out a set of dynamic mechanisms, and that these in turn produced in the individual an under-life of dreams and wishes and motives and possibilities, usually centered around the content areas that his culture and upbringing had taught him were to be sternly kept out of everyday awareness. A half-century or more ago in Vienna this meant Sex. For many persons, then as well as now, it also meant being angry or being afraid or—as Wilhelm Reich was to discover, to his own surprise— even being happy. In any case, it was whatever the person, as his own worst enemy, had taught himself that it was bad to do or think or feel or want—so bad, in fact, that keeping it out of awareness had long since become purely habitual, something that his own normal functioning took care of without his even knowing any more that this was happening. Within each individual, personal circumstances intermixed with this socially conditioned under-life to produce the patient's own public secret which Freud, without quite understanding the phenomenon, then labeled the patient's Unconscious.

From the vantage point of myself experiencing, the phenomenon of the public secret can be described in another way. As an example, consider what happens to me, in experience, in the course of carrying out an ordinary act in the world. When I do something spontaneously rather than from sheer, unthinking habit or from being ordered to do it, I have a kind of experience-in-advance of how it will go. But the consequences are never exactly what my experience promises me. I seem to be in a continuing state of mild wonder that things don't fall into place for my efforts. Because of this wonder, and because I have no way to prepare for the unexpected, it is as though I kept stumbling over the threshold of my own consciousness. Just at the point of stepping through the threshold into action I stumble again, and each time it is a little surprise.

From the point of view of an external observer it is easy to see what I am referring to here. The world offers resistance to most of our action; almost nothing of what we do is effortless. We are so accustomed to this fact that we have learned to put up with it and so ignore it, but it is easy to arrange matters so that we are once again forcibly reminded, as Lee Meyerson has shown: When subjects are required to physically incapacitate themselves and then report on their experiences, they remark on them with great surprise[37]—as did the subject who strapped one leg so that it could not be bent in walking. "I never knew there were so damn many steps in this building!" The resistance that had ordinarily been overcome as a matter of routine was now unexpectedly brought to his attention. The real world is mostly background for what we do in it and only appears noticeably when it breaks down—as when the ballpoint pen runs dry—or when we are weakened and can't manage to overcome the normal level of the world's resistance.

In terms of my own experience, there is a sense in which I always know that the world is there, a running comment on my ongoing efforts, just outside the threshold of my consciousness in the form of a covert resistance. Unless I choose to stay on the inner side of the threshold, I have to take my chances on what will happen whenever I act, and in particular when I act in relation to other people. Of course, I do have some alternatives as a recourse if I choose not to act in the world; both fantasy and dream provide me with exits without my having to cross the threshold. But aside from these, whatever I do is sure to bring me up against the world, stumbling a little and never being able to prepare for it, and thus continuously adjusting, adapting, forced to make my way because the world is not made for me.

This lifetime of adaptive acts is a real part of Me, but not in the way that my continuing inner experiences are part of Me. What is inner is known to me first as a continuing body-experience and then as it appears in me in emotion and wishing and immediate knowing. What is on the other side of the threshold is known sometimes immediately, but at other times only by hearsay; at times almost directly, at times by gossip and report or else mirrored back from its consequences. "Each of us," says Ronald Laing, "is the other to the others. . . . But what we think is less than what we know: what we know is less than what we love: what we love is so much less than what there is."[38]

All of it makes up the total Me, a primary my-experience and that other part of Me that, like a secret which I keep on display, I reveal without telling. What I am, to describe it in still another way, is "a network of significative intentions which are sometimes clear to themselves and sometimes, on the contrary, lived rather than known."[39] In the course of everyday behavior, dulled by routine and by the avoiding of risks, masked by the strictures of social convention, I am not likely to show much except what is overt and on the surface—directly observable actions, familiar behaviors, or outstanding expressions. But in the clinical session, where each of the two participants is kept alerted to the possibilities in every interchange, where they both risk the consequences of a highly charged encounter, action will be neither routine nor dulled. The patient in particular is free to parade his public secrets for the perceptive therapist to zero in on. The balance may not be even but to some extent each will see more in the other than the other sees in himself. Each one will appear larger than life or, more exactly, each will begin to appear as large as the true extent of his own life possibilities. Whether this phenomenon is called by its technical name, the Unconscious, or whether it is understood in terms of publicizing the outer aspects of one's experience and sharing respective public secrets, it would seem to provide a key to the data that are unique to the clinical session.

## PROSPECTUS

In this opening chapter I have introduced the notion of experience, which is what this book is about, and have started to discuss it in terms of its major characteristics. A distinction made at the beginning of the chapter will now be useful as a basis for outlining the remainder of the book. In my opening example, concerning two related approaches to understanding the activity of a village marketplace, I referred to a level of over-life and a concurrent level of under-life, and to an external view that focused on the former, as distinct from an inner, participant view that focused on the latter. The inner and the outer, then, are two ways of looking at almost any complex phenomenon, particularly those in which can be identified an interior realm of activity in addition to what is external, evident, or overt.

This is a distinction that applies most profoundly to aspects of the person, and indeed my chief reason for building my discussion around the notion of experience is to emphasize the inner aspect of persons that has for so long been ignored in psychological theory. But as the history of psychology has clearly shown, persons have their outer aspects as well. The conjunction of these two aspects will furnish the basis for the treatment of various issues that follows. I plan to discuss four major themes, in each case dealing with both the outer and the inner aspects. Together the four themes cover most of the significant issues in a clinical discipline and in treating each of them from both an outer and an inner vantage point, while declaring a bias for the inner or experiential, I hope to provide a clinical survey and at the same time to explore some clinical possibilities that have until now been underemphasized.

The first of the themes I will discuss, madness, provides the material for Part Two. In Chapter 2 I will discuss the phenomenon of madness from an outer viewpoint—its history and institutionalization, as well as contemporary critiques of current modes of treatment. Chapter 3 provides my own contribution to an understanding of the schizophrenic state and leads to an extended case study, in Chapter 4, in which the outer and the inner views are compared in regard to specific clinical data.

The second major theme, centering on the topics of neurosis, deviance, and identity, will be discussed in Part Three, in two chapters. In the first of these, Chapter 5, the history of some significant modes of deviance is treated, as a way of approaching this problem from the outer view, and in Chapter 6 I look at the problem of neurosis from the inside.

In Part Four, the third of the major themes, psychotherapy, is considered, first in Chapter 7 in terms of its rules and roles, and then in Chapter 8 in terms of the major changes in these respects over the past half-century. These two chapters constitute the outer view of the theme. The inner view is then discussed in Chapters 9 and 10, in which two major directions for clinical practice and theory are discussed: the body-oriented approaches pioneered by Reich and the new forms of theater introduced by Fritz Perls. Finally, in Chapter 11 I attempt to consider, in the light of the foregoing discussions of madness, therapy, and identity, some possibilities for a fourth theme, psychological theory. Here I discuss my-body-experience and the notion of Allowing as a basic concept for a personal, experiential psychology of the helping arts.

# part two

## on madness

# chapter 2
# the Stranger in our midst

The beginnings have been very well described by Michel Foucault.[1] By the end of the Middle Ages leprosy had almost disappeared, and madness very soon took its place as the great mysterious affliction of mankind. Within a few hundred years special institutions were established to define madmen as special types of outcasts. One of the earliest of these, now buried in the folklore of the past, was the Ship of Fools, a mythical vessel on which mad persons, set adrift and cast off from society, wandered endlessly, homeless as only the perpetual seafarer can be, yet serving as a continuing moral comment on their saner brethren.

As established cities grew and prospered, it became a matter of local circumstance or budget that determined the nature of the permanent institutions built to house madmen and other outcasts. Hellholes fully worthy of modern slum technology were in full swing in most countries by the end of the eighteenth century. In them the outcasts and dregs of society were immured, often for life, at a level of debasement far lower than was meted out to domesticated animals. In the less affluent communities, where funds did not allow for the construction of special buildings, the town or county almshouse served as a general refuse heap for the poor—particularly poor orphans, the alcoholics, the feebleminded, the crippled and maimed, the deaf, who were usually mute as well, the epileptics, the brain-damaged, and many of the malcontents, the criminals, the rebels, and the alienated, as well as the madmen themselves—a swarming dung pile of derelict humanity.

But in the eighteenth century a reformist spirit began to sweep over much of Europe and America. Fresh and radical political forms appeared in France and the new United States. The Quakers made their noble influence felt, first in England, and then in the States. At last the pitiful victims began to be unshackled, at the same time that the senses of the mentally retarded were beginning to be freed with the founding of special schools by Edouard Seguin in France. Thereafter a steadily more industrialized society found more efficient, less openly brutal ways of dealing with its outcasts. For the madman, prototype of the stranger and the deviant, the mode of treatment followed the winds of the prevailing social philosophy. So it was that beginning in the late eighteenth century a profession arose with the assigned duty of patrolling this portion of society's perimeter. That specialty of medicine now called psychiatry was called upon to preserve the walls against this incursion from some wilderness of the antihuman.

A strange quirk of history, indeed. Here was a condition that had been viewed, and often accepted, in a dozen different ways by as many societies throughout history. Out of this range of possibilities, we have increasingly chosen to see it, or explain it, as an illness. We decided that it can be diagnosed, like the common cold; that it has causes, symptoms, and appropriate cures; that it ought to be treated in hospitals or clinics by professionals dressed in long white coats; that it can take acute or chronic forms, like malaria; and therefore that it is best termed mental illness. To judge from the promotional literature sent out by drug companies or from the views of those who take an extreme position in this regard, the proper attitude toward this dread ailment is approximately that which was held in former centuries toward epidemics of the plague.

Why this choice of explanation for a condition that demonstrably has existed, in often remarkably similar forms, in every known society for thousands of years? There have been, and in some places still are, preliterate or nonindustrial societies in which being schizophrenic was regarded as like having great dreams or drug-induced visions; it simply meant that the person had stepped into another kind of world in which different things, great and wonderful things, even profoundly important lessons, might happen. The shaman, the witch doctor, the mystic or healer had an honored place because he had access to what was closed off to lives stuck in more commonplace orbits.[2] But the assumptions that made this explanation possible—whether valid or not we can hardly tell until we have experienced both their worlds and ours—are lacking in the society we have built in Europe and America over the past two centuries. Our idea of *explanation* and our notion of *understanding* have become restricted in scope. Today we mean by these terms the use of reason within a naturalistic framework, and we specifically rule out what cannot be verified by objective physical means. Faith is no longer accepted as evidence, nor intuition; and whatever falls outside the scope of "natural causes" is inadmissible as an influencing factor.

Thus being mad has become secularized, along with all the other visions that once shamed and exalted their possessors. In a world constructed neatly along rational, technical lines, the strangest, wildest, most odd of all human states has been diminished to the status of one more problem to be solved, and the further consequence of a politically powerful medical profession has enabled these practitioners to take over madness as their own special province, now redefined as mental illness.

## THE MAKING OF THE STRANGER

But all of this was not brought about without a process of socialization that took place over a number of centuries in Europe. How the citizens of a society look upon special individuals out of their own number is a complex and changing matter, the resultant of a wide array of powerful socializing influences. In order for a group of persons to be identified in a special way, to be plucked out of the population and put aside, and then to be looked on as so unique that the very stability of the society requires their special treament—all this requires that at least a number of steps take place. The social order must first of all have developed to the point where it has at its command the general concept of a deviant group within its midst. It must then be able to identify such a group—a step that is learned by practicing on earlier examples or prototypes. Finally, it must set up institutional forms, including special places and selected persons, for the express purpose of handling the group in a proper manner.

These are the four stages—the concept, the prototype, the institution, and the profession—which I will discuss in reference to the historical development of the madman as the ideal Stranger in Western society. In attempting such a survey, I may well appear to be describing a kind of history of collective villainy, to be pointing an accusing finger at the devilish persons in our history who set about doing this evil to their fellow citizens. At the outset, then, I want to disclaim any intention of making such accusations. I do not believe that history is the story of the good people arrayed against the bad, least of all in regard to such complex issues as madness. It is true that history has always seemed to conspire against certain subgroups that were unpopular in their day and that this goes on today as it did yesterday and the day before. Thus I am myself white, middle-class, male, heterosexual, and nonpsychotic, and so I am, perforce, part of a historic and continuing social campaign against the nonwhites, the poor, women, homosexuals, and schizophrenics. Am I therefore a villain or the companion of villains? No, I believe that I am at worst a knowing victim, not witless and not hapless, merely guilty. There are no villains, only the guilty and the victimized.

### The First Stage: The Concept

We have no term in English to refer precisely to members of the in-group who are treated as though they are aliens. Such terms as outcast, leper, scapegoat, outsider, or (incorrectly) pariah all refer to different though related phenomena. I have therefore chosen to use the word *Stranger*, since it may be used to refer to those either inside or outside a group. The Stranger-outside is familiar to us—

the alien, the true outsider. The Stranger-in-our-midst is perhaps less familiar as a concept, but as we will see it helps us to organize and understand much of the history of the collective treatment of those who are judged as deviant.

Human societies, like most infrahuman groups, spontaneously develop ways of identifying, marking, and dealing with those who are perceived as non-members or Strangers-outside. The Greeks had a word for such a person: the barbarian, meaning someone who spoke a different language and so was unintelligible, a stammerer. But they also possessed the concept of Stranger-in-our-midst—a subgroup within the society composed of those who were still members of the larger group but relegated to an inferior status, a subgroup who were not outcasts or barbarians but were treated as though they were. For the Greeks, as for all other societies since biblical times, this designation was retained for the largest of its subgroups, women. They were the first to whom the concept was applied and the ones who provided a training ground for males to learn the concept of Stranger. Women were the first inside outcasts.

It was not an easy concept to grasp and so its introduction, marking a major step forward in the complexities of social interaction, has led to a dialectic of love that necessarily includes hate. The male and female of the human species comprise all that there is of us; there can never be an effective way to split humanity in half and have the stronger part literally cast out the weaker. As a consequence, men's effective power over women has had to be exercised within the concept of Stranger-in-our-midst. They have had to subjugate women efficiently yet without pushing them toward open revolt. They have had to keep women down and at the same time make them even think that they preferred it that way.

How did this differ from the position occupied by slaves? There have, of course, been slaves for at least as long as women have occupied a subject position, and they were also in some sense Strangers within the group. Too, both women and slaves occupied their inferior positions by a decree of fate: the one fated to be born into that status, the other fated to be victim of the misfortunes of war. Neither had chosen their position, nor would have. Many women in all ages would have chosen to be men; but very few men would ever have chosen to be women. Women and slaves were alike also in the treatment they might get—good or ill, depending on their master. Some members of both groups have achieved eminence and distinction; many members of both groups became indispensable. In all these respects the position of women was like that of the slave, sometimes better, rarely worse. The one all-important difference is that every slave had within him the possibility, however remote, of one day being free. To be a slave was not all there was to being human. But a woman has never had this way out. She occupied her position not because she, a female human being, had been forcefully thrust into a special category to which some other females belonged. Rather, she was in the category precisely because of what she was, a female. There was no way out.[3] No woman could ever be free, as even a slave might, unless the society itself changed to make it possible and permissible.

By inspiring the invention of this concept, women thus provided the first step toward society's control of its Strangers. It was a major advance toward contemporary social organization, yet it carried with it certain ironies. The chief of these was that precisely as women were bound, inextricably, into their inferior status, so to the same degree was man bound to his position as master. The more tightly the slave is tied to his master, the tighter the master is bound to the slave. I suspect that this may explain in part the fierceness of the sentiments expressed against women, especially by religious writers; their venomous tirades seem like lust turned inside out. And it may also help to explain such curious offshoots as the Jewish mother syndrome, based on what has been described as "the ability to plant, cultivate and harvest guilt."[4] Here one of the most oppressed of all contemporary groups of women takes her revenge on the male closest to her by assuring his masculine ineffectiveness. His every action will be tempered by a memory of how, in some mysterious way, he has sinned by making his mother suffer.

One objection to my explanation should be mentioned at this point—that the basis for the bitterly antifeminist writings of so many clerics is really their latent or repressed homosexuality. But this makes no sense as a theory. If religious writers and thinkers had indeed wanted men so badly, they could have tried to take men instead of inveighing against women. And even if this had not been possible, even if they were left with nothing but an unfulfilled longing for men, it is hard to see how this would have led them to hate women. To assume so is to believe that to love, whether or not it leads to finding a lover, must necessarily be accompanied by hatred of those you choose not to love. On the contrary, a feeling *for* if it is at all genuine cannot be the source of a feeling *against*. Those who are capable of sustaining hatred can never be excused by the claim that their hatred is really an inescapable outgrowth of their love. Hatred, like love, is sui generis.

Once they were effectively subjugated, originally by the Old Testament Hebrews, the position of women remained fixed until major social changes began to appear at the beginning of the period we call the Renaissance. Women who

## THE MYTH OF WOMEN'S DESTINY

The myth that childbearing and rearing is by far, in my opinion, the most damaging and destructive myth that imprisons her. Having children is no substitute for creating one's own life, for producing. And since so many women in this culture devote themselves to nothing else, they end up by becoming intolerable burdens upon their children because in fact these children ARE their whole lives.[5]

We are familiar with this kind of woman. She is the one who signs her letter "Mother of Three" when she writes to the editor of a newspaper; who joins a group whose crusading banner reads "Mothers United Against. . . ."; who appears on an afternoon giveaway show on TV and identifies herself as a home-maker—just as though motherhood or being a household drudge itself conveys some remarkable status on her.

were both exceptional and fortunate—for example, Catherine of Siena—on rare occasions achieved distinction in a man's world of churchly affairs. In general they were universally assimilated to the character of friendly and domesticated animals. They were viewed as beasts of burden and workhorses, dumb but rather trainable, valuable as servants and drudges, sometimes strong but essentially powerless, childish in nature and spirit, and of course deeply committed to their ultimate destiny as women—the bearing and rearing of children. That men had some hand in conception and therefore ought to share whatever worth or blame might be found in such a destiny was not admitted and was often explicitly disavowed. Thus, in the sixteenth century a girl who had been made pregnant and who bore an illegal child was ostracized, while the man was at most reprimanded; if in her distress she killed the infant, she was beheaded and her seducer simply banished from the town.[6]

In a society in which, in spite of strict rules of conduct, a great deal of sexual license existed, only men enjoyed the resulting privileges. The status of women is well expressed in the fact that it was precisely when they were most female—during the menstrual period and at childbirth—that to their inferior position was added the additional stigma of being dirty. We owe this particular proscription, like so many others, to the Old Testament patriarchs, who made up for an unparalleled ethical contribution by devising a ban on sensuality unequaled in the ancient world. Perhaps as the price they paid for creating a human ethic of immense moral grandeur, they cut themselves off from their own animality. They developed an almost terrified concern with nakedness, they instituted the fiercest of punishments for almost any sexual transgression, they violently opposed such harmless forms of deviance as homosexuality and coitus interruptus —and they passed on to the Christians this entire package of taboos on any sexual activity not aimed directly at producing young.

So began the Christian heritage, with the view that the human body was a source of evil thoughts and acts. Who might now be blamed for encouraging, promoting, even originally causing this vast, almost inescapable realm of sin?

---

WOMEN, ACCORDING TO MEN

Do you know that each of you women is an Eve? The sentence of God on this sex of yours lives in this age; the guilt must necessarily live too. You are the gate of Hell, you are the temptress of the forbidden tree; you are the first deserter of the divine law.
[Tertullian, A.D. c. 150–230]

And the woman was arrayed in purple and scarlet color, and decked with gold and precious stones and pearls, having a golden cup in her hand full of abominations and filthiness of her fornication:

And upon her forehead was a name written, Mystery, Babylon the Great, The Mother of Harlots and Abominations of the Earth.
[Revelation 17: 4, 5.]

Woman was God's second mistake.
[Nietzsche]

Men have broad and large chests, and small narrow hips, and are more understanding than women, who have but small narrow chests, and broad hips, to

the end they should remain at home, sit still, keep house, and bear and bring up children.
[Martin Luther]

The fact of the matter is that the prime responsibility of a woman probably is to be on earth long enough to find the best mate possible for herself, and conceive children who will improve the species.
[Norman Mailer][7]

I judge impetuosity to be better than caution; for Fortune is a woman, and if you wish to master her, you must strike and beat her.
[Machiavelli]

. . . the work of civilization has become increasingly the business of men, it confronts them with ever more difficult tasks and compels them to carry out instinctual sublimations of which women are little capable.
[Freud][8]

Women. Nowhere in all the weird back alleys of unreason is there a better example of the cognitive mechanism that is called projection. A little child hits his playmate, knows that he is likely to be blamed for it, and so changes his report of the incident: "He hit me." At a more advanced developmental level, when he is capable of greater cognitive complexity, he is about to hit his playmate, but he knows that if he does so without cause he will be blamed for it. So he prepares himself in advance with the conviction: He is going to hit me. This then gives him license to strike out in self-defense. The same twist of logic is always there: if my own wish is likely to lead me into trouble, I simply shift the wish, along with its accompanying blame and guilt, over to the other person, preferably the person at whom my wish was originally directed. If I lust uncontrollably after women, my torment is eased and my line of conduct remarkably smoothed if I first turn my wish around to read: She lusts after me. Then, no matter what happens, I am at worst a victim; and if things go right, I might even satisfy my own lust, escape punishment and self-punishment, and see to it that the woman is punished for being the instigator of my original wish. The final touch was, as always, an additional burden on women: since they were in fact subject to the same sexual wishes as men, they often collaborated in the miserable game by doing their own share of seducing and no matter what happened then they were bound to lose.

One more aspect of women's position in Western society needs to be noted here. When the ancient world as it existed in Europe began to break up and new social forms came into being—a change that led to the development of feudalism—the position of women changed as well. For the first time in history an entire society, all of Western civilization that was then known, came under the sway of a single institution, the Catholic church. It now became possible to specify in great detail the place and character of women, and there resulted a new definition that in one stroke solved all the problems of their status as persons-who-were-not-persons. This was accomplished by inventing a new type of human creature and then assigning all noblewomen—peasants did not count at all, of course—to the newly defined class. The procedure was very much like what happened some centuries later when a new class of human creature, the *child*, was invented, and all persons below a specified age were then assigned membership in the class.[9] The new creature invented to accommodate women was the *maiden*. Conceived as an ideal, her characteristics widely popularized by wandering troubadours, she was specified as a lovely, untouchable creature, high on her pedestal, who was to be the object of a man's special longing. The new class of wish that was devised to describe man's urge toward this creature was *romantic love*; the term has served, until recently, as a euphemism for sex.

Thus in one neat stroke woman was both exalted and degraded. Though ostensibly given a very special status within the community, she was in actuality eased out of even the limited hold she had formerly maintained on being human. Idealized and unreal, woman as maiden was now no more than the heroine of a ballad, as mythical as the fabled unicorn whom, it was said, only she could tame.[10] And this was the position in which women were then held, astonishingly enough, until only a few years ago.[11] It is a fine lesson in how the human character, and even the body, can be patterned into the mode that society wills, in this case, to be feminine. As we will see in Chapter 9, what was done in this respect to women can be done just as easily to any one of us, and this procedure in turn will serve there as a useful basis for a discussion of our individual neurotic fates.

Thus the first step, always the hardest one to take, toward the development of social mechanisms for effectively dealing with those who are different. The remaining steps, as they succeeded historically, can now be dealt with more briefly.

### The Second Stage: The Prototype

In a society that was in the process of developing ways of picking out and even stigmatizing its deviants, what was needed now was a kind of living example. Ideally it should be an example so pure that it might serve almost as a metaphysical principle in concrete form, so pure, indeed, that immediate recognition, absolute segregation, and unmitigated persecution would all follow quite naturally once the example had been found and named.[12] But who could possibly serve such a function?

The Jews. Their story turned out to be one of the greatest of history's ironies. It was the Jews whose ethical system, monotheistic religion, and moral severity provided the basis for a Christianity that had come to dominate Europe totally. The Jews' mistake, however, was not to have died off as the Etruscans did. Instead they persisted, displaying the same fierce and unrelenting pride that had made them unique among the Neolithic desert tribes of the Near East. In the midst of a universal Catholicism they stood unchanged, different by their own choice from every Christian—and that meant every adult—of the Western world. It was not possible to excuse them, as one might the sick person, by saying that their moral fate showed only the hand of God visited on an innocent victim. It was not even possible to say, as one might say of women, that in any case their existence was necessary for the preservation of the human race. No, they were a living anathema, lacking any excuse. It was surely the sacred duty of a true Christian to wipe this curse from God's eyes—that is, unless they happened to be temporarily useful as mapmakers, international messengers, physicians, minters, teachers, scribes, astronomers, mathematicians, or traders.

Even when they were suffered to live they were hounded into ghettos, branded in every language and country. Everywhere they were examples of the pure alien, the heretics who were totally defiled and forever beyond hope of redemption unless they repented and were converted to Catholicism. The very idea of *Jew* took its place in the speech and the thought of Western man, and it has only been in very modern times, as religious dogma has begun to lose its hold in our culture, that anti-Semitism has faded away in all but the most regressive groups. Prejudice of this sort, of which anti-Semitism has always been the prototype, is the meanest of passions and does not necessarily require religious belief as its basis, but the intensity and rigidity of medieval religious thought made it by far the most likely foundation on which to build.

Although Jews as a group had been isolated and restricted as far back as Roman times, actual persecution of them did not erupt on a broad scale until the year 1095. Then, at the start of the First Crusade, when all the energies of the Church were mobilized to revive a flagging and uncertain support among the populace, Jews were discovered as a scapegoat, and a great massacre took place in the Rhineland. In this way a pattern was set that developed in its full flowering during the sixteenth and seventeenth centuries, in the Inquisition of Spain in particular. This too was a counterattack by the Church against its heretics, apostates, and the less than faithful. The merciless persecution of Jews would, it was hoped, spark a revival of Catholic faith and a return to the true Church. The model developed during these years was faithfully copied by the Nazis in a later century, when the Jews as a group were very nearly wiped out.

### The Third Stage: The Institution

Both a concept and a pure principle and example were now available. What the Western world needed at this point as part of an organized system of dealing with deviants was a formal, and preferably an institutional, arrangement. This would make it possible to enforce whatever degree of segregation was deemed necessary.

An early form of such an institution had already been known in many cultures, and all around the world, for as long as historical records existed. This was the zoological garden—its name shortened in modern times to *zoo*—in the form of a royal park, usually for the edification and amusement of the ruler and his court. When the Spaniards captured the Aztec capital of Tenochtitlan, one of the incredible sights they reported was just such a *paradeiso* filled not only with animals but also with a large collection of abnormal humans—midgets, hunchbacks, and albinos, among others.[13] The physically different were apparently treated this way in many earlier societies, either as victims of scorn and abuse or else as exotic deviants who might provide a moment's amusement.

Every village had its deaf-mute, its feebleminded or brain-damaged persons who were the butt of jokes; every town had its corps of amputees, palsied, crippled, and deranged, who were kicked aside as beggars not fit to be touched—and then there were always the lepers. Most of all, there were the lepers, the ideal type of physically deformed victim, pariahs in every settlement in Europe.

No one knows exactly where or when leprosy arose, but it has been known for a very long time. By the early Middle Ages, it had spread its fearsome touch through all of Europe; by the twelfth century, it is estimated, there were more than a million lepers in England and Scotland alone. No other affliction in human history has occasioned the horror and revulsion that came to be associated with this condition. Its incubation period in the individual being highly variable, no one could know when or whom the disease would strike next. It traveled mysteriously from victim to victim, and all that was known for certain was the dread fact that men were more likely to be cursed with it than women. No cure was possible against this "vile and loathsome crust," as Shakespeare aptly called it.[14] One of its forms resulted in anesthetic areas on the skin; in an age quite lacking in modern methods of treatment, it was all too easy for the leper to unknowingly injure or burn such an area and then to develop as a by-product an infected wound that was essentially incurable. Closely related was another form of the disease in which nodules appeared that easily became sites of secondary infection. The result was that the victim often came to resemble a creature rotting away while still breathing—the very picture of living death. It was truly death in life, and so it could only have come about as the direct result of the wrath of God.

No wonder the lepers were thrust away in a social gesture of spontaneous revulsion. Every city did the same: leprosariums were built outside the city walls, and the poor victims were herded there, to be kept totally segregated from others who were, miraculously, still untouched. The treatment of lepers by segregation in special institutions thus became the model for public reaction to a victim who must be banned, just as the word *leper* itself came to stand for an outcast and, with these connotations, still lingers in the underground recesses of our language. The leper was driven out of all the places that normal people inhabited, not because it was felt that he might contaminate his fellows (for the idea of the spread of infection was not yet clearly articulated) but because he represented in living form in their midst a running sore on the social collective, a continuing reminder of human sin and God's retribution. All that saved the lepers from swift and terrible punishment as creatures of the devil was a dim sense that they were victims and a hesitancy about interfering with God's righteous punishment. Thus, they were only exiled, but the form of their exile established for all time a specific institution meant to deal with the Stranger-in-our-midst.

Women were subjugated, but they could not be banished beyond the kitchen and bedroom. Even the harem, that classic instance of the purely male society in all its cruel arrogance, arranged that its women were kept within the institution's walls.[15] The Jew was often locked within the ghetto, but when his services were valuable he was frequently accorded high rank and freedom to travel. Only with the leper did there come about a specific device for total banishment without killing. With this step European society was nearly prepared to deal with those whom it selected as Strangers—by providing a place of confinement that was not built as a punishment but as a refuge. The leprosarium was meant as an asylum, a hospital, that is, literally a place of refuge and shelter. The victims who were banished there were told, in effect, that they were to be cast forever out of human society, but that it was really for their own good.

The same statement was to be applied to other groups, with equally damning effect, in the centuries to follow. But before this happened, an unexpected twist of circumstances changed the cast of actors in this historic drama. By the year 1400 the leprosariums of Europe were almost emptied. No one knows exactly why this occurred; certainly no cure for the disease had yet been found. But inexplicably, the majority of the inmates died off; progressively fewer were admitted each year; and the disease itself almost disappeared. The leper houses now stood empty, awaiting their next victims.[16]

All this happened five centuries ago, and more. But although the city walls no longer have any meaning as barriers and remain only as historical curiosities, and although the curse of leprosy has been prosaically renamed as Hansen's disease and is now known to be only mildly infectious, and although the bacillus that causes it has been identified—in short, although we no longer have a basis for the former widespread belief in the reality of God's wrath—the stigma remains. The very word itself, *leper*, still evokes an uncontrollable response. This is the legacy that was left to us by the Middle Ages, not in the meaning of a word but in a raw nerve that lies in some inaccessible region behind the meaning. We still banish the leper whenever we think of him; that is what has been built into our experience.

### The Fourth Stage: A Profession

By the fifteenth century the Catholic church, although ostensibly still in full control of the secular life of Europe, was beginning to be in organizational trouble. Opposition was starting to appear—in politics, in commerce, in intellectual life, and even within its own ranks in regard to religious dogma. There was only one thing to do. The best defense being a good offense, the Church mounted a major counterattack. What came out of this was nothing less than a major advance in political practice.

The basic maneuver was familiar enough: to find a good scapegoat. What better one than the subjugated group most available, women? The next step was to define at the very highest level the nature of the crime of which women were to be accused. In 1484, therefore, Pope Innocent VIII published a papal bull declaring witchcraft a heresy. The term *heresy* was by no means new, but it had never before been used on a broad scale for so ostensibly a political purpose. The offense that was now specified by the term consisted simply of opposition to the Church, but defined so vaguely, with the charge stated in so all-inclusive a manner, that any act could be used as evidence. As it soon turned out, even the absence of an act could be taken to be heretical, thus exhausting all possibilities in one masterly stroke.

Even with the heretics already named as a group—they were to be women, not men—and a general counterattack on heresy soon begun, the problem of pinning down the specific form of heresy, witchcraft, was not so easily solved. It is true that forms of pagan ritual were still known because they had never been completely uprooted even after a thousand years of Christianity. These formed the basis of most so-called witches' rites, but they were often trivial, even harmless, and more rebellious than sacrilegious—for example, the practice of insulting the priestly craft by reciting a mass backwards, much as young people today mock the military by using their uniforms for casual dress. There was also the fact that many women who were accused as witches had made the mistake of competing with male physicians by practicing as midwives and folk healers. But knowledge of these two kinds of suspect activity was not sufficient to mount a major campaign. What was needed was a formal method for describing and identifying the sin when it was presumed to have occurred. In view of the fact that the sin was a sheer invention, a fiction invented for the purpose, the method had to include ways of "proving" the existence of heresy even when it was not publicly evident. Clearly, the problems of diagnosis and treatment involved here were not simple. They were solved by another master stroke—establishing a profession of "experts" whose business it was to know what to look for, to look for it, and then, mirabile dictu, to find it.

The Church first used its own extensive power to develop a campaign to awaken the populace. Public feeling was soon aroused to the point where the mere possibility that a woman might be a witch was sufficient to inflame her neighbors and often even her family to accuse her and demand that she be tried. The influence of the established Church was such that routing out witches soon came to be, in and of itself, the surest way that a person of uncertain piety could bring himself to feel firmly on the side of the angels and in favor of justice, public order, and what was morally right. Most important of all, the Church established an impressive ritual including procedures for conducting examinations, methods for conducting trials, and specification of degrees of punishment so as to insure that the discovery and rooting out of the evil would be properly and fairly accomplished. As the capstone, the Church provided a rationale and philosophical justification as well: The holy crusade was not only for saving the souls of those who might be affected by witches, but even more for the purpose of saving the poor wretches who had fallen victim by becoming witches. The entire campaign, in all its suspect glory, was for a good and holy purpose; no one, no matter how much suffering ensued, could possibly lose.

The very heart of the campaign, however, and what made it a political development rather than just one more sad chapter in the history of religious zeal, was that a profession arose whose specialty was to identify the evil in order that it might be eradicated. This was the whole point: witchcraft and its practitioners were not out in the open, for in that case good and honest folk would be able to see and avoid the evil without difficulty. No, it was the apparent absence of the heresy in everyday life that was itself the surest sign of its presence and also the most damning evidence of how devious and ultimately dangerous it really was. The fact that most persons were unable to see signs of witchcraft around them was the clearest indication of how badly the professionals were needed. (The Nazis, engaged in a similar campaign of persecution during the 1930s, used a more straightforward technique: they required all Jews to identify themselves by wearing a yellow Star of David on the sleeve.)

One form of the new professional activity consisted then, as it does now, in the writing of learned textbooks. For the campaign against witches, the most influential of these was the *Malleus Maleficarum* (usually translated as *The Witches' Hammer*), written by two supremely dedicated monks, Spraenger and Kraemer, and published in 1489. A second professional innovation consisted of developing a new occupational specialty, which became known as witchpricking. One of the best-known of the witchprickers was Matthew Hopkins, who practiced in seventeenth-century England and whose success earned him the name of Witchfinder-General. Armed with his textbooks and the jargon of his guild, and equipped with a trained eye with which he could detect invisible marks on hidden areas of the skin, the witchpricker served as a powerful agent in the Church's campaign.

Every era needs its devil just as badly as it needs its gods; and so every age finds some embodied devilment that most closely conforms to its own deepest fears and personal anxieties. At the close of the Middle Ages, when the moral order was still ruled by the Church, men's deepest fears concerned those sexual impulses which had been ruled out of conscious life by a rigid dogma. In such a time the devil had to be embodied in Woman; she was the source of men's lust. So women, now identified and diagnosed as witches, became the logical targets of a counterattack, first by the Catholic church and later by the leaders of the Reformation, for neither education nor scholarly wisdom ever served as a counterbalance against the most fervent belief in witches, as evidenced in the writings of Erasmus, of Johannes Kepler, and of Martin Luther.[17]

The most important consequence of the campaign against witches was that for the first time in Western history persecution, organized officially and on a grand scale, had been enthusiastically pursued by the mass of ordinary citizens. It now became a recognizable tactic in the armamentarium of governments. Henceforth matters might be arranged at any time so that while the majority made war on a minority those in power could sit back and encourage the persecution. In small matters and large, the trick could be made to work so long as there was available a special profession that could define into existence the very evil that it proposed to eradicate.

## PLACES

The history that I have sketched has indicated the major stages in developing our modern means for dealing with deviants of any sort, those whom we designate as Strangers. There are, of course, some deviants today whom we prefer to execute—for example, condemned murderers or those found guilty of treason during wartime—using a punishment as extreme as that practiced by primitive groups on any member, from infancy on, who was unacceptable to the society.[18]

Others, even today, are banished from our shores—for example, criminals who are deported to their countries of national origin—just as the infamous Man Without a Country was once banished to wander, stateless.[19] But these are extreme cases. Aside from them, our society has managed to find a way to deal with all its deviants without either killing or banishing them: they are declared Strangers and then ruled out of our community of privilege while still remaining within the society.[20]

This notion of Stranger-in-our-midst belongs to the modern era. It could not have come about until, first, the historic position of women in a male-dominated society was purified, so to speak, by identifying the Jew as a prototype; second, the concept of asylum, a building that was outside the city's walls yet still within the society, was introduced; and third, the campaign against witches had taught its inquisitors how to create a profession of experts to identify the victims and then bring them to punishment. A thread of righteous and essentially dishonest self-justification runs through this sequence and binds its steps into a social ethic: the theme of controlling subversion while loudly proclaiming freedom. Stated in other terms, it is an arrangement for getting rid of those who are different by claiming to be doing it for their own good, thus satisfying both security and conscience at one stroke.

The social organization that resulted from this development proved hard to stop. Like all institutions, it had its own inner momentum that impelled it to grow even more influential. In a secular society, social control cannot be achieved simply by manipulating men's inner lives; only a completely religious society like that of medieval Europe can do this. Thus, a major consequence of the secularization of society during the past few centuries has been that what is effective as a social influence has come to be what exists outside of persons, in the places of their environment. Since the time of the Renaissance, then, such places have told the story of society's Strangers and how they were treated. Two of them, about which we now know a great deal, will serve here as examples.

### St. Mary of Bethlehem Hospital, London

In England, much of the seventeenth century—a time that we now refer to as the Jacobean era—was, like our own time, a period of marked instability, of widespread social and political unrest, of serious questioning of all the old standards and beliefs. It was also a period of transition and therefore of doubt and uncertainty. The world order, expressed in the Ptolemaic scheme of a universe revolving around the earthly home of God's children, was clearly coming apart, but nothing had yet taken its place. In the classical view, to be mad was to rave against the gods, to blaspheme as though trying to break down the order of things ordained in heaven. But by the seventeenth century this was hardly blasphemy, only intellectual courage. How could a man be considered mad at a time when the very world itself seemed to be coming apart? Who could appropriately be called deviant in thinking in a society whose most perceptive members were beginning to doubt that society's own foundations?

Hogarth's print Scene in Bedlam, from his series entitled The Rake's Progress, depicts very realistically the antics of the inmates and the attitude of visitors who came to watch them.

The Metropolitan Museum of Art, Harris Brisbane Dick Fund, 1932

When Bethlehem Hospital in London began as an asylum for the mentally disturbed it had surprisingly few patients, perhaps for just this reason—madness had not yet been efficiently redefined. There were twenty inmates in 1598 and only about thirty by the year 1632. The patients seem to have been a curious mix: some delusional, some depressed, some silly and prankish, and even some political prisoners.[21] As a consequence of a very stringent budget, living conditions for the patients were hard, the diet sparse, and the treatment methods harsh and punitive. Under these circumstances, it is understandable that the patients might have welcomed the additional funds brought in by curious visitors who, at the rate of 300 per day, paid a penny apiece to come and gawk at the madmen.[22] It is not surprising that the picture that has come down to us—summed up in the very word *bedlam*—is of a constant "mad fury" to which the visitors may have contributed by goading the patients.[23] But on off days, or when visitors were not around, the patients appear to have been much more like those we might find in modern mental hospitals—quiet, withdrawn, often unreachable, occupied with a tortured, inward journey of their own.

To the paying public who wanted cheap entertainment, madness at Bedlam was a kind of spectacular oddity. To a contemporary playwright, it was better described as "a gentleman-like humour, and in fashion." [24] The trouble with both these definitions is that they are correct, for they are descriptions not of what madness is, but of what form madness takes under specific institutional conditions. The paying public saw a group of hungry performers who had many reasons to act wild; the playwright saw and judged the times he lived in and some of the possible reactions to it. The lesson to be learned from the early history of Bethlehem Hospital is that an institution can mold its inmates as the time and place demand. We can now see what happens when major social forces become involved in the molding process.

### Worcester State Hospital, Massachusetts

Opened in 1833, the Worcester State Hospial very soon became a model; "being the first of its kind in Massachusetts as well as the prototype of the modern American state mental hospital, [it] was one of the most influential public institutions in the nation." [25] A law had been passed the previous year specifying the type of patient who had to be admitted as well as other types whose admission was urged though not required. It was this law that determined the purpose the hospital would serve and thus the role the insitution was to play. According to the law, insane persons who had already been committed to jail as dangerous to the community had to be transferred to the new hospital; "town pauper lunatics" who were more of a burden than a danger were to be admitted if a local township was willing to pay their keep; and insane persons who were harmless and thus able to live with their families might or might not be admitted, again depending on who would pay the bill. [26]

The purpose of this law, and therefore the role of the new state hospital, has been aptly summarized as "to rectify a socially undesirable situation" [27] by taking care of the "socially undesirable person." [28] For this reason potential patients were classified not on the basis of their illness but on the sounder legal basis of their supposed danger to society. The institution was essentially a device

---

PROFESSION, PLACE, AND MYTH

The institutional label of "hospital," together with the rapid development of medicine, culminated during the nineteenth century in the psychiatrist assuming more and more that mental illness was somatic illness, usually involving lesions of the brain, which was regarded as the organ of the mind. Yet psychia-

trists could offer no empirical evidence to substantiate this assertion. Consequently, "mental illness" was identified through a person's manifest behavior. This, then, required some normative standard by which to judge or evaluate behavior. The norm that they used (and it was generally an implicit, rather than an explicit, one) was the norm of their own reference group. The standard used was no longer a physical one (one that involved proper organic functioning) but, rather, was culturally defined: it was a standard that implicitly adopted middle-class, Protestant, agrarian values. Defining mental illness in terms of outward behavioral manifestations, while yet claiming that it was organic in nature, of course created serious theoretical problems.

Since "mentally ill" people were sent to institutions called "hospitals," classifying and labeling their social behavior became necessary. This act of classifying behavior was traditionally a function performed by a physician in the institution called a hospital. Thus, the social behavior of the inmates came to be categorized and labeled (judged) no longer as a form of social behavior, but now as a disease entity. . . . Such classification, in the medical tradition, was taken to be an essential preliminary step for the future discovery of a biochemical agent or a neurophysiological basis for these social or mental diseases.[29]

The term "mental illness" is widely used to describe something which is very different than a disease of the brain. Many people today take it for granted that living is an arduous process. Its hardship for modern man, moreover, derives, not so much from a struggle for biological survival as from the stresses and strains inherent in the social intercourse of complex human personalities. In this context, the notion of mental illness is used to identify or describe some feature of an individual's so-called personality. Mental illness—as a deformity of the personality, so to speak—is then regarded as the CAUSE of the human disharmony. It is implicit in this view that social intercourse between people is regarded as something INHERENTLY HARMONIOUS, its disturbance being due solely to the presence of "mental illness" in many people. This is obviously fallacious reasoning, for it makes the abstraction "mental illness" into a CAUSE, even though this abstraction was created in the first place to serve only as a shorthand expression for certain types of human behavior.[30]

In actual contemporary social usage, the finding of a mental illness is made by establishing a deviance in behavior from certain psychosocial, ethical, or legal norms. The judgment may be made, as in medicine, by the patient, the physician (psychiatrist), or others. Remedial action, finally, tends to be sought in a therapeutic—or covertly medical—framework, thus creating a situation in which PSYCHOSOCIAL, ETHICAL, and/or LEGAL DEVIATIONS are claimed to be correctible by (so-called) MEDICAL ACTION. Since medical action is designed to correct only medical deviations, it seems logically absurd to expect that it will help solve problems whose very existence had been defined and established on nonmedical grounds.[31]

for social control of the society's most extreme and unmanageable deviants. Indeed, when Worcester State Hospital first opened, and for a number of years thereafter, it was run not by medical men but by laymen—further evidence that it was conceived not as a place for dealing with illness, but as an institution for a special type of social control. I do not mean to imply that the Massachusetts gentlemen who pioneered the building of the nation's first state mental hospital were moved by any but the noblest and most humanitarian of motives. In fact, their enthusiasm and motivation were admirable, and they did in fact manage to treat their patients in an exemplary manner. But regardless of motive or intent, what they did was provide a means for institutionalizing the category of deviant; they built a place for the Stranger and then passed a law to make sure that he was incarcerated there. This pattern of using society's best motives for these ends and of doing it for the good of the afflicted patients has persisted unchanged.[32]

As state hospitals became the dumping ground for all manner of undesirables and incompetents—usually from the lowest and therefore the most helpless of socioeconomic groups—the medical profession began to carve out a specialty that claimed a unique competence in regard to these victims of a social organization. The field of institutional psychiatry was founded within a few decades, and in the course of the growth of its parent profession its practitioners came to consider themselves the arbiters of who shall be defined as a Stranger.[33] We may now turn, in some detail, to a major contemporary critique of this professional movement.

## THOMAS SZASZ ON INSTITUTIONAL PSYCHIATRY

The history of psychiatry . . . is largely the account of changing fashions in the theory and practice of psychiatric violence, cast in the self-approbating idiom of medical diagnosis and treatment. In this respect it resembles traditional religious and nationalistic history, which depicts the violence of ruthless and power-hungry leaders as a series of selfless struggles for God and Nation. (In the Communist idiom, the struggle is waged for the workers or the downtrodden masses.) The feared violence of the madman is thus best understood as largely the projection, onto the victim, of the actual violence of his persecutor. The aggression of society in general, and its physician-agent in particular, against the so-called insane begins in the seventeenth century, with the dungeon, the chains, physical torture, and starvation; continues in the eighteenth and nineteenth centuries, with the insane asylum, flogging, bleeding, and the physical strait jackets called waistcoats; and luxuriates in the twentieth century, with the vast state mental hospital (housing up to 15,000 inmates), the shock machine, the leuco-tome (the scalpel for severing the frontal lobe from the rest of the brain), and the chemical strait jackets called tranquilizers. Like all systematic, popularly accepted forms of aggression, psychiatric violence is authorized, and incorporated into, important social institutions, and is sanctioned by law and tradition. The principal social institutions involved in the theory and practice of psychiatric violence are the State, the family, and the medical profession. . . .[34]

With the decline of the power of the Church and of the religious world view, in the seventeenth century, the inquisitor-witch complex disappeared and in its place there arose the alienist-madman complex. . . . In the new—secular and "scientific"—cultural climate, as in any other, there were still the disadvantaged, the disaffected, and the men who thought and criticized too much. Conformity was still demanded. The nonconformist, the objector, in short, all who denied or refused to affirm society's dominant values, were still the enemies of society. To be sure, the proper ordering of this new society was no longer conceptualized in terms of Divine Grace; instead it was viewed in terms of Public Health. Its internal enemies were thus seen as mad; and Institutional Psychiatry came into being as had the Inquisition earlier, to protect the group from this threat. . . .[35]

The inquisitors who opposed and persecuted the heretics acted in accordance with their sincere beliefs, just as the psychiatrists who oppose and persecute the insane act in accordance with theirs. In each instance we may disagree with the beliefs and repudiate the methods. But we cannot condemn the inquisitors doubly—first for having certain beliefs, and then for acting upon them. Neither can we condemn the institutional psychiatrists doubly—first for holding that social nonconformity is mental illness, and then for incarcerating the mental patient in a hospital. In so far as a psychiatrist truly believes in the myth of mental illness, he is compelled, by the inner logic of this construct, to treat, with benevolent therapeutic intent, those who suffer from this malady, even though his "patients" cannot help but experience the treatment as a form of persecution.

Although the Inquisition and Institutional Psychiatry developed from different economic, moral, and social conditions, their respective operations are similar. Each institution articulates its oppressive methods in therapeutic terms. The inquisitory saves the heretic's soul and the integrity of his Church; the psychiatrist restores his patient to mental health and protects his society from the dangerously insane. Like the psychiatrist, the inquisitory is an epidemiologist: he is concerned with the prevalence of witchcraft; he is a diagnostician: he establishes who is a witch and who is not; and finally, he is a therapist: he exorcises the devil and thus ensures the salvation of the possessed person's soul. On the other hand, the witch, like the involuntary mental patient, is cast into a degraded and deviant role against her will; is subjected to certain diagnostic procedures to establish whether or not she is a witch; and finally, is deprived of liberty, and often of life, ostensibly for her own benefit. . . .[36]

The secret police of modern totalitarian states have faithfully copied this inquisitorial method. The Mental Health Movements of modern Therapeutic States have improved upon it: Institutional psychiatrists (and psychologists, social workers, etc.) act as and believe themselves to be the individual's ally, friend, and therapist, when, in fact, they are his adversary. Should the patient confide his fears or suspicions to them, they will interpret these as signs of "mental illness" and so report to their employer; should the patient fail to "co-operate" with them, they will interpret his refusal as itself a sign of "mental illness" and will again so report to their employer. . . .[37]

. . . the phenomena in question—called witchcraft during the Renaissance and mental illness today—are actually created through the social interaction of oppressor and oppressed. If the observer sympathizes with the oppressor and wants to exonerate him, while he pities the oppressed but wants to control him, he calls the victim mentally ill. This is why psychiatrists declare that witches were mad. Conversely, if the observer sympathizes with the oppressed and wants to elevate him, while he loathes the oppressor and wants to degrade him, he calls the tormentor mentally ill. This is why psychiatrists declare that the Nazis were mad. I insist that both interpretations are worse than false; by interposing mental illness (or witchcraft, as was the case formerly), they conceal, excuse, and explain away the terrifyingly simple but all-important fact of man's inhumanity to man. . . .[38]

In 1796, the psychiatrist knew that the Negro would have preferred to be white. Today, the psychiatrist knows that the alleged drug addict would prefer not to take drugs; that the homosexual would prefer to be heterosexual; and that the suicidal person would prefer to live. The upshot is the psychiatric discreditation of human experience and the therapeutic destruction of human differences. . . .[39]

Since psychiatry deals with personal and social conduct, and since such conduct cannot be described, much less evaluated, without anchoring it in a matrix of values, there is nothing to confuse between rules of mental health and rules of morality. The two are one and the same; they are two different sets of terms, two different languages, for describing and influencing human relations and personal conduct. . . .[40]

I hold that in each of the foregoing persecutory situations we are confronted with a relationship between oppressor and oppressed; the oppressor invariably resorts to both force and fraud in subduing and exploiting his antagonist; frequently he develops a therapeutic rhetoric, justifying his domination by claims of selflessness and a desire to help the victim; criticism of the oppressive practice is rendered impossible by persecution of the critic as a traitor to the existing social order; finally, the ideology of helpful coercion is institutionalized, stabilizing and perpetuating the persecutory practices over long periods of time. . . .[41]

Critical examination of the practice of involuntary mental hospitalization compels one to confront the basic moral dilemma of contemporary psychiatry: in a conflict between the values of liberty and mental health (no matter how defined), which should rank higher? The architects of the Open Society chose liberty; I want to re-echo their choice. The architects of the Therapeutic Society chose mental health; the present-day supporters of commitment procedures re-echo their choice.

The fundamental parallel between master and slave on the one hand, and institutional psychiatrist and involuntarily hospitalized patient on the other, lies in this: in each instance, the former member of the pair DEFINES the social role of the latter, and CASTS him in that role by force.

Wherever there is slavery, there must be criteria for who may and who may not be enslaved. In ancient times, any people could be enslaved; bondage was the usual consequence of military defeat. After the advent of Christianity, although the people of Europe continued to make war on each other, they ceased enslaving prisoners who were Christians. By the time of the colonization of America, the peoples of the Western world considered only black men appropriate subjects for slave trade.

The criteria for distinguishing between those who may be incarcerated in mental hospitals and those who may not be are similar: poor and socially unimportant persons may be, and Very Important Persons may not be. This rule is manifested in two ways: first, through our mental hospital statistics, which show that the majority of institutionalized patients belong in the lowest socio-economic classes; second, through the rarity and difficulty with which VIPs are committed. Yet even the sophisticated social scientists often misunderstand or misinterpret these correlations by attributing the low incidence of committed upper-class persons to a denial of the "medical fact" that "mental illness" can "strike" anyone.[42] To be sure, powerful people may feel anxious or depressed, or behave in an excited or paranoid manner; but that, of course, is not the point at all. . . .[43]

"Mental illness" of the type found in psychiatric hospitals has been investigated for centuries, and continues to be investigated today, in much the same way as slaves were studied in the antebellum South and before. The "existence" of slaves was taken for granted; their biological and social characteristics were noted and classified. Similarly, the "existence" of "mental patients" is now taken for granted; indeed, it is widely believed that their number is steadily increasing. The psychiatrist's task is to observe and classify their biological, psychological, and social characteristics.

This perspective is a manifestation, in part, of what I have called "the myth of mental illness"[44]—that is, of the notion that mental illnesses are similar to diseases of the body; and in part, of the psychiatrist's intense need to deny the fundamental complementarity of his relationship to the involuntary mental patient. The same complementarity obtains in all situations where one person or party assumes a superior or dominant role and ascribes an inferior or submissive role to another; for example, master and slave, accuser and accused, inquisitory and witch. (Sometimes people willingly assume a submissive role and cast their partners in a dominant role. I am not concerned with this aspect of the problem here.)

A basic assumption of American slavery was that the Negro slave was racially inferior. . . . Similarly, the basic assumption of institutional psychiatry is that the "mentally ill" person is psychologically and socially inferior. He is like a child: he does not know what is in his best interests and therefore needs others to control and protect him. Psychiatrists often care deeply for their involuntary patients, whom they consider—in contrast with the merely "neurotic" persons —"psychotic," which is to say, "very sick." Hence, such patients must be cared for as the "irresponsible children" they are considered to be.

The perspective of paternalism has played an exceedingly important role in justifying both slavery and involuntary mental hospitalization. Aristotle defined slavery as "an essentially domestic relationship"; in so doing, wrote D. B. Davis, in THE PROBLEM OF SLAVERY IN WESTERN CULTURE, he "endowed it with the

sanction of paternal authority, and helped to establish a precedent that would govern discussions of political philosophy as late as the eighteenth century." The relationship between psychiatrists and mental patients has been and continues to be viewed in the same way. The fact that, as in the case of slavery, the physician needs the police power of the State to maintain his relationship with his so-called patient does not alter this self-serving image of the oppressive institution.

Paternalism is the crucial explanation for the stubborn conflict about whether the practices employed by slaveholders and institutional psychiatrists are "therapeutic" or "noxious." Masters and psychiatrists profess their benevolence; their slaves and involuntary patients protest against their malevolence. . . .[45]

This is the characteristic dialogue of oppression and liberation. The ruler looks in the mirror and sees a liberator; the ruled looks at the ruler and sees a tyrant. If the physician has the power to incarcerate the patient and uses it, the relationship between the two will inevitably fit into this mold. If one cannot ask the subject whether he likes being enslaved or committed, whipped or electroshocked —because he is not a fit judge of his own "best interests"—then one is left with the contending opinions of the practitioners and their critics. . . .[46]

Oppression and degradation are unpleasant to behold and are, therefore, frequently disguised or concealed. One method for doing so is to segregate—in special areas, such as camps or "hospitals"—the degraded human beings. Another is to conceal the social realities behind the fictional facade of what we call, after Wittgenstein, "language games." While psychiatric language games may seem fanciful, the psychiatric idiom is actually only a dialect of the common language of oppressors. Thus slaveholders called the slaves LIVESTOCK, mothers

BREEDERS, their children INCREASE, and gave the term DRIVERS to the men set over them at work. The defenders of psychiatric imprisonment call their institutions HOSPITALS, the inmates PATIENTS, and the keepers DOCTORS; they refer to the sentence as TREATMENT, and to the deprivation of liberty as PROTECTION OF THE PATIENT'S BEST INTERESTS.

In both cases, the semantic devices are supplemented by appeals to tradition, morality, and social necessity. . . .[47]

A psychiatrist who accepts as his "client" a person who does not wish to be his client, defines him as a "mentally ill" person, then incarcerates him in an institution, bars his escape from the institution and from the role of mental patient, and proceeds to "treat" him against his will—such a psychiatrist, I maintain, creates "mental illness" and "mental patients." He does so exactly the same way as the white man who sailed for Africa, captured the black man, brought him to America in shackles, and then sold him as if he were an animal, created slavery and slaves. To be sure, in both cases, the process is carried out in accordance with the law of the land. The assertion that only the "insane" are committed to mental hospitals is, in this view, comparable to the claim that only the black man is enslaved. It is the most damaging evidence, for it signifies that the oppressor recognizes the "special" condition of his adversary. . . .[48]

The psychiatric profession has, of course, a huge stake, both existential and economic, in being socially authorized to rule over mental patients, just as the slave-owning classes did in ruling over slaves. In contemporary psychiatry, indeed, the expert gains superiority not only over members of a specific class of victims, but over nearly the whole of the population, whom he may "psychiatrically evaluate.". . .[49]

We know that man's domination over his fellowman is as old as history; and we may safely assume that it is traceable to prehistoric times and to prehuman ancestors. Perennially, men have oppressed women; white men, colored men; Christians, Jews. However, traditional reasons and justifications for discrimination have lost much of their plausibility. What justification is there for man's age-old desire for domination of his fellowman? Modern liberalism (in reality, a type of statism), allied with scientism, has met the need for a fresh defense of oppression and has supplied a new battle cry: Health!

In this therapeutic-meliorist view of society, the ill form a special class of "victims" who must, both for their own good and for the interests of the community, be "helped"—coercively and against their will, if necessary—by the healthy; and among the healthy, especially by physicians, who are "scientifically" qualified to be their masters. This perspective developed first and has advanced farthest in psychiatry, where the oppression of "insane patients" by "sane physicians" is by now a social custom hallowed by medical and legal tradition. At present, the medical profession as a whole seems to be emulating this model. In the Therapeutic State toward which we appear to be moving the principal requisite for the role of Big Brother may be an MD degree. . . .[50]

We can, and indeed must, choose between two mutually exclusive postures. On the one hand, we can define certain persons as helpless, requiring special treatment on the part of the State; those in the "helping professions" will then be able to bask in the glory of their own benevolence, while those being "serviced" will be stigmatized. On the other hand, we can strive toward the creation of a society in which the State, especially in its imposition of social controls through criminal laws, recognizes neither stigma nor status symbols or categories; the manufacture, with State approval, of stigmatized individuals and classes by professional degraders would then cease and, as citizens subject to control by the State, all men would be equal.

This need not be the end of charity and decency. On the contrary, it could be their beginning. For only then would charity be purged of coercion, and decency of domination.[51]

## THE HOSPITAL AS AN ASYLUM

Szasz's attack on what he terms the "benevolent coercion" that serves as the inner core of the practice of institutional psychiatry needs to be assessed against realistic attempts to develop an alternative treatment model. The central argument in favor of traditional practices of incarcerating the mentally ill is that they need to be locked up in order to protect themselves and those around them. If the evidence should support this argument, then the social good would demand that current practices be continued, no matter how much they might seem to resemble those of the medieval inquisition. On the other hand, if alternative approaches to treatment produce results that are satisfactory, and if the results can be evaluated in terms of reasonably "hard" evidence, then there would be a basis for accepting Szasz's conclusions regarding the apparent imperialism of the psychiatric profession.

The simplest question that might be asked is whether the mental hospital can be eliminated—or, to put the question in more realistic terms, whether potential patients can do just as well outside the community. In a major study addressed to just this point, Benjamin Pasamanick and his colleagues report on an extensive program with patients who had been diagnosed as schizophrenic but were treated at home.[52] Just as in most understaffed and underbudgeted institutions, the major treatment modality was tranquilizing drugs. This was coupled with the use of regular home visits by nursing personnel, the hospital itself being used only as a backup facility in emergency situations. Under these circumstances approximately 75 percent of the patients treated were able to maintain themselves satisfactorily at home. An additional finding, suggestive but not fully understood, was that one-third of the patient population were apparently able to make it on the outside even if a placebo was substituted for their medication.

There are other, related questions that might be asked about the hospitalization of the mentally ill. For example, is there any relation between the length of hospital treatment and subsequent adjustment? Or, more generally, are there grounds for saying that hospital care is good for a patient, or at least better than keeping him in the community?

Questions of this sort can hardly be studied by the use of control groups since treatment cannot be made to depend on research needs. Rather, the answers can be found only by an examination of existing statistics. In one such study, by Werner Mendel, the records of 2,926 patients were examined.[53] They all had been discharged from Los Angeles Hospital, after treatment of varying length, with the diagnosis of schizophrenia. Of this group 75 percent were able to remain in the community for at least some period of time. But the significant finding is this: The length of the hospital stay in each case (varying from seven days to one year) showed no relation either to their success in staying out or to their chances of readmission. Indeed, the briefer the first period of hospitalization, the shorter the period of treatment required on later readmission.

A second group of 443 patients similarly diagnosed was then followed for a two-year period following their discharge from the hospital. Their ability to function adequately with others, with family, and at work was found to be negatively correlated with the length of hospitalization. That is, the longer their hospitalization, the lower their level of posthospital functioning, and vice versa. Again, by this sort of evidence it appears that rather than being a help to a patient in his posthospital career, treatment in the hospital decreases his chances of functioning to his own best capacity.

In answer to these data it might be argued that nothing at all has been demonstrated except that people who are less sick to begin with require less hospitalization and then, of course, function better after discharge. But this line of argument misses the point. The question here has to do with the value of hospitalization in treating the mentally ill. If treatment in a hospital is of any value at all, it would follow that hospitalization would help the mildly disturbed as well as those who are more seriously ill, and in that case the less disturbed patients who had, for various reasons, been subjected to longer initial periods of hospitalization would benefit by requiring shorter periods of treatment on later readmission. In fact, precisely the reverse was shown to occur—that is, the shorter the initial period of hospitalization, regardless of any other factor, the shorter the treatment period required at a later date.

The only reasonable conclusion seems to be the one stated by Mendel: "The least number of days of hospitalization which fulfills the therapeutic intent is the optimum time of hospitalization."[54] Whatever else may be implied in these data, they do not support the proposition that hospitalizing a patient increases his chances of getting better; rather the less hospital treatment he is given, the better off everyone will be, for, as Mendel notes, there are also definite contraindications for hospitalization: "[it] causes further alienation of the patient from society and reification of the patient's failure in his adaptive tasks, reinforces the passive role in the solution of his problems, and mobilizes his remaining resources to adapt to the artificial society of the hospital rather than utilizing these for the task of conforming to the real world outside of the hospital.[55]

Finally, one other kind of evidence is relevant to the issue of hospitalization— the results of programs that utilize the mental hospital as an asylum rather than as the prisonlike institution that Szasz describes. If alternative approaches can be developed within the institution itself, then we would be tempted to agree with Szasz's claim that techniques verging on incarceration are unnecessary. One such alternative program is worth considering.[56]

In a typical state hospital, which was required to accept all psychiatric admissions within a specified geographic area, a total of seventy-two patients during one six-month period and ninety-six patients during a second six-month period were brought in, admitted, and treated. The treatment program was specifically designed to handle all incoming patients, treat them over a brief period, and discharge them. The results were as follows: during the initial six-month period, 92 percent of the patients admitted were discharged; of these 75 percent were returned to their families and 17 percent either to relatives or to live by themselves. The comparable figures for the second six-month period were 70 percent and 18 percent, for a total of 88 percent discharged. Of those discharged, the median length of stay in the hospital was twenty-one days; and of the total group, nine out of ten left the hospital in less than three months. These were not simply mildly disturbed patients but very similar to those who are routinely sent to state hospitals; more than half had been diagnosed as psychotic on admission.

A follow-up study approximately one year after hospitalization covered 98 percent of the patient group, and it was determined that one-fourth of them had required rehospitalization for psychiatric reasons.[57] This compared with the figure of 23 percent for a very similar comparison group in previous years who had not received the benefit of this special program. In addition, patients in the special program had not required greater care nor put a greater strain on community resources, and their composite record showed fewer arrests than would be expected in such a group. Further, their post-hospitalization careers showed that they were involved in significantly less family disorganization than was true of the comparison group. By most criteria, then, their adjustment was either equal to or better than that of patients who had left the hospital in former years, in spite of the fact that their length of stay was, on the average, less than half of what had been customary in this institution.

The program that produced these results consisted of two phases—an intensive treatment period lasting approximately one week, followed by a readjustment period of two to three weeks. The entering patient, regardless of diagnosis, symptoms, or presenting behavior, was taken first to the intensive treatment area and there greeted. All physical restraints were removed, and within ten minutes the patient was seen by a psychiatrist for evaluation. The patient was then given to understand that he was ill and would be accepted as such and that he was now to be treated as a sick person. He was given fairly heavy medication, the purpose and effect of which was first explained to him; he was dissuaded from talking about his problems or manifesting his symptoms; he was told that there was no need at the present for him to make any plans; and in general he was strongly encouraged to defer any action and to accept fully the sick role. During this phase of the treatment the patient often slept a great deal, at least initially; in any case he was under rather close and continuous medical supervision.

As soon as the acute phase of the patient's disturbance had died down and he showed that he was beginning to reorganize himself, he was transferred to the readjustment area, where he was treated as a responsible person who was recovering from an illness. Medical supervision was minimal and unobtrusive. The patient took responsibility for selecting his own room, arranging his own activities, visiting with family and friends, obtaining his own medication, and planning with his individual counselor for his posthospital course. In the course of this counseling the emphasis was on the future rather than on the patient's personality or his past difficulties; as far as possible, his family was included in his planning.[58]

The treatment program was deliberately built around what might be called the management of expectations, on the hypothesis that social behavior is to a large extent determined by one's expectations as to what the situation demands.[59] In the initial phase of treatment, the patient's expectations in regard to being sick were met and fully satisfied; in the second phase, his expectations were guided toward his return to a self-responsible role in the community. The results appear to show that the mental hospital may indeed be used by professionals, not as a device for controlling the lives and fates of helpless victims, but as a true asylum, like a helping hand and a place of refuge. When this is done, even the most disturbed patients can apparently be dealt with appropriately and very soon returned to their communities without the imposition of a lifetime stigma.

All three types of evidence that we have examined converge in supporting Szasz's position that as the mental hospital is currently constituted, it does the patient more harm than good, but that it can in fact be reconstituted for a more socially humane and effective purpose. When this is done, the traditional picture of mentally ill patients who need incarceration for the protection of themselves and everyone around them is seen to have very little foundation in fact. That picture, in fact, may be—as Szasz claims—fostered by a profession that has too often taken on the role of agent to identify and control whatever form of deviance is currently unpopular.[60]

# chapter 3
# schizophrenia
# as
# a
# way
# of
# life

The condition we call madness has many names; every language ever known has had its special terms, both polite and vulgar, for the phenomenon of being utterly deranged and inexplicably different. Yet as far back as written records exist the picture seems to have been very much the same. We can read the description on any police blotter, in the record of any hospital emergency room, and even in the Old Testament, and it will be familiar. Here, for example, is Nebuchadnezzar: "The same hour was the thing fulfilled upon Nebuchadnezzar; and he was driven from men, and did eat grass as oxen, and his body was wet with the dew of heaven, till his hairs were grown like eagles' feathers, and his nails like birds' claws." [Daniel 4:33]

In every age and every culture, no matter what the social conditions or the level of collective development, some people have fallen into this state and have immediately been marked by their fellows as so radically changed as to merit some special name and usually some special treatment.[1] Every conceivable explanation for the condition has been offered at one time or another and quite possibly every imaginable form of treatment has been tried. But it still happens and keeps happening to so many people every year, and some of them later change for the better while others do not.

## THE NAME FOR IT

The words for the condition seem to fall into three groups: (1) essentially descriptive terms with the common meaning of "wrong" or "awry"; (2) terms that imply an informal or primitive theory; and (3) formal terms derived from a theory. There may be slang as well as nonslang terms in each group.

### DESCRIPTIVE TERMS, NONSLANG

INSANE: not healthy (cf. the similar Spanish INSANO and the French IN-SENSE.) This term was more widely used in earlier centuries; today it is mostly restricted to that museum of fossil English, the law.

MAD: a very old root related to words meaning "foolish" or "hurt."

DERANGED: off the track. (cf. the similar German VERRÜCHT and Spanish TRAS-TORNADO.)

FOOLISH: having to do with FOLLY. (cf. the similar French FOU.)

CRAZY: crazed, cracked.

FRENZY, -IED: from the Greek PHREN, meaning "heart, mind." Closely related is DEMENTED: out of (one's) mind.

### DESCRIPTIVE TERMS, SLANG

WACKY: the origin is not certain; perhaps from a journalistic term referring to news that is not straight or ordinary.

UNHINGED; OFF (ONE'S) ROCKER; CRACKED UP, CRACKERS: the meanings of these are straightforward.

BATTY, BATS: of uncertain origin; perhaps a reference to the creature, in the sense of fluttering, or perhaps derived from the expression "bats in the belfry."

NUTTY, NUTS: related to NUT, an old term for "head."

DOTTY: from DODDER, meaning to quake or quaver; thus, "shaky."

CUCKOO, KOOKY: from an old term GOWK, meaning "foolish."

BONKERS: from an English naval term meaning "slightly drunk"; or from a similar British cyclists' slang term meaning "out of energy."

DAFFY, DAFT: one of those curious terms that gain their current meaning by way of a reversal. Originally from a root meaning "fitting" (cf. DEFT).

SCREWY, SCREWBALL: from a British slang term SCREWED, meaning "drunk"; the derivation seems to be along the same lines as the British TIGHT for "drunk."

FREAKY, FREAKED OUT: apparently from an old word meaning "capricious." A related word, taken over from the contemporary drug culture, is SPACED OUT.

CRACKED (UP): same origin as CRAZY.

### INFORMAL THEORY, NONSLANG

LUNATIC: from the Latin LUNA, meaning "moon."

PIXILATED: derived from PIXIE, or "fairy."

BERSERK(ER): from an Icelandic word for "wild warrior," perhaps in turn derived from BARESARK, referring to fighting without shirt of mail or armor.

AMOK: from the Malay AMOQ, or "wildly crazy."

DELUDED: from Latin LUDENS, or "game," meaning to be played with, to be "gamed" or deceived.

### INFORMAL THEORY, SLANG

LOONY: same origin as LUNATIC.

LOCO: (similar to Spanish LOCO, Portuguese LOUCO) from the locoweed, a plant that was supposed to make people crazy; its name, in turn, derives from Latin GLAUCUS, or "sparkling."

### FORMAL THEORY

PSYCHOTIC: from the Greek PSYCHE, or "mind."

SCHIZOPHRENIA: Eugen Bleuler's term, referring to a "split mind" (feeling versus thinking).

DEMENTIA PRAECOX: Emil Kraepelin's term, meaning "early derangement" or "youthful aberration."

## MADNESS AS A HUMAN CONDITION

It is the very universality of this condition—one of the very few true universals among human beings—that seems to have impelled thinkers to look for absolutely fundamental explanatory schemes. Since it occurs in all times and places under the total range of human living arrangements it can hardly be attributed to the merely local or temporary cause. Whatever makes it happen must be with us, as human beings, in every society we fashion, no matter when or where. There are not many aspects of our lives that are this universal. Our biological makeup is one; the existence of certain of our social institutions, such as marriage and the family, is another; and a third involves such characteristics of our lives as the fact that we have a language or do some sort of useful work. Theories about madness have therefore looked in these three directions, at least since educated persons gave up their beliefs in madness as either a visitation of divine wrath or the temporary possession of body and mind by some good or evil spirit.

In this chapter I will look briefly at some of the evidence concerning these major explanatory approaches, but before getting to that there is a preliminary step to be taken. In order to embark on a sensible comparative discussion, it is necessary to have the matter itself well in hand. There are real risks in trying to assign explanations and causes to a phenomenon before it has been adequately described so that we can all agree on what it is that we want to explain. As we shall see in discussing some explanatory schemes, arguing for a specific approach to understanding madness seems to be associated with emphasizing its distinctly different aspects—very much like the group of blind men whose individual positions led them to explore different aspects of the one beast and thus draw quite disparate conclusions about the nature of an elephant.

Some commonplace examples will point up what I mean here. Consider these two passages:

*Perhaps you have known someone like Roberta L. Soon after she turned 16 she became unruly, unpredictable and sloppy. Although she suffered violent mood swings, she was most often depressed and fatigued. Her world became distorted. She was unable to get along at school or at home. Her parents blamed themselves. . . . Roberta is not the victim of a poor environment. She is one of tens of thousands who each year develop a little understood disease called schizophrenia.[2]*

*Schizophrenia affects at least two million Americans and hospitalizes more people than cancer, heart ailments, and tuberculosis combined. In fact, patients suffering from schizophrenia fill one-fourth of all hospital beds. Until recently, there was almost no hope of recovery from this dread disease; but now, thanks to new research on the frontiers of medicine, hope is growing that schizophrenia can at last be cured.*[3]

The first of these passages is from a fund-raising brochure for the American Schizophrenia Association; the second is from a newspaper account of recent biochemical research on schizophrenia. Both passages represent an unquestioning view of this condition as a biochemical, and therefore purely medical, disease that, like the plague of medieval times, will be cured as soon as we are able to discover the appropriate medicine. The explanation proposed here may be closer to the truth than any other; that remains to be shown. But until such an answer is at hand, we would do well to avoid preempting the conclusion to our discussion by describing the condition of madness in so narrow and specialized a way. What we need, rather, is a heading under which all the existing approaches can be subsumed, a neutral concept that will enable us to describe the major characteristics and consequences of madness without committing us to any of the explanatory biases by which we customarily come to terms with it.

### The Concept of "Way of Life"

Consider first a familiar phenomenon about which we have fewer strongly held preconceptions—adolescence. Let us try to find the single term that describes this phenomenon. Is adolescence a condition? Is it a state? Should we refer to it, rather, as a process or a period? It seems to be all of these, you might say. To be somewhat more precise, then, we may ask: Is adolescence a disease? Is it a set of behavior patterns? A series of life choices? A collection of established social rituals and customs? Again, in some measure all of these concepts apply. But the difficulty with them, without exception, is that either as terms or concepts they imply too much at the outset. In their place, we may try to agree on a relatively neutral description of adolescence and see if this does not help us to find a handle for further discussion of it. Thus:

It appears that for some measurable time during the lives of most persons in modern societies, approximately between the ages of ten and twenty, they are identifiable as a group. During this period—or at least for a large portion of it—many of the most significant aspects of their lives are related to, and may perhaps be determined by, the fact of their "belonging" to this group. (That term is set off because there is no implication here that these persons have in any way chosen to join a group or are even aware of their possible group membership.)

Notice that I have said this much about adolescence without making any commitment as to what might cause the phenomenon or even indicating whether it is appropriate to speak here of causation. Nor have I expressed or implied any judgment about adolescence, whether it is good or bad, normal or abnormal, desirable or not. All that I have stated is that there appears to be such a phenomenon and that we can probably agree on identifying it. A most convenient term and concept, to sum up what I am saying here, is that for a certain period of time adolescence constitutes for most persons a *way of life*. I mean by this that being in this way of life affects just about every significant aspect of the person's mode of living. In this sense, the notion of way of life is much broader than most other descriptive terms. The way of life that we term adolescence affects where the person lives, how he spends his time, what other persons may think of him or feel about him, how others will act toward him, how he views himself and his person and body and day-to-day condition, how he sees his own past and future, his appearance and preferences and interests and activities, and even the small details of what he may wear or eat or say. All of these aspects are in some way related to, and are often determined by, the fact that his way of life is that of being an adolescent.

Many other examples of ways of life come to mind: being an adult rather than a child, or elderly rather than young; being female rather than male; being black or brown rather than white; being primarily urban rather than rural; being American rather than, say, Brazilian; or being very intelligent rather than mentally retarded. To some degree, and in some ways, many significant aspects of one's total mode of living will be affected by the fact of being in one or more of these ways of life rather than others. For we are all associated with a number of ways of life at the same time, so that they overlap and interpenetrate without mutual interference. As a consequence, we conduct ourselves within a complicated and highly individualized mosaic of allegiances and roles. But some ways of life are clearly of greater import than others and will override whatever others the person may at the time be identified with. In our own society, for example, it makes much more of a difference what skin color you were born with than whether your birthplace was city or country, and for many thousands of years it has made a lot of difference whether you were born female rather than male, but only some difference whether you were born bright rather than stupid or rich rather than poor. There are always hierarchies of ways of life in any society. The exact characteristics pertaining to the various ways of life may have changed through the centuries, but the fact of one way of life being more significant for the person than another has not changed. Indeed, this fact has largely determined the kind of culture that people in any age have suffered under or enjoyed.

Of all the ways of life with which we are familiar, large or small, surely the one which has caused the greatest concern, and recently the greatest puzzle-ment, is the condition that we now call schizophrenia. Its chief characteristic is simply that it is different; to enter it as a way of life constitutes, in almost every case, a radical change in some of the most fundamental aspects of experience and behavior—feelings, expression, perception, and even the patterning among these aspects, such as the normal relations between feeling and expression.[4] More than any other way of life, therefore, schizophrenia has literally demanded an explana-tion, in a way that one's sex, for example, or one's intelligence has not. And under-standably, the explanations offered for madness all through the centuries have tried to be as basic as the condition they described: the wrath of God, as in the case of Nebuchadnezzar, or possession by evil spirits, as in so many other instances.[5]

## The Natural History of Schizophrenia

Every way of life that is reasonably total in the sense that it encompasses in its unique way most important aspects of a person's life—for example, being female rather than male, or being schizophrenic—will also extend over some appreciable span of time. It will have its own particular background, its own special course of development, perhaps even its own typical outcomes—in short, what might appropriately be called its *natural history*. I mean by this term that identifiable course of events that is peculiar to some organism, or creature, or phenomenon simply because of what it is. A tree, for example, has its natural history: not simply the fact that it grows, but more particularly that it grows in its own treelike way, up and out rather than down and in; that it goes through cycles related to its own reproduction; and that it stays in one spot rather than getting up and moving to a new place.[6]

A natural history is, in a manner of speaking, each thing's way of saying that it knows its own place in some large scheme and that it will stay within the limits that define this. Thus, without stretching the term too much, it can be said that the common cold has its own natural history—hence the sage remark that if you treat a cold with medication you can knock it out in seven days, but if you just leave it alone it will go away in a week. On a level of greater significance, Hans Selye, having spent a professional lifetime studying diseases in a search for their common elements, concludes that a disease is always in some way an abbreviated history of stress on the organism and so it always falls into a specifically patterned sequence.[7] His theory of disease, then, consists of a natural history of biological stress.

But, you may object, this is so self-evident as not even to call for mention; of course a tree grows up rather than down; if it grew down and in, it would not be a tree at all. Most assuredly—and in this sense I am only stating what is self-evident. My defense, however, is precisely that by introducing the notion of the natural history of an organism or phenomenon I am enabled to deal, on a purely descriptive level, with what is self-evident. By discussing the natural history of schizophrenia rather than what causes schizophrenia, I hope to be able to explore in an unbiased way some of the more salient aspects of this particular way of life. In this area what we need, first of all, are some means for simply describing the phenomenon in an organized but unprejudiced way. Only then will we be in a position to examine some evidence about the supposed determinants of the phenomenon and what happens when we attempt to change it.

The natural history of schizophrenia seems to fall into three stages: a first phase that is anticipatory, perhaps preparatory, and that I will call *prodromal*; a second, *transitional* phase in which there usually occur those events that we identify with madness and call the acute symptoms; and a third phase of *adjustment* to the consequences of change.

*THE PRODROMAL PHASE.* Since the recognizable aspect of schizophrenia may occur at any age, beginning with early childhood, the prodromal phase varies in length from one person to another. Usually, however, it includes childhood and often adolescence as well; theories about the importance of early family environment refer to its effect on this phase. More ambitious theorists try to extend the prodromal phase back before birth, in a search for so-called hereditary factors. Whether or not any of these theories will turn out to be valid—and it is equally likely that schizophrenia will never be traced to clear-cut and universal patterns of early development—we can at least agree that genetic and early familial influences have their greatest chance, so to speak, during this phase. Thus, it may be helpful to extend this phase as far back as possible in order to examine every potential influence, rather than to assume a short prodromal period. Accounts of drug-induced behavior that seems psychotic often neglect this factor, implying that the drug itself, when taken in adulthood, constitutes the sole cause; but when a lengthy prodromal phase is considered, as Theodore Barber[8] has shown, the evidence in most cases indicates the influence of long-standing personality characteristics. The more seriously the prodromal phase is considered, the greater the likelihood that preventive measures, particularly on a large scale, can be developed.

*THE TRANSITIONAL PHASE.* What most people think of when they hear the word *crazy* is the transitional phase. It is a period usually of fairly short duration, rarely lasting more than a few weeks, and since the introduction of tranquilizing medication about 1955, in fact, it may last no more than a few hours. It is marked by overt and often bizarre symptoms and by very rapid change. Schizophrenia may sometimes even begin here, in a manner of speaking, without any recognizable prior phase. A sudden crisis of overwhelming proportions, a physical trauma, such as a blow to the head, or a neurological crisis involving coma and delirium may bring on the experience of world-reordering change, a fundamental and radical destruction of everything known and imagined. However, there is always the possibility that a mild prodromal phase, setting up the individual as a victim, actually preceded even a severe crisis.

In any case, the dramatic period of this second phase almost always serves to bring the person to the attention of those around him. It is at this point that his associates, his family, his friends, or someone in authority—whoever happens to be affected and in a position to do something about it—will take the steps that result in the schizophrenic becoming, at least in most modern societies, a mental patient. To accomplish this, a curious collection of state laws has developed in this country. One reviewer has surveyed them and concluded that they constitute at best "a mélange of statutory ineptitude . . . a display of 51 statutory criteria and definitions that were developed for the purpose of transporting certain human beings out of society and incarcerating them somewhere in something. These statutes are really not criteria or guidelines. They are conflicting labels that are the social excuse for incarcerating the gauche."[9]

Those who are closest to the patient, and even those who act as society's agents in implementing the decision to hospitalize him at this point, believe sincerely that this action is, in a sense, forced on them by the severity of his disturbance. But when the entering patient's condition is evaluated by independent and unbiased observers, the evidence seems to indicate that the crucial factor, though it may not be apparent to the persons concerned, is really the presence or absence of community resources for support of the patient and his family. On the basis of their study of 269 such decisions, made by 33 decision-makers, the authors of one study conclude: "This study presented data which provides further evidence for the point of view that hospitalization is not a necessary or even useful approach to the treatment of mental illness if adequate community resources are available, experienced personnel has sufficient time to evaluate crisis, and service can be offered immediately to the patient when he needs it."[10]

In any case, the result of collective action on the part of those immediately in contact with the schizophrenic patient is that he is branded, often for life, by means of a standardized set of procedures in which his whole way of life is radically altered. The institution through which this is accomplished is the mental hospital; and as such it plays a major role in determining the natural history of schizophrenia and other psychological life crises.

---

We'd like to know
A little bit about you
For our files.
We'd like to help you learn
To help yourself.
Look around you. All you see

Are sympathetic eyes.
Stroll around the grounds
Until you feel at home.[11]

---

If theoretical biases enter to some degree into consideration of the prodromal phase, they are even more pressing in regard to the acute, transitional phase. The commonest and most powerful of our current biases—that schizophrenia is a disease—is based almost entirely on data taken from this second phase. Schizophrenia is usually characterized in terms of the kinds of behavior shown here—confusion, hallucinations, inappropriate communication or lack of it, delusions, unpredictability, strange and different emotional expression, or violence. Thus a process with its own three-stage natural history comes to be identified with the special events taking place in only one of the stages. The events are, under the terms of a medical bias, understood as "symptoms" of the supposed illness, which is now considered to be in its acute stage, and by a proper reading of the more obvious and dramatic of these events, the practitioner is enabled to arrive at a "diagnosis."[12]

Behavior that is extremely deviant and uncommon is, of course, often frightening to the layman, and even to the experienced professional it is at least upsetting and puzzling. In addition, it often poses an immediate problem of interpersonal stability that takes on first priority for action—for example, if a member of a family threatens to burn down their house or a member of a small community begins to dance nude in the town square. For these reasons, the case is not likely to be studied and the person himself not likely to be allowed, much less encouraged, to proceed with what he is doing. As a result, we have surprisingly little information about what really does happen during this phase. Hospital patients who show continuing or recurring indications similar to their behavior during the transitional phase can often be shown to be either holding to a habit or using the "symptom" as a device to keep people away. When asked to talk about what happened or what they experienced, hospitalized schizophrenics are rarely able to furnish more useful information than can be gained from interviewing their family and friends—although the one intriguing item on which they seem to be nearly unanimous concerns their overall attitude toward the transitional experience. When asked if they would mind going through it again, they will almost always say, with great feeling, "No—absolutely not, anything but that!"

This suggests what we might have suspected—that from the point of view of the schizophrenic himself, the experience during this phase is of being a victim of intolerable change. Not simply that his world is changing rapidly, and not only that the changes are fundamental. Neither of these would necessarily and invariably produce the reaction we get when we talk to hospitalized patients about this phase. Only the fact of having felt victimized could account for their unanimous response. If this is so, it is a period different from anything most of us know during our lives—different from going along with change, even more different from helping it along. The experience must be one of total ego loss—for it is the ego that enables us to deal with change—and, related to this, being overwhelmed by the world. How the world appears in its all-consuming aspect, whether evil or threatening or collapsing or mysterious or impenetrable,[13] will probably then determine the precise events that to an observer appear as symptoms—delusional fantasies of world destruction, or violent attack on strangers, or disorganization of behavior, or frozen immobility.

*THE ADJUSTMENT PHASE.* Surprisingly, we have very little more uncontaminated data about the third phase than we do about the second since, in modern Western culture, it most often takes place in the confines of that total institution known as a mental hospital. Consider some of the factors operating in the hospital that are more decisive than those pertaining to the individual patient and his experience:

1. Every institution has its own continuing weight of tradition and custom, and the larger it is and the longer it has been an institution, the greater is this weight. Further, the more established and routinized are the customs, and the more they are encrusted with established habits and patterns of status, the more likely it is that most of the jobs in the institution will be sought and held by people who are most comfortable with unfeeling routine. These people, in turn, will hold to one chief purpose, which is to make sure that things keep being done

the way they have always been done; and this will further assure that nothing will change. Chronic patients may usually be found in chronic hospitals that are staffed by chronic help. The typical patient who is an inmate of such an institution is hardly in a position to do other than accept the rules, the rote, and the routine that mark his all-encompassing environment. As a result, he soon learns to act in ways that fit the role of the good patient, thereby convincing the staff or other observers that he must indeed be the sick person supposed on admission. (I do not mean to imply here anything as dramatic or crude as a conspiracy on the part of the staff to keep patients locked up, for the hard fact is that many hospitals are overcrowded and would gladly accept any inexpensive scheme for depopulating their wards.[14] Rather, I am pointing to the fact that the traditional structure of the mental hospital serves, even if unwillingly, to make and keep its patients in a chronic status.)

2. One way of describing what has happened to a newly admitted schizophrenic is to say that he has only recently learned radically new ways of acting. Here some of the evidence from the experimental literature is relevant. As the research literature on cognitive dissonance shows,[15] when something has been learned at some cost to the learner, he will go to great lengths to continue believing that things are really the way he now construes them to be; in fact, he may change his existing attitudes and even his perception rather than alter his hard-won attitudinal position. Thus, the newly admitted patient who has just passed through a period of intense and traumatic change is unlikely to make an easy surrender of his newly developed psychotic position, particularly since there is relatively little pressure on him to do so. He will keep on acting in the way that helped to bring him into the hospital in the first place.

3. With all its faults, the hospital does represent a haven from whatever crisis situation the schizophrenic has recently passed through. Whatever else it may be to the staff or to ousiders, for the newly admitted patient the hospital serves as a place for getting away from a situation of stress and as a place to rest and recoup. If certain ways of acting have brought him here he might be well advised, at least at the beginning, to keep acting the same way so as to assure his remaining until he has had a chance to work out a new life situation for himself. Much anecdotal evidence from older mental hospitals supports this view of the patient's symptomatology as a device that will assure his getting into or returning to or staying in the hospital.

4. Finally, and as a caution in regard to whatever we may say about the patient's hospital career, we have nothing but heavily biased accounts of what it is like to be a mental hospital inmate. Every attempt at fact-gathering is bound to be an intrusion, and a nonneutral one at that, on the complex pattern of coexistence developed by the inmates and staff. For all the reasons just discussed, there is a strong tendency on the part of inmates and staff to keep things more or less as they are—and so a nonneutral intrusion by an outsider often serves to precipitate the very kind of extreme or symptomatic behavior that initially brought the patient into the hospital. The picture that we have of the inside of a mental hospital today, in spite of decades of educational effort by mental health

groups, is not too far removed from that depicted by Hogarth; which in turn, according to independent evidence, seems to have been quite a false picture of how patients behaved most of the time—as false to the facts as are many contemporary accounts.

For all these reasons, the adjustment phase of schizophrenia is likely to be, for most schizophrenics, a period of hospitalization, often long-term and unchanging; and as the hospital patient stays where he is, cut off from all of his past life and with little influence on him to live a normal life, he settles more and more into the pattern of a back ward patient, a "burnt-out case." Behavior in any social setting is to a great extent related to interpersonal anchoring points, or standards of reference that are validated by the local group. These serve as helps in instances of social uncertainty, and learning them forms part of the normal socialization process. Thus, only very young children, who have not yet learned the indicators that help to constrain social behavior, will make such silly mistakes as talking loudly during a church service or telling family secrets in front of visitors. Unless they move to a completely strange society, adults are usually able to go through life using the standards of behavior that they learned while growing up. The schizophrenic, however, now radically changed in his life pattern, taken out of the society he knows and set down in one totally different, finds himself bereft of every known support. In addition, he is surrounded by an array of authority figures who treat him as though he is unable to make it on his own. To his problem of learning a completely new way of life are added the additional burdens of having to do it alone, without help or encouragement, and of being forced to learn what is essentially a degrading set of social customs if he is to survive. The ways that he adopts (Erving Goffman

---

## THE INMATE COPES

The privilege system and the mortifying processes that have been discussed represent the conditions to which the inmate must adapt. These conditions allow for different individualistic ways of meeting them, apart from any effort at collective subversive action.

First, there is the tack of "situational withdrawal." The inmate withdraws apparent attention from everything except events immediately around his body and sees these in a perspective not employed by others present. This drastic curtailment of involvement in interactional events is best known, of course, in mental hospitals, under the title of "regression." Aspects of "prison psychosis" or going "stir simple" represent the same adjustment,

as do some forms of "acute depersonalization" described in concentration camps and "tankeritis" apparently found among confirmed merchant mariners.

Secondly, there is the "intransigent line": the inmate intentionally challenges the institution by flagrantly refusing to co-operate with staff. The result is a constantly communicated intransigency and sometimes high individual morale.

A third standard alignment in the institutional world is "colonization": the sampling of the outside world provided by the establishment is taken by the inmate as the whole, and a stable, relatively contented existence is built up out of the maximum satisfactions procurable within the institution.

A fourth mode of adaptation to the

setting of a total institution is that of "conversion": the inmate appears to take over the official or staff view of himself and tries to act out the role of the perfect inmate. While the colonized inmate builds as much of a free community for himself as possible by using the limited facilities available, the convert takes a more disciplined, moralistic, monochromatic line, presenting himself as someone whose institutional enthusiasm is always at the disposal of the staff. In Chinese P.O.W. camps, we find Americans who became "Pros" and fully espoused the Communist view of the world. In army barracks there are enlisted men who give the impression that they are always "sucking around" and always "bucking for promotion." In prisons there are "square johns." In German concentration camps, a long-time prisoner sometimes came to adopt the vocabulary, posture, expressions of aggression, and clothing style of the Gestapo, executing the role of straw boss with military strictness. Some mental hospitals have the distinction of providing two quite different conversion possibilities—one for the new admission, who can see the light after an appropriate inner struggle and adopt the psychiatric view of himself, and another for the chronic patient, who adopts the manner and dress of attendants while helping them to manage the other patients, employing a stringency sometimes excelling that of the attendants themselves.[16]

---

calls the process "making out") will bear the stamp of his unenviable position— his aloneness, his uncertainty and terror, his confusion, the rigidity and authoritarianism of the setting, thus adding to the staff's conviction that he is sick and probably incurable. Given the shortage of staff in every mental hospital except those devoted to the care of the wealthy, the average patient is soon abandoned for newer and fresher prospects. He then languishes, in greater or less personal comfort, depending on the institution and its budget, until he becomes one more statistic supporting the homely observation that the best predictor of a patient's chances for cure is the size of his hospital folder, the thickness being directly proportional to his incurability.

### DETERMINING INFLUENCES: HOW IT COMES ABOUT

I have deliberately used neutral, even rather vague, phrasing in the heading of this section in order to emphasize that stronger and more precise terms such as *cause* or *determinant* are hardly appropriate to the present state of our knowledge. Indeed, it may even be argued that the notion of cause will never be appropriate to either the understanding or treatment of schizophrenia. Consider again, for example, that schizophrenia is in many ways like adolescence. Both phenomena consist of periods of varying length during which the person undergoes a radical change, out of his own control, in just about every aspect of his life. Both sets of changes are accompanied by many indicators of personal distress; both clearly have biological aspects though both are also in important ways a function of social custom; and both exist, in rather similar fashion, in a wide range of literate and preliterate cultures, ancient and modern. Therefore, since adolescence and schizophrenia are structurally so much alike, it seems legitimate to ask regarding adolescence the kinds of questions that are often raised in regard to schizophrenia:

1. What causes adolescence?
2. How would you suggest that we cure adolescence? Is it curable?
3. What do you think might happen in the following case?

A kindly but authoritarian father who has nearly absolute power over his adolescent son says to him, "Now, I know that you have not asked me to do this, and I'm aware that you may not like what I am about to do. I also know very well that you have achieved the relative stability of your present position by working through a period of severe personal stress. Anyway, this is what I plan to do for you—I'm going to cure you back to the way you were before your adolescence started."

The example is, admittedly, farfetched, but it does at least suggest that if we take seriously the analogy with adolescence the whole issue of cause and cure becomes suspect. In any case, the concept of causation, at least as it is used in science, ought properly to be reserved for a kind of mechanical relation that is determined to exist between two identifiable single events. By that definition, the concept is far from appropriate when applied to the whole complex of conditions that necessarily precede any existing way of life.

With these major qualifications, then, we now look at the most important kinds of life influences that take place at various points in the development of the person who becomes schizophrenic. Because of the relation of different types of influence to the three phases of the natural history of schizophrenia, I have grouped them into three categories: genetic and early family influences, social influences, and experiential and personal influences.[17]

### Heredity and the Early Family Years

Genetic factors, which ought to be the easiest of determining influences to pin down in unequivocal fashion, turn out to be the least satisfactory. The history of the social sciences, especially over the past hundred years, is replete with passionately argued "proofs" that just about every known human condition, both admirable and blameworthy, from poverty and prostitution on the one hand to musical genius and political eminence on the other, is "caused" by inferior or superior genetic endowment (to use a once popular catch phrase). Centuries of success in breeding domesticated animals for specific characteristics of behavior and temperament served to lend strong support to such claims—which were, unfortunately, usually associated with the most retrogressive political views.

It seemed evident that characteristics of many sorts were passed from generation to generation, and with the development of the gene theory the mode of transmission also seemed clear. Early workers from Francis Galton on began an elaborate game of counting, in which the number of persons in a given population who could be expected to possess a characteristic, if the characteristic were distributed randomly, was compared with the actual distribution. The results unequivocally favored the hypothesis that most significant characteristics of human social life were inherited, or at least that the distribution was not random. It was clear that political and social eminence, intellectual and artistic attainments, alcoholism, criminality, and poverty all "ran in families" or were not distributed at random in the general population. The "good" characteristics, as it turned out, were bunched in "good" families and the "poor" characteristics in "poor" families. But because the conclusions, thus neatly drawn, so obviously supported a conservative position in regard to social organization, the real problems involved were soon lost sight of in a developing quarrel between conservative-minded nativists and liberal-minded environmentalists. Nothing could be learned about the origins and growth of important human characteristics as long as the discussion took the form of a political quarrel.

The pattern of "proving" that complex forms of human behavior were inherited was thus set by early studies that were often motivated primarily by social prejudice. Elaborate programs of research, such as that of Franz Kallmann,[18] were greatly weakened by methodological difficulties—for example, by inadequacies in specifying the behavioral phenomenon in question; by sampling that was often suspect; and by unwarranted assumptions concerning the genetic mechanisms involved. The result has been that only recently have investigators given up the "counting technique" inherited from Galton[19]—in which, for example, it was shown that the more closely related were two persons, the higher the likelihood that the diagnosis appropriate to one was also appropriate to the other—and turned to more stringent methods such as those based on adopted children. The conclusion drawn by David Rosenthal, on the basis of a very complete review of the evidence, is that there is indeed an important genetic factor in schizophrenia[20]—but it should also be emphasized that much more confirmatory evidence is needed, that this conclusion says nothing about the mechanisms involved, and that we still lack a comprehensive theory as to how such genetic influences might interact with environmental influences. When a single patient is studied intensively—or even an entire family, as in the case of the Genains—the gaps in our knowledge become still more evident.

---

## THE CASE OF THE GENAIN FAMILY

In this study, which is unique in the clinical literature, six persons in one family—a father, a mother, and four identical quadruplet daughters—were examined intensively.[21] The family came to the attention of investigators of the National Institute of Mental Health (a branch of the Department of Health, Education, and Welfare) when it was learned that the four girls had become schizophrenic; they provided an unprecedented opportunity to study IN VIVO some of the complex modes of interaction between genetic and environmental determinants of mental illness.

The study itself consisted of a book-length case history of the entire family; intensive investigation of the zygosity of the daughters—that is, tests and studies to determine the probability that they were identical quadruplets; and long-term hospital treatment and follow-up of the girls.

The first question to be raised is whether the girls were in fact identical, that is, whether they were formed from a single egg. Since a wide variety of test results are available, the answer to the question must rest on combining probabilities resulting from individual tests. The results, for the entire life span of the girls since birth, are summarized as follows:

"Previous investigators, who studied the placenta, early physical resemblances, and qualitative features regard the Genain quadruplets as monozygotic. The addition of blood group tests to the criteria now tends to confirm the earlier conclusion. When probabilities are calculated by a modification of methods devised for twins, simple hereditary traits yield a probability above 99 percent that the quadruplets are monozygotic. Some quantitative differences, especially fingerprints, appear more consistent with a two-egg origin, but statistics on these traits in other quadruplets do not exist.

"The evidence from qualitative traits so strongly supports the monozygotic hypothesis that the observed quantitative differences can probably be taken as a measure of the variation that is possible in identical quadruplets."[22]

The variation is of especial interest, for evident differences among the girls were apparent from the moment of birth. Here are the figures on their birth sizes:

| Name* | Nora | Iris | Myra | Hester |
|---|---|---|---|---|
| Birth weight | 4 lb. 8 oz. | 3 lb. 5 oz. | 4 lb. 4 oz. | 3 lb. 0 oz. |
| Birth length | 17 in. | 16 in. | 16½ in. | 13¾ in. |
| Weight at 6 weeks | 6 lb. 15 oz. | 5 lb. 3 oz. | 6 lb. 4 oz. | 4 lb. 0 oz. |

They maintained approximately these relative positions all through school, for example, in the grades they received. Nora averaged out at about C, Iris at about C—, Myra at about D, and Hester at D—, and all repeated one or more grades. The only one of the four whose position varied was Myra, who was at times the "middle" one and in other respects the "best" of the four.

The home environment was, by any standards, very disturbed. Mrs. Genain did her best to maintain some sort of order and consistency, but she was neither very strong as a personality nor very perceptive and capable as a manager. In addition she was usually dominated by her husband, who became progressively more disturbed as the girls grew up. The consequence was that the girls became, in the description of someone who knew them well, "proper, precise, little old ladies" in a home atmosphere that was cold and fear-ridden. The girls were all bed-wetters until they were fourteen. Mr. Genain became a heavy drinker, was moody and violent, and became more and more paranoid and preoccupied with the supposed sexual activities of his daughters.

Hester had her first psychotic episode when she was a senior in high school. Nora was able to finish high school and go to work in an office, but at age twenty she too became nervous, upset, and mildly confused and had to stay home in bed for two months; after some improvement, she became worse and when she was twenty-two was admitted to a state hospital with the diagnosis of schizophrenia. Iris also became acutely psychotic a few months after Nora had

* The pseudonyms for the girls are based on the initials NIMH.

been hospitalized. A few months later Mr. Genain became openly psychotic, although neither he nor Iris was hospitalized. Finally, Myra began to show similar symptoms, to which, as Mrs. Genain reported, the response of her sisters was, "The other girls were glad that Myra was finally getting ill." At this time the family picture was one of five persons, in various stages of disturbance, affecting each other in an abrasive and hostile manner, with Mrs. Genain vainly trying to keep some semblance of order and harmony.

This continued for another few months, until the situation became unbearable for Mrs. Genain. Hester was now unmanageable: "She was frightened and kept saying that it was dark, even when the sun was shining. . . . She talked of a high flaming fire and kept screaming and moaning, 'Oh, oh, Mama, Mama, stop it, stop it, save, save. The fire is going to burn all of us.' She would motion with her hands around her head. When trying to sit up, she would make a distressful, moaning sound, saying, 'She hurts all over,' and fall in a faint for five minutes or more, have a bowel movement, and vomit."[23] Iris took to spreading laundry around the yard and clothes around the bedrooms, and the girls would then fight with one another. Myra tried to practice typing but had to stop because the noise bothered the others; and Mr. Genain continually criticized Myra and watched everything she did.

With the help of a psychiatrist who had treated Nora, the girls were ad-

mitted to the hospital at NIMH. Their reactions varied in a predictable manner: "Myra went with great hopes of recovery and with a great desire to help her three sisters. Nora did not want to go at first, but then changed her mind. Iris did not seem to care. Hester did not seem to be aware of what was happening.[24]

The course of treatment and response over the next five years, during which time Mr. Genain died, was also consistent with the patterning among the four. Myra began to improve after a year and a half and at the end of three years made an attempt to live out of the hospital. Although readmitted on her first try, she improved again, spent some time in a Halfway House and then at the YWCA. She was finally discharged as much improved and married a career man in the military.

As for Nora, she was discharged to a state hospital after a number of years at NIMH. She stayed in the state hospital for a year, and then moved home to live with her mother. She maintained a marginal adjustment, helped by her interest in music and dancing.

Iris also went to a state hospital after some time at NIMH, then tried living with relatives, but after four years was readmitted to the hospital. Her prognosis is considered guarded and pessimistic.

Hester has remained in the hospital. After five years she is in a regressed ward for chronic patients, with a poor prognosis.

---

It is almost impossible to separate so-called genetic factors from those which are operative in earliest childhood. This is true in part because those characteristics that a child is born with certainly predispose him as to how he will deal with the influences of his environment during the first few years of life, and in part because the parents who, presumably, passed on certain genetic characteristics to him are the same persons who will be the major influences on him during childhood. For both these reasons, genetic factors and influences from early childhood combine to provide the greatest influence on what I have called the first, or prodromal, phase in the natural history of schizophrenia.

The evidence from family histories of schizophrenic patients indicates that it is extremely rare to find a schizophrenic member in a family whose interrelationships are basically healthy. What this says is that "healthy" families do not usually produce schizophrenic children. However, it does not say that "unhealthy" families necessarily produce schizophrenic offspring, for many other factors are of importance in bringing about this condition. Nor does this generalization say very much about how schizophrenia might result from familial pathology. A few years back, it was almost a fad to put the burden of blame on the mother, and the clumsy term *schizophrenogenic mother* was used to refer to the type of woman who was both distant and oversolicitous, both cold and seductive, both hostile and inconsistently loving, and who therefore created an atmosphere of emotional confusion and uncertainty, particularly for her male children. However, the emphasis has now shifted to looking at a total pattern of family relations rather than at the character or behavior of only one member.[25]

A broad picture of pathological communication and interaction now emerges, the person who later becomes schizophrenic has most likely been subjected to its atmosphere since his very earliest years. The picture includes the following major features: (1) the formal structure of the family is not clearly and comfortably established, either because a key member is missing or because some of the key members either cannot fit into their roles or intrude on the roles of others; (2) as a result, the patterns of authority and discipline and the boundaries of acceptable behavior are either not well defined or not comfortably accepted; (3) these then become the object of strategic manipulation among the family members; (4) major gaps then come to exist on a permanent basis in regard to the handling of at least some possible emotional states; and (5) the bonds among the members of the family do not appear to be strong enough for them to develop serviceable means for covering over all the lapses of structure, discipline, and emotional expression that are bound to occur. With this background, the communication among the members tends increasingly to serve only inconsequential or formalistic or even irrelevant functions. No clear-cut model of what is considered acceptable behavior emerges. Under these conditions, the likelihood of deviant development in one or more of the family members is high, and it may take the form that we call schizophrenia.

---

THE FAMILY OF THE SCHIZOPHRENIC

For most people, family life is where they learn to form, and have freedom to practice, different kinds of relationships. The maturational defect in the family of the schizophrenic centers in the inability of the parents to let the schizophrenic child learn to experience complementary and symmetrical relationships, despite the millions of messages they exchange together over the years. Typically if the child behaves in a way which indicates he is initiating a complementary, or "taking care of," relationship, his parents will indicate he should be less demanding and so behave more symmetrically with them.

If he behaves in a symmetrical way, they indicate that he does not seem to appreciate their desires to take care of him. This constant disqualification of his bids for relationship is a theme of their life together. If the child seeks closeness he is encouraged to be at a distance. If he attempts to place some distance between himself and his parents, they respond as if they have been criticized and indicate he should seek closeness. If he asks for something, he is too demanding. If he does not ask, he is too independent. The child is caught in a set of paradoxical relationships with all of his responses labeled as wrong ones. . . .[26]

The child also does not easily accept the behavior of his parents; typically he disqualifies whatever they offer just as they do. Because of the family inability to maintain a type of relationship with the child, there is thorough confusion in this type of family over authority and benevolence. Attempts to discipline the child usually end in confusion, indecision, and conflict. . . .[27]

Self-sacrifice by the parents is con-sidered a virtue in these families; mothers will even say that they have done nothing for themselves in their lives and everything for the child. . . . Not only will they help adult children eat, but they will converse with a quiet child by carrying both sides of the conversation. . . .[28]

The problem of who is to control whose behavior is a central issue in this type of family. The parents appear to receive any attempt by the child to initiate a type of relationship as a maneuver to control them. However, if the child responds appropriately to a relationship initiated by them, the parents also respond as if this is a maneuver to control them. For example, if the child asks mother to do something for him, she indicates by her reluctance that he is too demanding. Yet if she initiates doing something for the child, and he accepts her behavior, she responds as if he is demanding too much of her. Similarly, if he indicates he wishes to do something himself, she will respond by showing him that she should do it for him.[29]

---

Two studies, one which pioneered in this area and one carried out recently, will indicate the kind of evidence that supports the general picture I have just sketched. In the earlier study, by Theodore Lidz and his coworkers, the pattern of thinking on the part of parents of known schizophrenics was investigated.[30] Their findings strongly suggested that at least one parent of such patients—even when not hospitalized nor even obviously disturbed—was significantly more deviant in regard to rationality of thought than were either of the parents of nonpatients. A careful and elaborate study along the same lines, by Elliot Mishler and Nancy Waxler,[31] came to much the same conclusions: interpersonal communications among members of a family in which one child was schizophrenic were markedly different from similar communications occurring within all-normal families; they were more stereotyped, less appropriately emotional, and in general less informally directed among each other.

The findings all point in the same direction, but what is obviously missing is a way of understanding how such results come about. Here, if anywhere, there is revealed one of the weaknesses in contemporary learning theory: it can often handle adequately the circumstance of one situation or event producing one measurable result, but it seems to be unequipped to handle what H. F. Hunt has called "the slow, accretive development of behavioral anomalies."[32] Many examples are at hand—the "behavioral sink," or pathological community of laboratory rats that John Calhoun produced through the continuing effect of small variations in environmental conditions;[33] the condition of depression and debilitation known as *marasmus* that René Spitz found among infants in orphanages and attributed to the long-term effect of lack of emotional stimulation and acceptance;[34] and, in adults, as well as children, the well-known condition that has been called *hospitalism*,[35] a result of the slow but cumulative effects of overcrowded and impersonal hospital conditions.

It is primarily because of the lack of a theory that we are unable to answer what should be the first question: Do the findings suggest that the primary influence on the later schizophrenic patient is the inheritance of parental characteristics or their social effect on his early development? A related question remains just as much a puzzle: Since all our evidence is gathered after the fact, when the family has come under scrutiny because one of its members has already become overtly schizophrenic, how can we tell whether he reached his present condition as a consequence of growing up in such a family, or whether the family itself represents the other members' reactions to having lived with someone who was so deviant?

## Culture and Its Consequences

Dividing up influences into neatly ordered classes—heredity, environment; genetic, social; early, late—is a game for theoreticians. In the complex and perhaps unpredictable arena of social living, determining factors shade into each other too imperceptibly to be distinguished. Heredity and environment mingle inextricably, beginning with the moment of conception; the prenatal environment of the fetus is as profoundly influenced by social, cultural, and economic factors as is the later environment of its childhood. And once the organism begins to develop, the results of every successive moment of living turn into the basis for the next moment. Whatever might have been distinguished as particular cause then fuses into the sum total of prior experience and learning, so that after only a few months it becomes a hopeless endeavor to trace out lines of specific causation in the individual. All that can be done with any confidence is to make statements about populations in general, while recognizing that once the problem has been shifted to this level new issues emerge to further complicate things— for example, that the phenomenon of madness, however it is determined, is also culturally defined, and that the definition may change across cultures and down through the years. What is cause as distinguished from effect and what is influence as distinct from result then become meaningless and even irrelevant questions.

Yet there remains the problem of how social factors might be studied in their influence on various kinds of deviant behavior and experience. Whole cultures can hardly be studied and compared. However, subgroups within a culture can, and of these the one that lends itself most easily to analysis and use as an independent variable is *socioeconomic status*—the equivalent of old-fashioned social class in our contemporary industrial culture.

Given some means for assessing the individual's socioeconomic status (SES), an orderly series of questions may be asked: (1) Can any differences in regard to clinical status be discovered between groups known to differ on SES? If so, (2) can the differences be attributed to SES-related differences in defining clinical status? And in that case, (3) who is responsible for such defining? Or if no definitional distinctions can be found, (4) can the differences be attributed to SES-related differences in behavior relative to a common standard? And in that case, (5) what is the nature of the standard, and on what grounds is it justified?

These questions comprise most of the major issues faced in cross-cultural comparisons, or cross-group comparisons within a culture, when the dependent variable is itself a phenomenon that is influenced by culture. We have here a kind of investigation in which the phenomenon whose distribution is being studied— mental illness—is itself heavily influenced by cultural factors. It is influenced, quite probably, both in the manner and frequency of its occurrence and in the ways in which it is defined and recognized. If this is so, then it is extremely difficult to be assured of carrying out a pure study, one that is not contaminated by the very influences under study. The problem is similar to that faced by a virologist engaged in work on a strain of bacillus but uncertain of how to test his instruments for sterility.

Thus, the very first question to be answered is simply whether, if the population of subjects is categorized by SES, differences not due to sampling error can be found between categories in regard to mental health status. In a classic and pioneering study of this question,[36] a "psychiatric census" of the urban area of New Haven, Connecticut, was taken by obtaining information on every resident of the area who was receiving treatment from a psychiatrist or from a psychiatric clinic or mental hospital—a total of 1,891 persons.[37] Three hypotheses were evaluated, the first regarding the relation between class position and being in treatment, the second regarding the relation between class position and type of disorder, and the third regarding the relation between class position and the kind of treatment received. The results supported all three hypotheses as to significant relationships: persons in lower socioeconomic classes were more likely to be in some form of treatment; more likely to be diagnosed as psychotic and less likely to be diagnosed as neurotic; and more likely to be in a public hospital and receiving care other than psychotherapeutic than in private treatment with psychotherapy.[38]

In a very practical sense, then, it makes a difference whether an individual is from one socioeconomic class rather than another, and the difference is analogous to what might be found in any other area of living: the upper classes have access to more of the desirable things of life. But the differences revealed in this study are a function of other factors as well, some of them quite subtle. To look at these, we turn to the second question above, whether the differences found can be attributed to SES-related differences in defining mental illness. In one respect, this question asks whether the different classes have varying definitions of mental illness, to which the authors of this study answered affirmatively: "We believe that far more abnormal behavior is tolerated by the two lower classes, particularly Class V, without any awareness that the motivations behind the behavior are pathological, even though the behavior may be disapproved by the class norms."[39] The lower classes, they found in an additional, intensive survey of a sample of fifty selected patients, were more tolerant than the upper classes of many kinds of disturbed and offensive behavior, and were also less likely to attribute such deviance to psychological factors or to mental illness.[40]

Curiously, however, a proportionately greater percentage of lower-class persons was found to be in treatment, the bulk of them in government-supported institutions. The authors did not explain this discrepancy, but we may venture the guess that if lower-class members resist sending their disturbed members for treatment while still contributing more than their share to the population under treatment, the total number who need treatment, if defined by upper-class standards, might be even higher than is indicated by the data of the study. This brings us to another aspect of our question: Is mental illness defined differently at different class levels? If by mental illness we mean that kind of behavior which subsequently results in being sent for treatment, then, as we have seen, the lower classes resist putting that label on this behavior. But such a criterion is not very useful for a study like this; it is illogical to define mental illness in terms of being sent for treatment, when the variable of being in treatment is itself what is being measured.

Fortunately, the authors had another criterion at hand. They had access in each case to the psychiatrist who was treating the patients who were undergoing private treatment and to the records of the institutions where patients were undergoing outpatient or inpatient treatment. The mental illness of the patients, then, was in these cases defined entirely by psychiatrists in private practice or on hospital or clinic staffs. By this criterion, results were obtained which were very similar to those in a study some years later in New York City, where the diagnosis was also made by a team of psychiatrists.[41] When psychiatrists, whose values are very largely those of the middle and upper socioeconomic classes, define whether subjects are mentally ill, the class of the subject is shown to be significantly related to the resulting definition; specifically, those persons who are more like the definers are defined as being less "psychologically impaired," or, if they are seen as impaired, are defined as being more similar to the kind of patients that the definers usually treat. Rightly or wrongly, a tight circle has now been set up— and so long as no completely independent definition of the dependent variable is available, the circle cannot be broken.

By the evidence from studies relating SES to clinical status, then, the answer to our second question above is that whatever differences are found between classes might well be a function of the class-related pattern of defining mental illness. The same might be said, as well, in regard to differences between one culture and another—that is, if members of one culture are found to be different from those of another in regard to their clinical status, the findings might well be a function of who does the defining. The prospect is discouraging. Nevertheless, some encouragement is at hand in the assumption—bearing in mind that it is no more than this—that the more severe forms of disturbance such as schizophrenia are so widespread and so similar in their manifestations across cultures that defining them can be accomplished independently of one's own cultural bias. If we accept this assumption as a starting point, we are in a position to look at the third of our questions above—whether the differences found between classes can be attributed to SES-related behavioral differences relative to some common standard.

What this question asks is whether in fact some general standard of behavior can be assumed and whether the behavior of any individual, regardless of class, can be compared with that standard. If so, it would then make sense to determine whether class differences in mental illness are revealed in class differences in behavior. In the preceding paragraph I referred to an assumption that there is in fact a universally recognizable behavioral pattern of severe disturbance, as in schizophrenia. If we start with this assumption, it would make sense to compare individual schizophrenics from different classes with our collective and universal picture of schizophrenia. One hypothesis would be that schizophrenics from every SES resemble the universal schizophrenic and therefore all belong to the same category, but that a disproportionately higher percentage will be found to come from the lower classes.

I am not aware that a test precisely like this has ever been carried out, and, indeed, the difficulties involved would be appreciable. However, some relevant data are available, and they do not support the hypothesis. Comparisons of the symptomatic picture of the acute phase of schizophrenia between ethnic groups or between subcultures within a group reveal rather striking differences. As Marvin Opler has shown, the acutely disturbed Italian does not resemble the acutely disturbed Irish patient in New York City.[42] Among many tribes of native Africans the probability of psychosis due to senile arteriosclerosis is very low among those who have not become acculturated to the white man's way of life, but it increases steadily as the individual's life more closely resembles that of the whites.[43] The delusions of a century ago were not the same as those of today. Specific cultures have their unique forms of going mad—*amok* among the Malays, for example, or *berserker* among Icelandic warriors, or any of the forms of trance peculiar to specific culture groups.

But these data are far from definitive, and other data can be shown to support the opposite conclusion, that there are in fact nuclear features which are common to the condition of madness the world over. The most significant aspect of this conflict of views may be, not that no firm conclusions have yet been drawn, but that on principle no firm conclusions can be drawn. The search for a definite answer is a self-defeating quest because there is no way to avoid going in a circle.

This assertion is sufficiently discouraging to require some justification. I have noted above, in reviewing the classic study by August Hollingshead and Frederick C. Redlich, that in order to compare social groups such as those differing on SES for differences in mental illness, one needs to be able to define mental illness independently of social-class bias. But their own evidence shows that mental illness is defined differently according to the definer's social class. Therefore it seems at least probable that the social class of the investigators influenced their own definition of mental illness—unless the curious proposition is advanced that the investigators were themselves completely free of social-class bias. The investigators, then, were caught in the web of their own logic; the net they cast to catch the thinking and behavior of their subjects fell, inevitably, over themselves as well. Now, one way out of this uncomfortable position is to begin by maintaining that there are universal, and therefore universally recognized, forms of mental illness, particularly its more severe forms such as schizophrenia. After all, data from cultures far removed from ours in time and place lend support to this claim, although still other evidence seems to contradict it. The essential point, however, is that there appears to be no way to settle the matter one way or the other, for the same dilemma arises, in more elaborate form, that confronted investigators who dealt only with SES differences in one city. The dilemma is this: How can the investigator be assured that his work is itself sufficiently free of cultural bias as to allow him to develop a universally applicable definition of schizophrenia, and who else is sufficiently free of cultural bias as to guarantee the universality of that definition?

Yet some such definition—whether we term it universal, or logically independent, or free of cultural bias—seems to be a necessary first step in designing a cross-cultural study of mental illness, for the most general reason possible: two phenomena cannot be compared on any dimension, or within any realm, unless the comparer has some independent grasp of the dimension, or realm, prior to dealing with the two examples of it. We cannot fall back into the comfort of a relativist position, making comparisons only among particular examples while ignoring the inclusive dimension or realm, when the matter concerns what are clearly fundamentals. Mental illness, and in particular schizophrenia, is clearly such a fundamental phenomenon in human life that comparing it against other, lesser instances of behavior will not help at all.

I have gone through a lengthy argument to lead to the point that on principle it is not possible to undertake cross-cultural studies of a fundamental phenomenon such as madness unless one somehow knows in advance what madness is like. The way in which this might be known requires some discussion, and I will devote most of the rest of this book to various aspects of this discussion. For now, however, we may note only that the point made above is not quite so strange as it appears at first sight; there are many familiar instances of such prior knowing. They are found, for example, in the realm of expression, and it may be that the general neglect of this topic in psychological theory results from the fact that the priority of expressive phenomena does not fit into most theoretical schemes. Erwin Straus remarks:

*Paradoxically, everyone in his understanding of expression is at the same time expert and ignorant. . . . Age, sex, group, race, color, epoch, language—these do not constitute obstacles. We take it for granted that a mother realizes how her*

*baby feels long before he is capable of pronouncing the simplest words. But also—
and this is more startling—long before he is capable of distinguishing a circle
from a square, the baby responds to the expression of the mother, whether she is
friendly or angry, cheerful or sad. . . . Expressive understanding even transcends
barriers separating species from species. We can talk to a dog in many languages;
he understands all of them, not because he is polyglot but because he responds
to the expressive values of intonation. . . . Verbal communication is limited to
those who speak the same language—a language that they once had to learn.
Expressive communication is universal; it does not have to be learned. There are
no schools that offer instruction in expressive motions; if they did they would
do more harm than good, for expressions are not intended as such.*[44]

An elaborate analysis of these phenomena has also been offered by Jean-Paul
Sartre as part of what he calls his existential psychoanalysis, as distinguished
from traditional, or empirical psychoanalysis. "The principle of this psychoanalysis
is that man is a totality and not a collection. Consequently he expresses himself
as a whole in even his most insignificant and his most superficial behavior. In
other words there is not a taste, a mannerism, or a human act which is not
revealing."[45] The chief "pillar of support" for human experience, according to the
scheme of existential psychoanalysis, is

*the fundamental, preontological comprehension which man has of the human
person. Although the majority of people can well ignore the indications contained
in a gesture, a word, a sign and can look with scorn on the revelation which they
carry, each human individual nevertheless possesses* a priori *the meaning of the
revelatory value of these manifestations and is capable of deciphering them. . . .
Here, as elsewhere, truth is not encountered by chance.*[46]

To insist on the necessity for considering a priori phenomena, however, is
not to discount completely the value of other kinds of judgments, such as those
made by Rosenthal in regard to genetic factors or those made by Hollingshead
and Redlich in regard to social influences. Both are legitimate, and often useful,
approaches to understanding the background and development of human conditions. I am merely arguing for supplementing them in order to avoid the
impasses to which social theorists, in particular, are often led. Theorists of genetics,
on the other hand, do not seem to run such methodological risks, and the reason
will teach us an important distinction between these two classes of determinants.

I have noted that the problem faced by investigators of social determinants is
that their own social class, which forces them inevitably into a partisan stance in
this matter, impels them to a biased view of the phenomena they investigate—
for example, the manifestations of mental illness. Now, why should this not
also be true in regard to genetic factors? Why, for example, should not my own
level of intelligence so bias me as to make it impossible for me to construct a useful
test for assessing the intelligence of those who are less gifted than I? The basic
reason, I would offer, is that genetically determined factors are stated in terms

of an implied hierarchy; being positioned at a lower level is then equivalent to saying that one has less of the characteristic in question. For this reason my greater degree of intelligence does not bias my testing of others, for they are being assessed on their lack, greater or less, of what I possess. But were I to investigate the effect of social-class membership on, say, mental illness, I would arrange the various social classes in a parallel fashion, so to speak—not one above the other on some dimension, but side by side. Under such conditions of forced equality, I would have no choice but to view the results of social-class membership from the only vantage point I know, which is my own position, and so my view of any other social class would be biased.

There is a way out of this impasse for social theorists too. It is to rest their assessment on some dimension that is spelled out by a theory. In the social sciences such theoretical constructs are not easily come by; a rare exception is the Stirling County study of Alexander Leighton and his associates.[47]

*In broad outline, the theoretical framework of the study assumes that there are two sets of factors in the social environment: those that create or foster mental illness and those that create or foster its absence. The two sets of factors are interrelated as they are used to specify an underlying construct, social organization-disorganization. The general theoretical hypothesis of the research is that social disorganization as opposed to social organization predisposes to mental illness.*[48]

One might quarrel with the specific construct, but its utility is an empirical matter to be settled in the field by seeing what it produces. Its value is that it enables the investigators, once they have defined the end points of their dimension, to assign every instance of their data to some point on a dimension so that comparisons are possible which are independent of their own partisan positions as social beings.

Two major suggestions have come out of this discussion of social influences. Both indicate that a purely empirical approach to assessing the place of such determining influences—an approach that pretends to no prior knowledge or commitments—is bound to leave the investigator caught in a net of his own devising. One way out, as I suggested, is to approach the problem with an explicit awareness of the sort of universal, a priori knowledge that all of us carry around as the basis for our equipment as socialized human beings. A second way out is to approximate this stance by developing some theoretical constructs that will then permit dimensional evaluation of the data. The first of these suggestions points toward that inner view of people to which much of this book is devoted; I will return to it again in the balance of this chapter, in the course of discussing a third major class of determining influences, and then again in the chapter that follows, where the outer and the inner kinds of data are compared.

### Influencing Oneself
The first, or prodromal, phase in the natural history of schizophrenia, as we noted above, is primarily influenced by the determinants we call genetic. The

second, or transitional, phase, when the schizophrenic way of life first becomes evident as an acute problem in living with others, appears to be influenced primarily by the determinants that we call social influences. If the schizophrenic individual arrives at the third phase, the stage of adjustment, what now affects him? There appear to be two major sources of influence: the nature of the social institution to which he becomes most closely related, and his own choice as to what he will make of his radically changed way of life. I will discuss both these sources as a part of influencing oneself although the second appears to be of greater importance.

THE INSTITUTION. For the past two hundred years or so, the chief institution for dealing with the schizophrenic in his passage from a transitional phase to one of adjustment has been the mental hospital. Only recently, however, has the hospital been studied as a significant sociological phenomenon in its own right; the first major study along these lines, by Alfred Stanton and Morris Schwartz, was published in 1954.[49] Investigators who were willing and able to look at the mental hospital with a relatively unprejudiced eye, simply trying to understand it as a complex social institution, revealed that the institution, its staff and employees, and the population of patients it contained, together formed a little society that was amenable to social analysis. None of the participants—and this included the patients—could properly be called so strange or beyond reason as to make a rational account of their behavior impossible.

With this background, analyses of participant roles as well as experimental studies of behavior change became feasible. Investigations in the tradition of contemporary learning theory were one fruit of this development: patients as well as staff were "engineered" for socially desirable ends,[50] and the "token economy" was established and flourished in what had been forgotten back wards.[51] It was demonstrated by very stringent criteria that the behavior of even the most unreachable of patients could be altered on the basis of principles identical to those which had heretofore been applied to normal human subjects and to animals in the college laboratory. The schizophrenic in the hospital, evidently, was not the alien, almost nonhuman creature of popular (and often of psychiatric) belief. but rather was an understandable fellow citizen engaged in the insuperable task of re-establishing himself in a strange setting where he had no personal rights, no antecedents, and no one to whom he could or would turn. Thus, if he did appear strange or even out of reach, it was highly probable that his behavior was his own meaningful response to the situation in which he found himself; perhaps he was simply reacting to what he now saw as attempts to interfere with the fragile adjustment he had begun to achieve.[52]

These insights called for large-scale social-psychological analyses for here, ready-made for study, was a living laboratory—an alien subculture filled with captive subjects. That so little was done in the next few decades may be attributed in part to the difficulty of making inroads in an institution that has always been completely dominated by one of the less progressive factions of the medical profession. More important, however, may have been the fact that potential investigators were themselves often conceptually partisan and lacked a theory to help them become independent of their biases. Those who accepted a vaguely stated conception of the hospitalized schizophrenic as a victim of some dread disease could hardly be expected to study the ways in which such patients acted reasonably and understandably. Nor could they have become aware of the way in which their own investigations might, from the point of view of the patient, seriously threaten the status he had achieved at such cost.

But once some social scientists had begun to free themselves from a partisan stance, many aspects of the patient's situation became clear. His resistance to imposed change became understandable in the light of the world-shaking change to which he had just been exposed. His fight to keep things the way they were and to maintain his own position in that arrangement made sense in view of the fact that the situation to which he might be returned, if he were to leave the hospital, was the very one in which his troubles had been precipitated. Until revealed by careful analysis, it was not fully realized that mental hospitals may function to exacerbate many of the factors that oppose a patient's recovery: they keep him helpless and ultimately dependent on the hospital way of life; they progressively isolate him from his background, his family, and his occupational ties to his community; they help to develop in him a kind of chronic, pointless disinterest in the world around him; and, as a last blow, they may finally thrust him back into society with little preparation for making his way and with the added burden of a stigma that cannot easily be erased in our culture.[53]

*THE SELF.*   There are two groups of people in a mental hospital, the staff and the patients. What happens between them—a set of events that is usually called treatment—is a complex function of how each group perceives its own situation and acts on that perception, and of how the group actions interpenetrate within an ongoing social institution and community. Alan Towbin has provided an excellent example of what happens when the staff group becomes aware of its own cognitive and behavioral operations and of how this awareness may affect the success of a project aimed at speeding up the discharge process with chronically hospitalized patients.[54]

A special, physically distinct unit was set up in the hospital and given a high degree of autonomy, freedom from staff intrusion, and patient privileges. Applicants were accepted for whom "an interim setting of maximal independence and minimal ties with the hospital would be of therapeutic value in assisting the patient to adjust ultimately to complete independence from the hospital."[55] In spite of some initial success, the project bogged down in about a year, and investigation revealed that the patients in the unit had simply used their new-found autonomy to continue institutional living under more preferable arrangements. The staff then re-evaluated its own role in what had happened and instituted changes which made possible a successful program. The author describes the original arrangement in the following terms:

*The members of the unit were told they no longer needed hospitalization. The staff would appear to have effected the transformation of inmate back to citizen. But what we took away with the right hand, we gave back with the left. We ordered no discharge, urged no one to leave, kept no check of members' plans, and capped it all by the paternal gesture of providing a staff advisor to the unit. . . . [Thus] since the staff ordered no discharges, and was not trying to get anyone to leave, they were tacitly endorsing the members' stay. Motivation to remain in the hospital had been added to the staff's list of indications of continued need for hospitalization. We tacitly affirmed the existence of something we had explicitly denied—the members' need to be inpatients.[56]*

But as soon as the staff attitudes were changed from providing a place for continued treatment of inpatients to assigning tasks and supervising task performance, the status of the patients changed. They were now redefined as temporary residents whose stay had a reasonable limit and who no longer had to show self-discrediting behavior in order to enter or remain in the hospital. By changing their own attitudes and perception of the situation, the staff had now redefined the situation of hospitalization—a change that should not surprise us since we are all accustomed to the fact that it is usually the staff which defines the situation as hospitalization in the first place.

A striking possibility begins to emerge from such considerations as these. If the behavior of the staff is the consequence of their own attitudes toward the situation, may not the same be said of the patients? Might we not speak of varying needs among patients and on this basis, as Jules Holzberg suggests,[57] begin to offer more than one kind of situation, each designed for a specific need? And in regard to those patients who are hospitalized because we have only one kind of institutional setting to offer them, is it not reasonable to assume that the setting is as much their doing as that of the staff?

One team of investigators has based a series of studies on the assumptions just stated.[58] They begin with their beliefs about mental patients:

*Mental patients, for all their pathology, are in most respects, most of the time, just like the rest of us; they want to live in a mental hospital in the same way that ordinary persons want to live in their own community—that is, they can be expected to try to satisfy their needs and, to a considerable extent, to be able to do so. But because a mental hospital, while a community of persons, is not just any community but one of a very special and potentially restrictive kind, the patient's attempts to control his own fate will often have to involve devious and indirect tactics.[59]*

One such tactic is "impression management"—the device of acting in a way that will produce a desired effect in an observer. On the basis of a number of experimental studies, the investigators conclude that patients do use this tactic, even to the extent of creating their own opportunities, and that they use it with admirable finesse and with great effectiveness. That is, the chronically hospitalized patients they studied were quite effective in giving the impression, as needed, that they were sick enough to be kept in the hospital but well enough to be accorded desired privileges.

In addition, these investigators found that patients were able to adopt, and to consistently maintain, one of a number of adaptational styles in the face of the hospital's demands: a style of keeping close to the ward, a style of working, or a style of "mobile socialization." These styles had the practical effect of determining the length of the patients' hospitalization and the degree of their involvement with therapeutic programs. The conclusion one is led to is that these patients, though supposedly kept in a hospital because they are incapable of managing their own affairs, are, on the contrary, "effective human beings, capable of employing subtle forms of counterpower (impression management) in order to meet their needs, and . . . they can live the kind of life they desire within the confines of an institution."[60] The "invisibility" of some patients, then, may not be a result of their untreatability, but rather the reverse; their choice of social isolation may keep the staff away and contribute to their reputation as unreachable.

In sum, a series of experiments furnished striking support for the thesis that the mental patient is involved, in what seems a purposeful manner, in finding the hospital as a haven, being admitted, settling into a desired style of living, and remaining there. Quite a different concept from "disease" seems applicable here. The central element in a more appropriate set of concepts would be *choice*, meaning by this the same thing that is meant when the term is applied to the average person: that fundamental act of will which, as far as each individual is concerned, defines the direction of his own experience. In the view being advanced here as an alternative to a disease concept of schizophrenia, the patient is seen as no different from the nonpatient when one takes into account his experience and is therefore enabled to take a fresh and unbiased look at his behavior. Because they are both human, patient and nonpatient can be fully understood only as choosing that way of life which serves, for them, to resolve the conflicting influences in the situations they face. In particular, in order to understand the special way of life that we call madness, we will need to stretch the limits of what we usually consider as acceptable solutions to life situations.

Laing has provided an exposition of one such stretching of limits.[61] He begins with the strongly felt conviction that the reality into which we all more or less comfortably fit, the social reality that we are pleased to consider as the framework and basis for sanity, is itself, by any rational standards of human fulfillment, quite insane. "From the alienated starting point of our pseudosanity, everything is equivocal. Our sanity is not 'true' sanity. Their madness is not 'true' madness. The madness of our patients is an artifact of the destruction wreaked on them by us, and by them on themselves."[62] And because we, the ostensibly sane, can have no basis for knowing either sanity or insanity, we are badly equipped to deal with a very special voyage when it occurs; we simply label it mad and brutalize the voyager.

What is the nature of this voyage? It can only be truly understood in terms of how it is experienced: "as going further 'in,' as going back through one's personal life, in and back and through and beyond into the experience of all mankind, of the primal man, of Adam and perhaps even further into the being of animals, vegetables and minerals."[63] It is a voyage back into a kind of death, with its own aeonic time, back from ego to self, followed by a return voyage out and back to mortality and time, to a new ego and an existential rebirth. Most of all, it is, Laing says, a "perfectly natural and necessary process."[64]

Are these merely metaphors out of a currently fashionable jargon, or do they really touch the core of the condition of madness? Whatever appeal, or lack of it, they may have for those who will see no farther than the surface of human behavior, they do seem to capture some of the quality of the schizophrenic experience. It is as though, for the very first time, an observer and theorist and clinician wrote about the madman's condition from the inside instead of from the outside. Laing may have it all wrong, but he has brought this, at least, forcefully to our attention: to do justice to a matter as fundamental as the nature of our own sanity, we will have to include in our thinking a realm of experience that is felt and shared, a realm that may be prior to whatever we know and therefore the very basis for whatever we know.

# chapter 4
# God and Nijinsky

In Chapter 3 I discussed the major determining influences in schizophrenia and introduced a notion that will now begin to serve as a general alternative to the concept of determinants. When schizophrenia or any other human phenomenon is considered entirely in its external aspects, as though it were being surveyed by an outside observer attempting to come to some kind of terms with it, what will be grasped is observable behavior, and what will be assigned are causes of that behavior. The problem will then become one of determining, as precisely as possible, what antecedent causes are to be assigned to what aspects of the behavior, and in what patterning.

But as began to be clear in the preceding chapter, this may be unsatisfactory for at least two reasons. First, in considering the class of social determinants, it appeared that handling such factors called for knowing in advance about some universal standard of either mental illness or mental health. Such a standard could not arise from observation, for on principle it must precede observation. Whatever this standard might be, wherever it might reside, it must be in any case a kind of mode of knowing to which we all subscribe, perhaps witlessly but with a preobservational wisdom nonetheless. A second reason for dissatisfaction with a purely external and observational approach was indicated in considering the major class of influencing determinants on the third phase of the natural history of schizophrenia—a phase that can apparently be best dealt with if we are willing to accept the special experience of schizophrenic patients as real and as determinative of their condition. We accept each others' experience in this way, usually unquestioningly, but our own doing so escapes our notice and is only brought home to us when we are asked to make the same admission in regard to the madman. Then there is impressed on us the presence of experience, pervasive and prior to all our organized knowing and fact-gathering. What is revealed in regard to the schizophrenic may well be true in every case—that only by accepting the other person's experience as real and as determinative will we be in a position to make observations that do not distort social reality.

## EGO LOSS AND THE NO-EXPERIENCE

For these two reasons, then, we now need to turn to emphasizing a dimension other than the one I have relied on in discussing the madman as Stranger. At the moment we are not prepared to compare the two dimensions, one based on an outer view and one on an inner view, but we do need to explore the consequences for understanding madness if we focus on human life as conceived internally, from within the person, in terms of his own experience. I will begin the discussion with an introductory statement, expressed from both an inner and an outer vantage point, and follow this with an intensive examination of a single case for which we have available both inner and outer kinds of data.

### The Ego and Ego Loss

When I consider in naïve fashion my own field of awareness, it is immediately apparent that I cannot both experience something and at the same time experience its cause. One or the other is available to me at any moment, but not both. All that goes on with me from moment to moment seems to be in the form of an existing manifold of trial and flaw and error, of things being and myself doing, nothing more. And nothing less, too, I may add. That is more than enough to fill my field of awareness.

However, although I cannot simultaneously experience something that matters and experience it as being caused, I know very well that I can perform many operations that are relevant to its cause. I can, for example, think about what caused it; I can decide between possible causes; I can draw conclusions on this basis. But these are, as operations, rather distinct from the naïve, usually unthinking, ongoing experience that I have just referred to. Essentially, such operations require my stepping back from my momentary position, as it were, and taking up a different stance in order to do something that refers to my direct experience. When I do this, I may then come to learn about causes, perhaps by comparing what is in my experience with what might be there. I have at my command a whole battery of these discriminatory operations to be employed whenever I need to reflect on my experience or to use my own experience as basic data for some other, behavioral end.

A convenient term for the set of mechanisms by which we perform these extraoperations is *ego*. I am using the term in approximately the same sense in which it was used by Freud, who also conceived of the ego as a kind of excrescence on the body of ongoing experience, functioning as the total set of processes by which the mind's important operations were carried out. As many writers have recently pointed out, the ego has been both the glory and the curse of Western civilization, as contrasted, say, with modes of life based on Eastern philosophy. By a more and more intensive concentration on ego operations, there has been built a civilization packed full of goodies from jet planes to electric toothbrushes, a standard of living and comfort that is the vague dream of every underfed nation in the world, and a steadily increasing distance within each person between his own ego and his own experience. The consequences of the latter may soon be tragic enough to convince people that the price demanded for an ego civilization is almost too much to pay: feelings of emptiness, a general malaise, uncertainty whether materialistic achievement is all that important; a world slowly being buried under the weight of its own junk and civilizations so productive that garbage piles up faster than it can be destroyed or rechanneled; the steady erosion of whatever is natural in our experience of ourselves, of others, of the immediate surround; and the near absence of any serious thought, within the human disciplines, about modes of awareness that need not depend on ego operations. The very epitome of ego processes can be found in contemporary science, with all its good and all that it leaves out of account as well. Technology, it has been well said, is the knack of arranging the world so that we don't have to experience it.

However, the ego is gained in a lifetime of adventures with the world, and so it may on special occasions be lost; perhaps there may even be ways to learn to give it up. When this happens, when there remain no ego processes to mediate the change, then the resulting experience is very special. It is then not a matter of changing but of being changed, of being a victim of the world. In total, overwhelming pain we say "It hurts," quite properly depersonalizing the source; for the source is the whole world. Episodes of confusion put the person in the same position; all his ego mechanisms are stripped from him, and he is lost to himself and victimized by what he experiences as happening to him. It can happen in pain or confusion, and it can also happen in certain stages of sleep, in the acute phase of developing schizophrenia, and in what may be a very wide range of states of ecstasy and superconsciousness.[1] Today we know very little about these last states, having become so tied to the necessity for ego control that we have neglected any fair-minded examination of positive and constructive ways to lose the ego completely. Our tendency, particularly in the academic disciplines, has been to equate every loss of ego with its counterproductive instances such as schizophrenia. Thus, Freud implied and many writers since have tried to argue that the state of psychosis is like dreaming. More recently, many kinds of drug-induced states of ego loss have been equated with being schizophrenic. In the anthropological literature, ecstatic states and visionary experiences have been "diagnosed" as nothing more than culturally accepted forms of psychosis.

### The No-Experience

To describe any phenomenon in terms of ego processes is to describe it externally, as something observed from outside. An alternative means, as I have said, is to describe it from inside, as it appears to the person himself. When the phenomenon to be described is ego loss, it is the latter approach that may be more appropriate. The description will then not be of a negative, that is, of a loss, but of a positive, of another kind of experience, unusual though it may be. I will call it *the no-experience*, not because the term is particularly apt but because at this point no better term is available.

To begin, we have to consider that experience is a curious matter that cannot be talked about in any simple or straightforward way; we may find, at least at the beginning, that metaphors will serve us better than declarative or factual statements. And much of what we will say initially will also be probing and suggestive rather than in the form of propositions that might be supported or refuted by evidence. But in this way, with patience, we may start to build a framework and a vocabulary for discourse in an area not yet explored.

As an example, consider the proposition that experience has no history. Each time that I become angry and allow it to happen to me (rather than imposing some ego operation on it, such as reason or guilt), it is as though I had never before been angry and were only now learning about anger for the first time. My experiencing of anger is like my experiencing of pain. It does little good for you to tell me that this is not the first time it has happened to me, that it will not be the last, or that time will pass and the pain is bound to go away. These are ego operations and whoever indulges in them is not, for the moment, himself in anger or in pain. They are relevant, they are sensible, and they are perfectly correct—but they have no place in my experience of the moment. The more direct and pure my experience, the more it is in a nontemporal world, outside the stream of my personal history.

This, at least, is what I would say about my-experience, about experience as I, individually, have it and can talk about it. (Whether I can talk about your-experience is a difficult question I would prefer to postpone until a later discussion.) There is another aspect of experience to be mentioned here—that as experience it is not bounded. If, for example, I were to ask the general question about human experience: What are its boundaries? I could properly expect a reply. You might say, "Well, speaking in general, I would say that experience is limited at any moment by the physical characteristics of the person. He cannot, for example, have the experience of sleeping and the experience of being awake at the same time." Or, speaking of a particular person, you might offer, "The experience of this individual, in my opinion, is limited to rather concrete and simple sets of possibilities, as a consequence of a childhood disease that appears to have left him severely retarded."

These are possible boundaries of experience when the view is from the outside. But viewed from the inside, as when I consider my own experience, the boundary is itself the limiting condition for me and therefore, as boundary, it eludes me. There is nothing but what I experience. This is a simple but very difficult notion to grasp and hold to. The horizon of my own experience is simply what-is-not-there for me—it cannot be a part of my experience and so it cannot be experienced; or if it is a part of my experience, then it is no longer not-there-for-me. The boundary of my experience is like my death; there is nothing I can say about myself dead; it cannot be a part of what I am. I am at a loss to imagine it, even though I have at hand some operations to imagine about it. I can talk about it, but not to it. Though I can, with an effort, address it, I can never speak its name.

Yet many have tried to describe the indescribable—observers, poets, and patients themselves. They talk of Nothing; they point to the void; they fill the

---

### THE NO-EXPERIENCE: THE
### SPACE BETWEEN THE SEPARATION
FROM A SYMPATHETIC OBSERVER

In over 100 cases where we have studied the actual circumstances around the social event when one person comes to be regarded as schizophrenic, it seems to us that WITHOUT EXCEPTION the experience and behaviour that gets labelled schizophrenic is A SPECIAL STRATEGY THAT A PERSON INVENTS IN ORDER TO LIVE IN AN UNLIVABLE SITUATION. In his life situation the person has come to feel he is in an untenable position. He cannot make a move, or make no move, without being beset by contradictory and paradoxical pressures and demands, pushes and pulls, both internally, from himself, and externally, from those around him. He is, as it were, in a position of checkmate.[2]

FROM A POET

And there, there overhead, there, there,
   hung over
Those thousands of white faces, those
   dazed eyes,
There in the starless dark the poise, the
   hover,
There with vast wings across the can-
   celed skies,
There in the sudden blackness the
   black pall
Of nothing, nothing, nothing—nothing
   at all.[3]

FROM THE BEHAVIOR
TYPICAL OF AUTISTIC CHILDREN

Symptoms of autism in children include: prolonged head-banging or head-rocking; an obsessive yet almost mechanical interest in some kinds of toys, often toys that spin; speech patterns that are essentially noncommunicative and may include whispering, a monotone, and the repetition of stereotyped phrases; a seeming lack of interest in persons or things of the environment, together with a resistance to change in the environment.[4]

FROM ONE SCHIZOPHRENIC PATIENT

People coming and going all the time —different times, different places.

FROM ANOTHER SCHIZOPHRENIC PATIENT

Nothingness. Is just plain blank. Its void. It has no affiliations with anything. It has nothing to do with anything. It doesn't involve competition or undue association. It involves a system of taking care of ones own affairs. It forms protection. It involves staying out of people's way. It concerns correct concern for ones self. It has nothing to do with science or engineering. It is a truism. If any undue stress is placed on anyone sometimes its nothing and sometimes it isn't. Various types of nothingness can be pushed out. It can be used for all sorts of things. Once one uses any sort of substitution it ain't nothing. It eliminates all abstract faults. Different things can blank people out. It concerns no undue affiliation with any mens clubs or front organizations. It allows membership in the YMCA. It means schizophrenia releif (sic) permanent. That is the thing called void. It means the use of positive force. It maintains no classification of leadership. It means no intermixture. It means straightness. It is the space between the separation.[5]

FROM A CONVERSATION
BETWEEN TWO SCHIZOPHRENIC PATIENTS
J: What do they want with us?
S: Hm?
J: What do they want with you and me?
S: What do they want with you and me? How do I know what they want with you? I know what they want with me. I broke the law, so I have to pay for it. (SILENCE)[6]

---

space between them with their Silence. I could not do this, but since these persons have tried to tell us about the no-experience, I will try to sum up their message. From the point of view of the stricken person, it appears that everything falls apart. He knows just what he is doing when he warns us that the end of the world is near, that great, unnameable forces threaten world destruction on every side. This is exactly what is happening to him, and this is how one truly knows anything—that it happens to him. What is inner and what is outer are no longer separate and meaningfully connected, but are independently powered, each side of the relation now racing off to its own doom. Nothing is sensible any longer, merely necessary; fate is naked and overt.

Cut off from the way things are, imaginings run wild; their anchor in the familiar is gone, and their tie to what one might do and mean and trust is lost. No neutral happening is possible. It is all one series of waves that overwhelm and trap, that suck and threaten, in vast shakings arising out of nowhere. In desperate restitution, the victim may work to pull it all together somehow. A world destruction needs a world reorganization—but if he succeeds, he has placed the capstone on his own symptomatology. He offers his delusion in order to save the world; we pronounce psychiatric sentence on him in order to save our own. Incarceration is always democratic: it represents the will of the majority.

The world, the body, all that the person has as his own, lose their moorings in radical ways. The ways seem to resemble what happens under the most powerful of psychedelic drugs. This is why for a brief period some investigators called these drugs psychotomimetic, or mimicking-psychosis, and thought they might become our key, found at long last, to "unlock the mysteries of mental illness" (I think that was the popular phrase at the time) by controlled experimental procedures. But the difference was clear and could have been pointed out by anyone with some background at being either high or crazy. Unlike the experience of being under the influence of a drug, the person who is cracking up can find no container to which he can point and say, "There it is. That's the source. As soon as the effect of that wears off, I'll be back to where I normally am, and I know what that state is, it's being normal, straight, not high. As long as I keep that in mind, I'll be all right; it is not me that is really experiencing all this, only what is happening *to* me." Without this assurance—and where would it come from?—the person who knows or feels that he is going crazy lives trapped in a doomsday machine careening ahead because it can never return to wherever it all began.

And when the worst of it is over, perhaps because exhaustion finally does what will and panic could not, all that remains for the person is to know that he is still alive, that somehow he has come through, and that nothing in all the world could ever persuade him to live it again. He will not go back, nor even look back. He will try only to keep things approximately as they are, and he will fight off any efforts to turn him around or to get him to take chances or to reach out on his own. He may or may not show the signs we now associate with his state; that is, he may or may not, depending mostly on the stresses placed on him, act like a crazy man. But he is now, in the layman's term, crazy.

## THE GOD OF THE DANCE

His name was Vaslav Nijinsky. He was certainly one of the greatest dancers who ever lived. In 1919, at the age of twenty-nine, he became schizophrenic. Thereafter he was either confined in a hospital or cared for privately by his wife, until he died in 1950 without ever having recovered. This, in summary, is his life story. In detail it is an instructive drama, and perhaps tragic as well.[7]

He was born February 28, 1890, of parents who were both ballet dancers of Polish ancestry but traveling as a touring troupe through czarist Russia. From a very early age his father, recognizing Vaslav's talent, gave the boy lessons, and he appeared on stage with his younger sister and brother when he was barely three. A few years later the father ran off, and so the mother settled with her family in St. Petersburg where they lived in near poverty while she worked to have her talented son admitted to the Imperial School of Dancing. He was finally accepted for training at the age of nine and stayed there for the next nine years, in an atmosphere of rigid dedication and restraint. Every aspect of the pupils' lives was ordained and regulated under the direct hand of the czar himself; the pupils were even formally "adopted" by him—such was the importance of the school for training future stars in the Imperial Russian Ballet.

By the time Nijinsky was sixteen, his teachers could teach him no more, but because these were the regulations he stayed on for another two years, becoming the leading soloist. Tamara Karsavina, herself already a leading ballerina, describes her first meeting with the boy whom she immediately called the Eighth Wonder of the World:

*One morning I came up earlier than usual; the boys were just finishing their practice. I glanced casually, and could not believe my eyes; one boy in a leap rose far above the heads of the others and seemed to tarry in the air. "Who is this?" I asked Michael Obouchoff, his master. "It is Nijinsky; the little devil never comes down with the music." He then called Nijinsky forward by himself and made him show me some steps. A prodigy was before my eyes. He stopped dancing, and I felt it was all unreal and could not have been; the boy looked quite unconscious of his achievement, prosy and even backward.*[8]

Just when he might have stayed on to become the leading figure of the classical Russian ballet, Nijinsky met Sergei Diaghilev and began with him the most fateful relationship of his life. Diaghilev was a great impresario—but much more than just that. He was an entrepreneur of the arts, a producer with a genius for discovering great artistic talent (Stravinsky, Massine, Prokofiev, Cocteau, among many others), an originator and integrator of artistic movements, the man solely responsible for bringing the modern art of Russia, its music and dance and painting, to the Western world. In 1909 Diaghilev invited the ballet of the Mariensky Theater in Leningrad and that of the Bolshoi Theater in Moscow to perform in Paris, with Nijinsky as his star as well as his lover. Their relation, sexual as well as artistic, lasted until 1913 when Nijinsky married Romola de Pulszky, a Hungarian girl who had recently joined the company as a pupil in order to be near him.

The proposal of marriage took place on board ship as the company, though without Diaghilev, headed for Buenos Aires and a South American tour. The two, Romola and Nijinsky, barely knew each other and had not even spoken, as they had no common language—he staying to himself as the star of the troupe, she merely a worshipful dancer in the chorus. Then one day the stage manager took her aside and announced, "Romola Carlovna, as Nijinsky cannot speak to you himself, he has requested me to ask you in marriage."[9] Astonished and fearing a practical joke, she fled to her cabin, but was persuaded later to go back on deck. As she relates in her biography of her husband, "Unexpectedly, from nowhere Nijinsky emerged and said: 'Mademoiselle, voulez-vous, vous et moi?' and pantomimed, indicating on the fourth finger of the left hand a ring. I nodded and, waving with both hands, said, 'Oui, oui, oui.' "[10]

They married when the ship arrived in Buenos Aires. She spoke no Russian at all, he spoke no Hungarian and very little French and so, in an inarticulate way, they came to know each other. A few days after the wedding ceremony she moved from her hotel room down to the suite that he occupied, the request again being made through the company's director. His suite, as she describes it,

*was composed of five rooms. The centre of the apartment was a large drawing-room, where we used to take our meals. On both sides the adjoining chambers were turned into living-rooms, and each of us had a bedroom at the opposite end of the apartment. . . . On our return from the performances Nijinsky used to write to his mother; he never forgot to do so. He seemed to be gay and happy and very proud when he spoke of me, and said, "Maia Jena" (which means "my wife"). I felt myself quite important. My fear of Nijinsky began to vanish. The charm of his personality, the tenderness of his whole being, radiated so much goodness, such beauty, that the evening he chose to remain I felt I was making an offering on the altar of happiness.*[11]

Diaghilev, when the news reached him, dismissed Nijinsky from his life with a curt telegram: "Your services with the Russian Ballet are no longer required. Don't join us."[12] The great dancer was now on his own, forced by circumstances to become his own choreographer and producer. His first productions in England were disappointing. Then, in 1914, his daughter Kyra was born—still another disappointment since he had badly wanted a son. When the nurse brought out the infant and announced, "It is only a girl, but a nice one," his feelings broke loose very briefly: "for one second he lost his self-control, and threw his gloves on the floor."[13]

Caught by the outbreak of World War I when they were visiting Romola's parents in Hungary, they were forced to live the next two years as internees, crowded uncomfortably in a small house almost under the noses of her mother and stepfather, who seem to have been rather unpleasant people. Nijinsky occupied himself with devising a universal system of notation for dance movements but did not show it to anyone.[14]

It was his international reputation as an artist that led finally to various intercessions on behalf of the Nijinsky family, with the result that they were able to leave for America by way of Switzerland in 1916. There Nijinsky resumed an artistic if not personal relation with Diaghilev. The Metropolitan Opera House organized his lengthy tour of the United States. It was a strenuous life, with Nijinsky himself as the star as well as producer and manager of the company. In January, 1917, for example, the company appeared at a gala performance in San Francisco, with Pierre Monteux as orchestral conductor. On the first evening Nijinsky danced the starring role in three complete ballets, *Les Sylphides, Scheherezade,* and a "comi-dramatic" ballet, *Til Eulenspiegel,* for which he had devised the choreography and created most of the settings and costumes. On the following evening four ballets were presented, with Nijinsky in the starring role in two, the sensational *Afternoon of a Faun,* which had almost created a riot at its premiere in Paris, and his own remarkable tour de force, *The Specter of the Rose.* In the climactic ending of the latter, Nijinsky leaped from front to rear of the stage in one bound and out an open window—where he was caught by four men and had his chest immediately massaged to help him recover from the strain.

It was during this tour that there appeared the first indications of the price Nijinsky was paying for the stresses of this period. He became more difficult to deal with, more demanding and unpredictable, less "natural" and, worst of all, acutely suspicious that a plot was being organized to ruin his career.[15] Both Nijinsky and his wife came to believe more and more firmly that the villain in back of this plot was Diaghilev, still determined to get his revenge for what he considered Nijinsky's betrayal of their relation. Were they right and was Nijinsky the unfortunate victim of the machinations of a more clever and powerful man—or is Diaghilev's biographer correct in shifting the blame entirely to Nijinsky?[16] High passions, strong feelings on both sides were aroused, and apparently can still be evoked,[17] but the truth now lies buried in the past. Whatever the facts of the matter, Nijinsky did indeed stumble into increasingly more difficult ways of behaving. He began to spend all his spare time in intense discussions with two men in the company, disciples of Tolstoi, apparently drawn powerfully toward the idea of throwing overboard his family and career, returning to Mother Russia, and living out his days in a state of deeply religious, peasant simplicity. Only his wife's angry attack on the other two men led him to drop the scheme and continue his efforts to create dances, manage a company, and perform on a rigorous schedule.

They returned to Europe for a rest and established the first real home their marriage had known in the village of St. Moritz, in Switzerland. With the war still on, no dancing was possible in Europe, and so Nijinsky began a period of enforced idleness. With increasing concern, his wife watched him turn more and more inward, except for occasional strange outbursts of anger, and spend his time writing long passages that he refused to show her. (These turned out, some fifteen years later on their discovery among his papers, to be part of a diary that he was keeping during this period, a very moving and revealing document that was first published in 1936, two years after his wife's biography of him.)[18]

The incident of the golden cross may have represented a turning point for his wife. It began when one of their servants alerted her: "Madame, forgive me; I may be wrong. We all love you both. You remember I told you that at home in my village at Sils Maria as a child I used to do errands for Mr. Nietzsche? I carried his rucksack when he went to the Alps to work. Madame, he acted and looked, before he was taken away, just like Mr. Nijinsky does now."[19] What he had been doing, according to the servants, was walking through the village with a big golden cross over his necktie, stopping passersby, and sending them to mass at the church. Frantically his wife ran down to the village and there confronted him: "What are you doing? What is this new nonsense? Vaslav, won't you stop imitating that old lunatic Tolstoi?" He immediately became contrite and sad, and tried to explain it away: "[since] all the foolish women copy my ballet costumes . . . why can't I teach them something useful, lead them to remember God. Why can't I set the fashion, since I do set fashions, that they should seek the truth?" And all she could say then was, "But you have a funny way of expressing your ideas."[20]

So preparations were made for medical supervision and advice. A physician was introduced into the house under the guise of examining Nijinsky for exhaustion. On his advice, a male nurse purporting to be a masseur in attendance came to live with them. But this careful plan came to nought when Nijinsky casually announced, a month or so later, that he had really been fooling them all along—pretending to be crazy, he said, even pretending to go along with their male nurse who passed himself off as a masseur.[21]

He had not danced in almost a year, but now he announced that he had to give one more great recital for his public. He set the date, insisted on sending out invitations to hundreds of persons, hired a hall, and ordered great bolts of black and white silk for his costumes, but he would not reveal in advance any of the details of the performance except to announce, a few days before, "I am going to show how dances are created. I will compose them there before the audience. I want the public to see the work. They always get everything readymade. I want to show them the pangs of creation, the agony an artist has to go through when composing, so I will even make the costumes in front of them." It was to be not a performance, but a happening.

When they arrived at the hall and his wife ventured to ask him what the accompanist was to play, he shouted at her, "I will tell her at the time. Do not speak. *Silence*! This is my marriage with God."

And so it began. Nijinsky came on stage in the ballroom, before about two hundred persons, and announced, "I will show you how we live, how we suffer, how we artists create." Picking up a chair, he sat down and stared out at the audience for half an hour, without moving. They sat quietly—perhaps waiting, hypnotized by the atmosphere. At last, when the accompanist began impatiently to play a few notes and his wife went over to whisper to him in anguish that he must begin, he thundered at her again, "How dare you disturb me! I am not a machine. I will dance when I feel like it." But now, finally, he did start to dance. With the black and white rolls of cloth he made a cross the length of the room, stood at the end of it with arms out like a living crucifix, and told his transfixed audience: "Now I will dance you the war, with its suffering, with its destruction, with its death. The war which you did not prevent and so you are also responsible for." It was, as his wife wrote later, "the dance for life against death."[22]

The dean of Swiss psychiatry was Eugen Bleuler, and Nijinsky's wife now made an appointment to take her husband to see him for a definite diagnosis. He seemed to be even more withdrawn, even more occupied with his secret writing—and besides, her parents were coming for a visit and she must have needed some definite word to face down their inevitable hysteria at the family situation. On a sunny afternoon they drove to Zurich and to the state hospital, where Bleuler met them and took Nijinsky into his office for an interview. When they came out ten minutes later, Bleuler seemed all pleasantries: "All right. Splendid." And to the puzzled wife, "Won't you step in for a second? I forgot to give you the promised prescription yesterday."

Once inside the office, Bleuler gave her the dread news, backed by all the weight of his profession and his authority. "Now, my dear, be very brave. You have to take your child away; you have to get a divorce. Unfortunately, I am helpless. Your husband is incurably insane." On and on: "I must seem to be brutal, but I have to be able to save you and your child—two lives. We physicians must try to save those whom we can; the others, unfortunately, we have to abandon to their cruel fate." And more: "I am an old man. I have sacrificed fifty years of my life to save them. I have searched and studied; I know the symptoms; I can diagnose it; but I don't know, I wish I could help, but do not forget, my child, that sometimes miracles happen."

In the outer office, when she faced her husband, "it seemed as though his face was growing longer under my gaze, and he slowly said, 'Femmka, you are bringing me my death-warrant.'"[23]

Her parents, who arrived the next day, tried vainly to persuade her to divorce the madman immediately and return home with them, but she refused. So her mother took her out for a walk and, while they were out, had their hotel in Zurich surrounded by firemen to prevent Nijinsky's escape and had a police ambulance called to take him by force. "They knocked at his door. Vaslav, thinking it was the waiter, opened, and was immediately seized. They tried to carry him out in his pyjamas. Vaslav, as I learned from the manager, asked, 'What have I done? What do you want of me? Where is my wife?' They insisted that he should come, and the doctor, seeing his quietness, asked the nurses to release him. Vaslav thanked him, and said, 'Please let me dress, and I will follow you.' "[24]

When his wife returned to find him gone, she raced to the state hospital where, with Bleuler's help, she found him in a group of thirty other patients "but, by that time, Vaslav, owing to the shock, had had his first catatonic attack."[25] It was a tragic sequence of stupidities and errors, as she later came to realize, compounded by keeping him in the hospital instead of taking him out immediately;[26] but it was now too late for that. Nijinsky stayed in the hospital for a day, then was transferred to the famous Sanitorium Bellevue under the care of Ludwig Binswanger, but he changed very little; he was always the quiet, docile, withdrawn, model patient. Consultations with every famous psychiatric figure in Europe, including Freud, gave no grounds for hope that he would ever recover.

Only Diaghilev, that great master of men's actions, was sure that he could pull off the trick that would baffle the medical authorities. He arranged to have Nijinsky brought to a gala performance of the Ballet Russe at the Opera House, where he might see his successor as soloist, Serge Lifar, dance the lead in Stravinsky's *Petrouchka*. A critic who was in the party has described the whole sad incident:

> *I cannot say that I did not recognize Nijinsky, but it was difficult to identify that baldheaded grayish little man (one always forgets how small dancers are) with expressionless eyes and a sallow, sick look on his face. . . . He did not greet us, nor utter a sound. . . . Throughout the performance Diaghilev continued to talk to Nijinsky in a nagging, insistent whisper, and once or twice I heard him say, "Skaji, skaji, tell me, tell me, how do you like Lifar? Isn't he magnificent?" He tweaked Nijinsky's ear, poked him in the shoulder, chuckling in the tone with which elderly men, unaccustomed to infants, usually bring about a prolonged tantrum. To all of it, Nijinsky remained silent, but when the poking turned into actual pinching, he mumbled something like, "Aie, ostav, stop it!"*[27]

After the performance, a group was organized to pose for a photograph that has become famous—with Diaghilev, Lifar, Nijinsky, some other artists, and Karsavina, prima ballerina of the company. In her description of the scene Karsavina says, "The crowd of artists fell back. I saw vacant eyes and a passive shuffling gait, and stepped forward to kiss Nijinsky. A shy smile lit up his face, and his eyes looked straight into mine. I thought he knew me, and I was afraid to speak lest it might interrupt a slow-forming thought. He kept silent. I then called him by his pet name, 'Vatza!' He dropped his head and slowly turned it away."[28]

After the photograph had been taken, and when it became apparent that Nijinsky was neither going to speak nor respond, he was taken back out to a waiting car. The return to his home:

*It was past midnight when the limousine stopped . . . and the ceremony of extracting Nijinsky from his seat began again. He looked paler than before. . . . I watched him from the car, saw him stop, turn around; and although the car's motor was on, I heard him say in a gentle, halting, and somewhat tearful voice, "Skajite yemou chto Lifar horosho prygayet—Tell him that Lifar jumps well."*[29]

He faded back into the shadows that surround the "incurables" of our society; word leaked out now and then of his quiet life, of occasional visits by his sister Bronia, who was herself a ballet dancer of some fame, as well as by his beloved child Kyra, also training as a dancer. His wife's biography of him, first published in 1934, created a small sensation and quickly became a best seller even though Bronia, newly arrived in the United States to create the ballet for the movie version of *A Midsummer Night's Dream*, immediately pronounced it full of inaccuracies.[30] Kyra made her debut as a dancer in 1932 in London. She and her husband visited her father in Kreutzlingen Sanatorium at Bellevue, Switzerland, where she danced for him. He was, according to the newspaper accounts, "entranced."

But he remained unchanged until his wife discovered the work of Manfred Sakel, a Viennese who had introduced the insulin coma as a treatment for hopelessly ill schizophrenics. The method consists of inducing acute hypoglycemia and finally a state of coma by the injection of insulin, with the dosage gauged so that the patient revives just short of death. Nijinsky was administered a total of 271 of the treatments. They enabled him, apparently, to recover to the extent that he could leave the hospital and live with his wife on the outside. Just before this change, he was visited in the hospital by Lifar, who went equipped with a phonograph and records in order to make his own worshipful attempt to "cure" his idol. He played the music of one of the master's greatest triumphs, *The Specter of the Rose*, and began himself to dance to it, until at last Nijinsky began to pay attention, to look, and to applaud: "Ah, that is so good! Very good, very good, magnificent!" And again, the tragic reminder of all that might have been.

*Then responding to the appeal of my leaps, my entrechat-six's, Nijinsky began to leap, without the slightest effort, without any preparation—not even the slightest plié! His elevation was an unforgettable thing to watch. . . . Though his feet were encased in heavy leather shoes, Nijinsky executed innumerable entrechat-six's in an irreproachable style. I continued dancing for him, drawing him after me into the magic circle of the dance. His steps took a more definite form: I could distinguish a graceful pas-de-bourée, cabrioles, perfectly timed beats. The record stopped, Nijinsky was breathing with difficulty. Deeply moved, in a sort of ecstasy, I threw myself on my knees before him. And again the genius of the dance responded to my emotion. He, too, went down on his knees and said to me, pointing to my foot:—"Good! Yes! Very good!" Alas, the miracle came to an end and the familiar, terrible, raucous laughter drowned out the last words of the God of the Dance.*[31]

The belief in miracles must end—but hope, and friendly efforts, continued. In December of 1939, Nijinsky's old schoolmate Anatole Bourman, who had established himself and his dancing school in Hartford, Connecticut, offered to furnish an affadavit in support of the Nijinskys' entry into the United States; Sakel had moved to the United States himself and would be available for continued treatment. But new signs of war were gathering over Europe; the American consulate in Zurich blocked the issuance of the visa on the grounds that Switzerland and even Hungary might be drawn into the war, the Nijinskys would then have no country to which to return, and the United States would be stuck with them. Permission was finally granted in 1940, but by that time the war was on. They could not think of leaving until December 1945, and at that time Nijinsky's wife decided to move to England instead.

The last announcement of Nijinsky's career as a dancer came in September 1945, when Sol Hurok, the impresario who had taken over the Ballet Russe after Diaghilev's death in 1929, announced that Nijinsky had—at the age of fifty-five—agreed to dance the leading role in *Petrouchka* the following season at the Metropolitan Opera House in New York. He was at this time living in the Hotel Sacher in Vienna, described by one reporter as a "bomb-wrecked hotel behind the gutted opera house;" a few months before, a wartime rumor had had him killed by the Germans. In a touching little drama of the postwar months, he was found by the Russian soldiers when they invaded Austria in August. Newly inspired by hearing his native tongue and the music of his childhood, he danced beside a Red Army campfire for hundreds of cheering soldiers, whom he so captivated that the Russian high command offered to return him to a haven in their country with the status of Hero of the Soviet Union. But his wife chose to take him to a quiet home in Surrey, where they lived until he died on April 8, 1950, at the age of sixty. In January 1953, his remains were transferred to a cemetery in Montmartre, not far from the scene of his first great artistic triumphs.

### The Person
These are the external facts of Nijinsky's life, the framework on which we might begin to hang our understanding of him. Other kinds of external facts are important too, in particular the social-cultural-historical setting in which ballet flourished as an institution; I will speak of these in a summary below. But in regard to Nijinsky himself, we now come to in-between sorts of facts; observations which are external in the sense that they are made by an observer, but internal in the sense that they refer to interior aspects of him as a person—his character, his manner, his personality, his special gifts as an artist.

What kind of person was he? How did he seem to others? Many writers and artists knew him; each took his turn at trying to describe an almost indescribable quality in him. Here are a few:

Paul Claudel, poet:

*He walked as tigers do, it was not the transference of an inert mass from one position of balance to another, but the supple alliance with weight, like a wing on the air, of all that machine of muscles and nerves, of a body that is not trunk or statue, but the complete organ of power and movement. There was no gesture so small—the one, for example, when he turned his chin towards us, when the little head swung round suddenly on that long neck—that Nijinsky did not execute with glory, with a vivacity both ferocious and suave, with overwhelming authority. Even at rest, he seemed to be imperceptibly dancing.*[32]

Once, asked how he managed to leap so incredibly, Nijinsky said, "You just have to go up and pause there a little."[33] His wife said: "He seemed to float. Every movement of his was soft and powerful, like those of a tiger, with an indescribable elasticity."[34]

Jean Cocteau:

*Nijinsky's height was below average. His soul and body were one single professional deformation. . . . His face, with its Mongol features, was linked to his body by a very long, very thick neck. The muscles of his thighs and calves stretched the cloth of his trousers so taut that his legs seemed to arch out behind. His fingers were stubby and looked as if they had been cut off at the second joint. In short, no one could have thought that this little ape, with thinning hair and dressed in full-skirted overcoat, topped by an unbecoming hat balanced straight on the crown of his head, was the idol of the public. . . . But he was, and with reason. Everything in him held itself in readiness to be viewed from a distance under lights.*[35]

It may have been his feet: it was said that they were like a bird's, with as much foot behind the column of the calf as in front.

In his studies at school he was slow-witted, in his relations with others, gauche, and he was prone to outbursts of violence, as when he "accidentally" wounded a schoolmate with whom he did not get along.[36] But over it all there was the order and control that marked him as a person, and particularly as a dancer. His reputation among critics was as a dancer of "exquisite neatness."

Robert Edmond Jones, the stage designer:

*a small, somewhat stocky young man walking with delicate birdlike steps—precise, a dancer's walk. He is very nervous. His eyes are troubled. He looks eager, anxious, excessively intelligent. He seems tired, bored, excited, all at once. I observe that he has a disturbing habit of picking at the flesh on the side of his thumbs until they bleed. Through all my memories of this great artist runs the recurring image of those raw red thumbs. He broods and dreams, goes far away into reverie, returns again. At intervals his face lights up with a brief, dazzling smile. His manner is simple, ingratiating, so direct as to be almost humble. I like him at once . . . I realize at once that I am in the presence of a genius. What, precisely, does one mean by this word, so often and so carelessly used? . . .*

*I sense . . . a quality in him which I can define here only as a continual preoccupation with standards of excellence so high that they are really not of this world. This artist, it is clear, concerns himself with incredible perfections. I sense, too, the extraordinary nervous energy of the man—an almost frightening awareness, a curious mingling of eagerness and apprehension. The atmosphere he brings with him is—how shall I say?—oppressive. There is in him an astonishing drive, a mental engine, too high-powered, racing—perhaps even now—to its final breakdown. Otherwise there is nothing of the abnormal about him. Only an impression of something too eager, too brilliant, a quivering of the nerves, a nature racked to dislocation by a merciless creative urge. And those raw thumbs.*[37]

He was totally an artist of the dance—and so it finally became impossible to say who the real Nijinsky was, so completely did he submerge himself, and then reveal himself, in his characterizations. The sheer perfection of his technical skill, of course, played some part; it was said, for example, that he could cross his feet back and forth in front of each other ten times while jumping in the air, a leap called the *entrechat*.[38] Most ballet stars do six; a very few have achieved eight. His leaps through space were equally stupefying, even to sophisticated audiences. And he was evidently a mime of surpassing artistry. But those who saw his characterizations sensed that it was more than virtuosity, more than great artistic achievement. One critic concluded that Nijinsky seemed to portray the very spirit or essence of the roles he played, so much so that the "real" person, Nijinsky, disappeared, was transformed—"the person of everyday knowledge vanished completely, absorbed in the evoked qualities of the character portrayed. He appeared to have the ability to contract or broaden his body at will."[39] Again, "Always he appeared to be of a race apart, of another essence than ourselves, an impression heightened by his partiality for unusual roles, which were either animal-like, mythological, or unreal. On the stage he seemed surrounded by some invisible, yet susceptible halo."[40]

There are no films of his dancing—presumably on Diaghilev's orders—and so the legend grows, built on inadequate still photographs, on words describing remembered scenes. The reports provide convergent evidence of what has been called "his extraordinary theatrical style, his peculiar and complete talent for spiritual identification with his roles, and his wonderful comprehension of balletic elegance and deportment."[41] Yet there was clearly some other quality, almost the quality of myth. His favorite role was *Petrouchka*, the "marionette with the living soul."[42]

Dancers, like athletes, must maintain quite specific relations with the limits and capacities of their own bodies. The body has to be on call for them, so to speak, either for uniquely precisioned movements or for sustained surges, often for special combinations of endurance and precision under stress; yet what they do must never be strained or deliberate. Their bodies need to serve them—the metaphor is the closest one can get—almost as ideal servants: always at the ready, perfectly skilled but not automatic. Nijinsky carried this quality far beyond other dancers. To his wife's comment that it was a pity he could never watch himself dance (there were no films, and he did not use a mirror), he said: "You are mistaken. I always see myself dancing. I can visualize myself so thoroughly that I know exactly what I look like, just as if I sat in the midst of the audience."[43] To be able to sit "in the midst of the audience" and at the same time to become so utterly submerged in a characterization that Sarah Bernhardt, watching his performance, was once moved to tears—perhaps only his own remark about himself can sum it up: he once said that he danced with love.

Speaking of a series of photographs of Nijinsky's most famous roles, an art critic has said:

> *It is interesting to try one's self to assume the poses on the pictures, beginning with arms, shoulders, neck, and head. The flowing line they have is deceptive. It is an unbelievable strain to hold them. The plastic relationships turn out to be extremely complex. As the painter de Kooning, who knows the photographs well and many of whose ideas I am using in these notes, remarked: Nijinsky does just the opposite of what the body would naturally do. The plastic sense is similar to that of Michaelangelo and Raphael. One might say that the grace of them is not derived from avoiding strain, as a layman might think, but from the heightened intelligibility of the plastic relations. It is an instinct for countermovement so rich and so fully expressed, it is unique.*[44]

To be an athlete, a dancer, is to sustain quite specific relations with one's body; it is, by comparison with all the rest of us, something quite abnormal. Nijinsky seemingly further compounded this burden of abnormality. He was able to put his body into service as a mechanism to a degree far beyond what even other dancers could do; he compounded this by enabling, or perhaps forcing, his body into "countermovement." Most athletic skills are essentially extensions of normal movements—the broad jumper's leap, the runner's endurance, the boxer's reflex defense or the power of his punch. Although they demand a body that responds perfectly as a mechanism, they do not entail the body's running counter to the normal direction or flow of movement. But Nijinsky demanded of himself— or perhaps discovered in himself—an additional dimension of artistic and bodily prowess. How could he ever hope to rediscover for himself the true nature of his own bodily functioning and the emotional states arising there?

In so many ways—and this was said of him over and over again—he simply was not of this world. His lifetime stance, even from childhood, was that of the alien: a Pole in the Russian motherland who never lost his Polish accent when speaking Russian, the Poles being in Russian eyes much like Mexican Americans are in the eyes of narrow-minded Anglos in the American Southwest. Even as a grown man he was helpless when required to do such simple but worldly tasks as buy a railway ticket or book a room in a hotel;[45] he had absolutely no sense of himself as a public personage. Fame rested on him, but awkwardly, like his ill-fitting overcoat; yet there was no way at all that he could avoid the contacts and eventually the responsibilities that went with being great and famous. For much of this he turned to his wife: "She was clever and taught me about the necessary things of life."[46] A curious little confession, with its implication that though he had learned the language of everyday behavior, he really never understood its meaning.

And then there is the question of his homosexuality, though that term is too easily misused. Diaghilev was homosexual in the sense that he was never known to have had a deeply personal or sexual relationship with a woman, and had on the contrary a succession of close personal and sexual relations of long standing with various younger men in his company. Nijinsky has described the start of their affair:

*Ivor introduced me to Diaghilev, who asked me to come to the Hotel Europe, where he lived. I disliked him for his too self-assured voice, but went to seek my luck. I found my luck. At once I allowed him to make love to me. I trembled like a leaf. I hated him but pretended, because I knew that my mother and I would die of hunger otherwise. I understood Diaghilev from the first moment and pretended to agree with him at once. One had to live, and therefore it was all the same to me what sort of sacrifice I had to make. I worked hard at my dancing and was always tired. But I pretended not to be tired at all in order that Diaghilev should not be bored with me. I know what he felt, he loved boys and therefore could not understand me . . . I admired him sincerely and when he told me that love for women is a terrible thing I believed him. If I had not believed him, I could not have done the things I have done.*[47]

During their first long separation, Nijinsky proposed marriage to a girl he barely knew, was accepted, and married her. The passage above was written five years later. Was it a truthful account of his liaison with Diaghilev, or was he trying to justify himself? Did he rush into marriage because it was the very first opportunity to assert his fundamentally heterosexual inclinations, once out from under the influence of Diaghilev? And what of the implications in this typical passage from his diary? "I know why men run after girls. I know what a girl is. Man and women are one . . . I am husband and wife in one. I love my wife. I love my husband."[48]

Was Nijinsky, then, a homosexual, and did the sources of his conflict over his sexuality contribute to his breakdown? The evidence is nicely balanced and so can be read either way. There is no possible answer to the question of whether he was a homosexual, and this fact should perhaps alert us to the possibility that the question itself may be meaningless. To say that someone is one thing or another is to assign him unquestioningly to a category and to assume that the category fully sums him up. Perhaps this can be done in the extreme case, and perhaps Diaghilev was such a case. But when exceptions arise, as when Nijinsky shows behavior that can be categorized as Diaghilev-like on one occasion and as non-Diaghilev-like at some other time, then questions about whether he belongs in the category of people like Diaghilev lose their meaning. An easy out is to make the mystery still deeper by introducing the notions of latent and manifest homosexuality and then by further claiming that one little instance of homosexual behavior, for whatever reason, is sufficient to tar the person with the pathological brush: he is then diagnosed as a homosexual, manifest as such on one minor occasion but latently so all the rest of the time. The trouble with this reasoning is that it makes too many assumptions about what kind of sexual preference is to be valued; it denies the equally logical possibility that it is the person's heterosexuality that may be latent during prolonged episodes of homosexual behavior. It can be argued both ways; no satisfactory answer is possible. Therefore we might begin to suspect that the original question, as in the case of Nijinsky, was meaningless.[49]

There was, however, a famous quarrel between Nijinsky and Diaghilev. It was for a time the talk of the ballet world; it deeply and continuingly affected both their lives and both their professional careers; it aroused great bitterness on both sides and forced everyone who knew them to choose and declare his allegiance. Our interest in the event at this late date is not in resolving the issues that divided them nor in determining, if that were possible, who was right and who was wrong, but in using the event to help us understand Nijinsky's inner biography. The fight, its setting, and its consequences, were deeply significant in Nijinsky's life.

### The Quarrel

Consider the setting for their high drama. Nijinsky became, at a remarkably early age, the most famous and promising of the stars of the Imperial Russian Ballet. It was a strange life, a hothouse culture, the very epitome of what was the most completely aristocratic society since ancient times. The setting has been well described by Diaghilev's biographer:

*We can have no conception of what fame meant to the dancer in Russia. It cannot be measured through any parallel with the great film star or the prominent athlete of our day. Life in Russia then was spacious and extravagant. Money flowed like water, and the wealthy spent a fortune to satisfy some whim—to recompense the tsiganes after a night's carousing, to make champagne flow from a fountain, to eat a banquet of meats and fruit out of season . . . Everything that we knew in the height of prosperity must be multiplied a hundredfold. Fame, to a dancer, did not merely on occasions offer the entrée into moneyed circles, but also a certain familiarity, however remote, with the court and the aristocracy that money itself could not always buy. The dancer was an expensive luxury maintained at the court's expense, and its most especial pride. Sudden success was enough to turn the best-balanced head, and to convey a set of entirely false values.[50]*

The ballet itself as a subculture closely paralleled the culture of aristocratic life. Both were closed in, with a great deal of inbreeding; one had to be born, or at least reborn, into the life. Its members knew themselves as a special, favored caste far above the level of the great Russian masses of workers. Isolated and turned inward toward their own center, they fed on intrigue and gossip; nourished by artificial yet traditional values, they were constantly seeking thrills that were unreal yet at a very high level of sensibility. Indeed, the ballet in its classical form could only have flourished within that world of the aristocracy which flowered prior to World War I. It was a world that we can now only read about in memoirs, for it disappeared for good with the first sounds of the guns of August, 1914.

Diaghilev was born and perfectly made for success in this atmosphere. His biographer has noted that he could not accurately be termed an impresario:

*An impresario, although he may be a man of exquisite taste and judgment, is a business man promoting an entertainment for gain. To be an impresario is to have a definite profession. That was not the case with Diaghileff. Whether he gained or whether he lost, his aims and outlook were totally different. He made for himself an occupation that did not exist previously, carving it out of his character and tastes . . . Diaghileff was always the aristocrat, organizing and creating work for his own satisfaction and that of his friends, and graciously allowing the public to participate. He was the host at his own performances, the descendant of those who had held serfs.*[51]

More than this, he was a master of men, a master of all the arts. Nijinsky's wife, hardly well disposed toward him, could not avoid saying it. "Diaghileff was a real man of the Renaissance. . . . He knew enough of everything to make his authority respected in each field, and he had the added alchemy of perfection, of suggestion, which drew out of everyone his greatest possible energies. He was, in the best sense of the word, a dilettante, but the dilettante raised to the *n*th power, the dilettante all-powerful, the dilettante whose career was the furtherance of other more intense talents."[52] No wonder that Nijinsky called him "the only man with universal talent that I could compare to Leonardo da Vinci."[53] And no wonder he confessed that "among all the people I have ever known, Diaghileff, of course, meant the most to me."[54] For they needed each other totally. The one a naïve, unworldly, mythic artist, the other effective, worldly, often cruel; the one an embodied dreamer, the other an imaginative doer. It was inevitable that they would find each other, meet and merge, feed on each other, and develop one another. Their relationship, as we now look back on it, was played out on the stage of Europe in the dying years before World War I, in a drama startlingly like one of their own ballets—perfectly plotted, handsomely mounted and exquisitely played, but laden with an oppressive sense of tragedy.

It is difficult now to be serious about their intrigue, their violent backstage passions, their lovers' quarrels, and their final nasty separation. Certainly Diaghilev never went beyond this level but remained sulking in his hotel suite, so to speak, until he died. But Nijinsky—and this is part of his continuing story—seemed to know that his affair with Diaghilev belonged to an older era, and he spent the next few tortured years, as choreographer and producer on his own, in a serious effort to make a bridge to a new world. The dances he created, with their angular movements and their strident sounds and rhythms, belonged not with the world of classical ballet, but with art forms just coming into being in Paris: the music of Stravinsky, the painting of Picasso, the writing of Joyce. But of course he had none of the abilities needed to turn his artistic visions into real productions on the world's stage; for this he needed the special talents of Diaghilev as partner. Born into one world, Nijinsky now found himself born out of it, but with no new one at hand and no gifts with which to construct his own.

The ardent proponents of one or another side of this quarrel have tended to see their antagonists as evil men, plotting to destroy the great institution of the Ballet Russe. But the truth of the matter—insofar as we can ever sum up the truth of any continuing relation between two human beings—should, rather, take into account the drama in which they costarred. Nijinsky was unworldly in the extreme (though hardly the complete oaf that his detractors have described); only Diaghilev's coaching and influence could have brought him to be more than a soloist in a St. Petersburg dance company. Only through Diaghilev could he have become a success; but whether this is to be praised or lamented can no longer be said with confidence. The answer may be tied up with the unanswerable question of whether any worldly success is worth its price. Surely some part of Nijinsky's personal tragedy was that he lived with this question and found no satisfying answer for it, a half-century before it was to become the agonizing personal issue it is for many sensitive people today.

In any case, Diaghilev exacted his price: whoever joined his company and became one of its stars had to commit his whole being to the Ballet Russe and its master. Even when the star was a man, probably only part of this demand was homosexually personal; the remainder of the demand (and here Nijinsky's wife may tip the balance too far) was probably a great producer's insistence on giving all for one's art. Nijinsky's flight from these pressures—into marriage, into managing his own affairs, into his own choreography and system of dance notation, into imitating Diaghilev as producer—was a necessary step that inevitably led to his downfall. But it makes no sense to assign strictly deterministic causes here, for the entire sequence, like a Greek drama, was marked by the inevitability of fate—its characters moving painfully, inexorably, and sometimes even knowingly toward their tragic ends. Nijinsky broke off from his lover but was hardly prepared to live with the consequences; equally, Diaghilev was unable to back down, to offer to share his authority, much less to forgive the insult to his personal and professional image. Together they fashioned what may have been the only authentic Greek drama of our century.

So much for the affair in its larger sense, historically and culturally. What has not been touched on, however, is the meaning that the affair and its termination had for Nijinsky, the part that it played in the history of his schizophrenia. When he composed his diary during that winter of 1919, he made Diaghilev into the prototype of everything worldly, everything managerial, therefore everything cruel and evil. Here is part of a letter that he never sent:

*To the Man,*

*I cannot name you because I have no name for you. I am not writing to you hastily. I don't want you to think that I am nervous, I am not. I am able to write quite calmly . . .*

*I am not afraid of you, I know well that in your innermost being you do not hate me. I love you as one loves a human being, but I do not want to work with you. But there is one thing I want you to know, that I am working a great deal. I am not dead. I am still alive. God lives in me and I live in Him . . .*

*You are organizing troupes, I am not. I am not interested in forming companies—I am interested in human beings.*

*You are dead because your aims are death.*

*I do not call you my friend, knowing that you are my bitter enemy, but even so I have no ill feelings toward you. Enmity calls for death and I am longing for life . . .*

*You said that I am a fool and I thought that you are one. I don't want to humiliate myself before you and you love people who do that. I do not want your smile, it is death. . . . I do not smile any more, I don't bring destruction. I am not writing in order to make you merry, I am writing to make you cry.*

*I am a person with feeling and brains. You have brains but no feeling. Your sentiments are pernicious. You want to annihilate me and I want to save you. I love you but you don't love me. I wish you everything good, you wish me everything bad . . .*

*Don't think, don't hearken. I am not yours, you are not mine. I love you now, I loved you always. I am yours and I am my own. You have forgotten what God is, and so had I, in the past. But I found Him. You are the one who wants death and destruction, although you are afraid of death. I am not afraid of it. Death is a necessary event . . .*

*I want to explain to you a great deal, but I never again want to work with you, as you have utterly different aims. You are a hypocrite, and I don't want to become one. I can only admit hypocrisy when a man wants to achieve something good and noble through this means.*

*You are a bad man, you are not a Tsar, a ruler. You are not my Emperor. You are an evil person. You wish me harm, but I do not want this for you. I am a tender being and want to write you a cradle song . . .*

*Sleep peacefully, sleep, sleep peacefully.*

*Man to Man,*

*Vaslav Nijinsky.*[55]

This letter was written during the most critical period of Nijinsky's acute illness. Yet it hardly sounds like the ravings of a man who is cracking up—even though the behavior that others saw every day was becoming more and more unusual. When the patient is given a chance, as he is here, to state his own case, what comes out is a message quite different from "crazy talk." He sounds—at least to me—as though he is terribly concerned with a statement that he must make. There is something that he absolutely must get across—to Diaghilev, to his wife, to friends, possibly to everyone in the world. The statement is not yet clear, perhaps not even clear to Nijinsky himself, but it seems to have something to do with a philosophy of life or, rather, with two contrasting philosophies, pairs of ethical opposites: life and death, love and hate, kindliness and power, good and evil, feeling and brains, God and man.

It is a curious document, as is Nijinsky's diary as a whole. He was no writer; he was not even a thinker who was unable to turn a phrase. The style is uniformly simple, almost banal. I find myself impelled to search between the lines; surely there is some deeper meaning here that I am missing. And having realized that I am genuinely moved by the spirit that animates these pages, I conclude that the meaning is not to be found clearly spelled out in the content of the diary. If Nijinsky had something to say to his family and friends, to himself, to the whole world—and if he struggled in his life and in his diary to say it—then we will have to look for it in its guise as expression, not declaration. I mean this: that if Nijinsky's personal tragedy has a message for us—and I think that it does, a message that he himself struggled to articulate—then it will not be found in some clearly stated declaration made by him but in what he expressed through his life, his art, and his painfully scrawled words.

### A Summary

To begin, we may try to summarize what we know so far. There are the external facts of his life; the many, often conflicting, views of him by others who knew him, met him, or worked with him; the story of his relations with Diaghilev; the society and the era in which his art flourished. One way to organize these data is in terms of the categories often used in case histories, and this might be a useful first step. That is, how do these data help us to answer the conventional clinical question concerning the relative influence of various kinds of determinants on Nijinsky's schizophrenia?

The commonest division of determinants is bipolar: they are either primarily biological or primarily social, either mostly inborn or mostly learned. A more complex breakdown would include hereditary influences, early family patterns and circumstances, sexual development and behavior, character and personality, general social and environmental background, and immediate situational stresses. We have enough material at hand to sketch in each of these briefly.

Nijinsky's background showed many signs of instability. His mother's father was a psychopath and compulsive gambler who finally committed suicide. His father was a passionate, moody, rebellious man who left Nijinsky's mother and three young children when the strain of supporting the family and apologizing for his numerous affairs became more than he chose to put up with. Nijinsky's older brother, Stanislaus, spent most of his life in an institution, where he died during World War I, apparently having suffered extensive brain damage from a fall, although Nijinsky himself always referred to his brother as "insane." Even before the father's desertion, the children's early years had been marked by insecurity and the lack of a permanent home. Settled in St. Petersburg after the father's desertion, Nijinsky fell into the unwanted role of mainstay of the family. It was not until he entered ballet school that he knew anything but insecurity and terrible poverty. He grew up as the type of schizoid character described in older textbooks: shy, quiet, withdrawn, socially clumsy, nearly inarticulate, with a tendency to murderous explosions of rage. Immature and ineffective in his relations with others, sexually naïve and inhibited even beyond the normal constraints of his day, emotionally both explosive and overcontrolled, he was totally unprepared for fame and for the gay, cosmopolitan life into which his artistic success thrust him. He may have had one sexual experience with a prostitute before meeting Diaghilev, but in any case this was the beginning of his sexual life; by his own straightforward statement, he did not choose homosexuality but was pulled into it by someone vastly stronger and more experienced. His later adjustment, in the marriage bed, can only be guessed at—but in spite of his wife's fulsome comments on his "godlike" performance, there is clear evidence that it took him at least some weeks after their marriage to invite her into bed for the first time.

Even in brief summary, this hardly adds up to a well-organized character with strengths and sources of stability on which to fall back in case of emergency. He had almost no resources within himself to be other than a uniquely gifted artist. When things went wrong for him he could only suffer or brood or become difficult with his associates. Cast adrift from Diaghilev, he was called upon to be a man of the world—a producer, director, and organizer, responsible for a large touring ballet company. Constantly strapped for funds—for he had none of the widespread financial resources that an established impresario would have—and with little knowledge of languages and a near-total ignorance of the world of business, he was assured of being a disastrous failure as a producer. Only his own artistic gifts saved him, at least temporarily. Then the only world that he knew began to collapse around him—the war stopped all international travel, the Russian Revolution cut him off from his homeland, and he found himself becalmed in Switzerland, all exits closed.

All the possible "causes," every known determinant, add up to nearly a diagnostic certainty. Whatever one's bias, he will find support in Nijinsky's case. What can we now conclude? Perhaps that schizophrenia has no causes as such, that all the supposed determinants are only pieces out of the same pie; each is related to all the others, and all may be present and influential in some way, but none may assume priority. This seems to be one lesson to be gained from a case such as Nijinsky's, in which we have access to facts from many different domains. But this is only half an argument; the question that still has to be asked is this: What, then, is the nature of the situation that finally overcomes him, that leads to changes so radical and irreversible? Why, then, and how, does he collapse in just this way, rather than into confusion or sleep or suicide?

## A VIEW OF THE INNER MAN

The diagnostic conclusion that we have just reached is essentially a view from the outside; it speaks of determinants and relates possible causes, all of them external to Nijinsky's experience as a unique individual. An alternative approach consists in getting at the inner person, either indirectly through the experiences that others had of him, or directly by looking at his own statements. Fortunately, we have access to both kinds of information.

To everyone who knew him, seemingly without exception, Nijinsky appeared as both remarkable and pitiable, as god and simpleton in one. Perhaps he was aware of this for he said that his favorite role, of all those that he created, was that of the puppet in Petrouchka—the not-quite-human doll with a spark of divine life, a figure both laughable and tragic, ridiculous and noble in one. Although he was an alien Pole to his Russian friends, others who were not themselves Russian explained his "difference" as the result of his Russian background. One of his teachers said of the Russians, "there is something about them that we Europeans can never, never penetrate";[56] and his wife said of Nijinsky and his daughter Kyra, "They were both essentially and fundamentally Russian. . . . Sometimes I felt as if I were intruding on them."[57] It may well be that they were all correct, the Russians and non-Russians alike: he was like his own roles, a clown, a doll, a puppet, a spirit, not quite either human or nonhuman. An artist who chanced to spend some time with him one summer in Maine when he was creating the role of *Til Eulenspiegel* described him as "so timid and reticent that I was scarcely able to draw a word out of him. He seemed to speak entirely with his eyes. He would examine a sketch of mine minutely, then look furtively at me, smile unexpectedly, and nod his head approvingly. He might have been a frightened faun."[58]

If his own identity was a mystery to himself, the problem was even more puzzling to those who worked with him. How could one relate to such a creature? His wife lavished on him a love so worshipful that it became quite unreal. Diaghilev manipulated him, sometimes doted on him, probably held him in mild contempt. Igor Stravinsky recognized his artistry but thought he was mostly a stupid child. Ernest Ansermet, the conductor, was even more frank:

*Observing him from a distance as well as at close quarters, I have always thought that he suffered from a latent conflict between his genius as a dancer—that grace which nature had bestowed on him—and his critical faculties . . . Diaghilev's ideas were capable only of upsetting him, and of contradicting his true nature. The latter was all too simple, one might almost say even too healthy, for aesthetic speculation. . . . The illusion of culture, which had enveloped Nijinsky while he was at Diaghilev's side, gave birth in him to aspirations which his intellect was incapable of realizing. . . . [He] was an instinctive choreographer. . . . He was endowed with a personality which on its irrational side possessed a marvellous power of communication with the world, of self-revelation, in dancing. On the rational side, however, it had remained in an infantile state, and closed.*[59]

The words here are embarrassingly reminiscent of explanations that used to be offered of the "instinctive musical gifts of the darkies"; they are terms that degrade the very person they purport to praise. Nijinsky wrote at one point in his diary: "I do not like praise because I am not a boy."[60] As he did so often, he uttered a startling and disturbing truth in terms almost too simple to be understood. I think that what he meant here was that whenever he was praised as an artist, the effect was to put him in the position of a little boy being patted on the head by adults. "You colored folks sure do have a natural rhythm in your feet," says Ansermet as he pats Nijinsky on the head. This, indeed, is all that most people can do when faced with an artist; they take advantage of his need to be appreciated and handle the problem of looking up at him by looking down on him. Nijinsky seemed to have sensed, even as a young boy, that this was all that the world could ever do with him. They would treat his person just as they dealt with his body, by training it, manipulating it, fondling it, patting it. What they would never do was, quite simply, come to terms with him as person. It was only much later—too late, in fact—when he was pouring it all into his diary that he found out what it was that he really wanted to take place between himself and the world. He wanted feeling, he said, true feeling and love.

A more ordinary man might have found love, person to person; a more gifted man might have arranged things so that love were possible. Nijinsky was neither, or both—not ordinary enough, not clever enough. Hence the ethic that in his extremity he struggled to express: for feeling and love and God and life, and against death and hate and power and knowledge. The diary is filled with instances of this one message. "I would prefer my writing to be photographed instead of printed, because printing does away with handwriting. Handwriting is a lovely thing; it is alive and full of character. I want my handwriting to be photographed because I want people to understand it as it comes from God."[61] Or this: "The mind is stupidity, but wisdom is God. You think that because I build everything on feeling, I have lost my mind. A man who bases everything on feeling is not horrible."[62] And this:

> For the first time I felt grieved three or five days after my wedding. I asked my wife to learn to dance, because dancing was the highest thing in life for me. I wanted to teach her. I never taught anyone my art, I wanted it for myself, but I wanted to teach her the real art of the dance, but she got frightened. Did she no longer trust me? I wept and wept bitterly, and already felt death. I understood that I had made a mistake, but it was too late to undo it. Had I put myself into the arms of a person who did not love me? I understood the whole mistake. My wife worshipped me above all, but she did not feel me. I wanted to leave, but understood that that would be caddish, and stayed with her. She loved me. Did she love me for my art and for the beauty of my body?[63]

And again: "Beyond this world there is no light, and therefore I am afraid of death and what is beyond. I want light, the light of twinkling stars. A twinkling star is life—and a star that does not twinkle is death. I have noticed there are many human beings who do not twinkle."[64]

There is only one way to get along in a world where everyone is too busy getting along to pause and make contact with each other. That one way, as Nijinsky knew in his heart, was to be clever and worldly and intelligent; feeling was a burden, simplicity only got in the way. By these lights he could only fail. He wrote: "I will remain alone, and cry in my loneliness."[65]

Once the message is understood, much of Nijinsky's supposedly psychotic diary makes sense. One conclusion, then, might be that the value judgment implied in our calling someone crazy is due to our inability to understand his unique message; if we could only grasp what it is he is trying to say we would realize that he may not be less "normal" than us but possibly far wiser. Such an argument disposes of craziness as a recognizable entity. It says that such people are off on their own trip or else embarked in directions for which the rest of us are not yet ready. It is an argument that has particular force at a time like the present, when conventional culture is in ferment, when new adventures in consciousness are announced almost every day, when many of us begin to be open to wonders and mysteries discoverable in our own potentialities.

But there is another facet of the whole picture, and in fairness we have to consider this as well. Some messages make sense. Now consider this one:

*I wish to explain what God is, to everyone, but I will not if people start laughing. I am talking about matters which touch the whole universe. I bring peace and not war. I want peace for everyone and want the earth to be full of love. The earth is disintegrating, and it is cooling down. It is still warm, but not for long, and God therefore wants love to be ever-present. People do not think of stars and therefore they cannot understand the universe. I often think of stars. I do not like astronomy, because astronomy does not explain God to us. Astronomy teaches us the geography of the stars. I do not like geography, as I dislike frontiers. To me the earth is one single state. The earth is the head of God. God is the fire in the head. I am alive as long as there is fire in my head. My pulse is like an earthquake. I know that if there are no more earthquakes the earth will get cold and all mankind with it, because people will not be able to exist.*[66]

And so on and on. This is how the diary runs, at least in some of its pages. One thought leads by a tenuous connection to another, one image or association weakly calls up the next, and though individually the sentences make sense, the effect of the complete paragraph is of a mind in a whirl.

I will confess that this is how my own thinking runs on sometimes if, for example, I am in a hammock, the sun dazzling my half-closed eyes, a faint buzz and murmur all about me as I drift in and out of a doze. I must also confess that there are times when I try very hard to loosen up my thoughts so that they will flow this loosely and my writing will improve. But even if it happens, I am never able to capture it in writing on paper; to do that I have to pull myself together again mentally. I have to stand firmly somewhere in order to catch all these fleeting images and associations on the wing. And when I organize to this degree, inevitably what gets down on paper makes sense, paragraph by paragraph. I can't arrange to be disorganized. The reason, I think, is that what I say or write is communicated, either to myself or to someone else. Using words is not like humming a tune; speaking is always speaking to. So I must take you, the listener, into account; I must have a continuing sense of what might be sensible to you. As speaker, then, I find myself always playing two roles, the talker and the critic, the one at work and the other aware of the work and keeping an eye on it. Only by this means am I able to keep clued in on the relative order of the world—for the world does make some kind of sense; it is in fact ordered in some way. Our collective comings and goings do mesh together so that the total panorama is not hopelessly random. The critic part of me has the job of keeping my communications roughly in tune with the relative harmony that defines the world.

If there should ever arrive on earth a message of such overwhelming and universal import that, immediately sensible or not, it would supersede all our accustomed needs for order, it might properly claim freedom from the restrictions under which we labor as individuals. But such a claim is rash as well as dangerous, and not everyone who offers it, therefore, has to be listened to. The chances will be that he is not reporting the end of the world but only the collapse of his own. When he does this, regardless of how moving is his personal message, we are entitled to call him crazy.

In sum, if we are all to make it together on the same planet, if we are to act as though we share something of the same world, we cannot deny some basis that is common and therefore binding on all of us. There is a final responsibility that each of us assumes as he enters the human community; it is the price he pays for being known to his fellows. This is the failing we can discover in Nijinsky; and the fact that it is revealed most acutely when we allow him to speak for himself, in his diary, lends even greater weight to its central significance.

The inner view, then, converges on the same conclusion as we reached in considering Nijinsky's case from the outside. But there is a special advantage to be gained from his own report of his experience. If we read it carefully enough, we may be able to understand the beginnings of his strange and tragic trip. Concerning the end, we agree that no matter how it is viewed he became crazy; but it was not this way for him when he started. Like all such persons—and indeed, in many ways like those who venture these days into outer space—he started his trip by breaking free of the hold that life has on earth. Once on the way, there was no turning back. Then, caught in an alien gravity, tossed and drawn by forces beyond his control, he plunged toward a strange place. What if he could have found an understanding listener at the very start—would that have changed his agonized trip into a meaningful search for a new identity?

One way to answer this question, both in general and for Nijinsky as an individual, is to consider how it is that persons arrive at the state that we call crazy and then to try to apply these generalizations to his unique case.

It is helpful, even if not absolutely necessary, to have had a lifetime of barren experiences with other persons, perhaps superficially rich in attachments but actually consisting of a succession of minimal ties and so of inadequate learning of ways to effect ties to others. It is equally helpful to have suffered an absence of chances to learn even the most elementary skills in recognizing and coming to terms with the tragic forces of life—the weaknesses of one's body, the losses, the failed hopes, and above all death. With the person thus truly disadvantaged, when crisis occurs it will serve only to further weaken the life structure rather than serving as a basis for learning and growth. In a general sense, the stage is now set for an acute and overwhelming situational crisis.

Almost any crisis situation will do, as often as not simply one that most persons will manage to stumble through. All that the crisis needs to accomplish is to bring the routine of living to a halt—by an unexpected turn of events, or a sudden disappointment or loss, even perhaps by an illness. Victimized, the person is now forced to ask, "And now what?" It is not a question he knows how to ask, much less to answer—not if his life pattern has kept him from ever knowing about himself or confronting himself or learning about himself from others. In a bind, finding himself blocked off in every direction, forced to look at himself and discovering only a stranger, he turns in desperation searching for any exit at all. It is the matter of exits that will determine what will happen to him.

Living, for most people, reduces to having choices. We start our lives with the experience of having unlimited options, all of them completely open. Ask a four-year-old boy about his long-term plans—not what he can do but what he will do when he grows up—and he will rattle off, with all the innocent confidence in the world, a list of achievements that adults cling to only in fantasy: he is going to be a fireman, a major league ballplayer, a cowboy, and the president of the United States. To the four-year-old just beginning to be able to think about his own future as such, everything is possible for him. What lies ahead is real because he wants it; he has yet to learn that a choice means gaining one alternative only at the cost of giving up another. To choose means to gain, but it also means to lose. This is what growing up is all about: learning to live with the hard fact that life is a succession of options gained and lost. From one perfectly valid point of view life is a sequence of achievement piled on achievement; from the opposite and equally valid point of view life is also a series of things given up. Thus, to decide to play baseball is to decide not to go out for the track team; to choose to finish high school is to give up the chance to go to work at the age of sixteen; to major in premed in college quite probably means never being a lawyer. Life may become richer as it goes on, but progressively it narrows down.

What keeps life meaningful and worthwhile, what keeps us going after all, is in part the gains that we experience from having made what we feel are the better choices. In part, too, we are continually sustained by a kind of implicit knowledge—that behind it all, even if everything now present should fail us, some little-used exit doors are available, many of them ready to be used in almost any situation of stress. They serve as typical escape mechanisms, and when they help to determine our character as individuals they are called coping devices[67] or releases from stress. In the simplest case, we get mad; we blow up and so blast our way out of a situation or, contrariwise, we clam up, close in on ourselves, bury our anger, and sulk. Drinking serves as a generally useful exit, wide enough to accommodate the passage of any life event; more and more frequently, addicting drugs tend to serve the same purpose. Some people turn to hard work as an out, some to cleaning the closets, others to masturbating or playing golf—each one constructs an exit door to fit his own internal architecture. The many ways out cover as wide a range as the besieged imagination can fashion, and they also vary in terms of generality—some specific to the individual or to the moment, some able to serve as exits out of almost any situation and thus functioning as last resorts. In my own case, when all else failed me, what might I do? In the extreme case, I think my body would demand sleep and then illness, and I would end up helpless, totally dependent on those who care for me. Other persons, reacting differently, might drop everything and run, run wildly and with no goal, just getting away from it all.

Nijinsky seems to have been one of those failed persons who lacked any ways out of whatever extreme situation he was in. He could allow himself only a limited range of emotional expression and certainly none of the emotional extremes that help one to overcome a situation by tearing it apart—the temper tantrum, the explosion of delirious joy, the depressive mood, the orgasm. I suspect that he had a very limited fantasy life, that on the contrary he was usually occupied almost completely with the operations through which he put his body. He enjoyed no real sexual life, no outside activities, no contacts with other persons, no accomplishments from hour to hour. He was deathly serious about life and so, finally, psychotically serious as well—having no usable exits out of a crisis situation short of death or psychosis, he ended up quite properly equating the two.

The year of the diary seems to have been for Nijinsky a time when things slowly closed in on him, in a crisis that gathered like a thunderstorm. Brought finally to asking himself the unfamiliar question, "And now what?" and unable to discover an answer in his current situation, he must have turned in a desperate search for exits. All possible life avenues closed, he turned inward, perhaps for the very first time in his life. The diary, that agonized but hopeless appraisal of himself and his history and his world, was the result. But because he was the man that he was, it had to be a message that no one understood. In his writing, in his thinking, and in his behavior, he was demonstrably crazy. The rest is a familiar story: the panic that he evoked in his wife's family, the hasty reliance on psychiatric authority, the grim and almost punitive diagnosis and commitment, the consequent shock and proof to the patient himself that he was hopelessly insane. In all, it is a sad and unfortunately common story of how irreversible results can come from the mishandling of a life crisis.

At the point where he turned inward, wrenching his own stance so as to take a first long look at himself as a person, Nijinsky was forced on a new tack, one based totally on the news about himself that he received from himself. That was the nature of the diary's content. Its guiding vision, for the same sound reasons, was an absolute, last-ditch honesty with himself, as though he had now said to himself, "I can no longer lie to myself or hide from myself. As far as I am able, I must now say it the way I see it." The results of this vision are often surprisingly rich and profound, particularly from a man who is clearly and admittedly not at home with either thinking or its expression in words. What comes from him, given the miracle of a total and utterly honest expression of his experience, can only be described as a baring of the soul. One passage in particular deserves examination:

*Whenever I have a feeling I carry it out. I never fight against a feeling. An order of God tells me how to act. I am not a fakir and a magician. I am God in a body. Everyone has that feeling, but no one uses it. I do make use of it, and know its results. People think that this feeling is a spiritual trance, but I am not in a trance. I am love. I am in a trance, the trance of love. I want to say so much and cannot find the words. I want to write and cannot. I can write in a trance, and this trance is called* wisdom. *Every man is a reasonable being. I do not want unreasonable beings and therefore I want everyone to be in a trance of feelings. I am in a trance of God. God wants me to sleep. People will say that all that I write is stupid, but in reality it has a deep meaning.*[68]

## GOD IN MAN'S BODY

Truth's got so much energy and so much juice in it . . . I really feel good when I find out that I can say something true once in a while, because when you say something true you can hook in behind it and . . . what comes out of your mouth is the word of God, because that's what the word of God is, is truth. . . . We are energy. This stuff is energy . . . also this sort of feeling that we have here of being this many people stonedish together . . . is energy. Energy's more specific than that, though—I believe that energy's the Holy Spirit, I believe that it's the body and blood of Jesus, Krishna, Buddha, and anybody along that line. We're a dance of energy, arranged and held in the mind of God. . . . We're each one creating our own self and our whole universe. You are all God creating your own universe. . . . You're God without doing anything . . . without trying, you see, for openers . . . right off the top you're God. But if you're uptight about it, well then you're not being . . . you only gain as much percentage of God as you let yourself be. If you can relax into it you're going toward your godlike state.[69]

"You grok," Smith repeated firmly. "I am explain. I did not have the word. You grok. Anne groks. I grok. The grasses under my feet grok in happy beauty. But I needed the word. The word is God."

"Go ahead."

Mike pointed triumphantly at Jubal. "THOU ART GOD!"

Jubal slapped a hand to his face. "Oh, Jesus H.—WHAT HAVE I DONE? Look, Mike, take it easy! You didn't understand me. I'm sorry. I'm very sorry! Just forget what I've said and we'll start over another day. But—"

"Thou are God," Mike repeated serenely. "That which groks. Anne is God. I am God. The happy grasses are God. Jill groks in beauty always. Jill is God. All shaping and making and creating together—"[70]

I say no man has ever yet been half devout enough,

None has ever yet adored or wor-
ship'd half enough,
None has begun to think how divine
he himself is, and how certain the
future is. . . .[71]

I believe in the flesh and the appetites,
Seeing, hearing, feeling, are miracles,
and each part and tag of me is a
miracle.
Divine am I inside and out, and I make
holy whatever I touch. . . .[72]

"I was six when I saw that everything
was God, and my hair stood up, and all
that," Teddy said. "It was on a Sunday,
I remember. My sister was only a very
tiny child then, and she was drinking
her milk, and all of a sudden I saw that
SHE was God and the MILK was God. I
mean, all she was doing was pouring
God into God, if you know what I
mean."[73]

---

This is disturbingly close to what we hear from many writers today, from
Robert Heinlein and Steve Gaskins to Walt Whitman. Every one of us is God
locked up in a body, though few find even the hope of a key to unlock their
own limitless potential. Some call this view of man a new kind of spiritual
approach, and when it derives directly from Eastern philosophy that term may be
appropriate. But *wisdom* may be a better, more general, and more sensible word
to describe the trance from which or into which we can wake. It is all there—
unless I am optimistically reading too much into the ravings of a madman—and
if it is, then Nijinsky had these insights a half century ago, alone and tortured,
talking to himself because there could not be anyone in all the world who would
hear him or understand him. Alone, and crying in his loneliness, he finished his
document with these words:

> *I know that Socialists would understand me better—but I am not a Socialist. I
> am a part of God, my party is God's party. I love everybody. I do not want war or
> frontiers. The world exists. I have a home everywhere. I live everywhere. I do
> not want to have any property. I do not want to be rich. I want to love. I am
> love—not cruelty. I am not a bloodthirsty animal. I am man. I am man. God is
> in me. I am in God. I want Him, I seek Him. I want my manuscripts to be
> published so that everybody can read them. I hope to improve myself. I do not
> know how to, but I feel that God will help all those who seek him. I am a
> seeker, for I can feel God. God seeks me and therefore we will find each other.*[74]

Did he sense the wave of hate that was already beginning to spread across the
world? How many of us today, at this precise moment of our natural history, can
find it possible to quarrel with his vision? Was this only the ravings of a man
going mad, or did he indeed begin to touch depths in himself, in human experience, that are only now becoming evident to most of us? All that we can say is
that this was his own true document. He finished it, signed and sealed it with
the fitting signature, "God and Nijinsky," and on February 27, 1919, closed his
book to await his fate.

# part three
## the politics of identity

# chapter 5
# varieties of Sainthood

There is no end to the continuing warfare between, on the one hand, those who do not conform and, on the other, those who insist on doing something about nonconformists. My interest in this chapter and the next in looking at types of deviance or nonconformism is that they often seem to end up as clinical problems when they should not be.

## ON THE SOCIOLOGY OF DEVIANCE

Madness is one of the best examples of the phenomenon I am calling the sociology of deviance; that is, an issue which ought to be resolved by social regulation is, for sociological reasons, defined in psychological terms and then dropped in the laps of clinicians. It is a phenomenon that Joseph Gusfield has appropriately called *deviant designation*; its source, he says, is most often in the "disinterested indignation" of a self-righteous, angry reformer who is impelled to act against some act or person even though he himself has not been harmed, directly or indirectly.[1] In American history our prize example was the notorious Anthony Comstock, who took it upon himself to protect the morals of the entire citizenry although very few of them, we suspect, would have petitioned for his assistance in this regard. He parlayed his own moral indignation into a far-reaching social movement and a series of laws from which we are not yet freed.[2] It is Gusfield's thesis—bolstered by such evidence as the history of the American temperance movement—that the legislating of morals will occur when deviant designation is accompanied by the expression of power. Thus, middle-class abstinent Protestants during the nineteenth century expressed their power over lower-class, hard-drinking Irish Catholics through the symbolic act of indignation over moral standards and then through the political act of legislating temperance. The consequence was that alcoholism was created as a condition and alcoholics as a group; and from there it was only a short step toward total control of the group by renaming the morally bad habit of drinking as the psychological illness of alcoholism.

There have been since the time of the prehistoric Egyptians many persons who drank alcoholic beverages. Some of them drank more than others. A few of these, in turn, drank very much; and some of those few could not get along without drinking very, very much. This has also been true, probably for just as long a period, in regard to the ingestion of coffee, tobacco, beef, and fattening starches. The selection of alcohol as one of the very few substances whose extensive use is supposed to constitute a psychological illness is a matter of historical accident, traceable to social forces unique to this country. It has very little to do with the actual facts concerning alcohol's supposed dangers—as we shall see below in considering the entire problem of drug users as deviants.

To state this issue more generally, amid all the myriad cross-purposes of any society, a kind of order can always be seen. It takes the form of a limited number of very general themes to which most of its members agree to submit—the acquiescence among most of the members about what is right and what is wrong, about what should or should not be done in the ordinary course of life. In our contemporary society the major themes are few in number and reasonably simple: don't stand out too much from the crowd; overtly, at least, stay within the law; accommodate yourself to the characteristics appropriate to your own age and sex and station in life; and, if you are past childhood, work to support yourself.

The rules by which these unspoken prescriptions are enforced are almost universally negative in format. Ever since the formulation of the Ten Commandments, society's laws have consisted of Thou Shalt Nots; it is difficult to think of a law that begins "Everyone must . . ." with the exception of such regulations as paying taxes—and these too are negative in sense even though positively phrased for convenience. From the point of view of the person who lives in it, the order of society is built upon an elaborate code of Nos.[3]

If social rules were, rather, phrased in the positive, in the form of Yes, the members of society who did not conform would not be outlaws but more like failures. Suppose, for example, that one of our laws stated, "All citizens are required to drain off their hostility by publicly, in the presence of two witnesses, insulting one other citizen at least once a day, Sundays and holidays excepted." Some of us, given to good thoughts and peaceful intentions, might find ourselves unable to conform to such a demanding regimen; we would soon fall behind in our daily count. Now, society, as we all know, is built on law. Where would we all be, we might ask, if people fell behind in conforming to a law? The authorities would clearly have no choice but to enforce sanctions or punishment against those of us who were deviant. We would be singled out, pointed to, held up to public ridicule, ostracized from the company of our fellow citizens. If ours were a modern, enlightened society, we might even be incarcerated in special institutions—they might be called schools—where attempts would be made to raise the level of our performance to an acceptable standard.

A most peculiar kind of punishment, you will say. True. We are simply not accustomed to referring to this kind of training by the term *punishment*. What this example emphasizes is that in talking about punishment, our reference is to exactly the converse of what I have just described. When the law begins "No one shall . . . on pain of . . ." the person who breaks the law will be punished for something he has already done and not for what he has failed to do. This has a most important consequence in regard to the nature of punishment. If laws were phrased in the positive, the punishment for lawbreakers and deviants would be, as in the example I gave, some form of training, and that training would have to be fitted to the particular failing in each instance of misconduct. But since our laws are in the form of prohibitions, the punishment need not fit the crime except perhaps in degree, and even that occurs infrequently and haphazardly. The punishment, rather, is likely to be a reflection of society's attitude toward transgression and more particularly, a reflection of the specific power relations existing between the dominant group and the miscreants who are thus identified.

In harsh societies justice is swift and stern; a thief might get his hand chopped off for stealing the equivalent of a penny. In more easygoing times the law winks at such wholesale transgressions of the law as the making of bathtub gin in a million households during the Prohibition era. The difference is in part a matter of the temper of the society, but equally it is a matter of the way that those in power feel about others whom they are in a position to judge as lawbreakers. A child who was hungry enough to steal a loaf of bread might have been executed for the heinous crime in Elizabethan England, but would probably be viewed as a pitiable victim today; whereas in our time the same series of misbehaviors that will lead to a black adolescent from a ghetto being jailed as incorrigible will, in most cities, lead to a white adolescent from the suburbs being placed on probation with a relative. These marked differences in how the culprit is identified and the punishment applied may make the picture seem confusing; but the very heterogeneity of result indicates that society adjusts its punitive force rather precisely as needed not for the possible training or retraining of its criminals and deviants, but as an expression of how the lawmakers view the lawbreakers or how the conformists view the nonconformists. The point that I have made in the historical survey in Chapter 2, as well as the point that Szasz made in his attacks on institutional psychiatry, is that increasingly our society's view of its deviants, and increasingly what society does about its deviants, seem to be determined by considerations advanced by the clinical psychiatric and psychological professions. Their gambit is to call every deviant some kind of madman—that is, to use the approach, the methods, and the institutions originally developed for the identification and treatment of that most obvious of Strangers, the madman.

It would be good to reflect on a system of social classification that groups together blacks, drug addicts, homosexuals, Chicanos, alcoholics and the poor. They are, taxonomically, a one, a unity. The radicals say they are oppressed, the liberals say they need medical attention, and the reactionaries say they are criminals.[4]

### Strangerhood and Sainthood

I have used the word *Stranger* to refer to a number of subgroups of the human community—women, lepers, and Jews—meaning by this term that they have, in greater or less degree, been identified as a group and then, on the basis of this identification, have been restricted from a social participation equal to that enjoyed by others of their station in life, that is, by men, nonlepers, and Christians. There is one characteristic that these three kinds of Strangers have had in common—they had no opportunity to choose the unpleasant fate thrust on them. Women are born female, and in a world dominated by men they find themselves, without having asked for it, in the position of the inferior sex. Jews are born into their religious and cultural group. Lepers fall victim to the disease that distinguishes them. It is a characteristic of all three groups that its members have no chance to decide for themselves whether they wanted to be chosen in this way; their fate, their strangerhood, happened to them.

But this need not necessarily be true of all deviant groups. It is certainly possible that one person or even a large group might choose a deviant status. The term that I will use for those who choose the role of deviant or outcast is *Saint*.[5] In the history of human culture, in particular the culture of Western society, there have been the three important groups of Strangers I mentioned above— women, lepers, and Jews. There have been some important groups who can appropriately be called Saints—notably homosexuals, drug addicts, and certain kinds of social rebels. There has also been one major group whose members may be either Strangers or Saints or both—the madmen. Fashions change in Strangerhood and Sainthood. The time chart summarizes the approximate periods during which each of the groups experienced varying degrees of deviant designation. It is tempting to look for some simple pattern in these lines, but I am afraid that the main conclusion to be drawn from the chart is simply that every age, no matter how enlightened, will manage to pick out some Strangers and give rise to some Saints.

The madmen, however, seem to be unique, and so I have left open on the chart the question of whether they belong with Strangers or with Saints. This is not a mere matter of terminology or labeling; rather, it points to a basic question about madness. When I say that I am uncertain as to whether the madman should be called a Stranger or a Saint, I mean that the evidence is unclear as to whether the person who is insane is completely a victim of certain causes or whether in some way and to some degree he himself chooses his state.

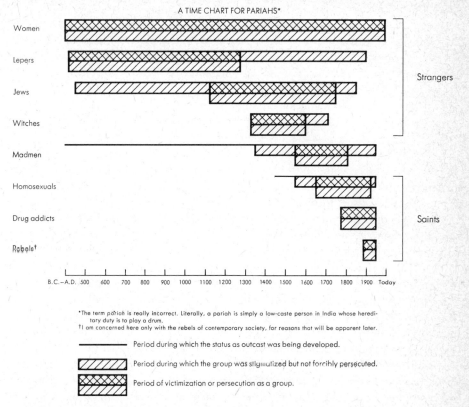

A TIME CHART FOR PARIAHS*

Women | Lepers | Jews | Witches | Madmen | Homosexuals | Drug addicts | Rebels†

Strangers

Saints

B.C.—A.D. 500 600 700 800 900 1000 1100 1200 1300 1400 1500 1600 1700 1800 1900 Today

*The term *pariah* is really incorrect. Literally, a pariah is simply a low-caste person in India whose hereditary duty is to play a drum.
†I am concerned here only with the rebels of contemporary society, for reasons that will be apparent later.

———————— Period during which the status as outcast was being developed.

Period during which the group was stigmatized but not forcibly persecuted.

Period of victimization or persecution as a group.

According to most views, madness is so deviant a condition and runs so totally counter to all we consider reasonable or understandable behavior that the person who is in such a state must be a victim of some truly fundamental error—a developmental pattern that gave him no chance to become normal; or an early rejection so total that it conditioned all his subsequent relations with other persons; or a biochemical fault in the synaptic connections of the brain itself. He is the epitome of the Stranger. A recent alternative view, influenced largely by Sartre,[6] would argue another way: If madness is a universal condition as it seems to be, occurring in all times and in all places, then it must be related to the very founding conditions of being human; of these conditions, surely the most basic is that human existence rests on the freedom which is the essence of consciousness, the freedom to choose what one is; and therefore to be mad is ultimately to choose to be mad, even though the choice appears to lead to being almost non-human. The madman is then the perfect Saint.

Every view of the nature of madness will fall somewhere between these two alternatives. My own bias is toward the latter, but I must admit that it is a bias rather than a reasoned or well-supported conclusion. We need to be able to study madness under many circumstances other than in the confines of the mental hospital; at the same time we need to explore many more realms of experience, many more levels of consciousness, before we can confidently answer some of the fundamental questions posed by the presence of the madman among us. At the moment we can only say that he seems to be the most obvious of Strangers, but that equally, he may be the most significant of Saints. In chapters 2, 3, and 4 I have tried to present a framework and some evidence, both historical and clinical, as a basis for considering this issue. In the present chapter I would like to turn in the other direction and discuss three groups of Saints and their respective fates in Western society: rebels, drug addicts, and homosexuals.

## HEROES OF THE NONREVOLUTION

It is a truism, repeated to the point of wearying us, that the young have always rebelled against their elders. They have little to lose, we are told, and besides they are prone to idealism, they are inexperienced, and so they are quick to leap on any bandwagon of romantic causes. Plato complained of the same faults in the young that Spiro Agnew does today and attributed the sorry situation to the same misplaced and overdone permissiveness. Young people probably did not listen to the criticism then and probably do not listen now.

But during the last half of the twentieth century, after so many generations of playing the same old tune, the rebellious young seem to have added something new to the old mix. Things have changed for both better and worse, and the situation is different from what it ever was in the past. Doom is closer, for one thing; there was never before in history a time when it was literally possible, and even quite probable, for the world to be blown to bits. In addition, the situation of young people has in fact progressively changed: they now become physically mature and educationally adult at an earlier age than has any generation in history, and so their time of transition, tension, and uncertainty called adolescence is stretched out almost interminably. Incomparably knowledgeable about their world, they are shunted off in increasing numbers to a four-year experience of college that only serves to delay still further their right to act as adults. And many of the young, particularly in America, have had at least a familiarity with a level of materialistic affluence that would have been unimaginable even a century ago. They have grown up in a society in which, quite simply, there seem to be no limits to what can be done, technologically, to make life more comfortable but in which, at the same time, they have heard—and often participated in—the loudest cries of despair that this technological genius is used for corrupt and indecent purposes.

It would be impertinent for someone of an older generation to venture a general statement as to whether the rebellious young are correct in the assessment of the world that results from their situation. The basic tone of their judgment is suspicion; and even a minimally sensitive adult must often feel that their suspicions are justified. The voices that speak for the young make the same point, from Bob Dylan's taunting reminder, "Something is happening, Mr. Jones, and you don't know what it is," to Cass Hodges' pronouncement, "Everybody's hustlin'"; and Johnny Cash sings to prisoners that everyone in the straight world is really also a thief but most of them haven't yet been caught. A gifted artist, Jean Genet, now finds it possible to proclaim an absolute rejection of the moral standards of society, and to fashion this stance into a moral and philosophic position.[7]

## SAINT GENÊT, THE SELF-CHOSEN DEVIANT

Treachery, theft and homosexuality are the basic subjects of this book. There is a relationship among them which, though not always apparent, at least, so it seems to me, recognizes a kind of vascular exchange between my taste for betrayal and theft and my loves. . . .[8] Repudiating the virtues of your world, criminals agree hopelessly to organize a forbidden universe. They agree to live in it. The air there is nauseating: they can breathe it. But—criminals are remote from you—as in love, they turn away and turn me away from the world and its laws. Theirs smells of sweat, sperm and blood. . . .[9]

It is said that leprosy, to which I compare our state, causes an irritation of the tissues; the sick person scratches himself; he gets an erection. Masturbation becomes frequent. In his solitary eroticism the leper consoles himself and hymns his disease. Poverty made us erect. All across Spain we carried a secret, veiled magnificence unmixed with arrogance. . . .[10] It proved to have been a very useful discipline for me and still enables me to smile tenderly at the humblest among the debris, whether human or material, including vomit, including the saliva I let drool on my mother's face, including your excrement. I shall preserve within me the idea of myself as a beggar. . . .[11] The atmosphere of the planet Uranus is said to be so heavy that the ferns there are creepers; the animals drag along, crushed by the weight of the gases. I want to mingle with these humiliated creatures which are always on their bellies. If metempsychosis should grant me a new

dwelling-place, I choose that forlorn planet. I inhabit it with the convicts of my race. Amidst hideous reptiles, I pursue an eternal, miserable death in a darkness where the leaves will be black, the waters of the marshes thick and cold. Sleep will be denied me. On the contrary, more lucid than ever, I recognize the unclean fraternity of the smiling alligators. . . .[12] In short, the greater my guilt in your eyes, the more whole, the more totally assumed, the greater will be my freedom. The more perfect my solitude and singleness. By my guilt I further gained the right to intelligence. . . .[13] In order to weather my desolation when I withdrew more deeply into myself, I worked out, without meaning to, a rigorous discipline. The mechanism was somewhat as follows (I have used it since): to every accusation brought against me, unjust though it be, from the bottom of my heart I shall answer yes. . . .[14]

If I had to live—perhaps I shall, though the idea is untenable—in your world, which, nevertheless, does welcome me, it would be the death of me. At the present time, when, having won by sheer force, I have signed an apparent truce with you, I find myself in exile. I do not care to know whether I desire prison so as to expiate a crime of which I am unaware. My nostalgia is so great that I shall have to be taken to it. I feel sure that only in prison shall I be able to continue a life which was cut off when I entered it. Rid of preoccupations with glory and wealth, I shall achieve with slow, scrupulous patience the painful gestures of the punished. Every day I shall do a job governed by a rule which has no other authority than that of emanating from an order which presents the penitentiary and creates it. I shall wear myself out. The men I find there will help me. I shall become as polished as they, as pumiced. . . .[15] As I write these notes, I am thirty-five years old. I want to spend my remaining years in glory's opposite.[16]

---

What is intimated by these developments is a new kind of possibility in the long history of social deviance. In every previous era, the young who shouted rebellion across the generation gap were not seceding from the human group but simply protesting its current form. Their revolution aimed at changing the world; their efforts always rested on the presumption that improvement was possible and that the effort was thus worthwhile. This is just how the rebels of our day may be radically different. Today a fair number of them, and often the most talented and perceptive, seem to be saying that they want no part of the world as it is and have no particular desire to improve it. They drop out, but not as a step toward changing things. Theirs is the first nonrevolution in history.[17]

Ivan Illich distinguishes the true revolutionary act from "the odd, the weird, and the simply criminal, [which] are the major categories developed in all societies to 'rationalize' radical renewal into tolerable, and culturally innocuous limits: commitment to the mad-house, the monastery or the penal colony are institutional forms symbolizing 'mad,' 'supernatural,' and 'aggressive' communities which still lie within the extreme boundaries of society."[18] Society, he notes, thus always has ways to handle the madman, the religious deviant, or the criminal, but it cannot contain the revolutionary; it must destroy him or else change itself. But now, in our day, a new possibility arises. Here is a revolution that does not tear down the established structures but only ignores them; a revolution whose participants simply remain where they are, not fighting but not running. They choose to take no part, they choose to let the world go its way, whatever happens.

The reaction they provoke is part exasperation, part anger, part disappointment, and perhaps even part admiration. Some of their elders are tempted to allow the younger generation this stance, at most to berate them for their impracticality, and to hope that finally they will change their views and get on with the necessary job of assuming responsibility for society. But even the most accepting reaction to their nonrevolt seems to be both fruitless and embarrassing; and so even the most sympathetic of older persons end up shaking their heads or helplessly throwing up their hands. What can be said to the utterly crimeless criminal?

Because this nonrevolution is essentially a psychological response to a sociological situation, many of the older generation are also tempted to deal with it as though it were merely a novel variant of more familiar forms of psychopathology. Kenneth Keniston, for example, who is certainly both sympathetic and understanding in his approach to the radical young, looks for explanations in familiar patterns of psychodynamics;[19] he feels that since this is a form of rebellion, it will have to be understood as one more instance of the sons rebelling against the father. But as one sensible psychiatrist points out, "to diagnose student unrest

## THE CRIMELESS CRIMINAL

Picked up by the campus police for sleeping in a field, a young man was questioned in order to determine if he was a fugitive from some crime. The police stated that they became suspicious of him because of his "evasiveness," a sample of which they reported as follows.

He gave his address as "Planet Earth," and on further questioning stated that: "he had no local address, that he had no permanent address, that he had never had a driver's license, that he had never had a social security card, that he did not have a job, that he did not know the name of anyone who works for the University, that he did not remember where he went to grammar school or high school, that he did not know his selective service number, that he had not had a selective service card for the last seven years, that he did not remember his father's or mother's middle name, that he had a sister but he did not know her married name or where she lived, and that he had been a transient for the past seven years and had never had any contact with the police."[20]

At first glance, the police term EVASIVENESS certainly seems justified. However, only when this young man is questioned in a particular way—as a police officer, or perhaps a psychiatrist, might do—does he produce answers that can be thus diagnosed. On the other hand, what if he, and his actions, were simply taken at face value—that is, accepted for just what they are, exactly as presented? Might he not then appear simply as an amiable person who chooses to have none of the conventional attachments or indicators which define the rest of us?

as though it were symptomatic of individual psychopathology is to fall into the error of confusing history with biography."[21] The nonrevolution of the young today can be reduced to patterns of individual behavior only if it is abstracted from current history; but as long as one maintains a position about their stance, about whether they are justified, and about the historical conditions that gave rise to their total rejection of society, then their nonrevolution remains a social event and cannot be explained away as individual pathology.

However it is judged, this is something new in history. For the first time in more than three thousand years of recorded deviance, a society has in its midst a large and perhaps increasing population of Saints—outcasts who have willingly chosen their status. Individual hermits, rebels, or madmen may have done this before, but to do it they had to cut themselves off from meaningful relations with other persons. The nonrevolutionary Saints of our day have not so much cut themselves off from participant citizenship as relegated it to a position of no importance to them. What they seem to have substituted is a combination of deeply felt individual experiences and "tribal" relations with a small group of intimates.

### On Caring for Others

There is one aspect of the nonrevolution that appears to offend even the most understanding members of an older generation. They ask: "But don't they care at all what happens to the world? Are they really willing to let the world go to pot without lifting a finger to change things? What kind of authenticity can this be that denies the caring that links human beings in a universal brotherhood?"

It is an issue that cuts across almost everything I have been discussing in this chapter. One may ask with equal vehemence: "All these ordinary people who participate, if only by looking the other way, in campaigns of derogation and victimization of deviants—don't they care about their fellow men?" How can we make sense out of the terrible history of human cruelty to humans? Specifically, how could the upper-class gentleman of a hundred years ago, though genial and kindly to his intimates, be so unfeeling in his dealings with those of inferior station?

I need to bring this issue still closer to home, to keep it from getting lost in a rhetoric of history and culture. To restate it, then, in personal terms: I don't hate Biafran nor Bengalese children, not at all. It is true that I eat well while reading about how they are starving, and I fail to recall an instance when I cried over their plight. But I don't hate them. The emotion that I discover, on looking into my own state, is like a feeling of regret: it is a terrible thing that's happening to all these children and I truly wish that it were not so. And if I am to be honest about it, I must confess that my feeling of regret is tinged, ever so slightly, with self-satisfaction, as though I were just a bit proud of my gentlemanly concern.

What I do not feel is perhaps more important. I do not feel any of the arousal, the shock, the level of excitement that I might experience if I were actually face to face with one of these anguished children. I look at the television screen and accept it as the image that it is, so I can examine the scene with interest and not feel impelled to close my eyes and ears against its impact. I am a kind person. I mean well to people in general and to children in particular; and I would not ever intentionally hurt someone else. My Biafran experience, now, tells me for the first time what my kindness really means. It means that I will always avoid the direct experience of being cruel or hostile, but that I am quite capable of living with the indirect experience of knowing about cruelty and condoning it by my inaction. And so I can go on priding myself on my gentlemanly concern, for not only do I refrain from direct cruelty but I truly feel sorry for starving children. Indeed, one might ask: What more can be expected of me?

Well, what might be expected of me is that I rise to the same level of arousal over what I see on television as over what I might confront face to face. But we all know that this is not what happens. To keep it from happening, I maintain

---

In 1924 a sociologist, Robert E. Park, introduced the concept of SOCIAL DISTANCE as a way of describing a central characteristic of ordinary relations between groups.[22] He pointed to the fact that different groups tend to maintain fixed distances from each other, economically as well as socially, physically as well as culturally. The disparity between a Negro ghetto and a middle class suburb restricted to whites finds its parallel in the obvious differences between their habits, their speech, their position on the economic and political ladder, and of course their patterns of social activity. Two families from such widely differing backgrounds are not likely to be found sharing a mode of speech or a living-room at a party, any more than their children share a classroom at school. In his term 'social distance' Park expressed succinctly and vividly this kind of socio-logical phenomenon; and there is little doubt that it has been a useful concept for the social sciences.

. . . another social scientist, Emory Bogardus, translated this notion into psychological terms.[23] Whereas social distance had been conceived by Park as a way of thinking about distinctions in social position or along some dimension of group activity, Bogardus devised a

technique by which social distance became a measure of how far apart people FEEL from each other. The technique consists of asking persons to indicate their relative preferences for specific groups—for example, to rank Negroes, British, Persians, Jews, and Chinese in terms of preference in sharing a neighborhood, working together on a job, marrying, and so on. Just as we might expect, the results are quite predictable, and they are remarkably stable even from one generation to another.[24] People do have definite, ordered preferences with regard to national and ethnic groups.[25]

---

distances between me and them. It is a wonderfully useful defensive maneuver, so natural and effective that an inquiring social scientist can tell my attitude toward groups of people simply by having me state how distant I feel from them. Like all adults, like all good and reasonable citizens, I carefully husband my involvement, restricting my intense experience to those few persons or situations that belong to my very personal life. All the rest is out there somewhere, at a greater or less distance. The gap can easily be crossed by sending a check through the mails.

The embarrassing truth is that this arrangement, with which most of us, I suspect, manage to live rather comfortably, is not very different from that of the nonrevolutionary Saints described above. What is an unacknowledged convenience to most of the elders seems to have become a living philosophy for some of their children.

## THE BOTTLE AND THE NEEDLE

Of all the characteristics that set man off from his animal brethren, none is so long-standing, none quite so perversely human, as his propensity for ingesting substances that have negligible food value and will ultimately do him in. In the culture of the West, by far the best known of these substances is alcohol. Our history, our religions and our social lives have been reflected in the bottle since the precursors of our civilization founded the first brewery in Egypt about sixty centuries ago. By contrast, Orientals are more familiar with a second group of substances consisting of various narcotic compounds derived from hemp or poppy plants; since the invention of the hypodermic syringe shortly after the Civil War, these opiate substances have been ingested mainly by means of the needle.

Very few forms of alcohol actually taste good, and a needle is an unpleasant way to take a substance into the body. Why, then, do some people go to such great lengths to use them? Why do very many people use them at all? The

ON ALCOHOLIC BEVERAGES
It sloweth age, it strengtheneth youth, it helpeth digestion, it abandoneth melancholie, it relisheth the heart, it lighteneth the mind, it quickeneth the spirits, it keepeth and preserveth the head from whirling, the eyes from dazzling, the tongue from lisping, the mouth from snaffling, the teeth from chattering and the throat from rattling; it keepeth the stomach from wambling, the heart from swelling, the hands from shivering, the sinews from shrinking, the veins from crumbling, the bones from aching, and the marrow from soaking.
[From a thirteenth century manuscript]

answer can only be, as Freud guessed, that we utilize our various modes of intake for many other pleasurable purposes than to satisfy hunger. He called these tendencies oral, because their prototype is the infant whose life-style is centered around its mouth, so much so that it can well be defined as a complex sucking mechanism. In Freud's view—and the argument is still worth considering seriously—the basic human experience is not hunger but orality: the experience of drawing the whole world into an embrace, of reaching and clutching and holding on and, yes, sucking it all in, incorporating all there is, without distinction and without limit. In adults it all becomes refined into hunger, even into good taste; joy turns into discrete kinds of pleasure; the gain is neatly balanced by the loss.

Even more puzzling than the fact that people ingest various forms of alcohol and opiates is the phenomenon of addiction—becoming hooked on the substance to the point that the experience is not simply wanting it but needing it; "I wish" becomes "I must." The addict is in one sense both Stranger and Saint. If he is addicted to either drinking or drugs to the point where he is identifiable in terms of his craving, he quickly becomes one of society's outcasts, a Stranger. And if he continues as an addict in the face of the fact that he must inevitably organize his life around his craving (and this will be true whether the substance is legal like alcohol, or illegal like heroin), he will have chosen his deviant status, a Saint. We are not accustomed to thinking of the addict as showing a choice in this matter, but choose he does. Any alcoholic can stay dry simply by choosing not to take the next drink—an insight that led to the founding of Alcoholics Anonymous.[26] Similarly, the drug addict can quit by choosing to stay off drugs for about a week. The choice in both cases is very difficult for the addict to make so it rarely occurs unless it is helped or enforced by others; nevertheless it remains a choice.

Consider, now, the use of alcohol and the experience of using it. Some sixty-five million Americans, far more than ever vote in an election, are estimated to enjoy at least an occasional drink—and the same situation apparently also occurs in countries with quite different traditions and forms of government. The practice of drinking alcoholic beverages may well be the one bond linking human beings throughout the world; as a custom it possibly antedates even such hoary institutions as the family or prostitution. This should hardly be a matter of pride, for the fact is that in any of its forms the alcohol we consume is a dangerous drug.

We are all familiar with how a drunken person looks and acts but, not surprisingly, there is very little systematic data on the experience. What is it like to be drunk? On this matter it is easy to become experienced but impossible to be an expert; and so the reports that are available, telling it like it is from the inside, are usually vague, confident, and incomplete. What they seem to sum up to is that in a state of mild alcoholic intoxication, before the anesthetic properties of the drug take over, all the boundaries that customarily restrain and set limits for a person tend to blur, to recede, even to disappear. He discovers an unexpected freedom to move when and where and how he pleases. If the whim just happens to strike him, he dances instead of walks, or he sings when he ought to talk; in either case he seems to be able to bypass the problem of deciding, and thus experiences the happy choice as though it were handed to him as a gift. Ignoring the restraints that determine the sober movements of his everyday behavior, he talks louder, longer, and looser. Both literally and figuratively—for they may well be the same thing—he oversteps just as though all the limits, the standards of his ordinary routine, had lost their definite and demanding character. He laughs more easily, he cries at next to nothing. He may pick a fight or make passes at a friend's wife—he, who was always so mild, so sober. Where there once were boundaries now appears mostly a melting, rosy glow.

In a way, it is like being mildly anesthetized to the obstacles and resistances of the everyday world; in fact, many persons also feel a numbing and tingling of their extremities as a part of the drinking experience. But we need only turn to the other side of the picture, to the behavior that is observed by others, to see that alcohol in small quantities does not function as an anesthetic. Indeed, its outward effects are just the opposite. The mildly drunken person does not fall backward into sleep but moves outward in unaccustomed action. He begins to encroach on all the areas that are probably taboo for him when sober: the boss's character, the friend's wife, the role of dancer or comedian. He becomes more outgoing, not less, often to the point of appearing to others as boorish or aggressive. He not only does, he overdoes. For the most obvious of reasons, almost half of all fatalities in automobile accidents—about 25,000 per year—directly involve alcohol.

The hallmark of drunken behavior is that, far from being an escape from reality, alcohol provides a cheap means for tangling actively, but at little experiential cost, with reality. This is just why people get drunk who are generally unable to be courageous or confident when sober. In English we call the phenomenon Dutch courage (to the chagrin of Hollanders), but we really ought to find a more universal term that recognizes alcohol for what it is. Liquor is everybody's license.

And now consider the opiate drugs. They are all either natural or synthetic versions of the narcotic element found in the unripe pods of opium plants, and they are used in various derivative forms as alkaloids, under the familiar names opium, morphine, heroin, and codeine. Stated most simply, what these substances have in common is that they are anesthetics; long-term users become so accustomed to the absence of most bodily sensations that after withdrawal of the drug they may panic at the flood of unexpected feelings.[27]

Morphine, the first of the opium derivatives to be produced on a large scale, was first used in the United States just before the Civil War as a cure-all for nearly every known physical ailment, since it quickly eased pain and other distress. Similarly, heroin was introduced in 1898 as a very efficient cough suppressant—which it undoubtedly was. Both drugs were touted in their day as medical miracles, just as methadone, another synthetic opiate, is sometimes touted today. During the half-century following the Civil War, the active ingredient of just about every successful patent medicine was some form of opium. What was discovered only slowly was an additional characteristic of these drugs—that they are highly addictive; the steady user will undergo physiological and psychological changes so that he will experience acute distress if he is forced to go without his accustomed dosage.

If one is sufficiently accustomed to the dosage so as not to become ill, the experience of taking an opiate is in some ways similar to drinking alcohol. Things blur; troubles recede; pointed demands become less demanding; pain disappears; and peace, even a mild euphoria, floods over one. But in other, more important ways the experience of taking narcotic drugs is quite unlike that of being drunk. One drifts easily into a half-waking doze, in contact with what is going on and usually able to cope with the environment if necessary, but without any desire to do so. One has no urge to go out toward the world, to engage reality, to exercise one's abilities, to test limits or act out pent-up desires. There is no intoxicating desire to talk, sing, or be the life of the party, to demonstrate sexual prowess—certainly not to fight. On the contrary, the person who is drugged with an opiate wants above all to stay just as he is, to continue experiencing the feeling that contains him. He wants to extend the peace into which he has drifted, not to break it up by becoming active. Things seem right, and he would like to keep them that way.

Understandably, the behavior of the drunk and of the drugged person are almost precisely the opposite. The drunk becomes more active, crossing unaccustomed boundaries, often to the extent of causing trouble to those around him. The person who is drugged, on the other hand, stays to himself; he is turned inward, becomes passive, bothers no one. If he goes through his day's work, as some addicts do, a casual observer might not identify his condition. This is particularly true if he is on no more than a medium dosage, as usually occurs with physicians or nurses who are addicts, or if the drug fits in with his normal activity, as often happens in the case of musicians or actors. This useful trick, to be able to go through the day's activities without being spotted, is one that can be carried off by only the most careful of alcoholics and in the most permissive of settings at that.

In its intense form, when the experience is at its peak, the drugged state is therefore highly personal, a kind of heightened dreaming that may finally fade off into a benign near-stupor. The intense form of drunkenness, however, is almost totally a public event—a highly demonstrative exhibition of the drunk's changed experience. In the end, of course, since most bodily conditions converge toward a common state when natural limits are exceeded, both the drunken and the drugged episodes become the same: first a state of unconsciousness, then stupor and coma, and finally death.

If we think about people who get drunk, it will occur to us that they are unable to act forcefully when sober but can do so when they are fortified by alcohol; and this may be just the reason they drink. Equally, it would seem that others become addicted to opiates because the drugs guarantee them just the kind of nonaction and associated experience that they would prefer. If liquor is Dutch courage, then perhaps opiates should be called Holland passivity. But by whatever names we call them, these two states are quite different. They ought to be viewed in very different ways by the average citizen, by the standards of society, and by the law. And indeed they are.

### Let's Play a Game: Volstead

The basis of the Volstead game is this: If you have two different choices, and you are permitted to accept or reject either or both choices independently, then four combinations are possible—to accept both, to reject both, to accept the first and reject the second, or to accept the second and reject the first. If three independent choices are available, there are eight possible combinations; if four choices, then sixteen combinations, and so on. For convenience in playing our game, we will suppose that three choices of substances to ingest are available to us; two of them, alcohol and the opiates, have already been discussed, and the third, the psychedelic drugs, is added because of their current relevance. We will refer to the first choice as the bottle, the second as the needle, and the third as the cube.

Andrew J. Volstead (R., Minn.), after whom I have named this game, never had the opportunity to pass judgment on the cube or the needle, but he left us a national legacy in the form of a very firm choice in regard to the bottle. He wrote the bill implementing its prohibition in 1919, and so our game honors him in the breach, as it were. Of course, I might just as well have called the game Anslinger, in reference to Harry J. Anslinger, the now-retired commissioner of the Treasury Department's Bureau of Narcotics, who was for thirty years the country's most influential force behind our policy toward the use of narcotic and addictive drugs. Or, to be fair about it, the name of the game might be Leary, in deference to the Timothy Leary who is currently the best-known proponent of the cube.

To take full advantage of the significance of the game of Volstead, it is necessary to make a choice about all three, in some combination. This is what makes it a revealing exercise rather than merely the parading of prejudices, for a preference for some combination is a subtle matter that goes beyond individual bias. For example, what kind of person would insist on banning all three substances? The worst kind of Puritan, perhaps—or the best kind of moralist? And contrariwise, who would be likely to opt for legitimizing all three? Just as interesting is the question of the various kinds of society that might legislate each of the eight combinations. Indeed, such a choice may quickly tell us as much about the society as it does about the single individual. Some possibilities lead to easy predictions, such as the repressive society that would ban all three—but would the quite different society that accepts all three be considered decadent or merely hedonist? And what about such unlikely combinations as accepting the bottle and needle while banning the cube?

As we know, the combination of choices existing today in most of the Western world consists in accepting the bottle while banning the needle and cube. In the Orient, on the other hand, the preferred combination seems to be to accept the needle in some forms while banning the bottle and cube. My hypothesis is that the choice of combinations in every case provides a clear window into the national psyche. As evidence, consider only our contemporary attitudes toward the bottle and the needle.

In the United States and in Europe the attitude toward alcoholic beverages is, to say the least, rather positive, and in European countries in particular, where beer is often sold to elementary school children for their lunch, there are in some localities almost as many alcoholics as nicotine addicts at these age levels. True, there was a brief and curious episode in American history in which a minority view triumphed over our ingrained tradition and wrote into law a legal ban on any drink stronger than 3.2 beer; and even today there are some places in the South and Midwest where liquor cannot be sold except through elaborate para-legal subterfuges. But the evidence from our public behavior, even from 1919 to 1933 when Prohibition was purportedly in effect and in the areas where strong liquor is still legally banned, indicates that we are overwhelmingly a nation of drinkers and that we feel fine about it. There is, of course, one exception to our whole-hearted endorsement of our professed standards: it is forbidden to depict someone in a TV commercial who actually drinks the beer so irresistibly foaming, and there has not yet been permitted a TV or radio commercial for whiskey. But in every other media meant to influence public habits, the drinking life is shown as it exists; alcohol is treated as an indispensable adjunct to zestful living.

More precisely, in this country drinking is treated as a useful sort of comic relief to the drama of everyday life. In our eyes the drunk is a funny figure, and so we scoff at a melodrama in which liquor is treated seriously as the cause of a wage earner's downfall. On New Year's Eve we pay fleeting attention to the solemn warnings given us about mixing alcohol and gasoline, and if pinned down we would admit to knowing about the true plight of the alcoholic and his family, but our real empathy goes out to the character in the Western who gets drunk and wrecks the saloon. We are in favor of the bottle except—and here is the critical distinction—when its user is affected by it as though it were an opiate and by virtue of continued use ends up on Skid Row.

But if we strongly favor the bottle, we are even more vehemently opposed to the needle. Not too many years ago the Sunday supplements thrilled their readers with exposés of opium dens, complete with excitingly veiled implications about white slavery and other examples of human degradation. Styles may have changed since then, but the basic attitude of the public has remained substantially the same. We still give our unqualified support to a stand on narcotics which is compounded equally of fear, anger, and fascination. The prevalence of this attitude may help to explain why an otherwise innocuous law, the Harrison Act of 1914, which was originally passed only to facilitate the collecting of tax revenues came to serve, without much opposition, quite a different purpose. It has been the basis for an essentially punitive policy of control and punishment under the authority of a major division of the Treasury Department. Although the public has long since come to accept the notion that alcoholism may be a disease and should be treated rather than punished, a similarly enlightened attitude toward the use of heroin has only surfaced since drug addiction began to affect white, middle-class youth. Public pressure to repeal the Prohibition laws finally became overwhelming; but there was never any public clamor, nor is there any now, to do the same with narcotic drugs. We still view the opiate drugs as a menace and their dealers as lower than the beasts, and a very large majority are prepared to support any policing efforts based on this view.

There must be a good reason for this difference in attitude, persisting through an era of rapid and even shocking changes in public standards in most other areas. One more look at the two substances may help to indicate the nature of our national choice in the game of Volstead.

The central distinction between the bottle, which we accept, and the needle, which we reject, comes down to the fact that under their influence people act in different ways. The effect of alcohol is to turn the person into, at worst, an active nuisance, whereas even large doses of the opiates result in negligible interference with others. From the point of view of the user, an analogous distinction can be made. Alcohol breaks down the articulated structure of the world in the way that an active and angry person would like; whereas the opiates break it down in the way that a passive and receptive person would like. This, finally, may be the clue to our collective attitudes. The distinction suggests that in Western countries, and in America most particularly, the welcome is out for any substance, almost no matter how harmful, if it helps a person to turn out toward others, to deal more vigorously with the world, to become engaged with things and sociable with others—in short, to come closer to our ideal of the well-adjusted person. On the other hand, the substances that we reject, that awaken our strongest feelings of fascination and horror, that set us to virtuously resisting temptation and fighting sin, are those, no matter how harmless (such as marijuana),[28] that turn the person inward on himself. The drug that we will ban is the one that leads its user to withdraw from active participation in the world's work, the one that helps him either to turn toward his inner self or to drop out, as he uniquely chooses.

The choices that a nation makes are, as we should have expected, clear indicators of the values that are most deeply held. An expatriate American writer summed up our national use of alcohol thus: "The French are dishevelled and wise, the American tries to approximate it with drink. It is his only clue to himself. He takes it when his soap has washed him too clean for identification."[29] By contrast, a medical expert, the former head of a federal institution where drug addicts were incarcerated for "cure," once remarked that the real danger in a drug habit was not physiological or medical or even criminal, but that it "may change an energetic, efficient, valuable member of Society into a regressed, valueless person who has side-stepped life." Fittingly, then, alcohol, which was once the hallmark of the Western frontier, is today the sign of all-American good times, the icebreaker for every social gathering, while the opiates are associated with the outcasts of society and the psychedelics and marijuana with its rebels. To hold up the bottle, and to put down the needle and cube, are thus perfectly reasonable, for they are consistent with the basic value orientation of Western society.[30]

### The Addict
But addiction is also an individual matter. Not everyone who takes a drink, not everyone who gets a shot of morphine, certainly not everyone who is merely exposed to the use of these drugs, takes up one of them as a habit. Who gets addicted, and why?

Since the early work of Lawrence Kolb,[31] it has been argued by the medical profession that drug addiction is essentially a psychiatric problem. This argument may be plausible in regard to alcoholism, which affects all segments of the population indiscriminately, but not in regard to narcotic drug addiction. The universally positive attitude toward alcohol in this society makes it understandable that problem drinking is primarily a psychological phenomenon and therefore is properly treated by one of the clinical professions. But the case with narcotics is quite different. The consensus toward them is almost universally negative; therefore the user commits both a personal and a social act by his habit. It is this distinction that removes the problem of narcotic drug addiction from the exclusive province of psychiatry or psychology. We shall have to look elsewhere to fully understand the nature of addiction.

As far back as the 1930s, studies of drug users showed that they tended to come from the most deprived and blighted sections of large cities, or else from economically deprived small communities in the South. This general finding held true until the sudden increase in narcotic usage among segments of the population who had been soldiers in Vietnam during the last of the 1960s. Even when the soldiers are also considered, one curious fact stands out: the most expensive possible form of addiction has tended to occur among those who have the least to spend on their habit, and the ready availability of another habit-forming drug, alcohol, made no difference. Apparently the opiate drugs satisfy a quite particular need uniquely related to the total life situation of the user.

The typical young drug user in large-city ghettos is likely to be a member of a minority group—black or Spanish-speaking. The typical user among the enlisted men in Vietnam may well be white and from a middle-class background. However, in many other respects their psychological situation is strikingly similar. They both find themselves trapped in what is for them a meaningless situation; they feel exploited, endangered, and bored, all at once; there is for them no way out; and it is all for no purpose that has any meaning to them. The victim, in Harlem or Saigon, no matter where he looks finds nothing but corruption around him, without end and without excuse or rationale. Worst of all, there is no way he can identify and personalize who it is who is doing this to him, for it seems part of a national way of life; it seems to be the way things are; and as far as any resources of power or understanding are concerned, he is both locked out and exploited.

Now let us add a speculation—that there are many possible ways to respond to this kind of situation, just as there are many different ways to be a prisoner in jail or a student in a university. The impulsively angry man in Vietnam may pick on one officer and toss a fragmentation bomb at his tent. The more intellectual or politically minded black rebel on Chicago's South Side may choose to join the Black Panthers. The one with a great fund of inner strength may wait out his time by concentrating on individual and personal growth. But there are many others who are not rebels nor loners nor students of their own inner resources. They want desperately to join the bandwagon, but they are not even fully aware of how it is that they happened to miss it. Those who are strong enough or angry enough will rebel or drink or draw on inner resources, but those whose strength and purpose could only be gained from society (which has refused this to them) can find at least a small salvation in a substance that, in effect, provides them with the experience of a happy defeat. This is essentially the experience that they can enjoy each time they get a fix.

There is some evidence to support this speculation. One of the few extensive studies of the heroin user concludes that his view of life is typically marked by unhappiness and pessimism, a distrust of authority, and an overriding sense of futility—all characteristics of the user whose profile I have sketched.[32] The timing of drug usage provides further supportive evidence, for it usually begins at just the point in life when adulthood looms, suggesting that the need for something like opiates increases as the person is faced with making his independent way in the world. Evidence from physician users of drugs also supports this position, particularly in regard to the lower frequency or even the absence of addiction among black or Puerto Rican physicians, among British physicians, and among pharmacists, all of whom have access to drugs. Their pattern of drug use suggests the hypothesis: Addiction will occur to a lesser extent among those members of a group who do not experience a need to achieve or maintain high status or whose experience is that they have already achieved status; and addiction will occur to a greater extent among those members of a group who experience a

PHYSICIAN DRUG ADDICTS

It has been estimated by the U. S. Commissioner of Narcotics that approximately one in every hundred physicians in the United States is addicted to morphine or heroin. This compares with approximately one addict per 3,000 persons in the general population, one per 550 physicians in England, and one per 95 physicians in Germany. From 1942 through 1956, 1,012 physicians in this country were reported as addicts, including one dean of a medical school and one head of a state medical society; the "new" addicts each year among physicians equaled in number an average graduating class of a medical school.

Interviews with a sample of ninety-eight opiate addicts revealed that the duration of their habits ranged from one to twenty-two years, with a mean of six years. All were successful in their medical practice and were judged to be functioning at an above-average level both as physicians and as citizens. In 74 percent of the cases, the addiction was known to the wife. Since none of these physician addicts made it a practice to prescribe for other addicts, they needed to supply only their own habits; only one had ever been charged by the law. However, many are finally caught, in which case their problem is usually handled privately by the local medical society. Of those who are caught in this way, approximately 85 percent manage to stay off drugs, and the remaining 15 percent are unable to kick the habit and are either hospitalized, jailed, or commit suicide. There appears to be almost no instance of addiction among pharmacists or among physicians who are black, Puerto Rican, or former inmates of a Nazi concentration camp.[33]

---

serious problem about their own status. Thus, persons of low-status origins who become successful in a high-status profession, as do black physicians, will not become addicted, nor will members of relatively low-status groups, such as physicians in England or pharmacists in America.

Within the addiction-susceptible groups who are defined by the hypothesis just offered, however, there will be wide differences on many dimensions of personality. The available material on individuals who become addicted suggests that the group conditions I have mentioned will peculiarly affect some persons in the following way: if such a person lacks a wide range of effective options in dealing with his environment; if his tendency is to accept and fit into his environment rather than question it or resort to independent thinking or consider rebellion; and if he is then faced with what is for him an untenable life situation in regard to establishing himself as an independent adult with some status, he may resolve the conflict by adopting the pattern I have described as the happy acceptance of defeat.

It is noteworthy that rehabilitated drug addicts tend to be surprisingly, sometimes embarrassingly, "straight" people rather than the rebels that their popular image calls for. Both Synanon[34] and Alcoholics Anonymous,[35] the most successful of the programs for addicts, are quite traditional in their value orientations. This suggests a practical conclusion to this discussion: unless they can be turned into Zen monks or political rebels, the most promising approach to "curing" drug addicts would be to involve them in a stable community to which they feel an attachment. Rehabilitation might then succeed because the usual order of treatment would be reversed; instead of the traditional sequence of eliminating the drug habit and then attempting to make the addict into a respectable citizen, this procedure would accept him as an addict and deal first with the problem of reconstituting his status as a citizen. It may well be that this is the common element in two such diverse treatment approaches as Synanon and methadone.[36]

## THE COMING LESBIAN REVOLUTION

The history of homosexuality is deeply intertwined with the history of human sexuality, a topic that is only now being accorded the serious attention it deserves.

Most of the story of sex has been kept carefully buried, but no part of it has been more effectively kept from study than homosexuality. Kinsey's famous finding in his study of male sexuality—that about one-third of his sample of adult males admitted to having had at least one homosexual contact to orgasm[37]—understandably came not only as a shock but as an overwhelming surprise. The discovery upset a consensus that had tried to make the homosexual into a prototype of the contemporary Stranger, so deviant that for the protection of society his preferred practice had to be forbidden. Spelled out, the consensus went like this: the normal and healthy preference in an adult is for someone of the opposite sex as a sole choice; there are a very few adults who develop a more or less exclusive preference for someone of the same sex; they are very often inducted into this strange and perverse group by the seductive activity of an older member, in an evil caricature of the normal socialization process; and however it comes about, the end state is pathological.

Stated in this way, without too much moralizing, the consensus has always seemed reasonable—but the trouble with it is that it is also profoundly antihistorical. It flies in the face of easily available evidence from the history of every culture including our own. Male homosexuality was neither a sin nor a weakness in other times, but rather a customary practice among young men before they settled into monogamous heterosexual arrangements. In some places it was exalted as the highest and noblest form of love. Alcibiades' account of his "affair" with Socrates, almost 2,500 years ago, would not have been permitted in a novel about two young men if it had been written in 1935.

How is it that the Western cultural bias of the nineteenth and twentieth centuries has been so different? We owe this change, as we owe so many other instances of eroticizing our sins, to the cumulative effect of our religious traditions, expressed currently in the severe moralistic constraints of the Puritan stance and,

---

### ALCIBIADES TELLS OF HIS "AFFAIR" WITH SOCRATES

And believing he had a serious affection for my youthful bloom, I supposed I had here a godsend and a rare stroke of luck . . . for I was enormously proud of my youthful charms. So with this design I dismissed the attendant whom till then I invariably brought to my meetings with Socrates, and I would go and meet him alone: I am to tell you the whole truth; you must all mark my words, and, Socrates, you shall refute me if I lie. Yes, gentlemen, I went and met him, and the two of us would be alone; and I thought he would seize the chance of talking to me as a lover does to his dear one in private, and I was glad. But nothing of the sort occurred at all: he would merely converse with me in his usual manner, and when he had spent the day with me he would leave me and go his way. After that I proposed he should go with me to the trainer's, and I trained with him, expecting to gain my point there. So he trained and wrestled with me many a time when no one was there. The same story! I got no further with the affair. Then, as I made no progress that way, I resolved to charge full tilt at the man, and not to throw up the contest once I had entered upon it: I felt I must clear up the situation. Accordingly I invited him to dine with me, for all the world like a lover scheming to ensnare his favourite. Even this he was backward to accept; however, he was eventually persuaded. The first time he came, he wanted to leave as soon as he had dined. On that occasion I was ashamed and let him go. The second time I devised a scheme: when we had dined I went on talking with him far into the night, and when he wanted to go I made a pretext of the lateness of the hour and constrained him to stay. So he sought repose on the couch next to me, on which he had been sitting at dinner, and no one was sleeping in the room but ourselves. . . .

Well, gentlemen, when the lamp had been put out and the servants had withdrawn, I determined not to mince matters with him, but to speak freely what I intended. . . . [On finishing, I said:] "You have heard what I had to say; not a word differed from the feeling in my mind: it is for you now to consider what you judge to be best for you and me."

"Ah, there you speak to some purpose," he said: "for in the days that are to come we shall consider and do what appears to be best for the two of us in this and our other affairs."

Well, after I had exchanged these words with him and, as it were, let fly my shafts, I fancied he felt the wound: so up I got, and without suffering the man to say a word more I wrapped my own coat about him—it was winter-time; drew myself under his cloak, so; wound my arms about this truly spiritual and miraculous creature; and lay thus all the night long. Here too, Socrates, you are unable to give me the lie. When I had done all this, he showed such superiority and contempt, laughing my youthful charms to scorn, and flouting the very thing on which I prided myself, gentlemen. . . . that when I arose I had in no more particular sense slept a night with Socrates than if it had been with my father or my elder brother.[38]

---

in America, to a very special stand on sex that harks back to a decayed pioneer influence. The bigoted person in this country would have had contempt mixed with pity for women; would have felt fear and mild loathing at the thought of contact with leprosy; would have disliked and dismissed Jews; would have been horrified at the thought of drug addiction and angry at youthful rebels—but he would always have reserved the full measure of his irrational, shuddering disgust for the homosexual. No one until recently dared protest the silent and relentless campaign against homosexuals in public life; not a voice was raised less than a generation ago when a political witchhunt selectively attacked suspected homosexuals in federal employment. Merle Miller, a successful author who recently broke the barrier of silence by becoming the first public figure in this country to publicly announce his homosexuality, reports that when the American Civil Liberties Union chose to be silent on this issue, he too was silent—although he was then a member of ACLU's national board of directors.[39] How many others, one wonders, out of Kinsey's one-third, lent their support by silence to the continuing conspiracy against homosexuality?

Homosexuality as a sin, like Judaism as a heresy, died away during the nineteenth century as religious belief gave way before a scientific rationalism and agnosticism. Unlike the sin of being a Jew, however, homosexuality found a new home in a contemporary catechism based on sex. The story of how this happened is a perfect example of the workings of the psychopathological game: define an entity, then deal with it as though it really exists; develop an expertise in regard to it; and then present yourself to the public as the only one equipped to do something about its dangers. The gamesters in this instance were psychiatrists who used psychoanalytic theory for their purposes.

Freud may or may not have intended to found an empire. Perhaps he wanted only to spread the truth among men. But even ideas, ethereal though they may be, need some institutional form if they are to take root in a culture and exercise influence. Freud's innovative ideas, resisted initially by the medical profession, finally found their institution in the developing profession of psychiatry and in the theory that it taught and practiced. As the proper subject matter of religious dogma was sin, so the chosen topic of psychiatry's theory was sex: good sex, bad sex, proper sex, improper sex, healthy sex, diseased sex, where sex came from, how it intruded on human activities, and what sex looked like in all its variants. Following Freud, whose own sexual activity was, according to his biographer, always under careful control and in fact seems to have been voluntarily relinquished when he was not yet fifty years old,[10] the accepted theory in what were termed scientific psychiatric circles was about as follows: As a result of a lifetime of struggle, growth, and development, the human adult achieved, if all went well, a pattern of sexual performance remarkably similar to that practiced abroad by missionaries to the great wonder and amusement of many of the preliterate tribes who heard about it. This performance consisted of two or perhaps three occasions a week when a man and a woman who were approximately the same age and married to each other would, late at night in their bedroom with the lights out, assume a position with the man on top of the woman. With a minimum or even absence of foreplay, they would commence quietly sweating palm to palm (in Aldous Huxley's expression), the man moving his penis in and out of the woman's vagina, while she lay still, until he ejaculated; her orgasm, if it occurred at all, was accidental and unnecessary. They would say very little if anything during the sex act, would indulge in no afterplay, would not talk about it after it was over, and would never under any circumstances refer to it outside the bedroom, not even when alone with each other. The act would be discontinued during the period of the month when the woman was menstruating, as well as for the final four to six months of any of her pregnancies; and the practice would drop in frequency with the passing years, usually at the woman's behest, so that it would be infrequent when they were in their fifties and would usually be completely discontinued by the time they had reached the age of sixty.

According to this particular dogma, one of the many errors to which the developing human was subject was an abnormality of final object choice. If everything went right, the person passed through normal stages of body centeredness, attachment to the parent of the opposite sex, temporary suppression of the sexual drive, attachment to peers of the same sex, and finally, in glorious "genitality" (as it was called), sexual attachment to a peer of the opposite sex. But things did not work out right for some unfortunates. As Freud summarized it in his famous letter of April 9, 1935, in answer to an American mother's question about her homosexual son: "Homosexuality is assuredly no advantage, but it is nothing to be ashamed of, no vice, no degradation; it cannot be classified as an illness; we consider it to be a variation of sexual functions produced by a certain arrest of sexual development." But though not an illness, homosexuality was still a deviation from what was normal and right; and so in standard textbooks of the time, which were largely based on Freud,[41] the condition was understood as either a symptom or a contributing cause of more general and severe disorders, such as paranoia, depression, alcoholism, or schizophrenia.

In the 1930s there began to appear in the psychiatric literature the first discussions of homosexuality as a form of psychopathology, a disease in itself. This may be related to the fact that at just about this time the American psychoanalytic group was entering its second generation and developing all the appurtenances of a professional society—admission requirements, training procedures, certification rituals—and so they felt a need to embark on a self-appointed mission of defining evil and then protecting the public from it. The diagnostic formulations of the psychiatric profession at about this time began to be increasingly political: any behavior that did not conform to the accepted standards of the day was defined as pathological and therefore treatable, including delinquency, criminality, alcoholism, prostitution, drug addiction, and above all homosexuality. Thus, today homosexuality is considered by many psychiatrists—and by psychologists, too, who pattern their practice on the medical model—as a serious and stubborn but not incurable form of psychic pathology.[42] Patients are accepted who express dissatisfaction with what Martin Hoffman[43] aptly calls the "sad gay life" and who wish to be "cured" of their condition. Elaborate theories are developed to explain how the diseased condition came about; which parent was, according to the current fashion, mostly to be blamed; and to what degree, depending on the theoretician's bias, constitutional or environmental factors were accountable as determinants.

Is there an alternative view of homosexuality, one which does not rest on either the moralizing traditions of our culture or the political history of the psychiatric profession? A more modern view of human sexuality would say that in general the true sign of psychopathology is a loveless, rigid, or manipulative relation with another person, regardless of the sexual content of their mutual activity. This, in summary, is the message of the majority of contemporary theorists in regard to sexual adjustment and mental health. As for homosexuality in particular, there is a possible alternative view that starts from no moralistic preconceptions. Human beings are creatures of very great complexity, and so they start out possessed of an enormously wide and varied potential; as a result of life circumstances as well as their own choices and talents, they may emphasize some of these possibilities relative to others or even to the exclusion of some; in regard to sexual objects and related sexual role identification, the key choices appear to be made in early adolescence, when the person is forced by society into fairly sharply defined relations with both sexes; and these choices may include, if circumstances permit, any of the almost infinite shadings between pure heterosexuality and pure homosexuality. Once the major choice is made—and it need not be a permanent choice, stamped in and marking the person for life—the individual's path through adolescence is fairly well determined; styles of life, identity of friends, major interests, sexual activities, and experiences of pleasure and pain, will all vary as a consequence.

In a sexually free and open society, as perhaps no society in Western history has ever been, an individual might make and unmake his choices any number of times, living at each point in his life history in terms of whatever experiences most appealed to him. But in our own society, to have made one choice rather than another imprisons the person in an identity trap that he then, out of fear and guilt and need for acceptance, may defend rigidly or even frantically. Thus, the most masculine male or the most feminine female, though seemingly secure in their roles, may nonetheless be haunted by the half-realized wish that has been deflected, the opportunity once offered but fearfully refused. In particular, even a partial choice toward homosexuality usually results in a life pattern of hiding, deception, and lack of self-fulfillment, of guilt and self-torment, if not ostracism or the threat of it. The strain of knowing oneself to be "queer" in this way is more than most persons can bear, and so they rapidly head toward one of the easier alternatives: to live a heterosexual life, at least on the surface and at whatever cost; to live on the fringes of a homosexual life, perhaps participant in gay styles of life but never daring to make an open declaration; or pounding desperately on a therapist's door and asking to be "cured."

Whatever the choice that is made, and however it is lived out, the result is that for some persons who cannot choose heterosexuality an entire set of possibilities, not simply for sexual activity but for the range and patterning of every human relationship, is distorted or smothered; what remains is only part of a life, neither man nor woman, unfulfilled at best and damned at worst. And the greatest tragedy of all is that as long as our current psychopathological myths are held and respected, none of us can be free. Each one of us, regardless of overt preference, must be burdened by the questions that are common to all. Am I really a complete man (or woman) and not latently a little queer? Are some of my troubles with my lover due to my hidden wish for a partner of another sex, a wish that I cannot admit even to myself? Am I, indeed, living this life more as a rebellion, or as a passive acceptance, than out of free choice?

I must emphasize that I am not making a case here either for or against a homosexual way of life, but rather a case for freedom. At many stages of our lives, but during adolescence in particular, we are occupied with that question of identity which is stated as: Who am I? This question, of all questions, can never be answered in the abstract. It can only be answered in the course of ongoing experience. When some modes of experience, either in activity or fantasy, are so tightly closed off that even the possibility of them is ruled out, then the question of identity is unanswered because it is unasked. And this is especially and often devastatingly true in regard to sexual identity. Only the freedom to wish or to do can make possible the experience of knowing one's identity.

The most striking of all the facts about homosexuality—if it is a fact rather than just one more myth—is the disparity between the frequency of male and female homosexuality. One explanation, consonant with psychoanalytic theory, is that the developing female is much less likely to veer from accepted paths and more likely to become just what society says she ought to become, but this explanation has relatively little force in an age of increasing freedom for both sexes. An older explanation, which can now be dismissed almost completely, would have it that women don't like sex as much as men do anyway. A more likely explanation, on the other hand, is that society has never allowed women to act on their wishes, sexual or otherwise, and so they have simply never had the opportunity to seek each other out as sexual partners.

One fact of social organization lends support to this argument. It is that the history of any group is always written by those who are in power in it. There were no slave historians in ancient Rome; the extensive material we have about slaves was written by their masters. Those who run a society determine the way its history will be written and who will be mentioned in what way. The more removed a subgroup is from the power center, the less are its chances of being written up unless its members are foolish enough to keep coming to the attention of their masters. And even if this should happen, the voice that tells about them will not be their own but that of their betters, looking down at them.

This tells us, I think, something significant about the unwritten history of lesbianism. Although male homosexuality was openly practiced in every ancient society and in Oriental societies until very recent times, as the histories attest, it is unlikely that there would have been a literature about female practices even if these had existed on a wide scale. Men rarely wrote seriously about women in their own right, and the one intriguing account that we have from classical Greek society, the story of Sappho and her group of cohorts on the isle of Lesbos during the sixth century B.C. (from which comes our modern term for female homosexuality), describes not so much a homosexual society as an intellectual, artistic, and political association.[44] The account would serve better as a model for the women's liberation movement than for a sexual community.

But even if all these factors are taken into account, it is quite probable that sexual behavior in other than normatively accepted ways was always more prevalent among men than among women. One good reason is easily found. Oppression has the effect of restricting the range of actual behavior in its victims and, more importantly, the range of possibilities that appear to them. Slaves live routine lives and, more important, slaves seldom dream about other than routine lives. Oppression serves to dull and limit both the actuality and the possibility. It is the taste of freedom, on the other hand, that makes for great dreams, brave trials, daring forays in imagination and action. And it is freedom, and the power that can be associated with it, that makes it possible for one sex to develop ways of expressing its homosexual preferences. Thus only men, and never women, have all through history had the chance to develop institutionalized forms of homosexuality.[45]

If this is so, if we do not accept the view that there exist some mysterious and inborn differences between male and female sexual organization, an interesting prospect opens up. It is a prospect as yet unsuspected—or at least unreported—among even the most vocal advocates of complete social and cultural equality for women. What we have not yet heard is a demand for women's right to be homosexual, yet the logic of the matter seems to suggest that something like this must happen if our society continues to open up possibilities for women in general and for the individualizing of their sexual choices in particular. In all probability an increasing number of young men will discover for themselves a homosexual option for some period during their development; they may as a consequence invent various modes of living-out this option in combination with other sexual choices. To the same degree, I suggest, the next generation of women should become increasingly free to make analogous choices. Indeed, the option is even more likely to occur in the case of women if only because this will be their most arresting opportunity in five thousand years. To have the complete freedom to choose on an individual basis the nature and variety of their sexual partners and not have that choice dictated by male needs or power will surely represent the most clear-cut statement that the long age of male domination is at an end. The temptation may well be to emphasize, perhaps even to overemphasize, those sexual choices that effectively rule out the male as partner. In that case we would see, for a shorter or longer period of time, an era that will have to be called the Lesbian Revolution.

And that period, at long last, should mark the beginning of the end of the social phenomenon of outcast-in-our-midst, the social sin that has always determined how the dominant group has collectively understood (and misunderstood) any group whom it has been profitable to select as distinctive and alien. At last the Saint will no longer need to make this painful choice, and we may finally welcome even the Stranger back home.

# chapter 6
# the split within

"I said people don't seem to like me for some reason—open your ears, fathead!"
Drawn by Al Johns                                    The Saturday Evening Post

It's all too easy to laugh at this man. His problem, poor fellow is painfully obvious. Seemingly he cannot even realize that all the while he is complaining that he has no idea why people don't like him, his very manner of making his complaint reveals exactly what the trouble is. He doesn't even appear to know that he is answering the very question he wants to pay the therapist to answer for him. How blind can a person be?

## THE NEUROTIC SPLIT

Or is he? Before drawing any conclusions, let's back up a bit. I'm sure that if I were a therapist and were to hear a patient make a remark like that, I would immediately know something about him that he doesn't seem to know about himself. I would know that he is a loudmouth who pushes people around by yelling at them. I would know it, just from looking at him and listening to him— and I would also know that he doesn't know it, because if he did know it he wouldn't be telling me that people don't like him "for some reason." So I am immediately one up on him: I know something significant about him that he does not—and perhaps cannot—know about himself.

This would be my thinking if I were in the role of therapist; and professionally this is what I sometimes do. I would probably even be tempted to leave the matter there and not pursue it any deeper. As a therapist my position is uncomplicated. You, as my patient, have a problem that you can't correct by yourself, so you come to me for help. We will probably start out by my knowing some significant things about you that you can't know about yourself, and when you get to the point where your knowledge of, and relation to, yourself is much more like mine, then we'll agree that you have achieved "insight" into your problems and are changed for the better. It won't be quite this crude, but this is the basic principle involved.

But, as it happens, I have also on some occasions been in the role of patient. So now when I think about these same issues from the other side of the therapeutic encounter, it seems to me that the matter may not be as uncomplicated as the therapist would like to have it. From my point of view as a patient, I know something about myself that my therapist doesn't know and perhaps even can't know. I know, more directly and truly than he can ever know, the ways in which I'm bothered, upset, panicked, beaten down, or torn apart. I know that something is wrong with where I'm at. What I know, in ways that no one else in the world can ever know, are the specifics of my condition. Most important, it is this knowledge that I have about myself, and not my symptoms or my inner psychodynamics, that brings me to a therapist. I think it is fair to say that most of what other persons know about me may, in fact, be a spin-off of the very great deal that I know about myself. It may, then, be at least an even match, my knowledge and that of others.

Coming back to the patient in the cartoon, we may ask which of the two kinds of knowing—what the patient knows about himself or what the therapist knows about him—is the key element in his needing a therapist? The therapist knows a secret truth, that the reason people don't like this man is that he is an obnoxious loudmouth; whereas the man himself knows a distinctly different secret truth, that things aren't right for him and that somehow he is different from what he might be or wants to be.

There is another way to put the same question. We may ask which it is that brings this man to a therapist's office—the divergence between his behavior and the standards of those around him, or the split between his behavior and his dream of what he might be. Both are apparent, of course; on the basis of my own experience, I would guess that this patient is in some way aware of the first. That is, I would guess that he knows that his behavior does not come up to the expectations of those around him; in fact, he begins by telling the therapist that people don't seem to like him "for some reason." He knows that his behavior diverges from social standards. But I would offer that this alone will not bring him to a therapist's office for help. He will only make this confession, and ask for help, at the point where this first divergence is translated into a second one: his "failure" as a person leads to a gap between what he is and what he might be. Only when the split becomes an inner one will he feel a need to change.

I propose to use the term *the neurotic split* to refer to this condition—the inner sense that what I am or do runs counter to what I could, or might, be or do.

---

## OTTO RANK ON NEUROSIS AND CREATIVITY

Rank was the only major follower of Freud whose personality theory explicitly made a place for creativity. He saw the personality as the ground where two fundamental and determining forces met: a fear of life (based on the birth trauma and subsequent separation anxiety) and a fear of death; or in very general terms, a fear of independence versus a fear of dependence. The energy, or power, that molds the personality and effects some resolution of the basic conflict was called by Rank the WILL.

The commonest type of adjustment, and the one that is worked out by the average person, is the ADAPTED type, whose development of will is such that he conforms to his own demands and those of society. The price he pays for a harmony of spirit is that he lacks creativity. At a more complex level is the person who experiences an inner struggle between will and counterwill. He sets up his own standards; he moves against social norms. If he manages to achieve a fusion of will and counterwill so that his life fears are integrated into his personality, a new Gestalt may be formed, an "ideal formation" that becomes the driving force for the CREATIVE personality type. But if he tries and fails, he may end up in conflict between what he would be and what he cannot be, that is, the NEUROTIC type:[1]

---

I should also disclaim immediately any pretense to the originality of the concept. A closely related idea was richly elaborated by Otto Rank; it bears more than a passing resemblance to Karen Horney's view that a person is neurotic when he, or others he can trust, see his behavior as unsatisfying;[2] and it is not inconsistent with Carl Jung's notion that neurosis is not necessarily an illness but may in fact be the curing agent for one's illness. However, the concept of neurotic split that I offer here is meant to be different from the notion—which runs through Freud's writings and has recently been revived by Laing[3]—of one part of a self somehow in conflict with another part. Experience, as I conceive it here, is always a totality; only theorists can, and do, break it up into parts and then create inner dramas among them. One possible mode of experience, in its totality, is a split—that is, to experience oneself as caught in a space between what one is known to be and what one can imagine being.[4]

Nor do I mean by this concept nothing more than being unhappy. The neurotic split is both broader and deeper than the familiar circumstance of an

---

THE SYMPTOM
PROBLEM AND THE LIFE PROBLEM
A STUDENT WRITES ABOUT SOME SYMPTOMS

It is surprising that I am still afraid of the dark—that is, when I have my own flashlight. I have tried to explain to myself that I am being ridiculous—but I still have to close my closet doors before I can go to sleep, and I still have to have the blanket pulled up over my ears. Another fear is a dread of spiders—I can only remember one day in the Spring when I walked past a vacant lot on my way to school—and a huge garden spider scurried out behind me as though he was chasing me. I also suffer from acrophobia —I cannot trace the origin, but I fear tumbling down to the bottom.

ANOTHER STUDENT
DESCRIBES A LIFE SITUATION

I feel at times that I am watching but not participating in the world around me. I feel that I am alone even when I am in the company of "friends." Other people seem to have lasting relationships but it seems impossible for me. I am continually on the outside and I find that I am hardened to a point of losing my emotions. I cannot evoke any feeling at times, I am emotionally numb. I believe I could do mean and harmful things and feel no remorse or emotion about them. My thoughts are broken much of the time and much of my thinking is inconsequential ideas that bear little relevance to the topic. I am very frightened and very tired of fighting a world that has screwed me.

---

unhappy mood or even a simple recognition of one's problem. To have a symptom, such as being afraid of the dark, and to be unhappy about having it, or to experience an unpleasant mood, such as being frightened or despairing, are straightforward conditions that affect the person partially or for a limited time. They do not necessarily encompass the totality of experience. But if they describe a general life situation, if they begin to define one's total experience, and if they are experienced as coming up against a dimly intuited sense that things ought to be better than this—then the condition becomes what I am calling the neurotic split. To some degree, as well, the standards that the person has picked up from society may play some part in the experience of the neurotic split, helping to color it with powerful, moving terms such as *Should* and *Might* and *Ought*.

Does this, in turn, sound like the activity of my conscience? Not quite. The typical notion of conscience is too narrow for what I mean here. Consciences are specialists, dealing mainly in moral prescriptions that are expressed as Right/Wrong, Proper/Improper, or Good/Bad. Consciences are much closer to the long-lost and forgotten, but still remembered, voice of a punishing parent, a voice that said sternly, behind a warning finger, "No, you shouldn't. You mustn't. Don't you dare. That's bad." (How curious that we have so little memory of a voice saying, "But of course you should. You must. It's good." Were all our parents that restrictive? or does the threat of punishment stick deeper than the promise of reward?)[5]

The two elements involved in the neurotic split may strain endlessly, not to narrow but to widen the split. The commonest name for the inner experience of this strain is *anxiety*, which may be why it is found as the accompaniment of most cases that appear in a therapist's office.[6] Its most common and most devastating form is one in which the no-no conscience is superimposed as coloring on the strain of anxiety. This is the condition we usually call *guilt*: not only do I see myself as not the person I might be, but I myself am to blame for my desperate straits, I and no one else. If my standards, based on my conscience, are high to begin with, perhaps almost impossibly high; if I have an exquisite and sensitive capacity for imagining what I might ideally be; if I have come to believe that what I am runs counter to any decent person's ideal; and if I have been carefully programmed to blame myself and never the world for this situation; then I am set up for endless and bottomless guilt. Does the portrait sound familiar? It should, for it describes the typical, intelligent, middle-class neurotic of our time, for example, the victim of Momism in its current reincarnation as the Jewish mother.[7]

By now there should be apparent more than a family resemblance to the formulations that are found in contemporary psychoanalytic ego psychology. At the heart of the theoretical structure that Freud developed to depict the human personality, there were three functioning elements: a biological reservoir of drives, called the *id*, whose slogan was simply "I want"; a guarding and warning and punishing element, the *super ego*, which kept saying, "Don't you dare"; and a mediating agency, the *ego*, with its words, "OK, I'll see what I can do about it." The task of the ego—and the only correlate of it that is finally seen in behavior— is to serve as executor among the conflicting demands of id, super ego, and world. For this, in current ego psychology, it is provided with its own major sources of energy, and its resultant efforts constitute the person's own sense of who he is and what he does. Neuroses, and defenses against their appearance, are ego functions; what I have called the neurotic split would be, in psychoanalytic terminology, an unsatisfactory ego resolution of demands by id, super ego, or ego ideal forces.

What I have described as the neurotic split, then, is a major portion of the ego psychology model, but here described from the inside looking out. Where theory builders, including those in the Freudian tradition, step outside of individual experience and so must resort to depersonalizing, abstracting, and generalizing, I have tried to stay inside the only subject whose experiential data I will ever know, myself. But there does appear to be a rough coincidence between the formulation arrived at externally, so to speak, and the one that I have offered from an internal base.

## NEUROTIC CHARACTER AND THE NEUROTIC SPLIT

Given the nature of human experience, there is an inevitability about the development of the neurotic split. To some degree at least, everyone is threatened; anyone may become its victim. This would seem to hold true whether it is oneself or another who sets up the standard against which one's behavior is compared.

The condition I have described is one in which I sense, however dimly or even without justification, that I have gone against my own true nature. Now, experience of any sort is a private matter. Experience is always modified by a possessive pronoun—always mine, never someone else's, certainly never belonging to no one at all. There is no way that experience can be assessed, for there can be no collective standard against which to compare it. I can only compare my own standards with my own experience; or at best I can compare my experience with what I see are the standards of the community. The calling to account, the judgment, and the final sentencing, all take place inside me; this is true though they all seem to be concerned with what goes on outside of me.

If I am now defined by someone else, and he tries to assess my action against contemporary standards, he will almost certainly be able to find ways in which my behavior is less than adaptive. He will detect at least some instances of the neurotic split. This is the best possible case. If, on the other hand, I make my own assessment of myself, the case is likely to be somewhat worse. No one, certainly not I, judges his own self to conform to his own ideals. By either standard, every one of us will come out at least a little tarred from the diagnostic brush.

This, then, is the threat, or perhaps the possibility, that haunts human experience. However, this is not to say that it must inevitably happen, or that there are no ways out. Rather—and here is the argument that I will be pursuing in the present chapter—much of human character as well as human social behavior may be understood as ways out of the neurotic split, as ways to avoid the experience in the first place or else to live more or less comfortably with it. Ours may indeed be the age of anxiety—which is surely one of the major fringe benefits of the neurotic split—but it is equally the age of learning how to avoid anxiety.

One reason that most persons are not trapped in the neurotic split is a most general one; the human being is simply far too adaptable a creature to be trapped for good in any condition. Man's ingenuity and creativity, unique in all the animal kingdom, often seem to serve no higher biological goal than to keep him at least one step ahead of that final checkmate position from which (as in the case of schizophrenia) he sees no way out. This does not mean that the person actively or deliberately plans to escape from a given condition, as though once grasped it were a problem to be solved. It means, rather, that if the possibility of the neurotic split is built into the experience of being human, so also is the major way to avoid its consequences. Since the neurotic split consists of the experience of oneself as less than one might be, a fundamental way of avoiding most consequences of the split is to block off major areas of experience.

As we shall see in some detail in a later chapter, the discovery of this phenomenon of blocking as the central problem in the clinical treatment of neurotics was made by Wilhelm Reich, although it had been anticipated by Freud's circle of analysts in their work on character. For this is essentially how the maneuver of blocking-off experience is carried out: the person's whole being, in the form of his character, is so arranged as to transform major areas of experience into sensing.

The three major targets of experience, as I noted in the opening chapter, are body, head, and world. A major form of character may be found to correspond to each of these targets—the hysteric to body-experience, the obsessive to head-experience, and the paranoid to world-experience. For the hysteric, the immediate and direct experience of the body is given up in favor of sensing the body; it is made into an object, to be known and used and even exploited. For the obsessive, the natural and directly experienced rate and manner of thinking, the immediate fusion of thinking and behavior, is forsworn in favor of planning, organizing, or scheduling; the present disappears and in its place appears a past to be relived endlessly as guilt and remorse, or a future to be filled emptily with plans that are never lived through. And for the paranoid, the risks involved in unmediated experience with the world and with other persons in particular are avoided by keeping others away and by objectifying human relations into predetermined categories, closed and fated and not to be tempered by interpersonal contact. To some extent, of course, we are all a little tainted, a little closed-off to completely pure and direct experience. We dress up our bodies for display, and we ham it up for others on occasion, as the hysteric character does in the extreme. We are organized and punctual, neat and orderly, and we are a little bit proud of what it does for us, though not to the overwhelming degree that marks the obsessive character. And we cannot bring ourselves to be completely open, trusting, and naïve, even if we do not carry this reluctance to the lengths that mark the paranoid personality.

In great degree or small, however, character traits serve as a way of dismissing experience without expending energy on a continuing basis. Energy is available for the sensing of a major target, but without the risks involved in direct experiencing. The target is then dealt with, often effectively, but at one step removed, so to speak, with character traits and their associated devices automatically interposed between experience and its target.

What was accomplished, apparently, in the early practice of psychoanalysis was to guide patients out of the rigid traps of their neurotic characters and toward at least attempting the challenge and luxury of direct experience. In effect, Freud and his followers seem to have taught their patients how to recapture for themselves a head-experience that had previously been avoided and obscured. It was done by the method of free association, in which the analyst said, in effect, "Trust me, and trust yourself. Allow yourself to be just exactly what you are. Let it happen exactly as it happens, at the rate and in the way that your experience occurs. Don't block off your experience by means of your knowing, your fearing, your judging, your arranging—just allow your expression to correspond to the pure experience of the moment." In very different words, this antedated the strikingly similar advice of contemporary mystics.

THE RATE IT HAPPENS
You've got to go at the rate you can go.
    You wake up at the rate you wake
      up.
    You're finished with your desires at
      the rate you finish with your
      desires.

The disequilibrium comes into
    harmony at the rate it comes
    into harmony.
YOU CAN'T RIP
    the skin off
    the snake. The snake must moult
    the skin. That's the rate it happens.[8]

What Freud's followers left out of this formula was supplied a decade later by Reich, with the technique he called vegetotherapy.[9] By means of radically new methods of clinical practice, he was able to reconstitute for his patients that body-experience against which they had blocked themselves during a lifetime of constructing their individual neurotic characters. When he worked directly on the physical constraints that could be found in their bodies, a sudden and powerful release of energy was almost invariably the result; this in turn suggested that great individual stores of energy were often bound in the neurotic character structure, with the door tightly closed, so to speak.

Extreme cases of this sort are rather rare. They occur primarily among those who are specialists in objectifying their own bodies—the professional model, for example, the dancer, the athlete, or perhaps the prostitute. Unfortunately, interviewers talk to these gifted persons about everything except the most important issues, and so we have very little information from them about what it is like to take this controlled and antiexperiential stance toward one major target of experience. But occasionally we are privileged to hear the report of someone who uniquely combines a near-total rigidity, an almost absolute objectifying of

THE PRICE OF EXPERIENCE

I am a sufferer from migraine, as were my mother and her mother before her. This has also been true of three of my sisters, and my eldest daughter, now twenty-one, since she was eight years old. . . . The attack is usually initiated by a mild but persistent ache in either temple. This grumbling ache may last several hours, even half a day, and sometimes fluctuates in intensity, although it usually increases steadily until the peak is reached. . . . I have built up a rather elaborate mechanism of ignoring the early stages of an attack, which consists of redoubled effort at concentration on any work that I may be doing. If the pain increases, however, the effort is very costly, and may actually become quite grim, accompanied by setting of the jaws which eventually only serves to increase the pain. This system usually fails in the end, but does succeed in delaying the climax of the attack; on other occasions, when the absence of pressure from work makes it possible to recline in a chair or lie down, the greatest intensity of an attack is reached much earlier, but may be less severe.

Sometimes the early stages of an attack occur during some morning just prior to a scheduled brain operation. My operations usually begin at 1:30 in the afternoon. When this occurs, I tie the sweatband which I wear around my head during operations, more tightly than usual. This, plus the firm contraction of the jaw muscles, makes it possible to go through a three- or four-hour operation, during which the numerous precise and meticulous maneuvers demanded . . . become more precise and more meticulous than ever, as if to show the demon of migraine who is boss. But the payoff comes when the operation is over. As soon as the sweatband is released and the jaws drop open from fatigue, all hell breaks loose. The pain seems to tear away from its moorings like a torpedo and great, swollen, humming pulses of pain streak through my temples and the base of the head. My face assumes a greenish pallor; I break out into a cold perspiration; my hands and feet feel cold and I feel chilly all over. Even a dim light in the room sends additional shafts of pain through my eyes. My stomach seems to turn over, and I wish that I could vomit but usually cannot, and the thought of food is a revulsion and a mockery.

The effort to bathe and dress, dictate the operative note, discuss the operation with my assistants, and often make ward visits, seems almost superhuman. At last the strife is over. I crouch into a corner of a taxicab to be driven home, crawl under the blankets without putting on the lights and often without undressing. Sleep is difficult to induce, and localized pressures of my head against the pillow cause additional pain. . . . On awakening, I feel unsteady, weak and hungry, but as if purged of something evil. I usually pass a large quantity of colorless urine. Breakfast has a remarkably restorative effect, and the world becomes bright and cheerful. All irritability is gone and being calm, patient and understanding no longer seems an impossible task. . . .

. . . the underlying causes, I am convinced, are anxiety and tension. . . . It may be a period when a series of major and difficult cases are being operated upon, and when at the same time that I am anxious about the success of the operation scheduled for the following day, I am worried about the postoperative course of the patient of today and perhaps, even more, that of the one who was operated on the day before. . . . The night deteriorates into a marathon of tossing and turning. Then the alarm clock finally rips into the peace of sleep attained, after complete exhaustion, during the last few hours before morning. On awakening, unrefreshed, the first dull ache in one temple gives warning of things to come. Breakfast is a desultory affair. The habitual elimination does not materialize. Irritability, which if unrestrained would estrange the whole world, must be controlled, and in spite of large doses of aspirin, the course of events may not be interrupted. . . .

There is no doubt in my mind that the migraine victim belongs to a personality group which, while varying in detail from person to person, nevertheless adds up to a "type." . . . One of the outstanding characteristics of the group . . . is "perfectionism." . . . There is no doubt that "perfectionism" is a burden, especially if it is accompanied by migraine. Fortunately for the perfectionist, the world has a place for him by virtue of this trait; and fortunately for the world, it has perfectionists to call upon for the performance of certain tasks in which anything less than perfection is failure.[10]

---

the body, a nearly complete substitution of sensing for the experience of his body, and the ability and training to discuss his own case. Perhaps this is his own way of living up to the familiar physician's dictum concerning healing himself. He may well be right; there may be scientific and professional advantages to be gained—as our migraine sufferer clearly believes—from being able to stand back, calmly view the emotional wreckage that constitutes a severe attack, thoughtfully consider the relevance of associated circumstances and the relative probability of different causative factors, and even weigh quite accurately the gains and losses that accumulate out of suffering on the one hand, and achieving near perfection in his work on the other. There is surely something to be said for the man who can make his own body, the very source of his own real pain, so much an impersonal object to be viewed, discussed, and analytically dissected.

And see how this stance shows up even in such small details as his description of his own case. Most of it reads just exactly as though he were describing the sensed but not really felt or experienced pain of another person, another body which is not his own. The grammar of his body language has almost eliminated the first person in place of the third. At key moments, in fact, the split between a self, now totally encapsulated as pure will, and a body, now utterly overcome with pain, becomes as complete as it could ever be, "during which the numerous precise and meticulous maneuvers . . . become more precise and more meticulous than ever, as if to show the demon of migraine who is boss." When finally the job is done, the will no longer needed, he sums it up again: "At last the strife is over."

As Leo Davidoff himself notes, the clinical literature on migraine, when it has considered at all some of the psychological issues, has restricted itself to the personality characteristics of typical migraine sufferers. Perhaps clinicians such as Harold Wolff are right, although the problem with such typologies is that the discovery of only one person who suffers from migraine but is not a perfectionist is enough to discredit the whole elaborate set of findings. But even if this search for parallels between psychic and somatic types is successful, as it surely seems to be in the present case, it does not touch on a more fundamental matter: the sufferer's relation between his experiencing and his sensing of his own body. I think it is no exaggeration to say that Davidoff, by his own admission, has managed to carry over into his dealings with his own body the complete set of attitudes and approaches appropriate to his dealing with the bodies of his patients; he is no closer to himself than he is to them. Only when pain, sheer pain, overrides this split—and this occurs only when the pain becomes overwhelming, literally uncontrollable—does he become capable of experiencing his own body. At this moment he becomes at last a creature of experience, even as you and I; he is now one with his own body, the will and the flesh trapped in an unbearable unity. But up to that point, as we see, it is never permitted.

Consider, for example, the problem he faces in regard to that everyday feeling-state, anger. Like all such states, anger can be a liberating experience of the moment, at least as long as the person lets it happen, goes with it, and allows it to take him for the moment out of the limits of his situation. A little boy of about four gets very angry with his three-year old sister. He stands face to face with her, his face about six inches from hers, and screams at her: "I hate you! I hate you! I wisht you was dead!" The little girl looks up at him, takes the full force of the attack, and then turns away, shaking her head a little as if to say, "Well, I guess that's the way it is sometimes." In a few minutes they are playing together again, quite peaceably. He was angry, no question about that—but he accepted it fully, and so did she, and that was that. Like those little children, adults are sometimes able to be angry (or sad, or afraid, or even happy) without stint, without holding back or questioning, with nothing at all interposed between the feeling-state and its expression. When this happens apparently the recipient does not feel bruised either. When it happens self and target are one; I and world fuse into one high-energy state.

But this is not at all true of our migraine patient. He is so unable to accept the bare possibility of his own anger that even a little indication of it, that preliminary stage which we call irritability, appears to him as fraught with almost world-shaking possibilities: "Irritability, which if unrestrained would estrange the whole world, must be controlled . . ." The preliminary stages, even though they could serve to defuse a potential explosion, may not be permitted. With the doors thus tightly and desperately shut for him, it is no wonder that he lives a controlled life, strung out between the two poles of perfection and failure—the one not attainable in our world, and the other not forgivable in his. Nor is it any wonder that his only access to pure experience is at the cost of unbearable pain. It is pain that shatters the order of his carefully made and precisely arranged life of sensing, pain that forces on him that body-experience which his whole life is arranged to deny.

## SOME AVENUES OF ESCAPE

Not everyone is capable of dismissing all experience by means of a character structure which was composed to this end through a lifetime of sensing. Fortunately, many other ways out of the neurotic split are available to the rest of us; taken together, they define most of our pathologies of being and doing.

### Being a Victim

One way to find happiness of sorts in the face of the neurotic split is to subtract from, rather than to add to, the strains of everyday life—that is, to become a victim. In the victimized state, when the person has been made into something less by some external influence, it may well be possible for him to experience the neurotic split and yet not be bothered by it. According to most reports, some such condition can be achieved by the brain surgery known as prefrontal lobotomy; the patient, now become a victim, acts as though he knows what used to bother him (his "voices," or his delusions, or his intractable pain) but he does not experience it as personally distressing, and perhaps not even as personally meaningful.

The mentally retarded person, on the other hand, though he may appear to be a victim, is not usually able to find surcease by this route. He is often doubly anxious—first because of the kind of split that afflicts us all, and in addition because of his continuing distress over his own limitations and frustrations. It seems to be, by contrast, only the direct assault on the nervous system that produces a state of hapless, but unconcerned, victimization: the split not really healed over, but rather ignored because of an incapacity to handle its two alternative possibilities at once. If the person has not chosen to be victimized in this way, and if the result of his condition is that he has lost the capacity to compare what is with what might be—a condition that Kurt Goldstein and Martin Scheerer call concrete behavior—then he can be described as both hapless and happy.

---

## THE "CONCRETE" ATTITUDE

The analysis of the behavior and performance changes in [brain-injured] patients led [us] to make a distinction between two modes of behavior—the abstract and the concrete. The normal person is capable of assuming both, whereas the abnormal individual is confined to but one type of behavior—the concrete. The abstract and concrete behaviors are dependent upon two corresponding attitudes which are psychologically so basic that one may speak of them almost as levels.

The abstract and the concrete attitudes are not acquired mental sets or habits of an individual, or special isolable aptitudes, such as memory, attention, etc. They are rather CAPACITY LEVELS OF THE TOTAL PERSONALITY. Each one furnishes the basis for all performances pertaining to a specific plane of activity. In other words, each attitude constitutes one definite behavioral range which involves a number of performances and responses.[11]

The abstract attitude is the basis for the following CONSCIOUS and VOLITIONAL modes of behavior:

1. To detach our ego from the outerworld or from inner experiences (e.g., to be able to say, "The snow is black.")
2. To assume a mental set (e.g., to initiate an action, or to proceed spontaneously if interrupted in a sequential task.)
3. To account for acts to oneself; to verbalize the account (e.g., to have an abstract grasp of spatial relations and be able to talk about this.)
4. To shift reflectively from one aspect of the situation to another (e.g., to change a task from the usual one, or to change topics rapidly in a conversation.)
5. To hold in mind simultaneously various aspects (e.g., to alternate counting with telling off the letters of the alphabet).
6. To grasp the essential of a given whole; to break up a given whole into parts, to isolate and to synthesize them (e.g., to do a jigsaw puzzle.)
7. To abstract common properties reflectively; to form hierarchic concepts (e.g., to use analogies or metaphors, or to understand a syllogism or the number system.)
8. To plan ahead ideationally; to assume an attitude toward the "mere possible" and to think or perform symbolically (e.g., to draw a map of a known route, or to pretend to drink out of an empty glass.)

Concrete behavior has not the above mentioned characteristics.[12]

---

It is an enviable state, at least in its results. The trouble is that few of us would be willing to pay the price required to reach it—to be free of the human necessity to compare self with ideal; to watch, more or less unconcerned, as standards drift away into meaninglessness; to be occupied solely and simply with what is, concretely and immediately. I must confess that I have mixed feelings; there are times when I face all the demands and decisions that push me from within and tug at me from without—but wait, help is at hand. I know, everyone knows, and people have always known for as far back as human society has existed, that there are ways to achieve this blessed state. There are chemical substances, a marvellous and magical array, to relieve me of the split that affects my every waking moment as a self-conscious member of my community. No wonder the use of drugs, particularly as some form of alcohol, is as ancient and established an aspect of human culture as those other ancient institutions, marriage and religion. Judged on the basis of these criteria, it is man's basic nature to be wedded, prayerful, and drunk.

Drugged states seem, indeed, to resemble being a victim. Under the influence, the happy victim acts as though he is not in control of his faculties. He may lose his inhibitions and overstep many of the normal boundaries that hem in his everyday life, or he may find his reactions enormously intensified without his exerting any effort to bring this about. During the drugged period he experiences neither anxiety nor guilt over what is going on with him. The neurotic split fades away in a rosy alcoholic glow or a delicious opiate haze.

But I believe that the case of the drugged person is really quite different. Recall that he drugs himself. He gets the substance, he takes it, he even has a reasonably good idea of what is going to happen to him. Even when high, he retains at least some notion of the fact that he is under the drug's influence, and he somehow knows that the effect will last only until the power of the drug wears off. He can look at the bottle, the syringe, the sugar cube, and know that whatever his present experiences of no-anxiety and no-guilt, they are terminable. He knows, too, that the terminal point has already been predetermined by the size of the dose that he chose to take.

I suspect that this psychological factor is, as much as any physiological factor, the reason that heroin addicts need to take larger and larger doses in order to keep producing the same level of effect. They need the larger doses in order to keep trying to mask the increasing realization that their self-chosen state is their own choice, is terminable, and is limited by the amount of the drug they have chosen to use.

In addition to this basic reason that drug users cannot be classed as hapless victims, there are the relevant social conditions. Except in the most unusual cases, a drug is taken under socially familiar conditions. The user is pretty well aware of what happens, how the drug affects people, and therefore how far from his own standards he is likely to deviate. In fact, the more habitual a user he is the more of this he is likely to know. The chronic alcoholic thus has the weakest possible argument when he says that he couldn't help himself because he was under an influence that overcame him. And if he claims to have forgotten what happened during his drunken period, we will have to conclude that his forgetting was also his own choice, motivated in the same way as his coming to the bottle yet once again.

This seems to have been the great lesson that finally came home to Richard

Alpert and Timothy Leary when they were using themselves as subjects in a vain search for some ultimate and endless psychedelic high. As Alpert (now Baba Ram Dass) describes it in retrospect:

*At one point I took five people and we locked ourselves in a building for three weeks and we took 400 micrograms of LSD every four hours. That is 2400 micrograms of LSD a day, which sounds fancy, but after your first dose, you build a tolerance; there's a refractory period. We finally were just drinking out of the bottle, because it didn't seem to matter anymore. We'd just stay at a plateau. We were very high. What happened in those three weeks in that house, no one would ever believe, including us. And at the end of the three weeks, we walked out of the house and within a few days, we came down!*[13]

Ironically, this became, for Alpert, a first step in his long journey toward a permanent, drug-free level of personal fulfillment. The lesson that he seems to have learned in those three fateful weeks was that his drug trip came from a container and therefore was limited by the quantity of drug that he himself chose to put in the container. Thus his being drugged was not equivalent to being a victim but rather a special kind of free agent, one who will not recognize his own freedom. The lesson can be generalized to every instance of choosing. I can choose a state in which choice seems to be ruled out—but then I am bound to know, at some level, that the no-choice state is my own choice to make. In this way I may learn that I can never give up my own freedom. It can only be taken away from me.

### Being a Rebel

The neurotic split can also be eliminated in advance simply by giving up one's ideal—nothing more than that. If the neurotic split consists, for me, in a disparity between what I am and what I might be, I can live out the former by giving up the latter. This will entail a reordering of my whole relation to society, but everything has its price. Among the range open to society's outcasts this seems to be a small enough price to pay.

There is a kind of person who in the clinical literature is called the *psychopath*, or more recently and perhaps a little more precisely, the *sociopath*. Here is one of the many blanket, or cover-up, terms used in the clinical professions to

---

THE PSYCHOPATH—
AN EXISTENTIAL VIEW

The psychopath tends to evoke from other people some measure of fear and moral repugnance. The psychopath, more than even the psychotic, reveals to us the intricacies of our own sensibilities and feelings of propriety. He does this because he does not share them and seems to violate them without the discomfort that his behavior causes us. For example, it may never have occurred to us that we place a value on the integrity of natural objects until a psychopathic companion repeatedly violates that integrity by carving into tree trunks, kicking apart rock formations, and destroying birds' nests. The experience of our own repugnance reveals to us a layer of sensitivity and sensibility that may have no counterpart in our verbalized world-view. But in the presence of a psychopath who does not share this existential platform, we discover not only that this sensibility is there, but also that it is a powerful part of our being.[14]

The world of the psychopath is unique in its peculiar omission of other PERSONS. Of course the psychopath knows the difference between people and things, but the "normal" tendency to treat persons as essentially like oneself, as having feelings that are as real to them as experience is to oneself—to identify with others, have empathy, feel their suffering, to put oneself in the role of the other—these processes seem strangely absent. . . .[15]

The psychopath experiences people much as most of us experience objects, i.e., as instruments of our purpose. The psychopath experiences objects, then, in yet a different way than we do. . . .[16] There seems to be no "respect" for things. We do not mean here the kind of respect that is paid to persons; it is more like the respect the carpenter has for his tools. Tools have a kind of otherness, a kind of presence, a kind of integrity that is independent of one's wishes. A screwdriver does not make a good hammer. . . . For the psychopath, every thing is reduced to its usefulness to him and his purpose. There is no world that stands there, to be confronted in its own terms. The entire world of things is subordinated to the one giant subjectivity, his atemporal self. . . .[17] What is missing most of all is the openness to reality. . . . a give and take attitude with people and with things.[18]

---

refer to a mixed bag of patients and to hide existing deficiencies in understanding them. What the term seems to refer to is the person, most often seen in the role of the juvenile delinquent, who is asocial if not antisocial; who appears to be bland, mirror-smooth, almost free of anxiety; who maintains minimal relations with others on other than a superficial or role-determined basis; who shows a very fine sense of the intricacies of power relations; and who is very difficult to reach or to change by traditional psychotherapeutic methods.

On closer examination, it appears to be his time sense that marks him as special: the way he uses time, and in particular his relation to his own past, present, and future. He acts as though time were nothing more than an endless repetition of whatever his own present moment is. He seems to be able to discount that sense of his own historic experiences and obligations that we call a past, as well as that network of expectations, wishes, fears, and hopes that we call a future. In the extreme case, he will keep giving evidence that he is not accumulating a personal past, for he will keep repeating the same reckless act as though he has no way to learn from experience; and he will appear not to be in the process of constructing his future, for he will act impulsively, ignore possible consequences, and fail to plan. Unweighted by the past and untrammeled by the future, he lives freely and rapidly just as though time were structured as an endless series of moments like the one in which he now acts.

Given this orientation, the psychopath has a made-to-order basis for not experiencing a neurotic split in himself: he moves fast enough so as to be always one jump ahead of it. He does not leave a track in his own awareness well enough defined to provide a basis for one half of the split; stated in other words, he gives up the action basis for sensing himself in any way that has import for himself. He is, by his own lights, whatever the moment calls forth in him; there is no other-thing that he might be, could be, or ought to be. He travels light, without the baggage of personal history that weighs down the rest of us, and so he travels fast, too fast for himself to see. In his own shifting and flickering way, he is just what he is—as flashing, often as glittering, and finally as untrappable as quicksilver.

For many psychopaths, the trick works. They spend their days relatively free of the anxiety that besets all the rest of us, and if they have some natural talent they are able to make amazingly good use of it, particularly if it involves relating to others in a manipulative way. The trick works—that is, until the sad day when the only underpinning they must have, the raw energy of their bodies, begins to run down. There are thus very few middle-aged psychopaths, very few menopausal playboys. Their character changes at this point, and they either fall into a depressive state, resort to artificial supports such as drugs, or simply turn into one more group of ordinary, anxiety-ridden citizens.

The psychopath avoids the neurotic split by a device for which his whole character was formed—which is why he is identifiable as a type. But this specific character is not necessary, for the same end can sometimes be accomplished directly, almost as an act of will. Again, the neurotic split is eliminated in advance by abandoning one's ideal and thus becoming free to change one's behavior.

Consider, in this connection, the hair-length problem, an issue that not too long ago brought many a school administrator into fierce confrontation with hitherto docile pupils. We start with the strict and unarguable standards that might have existed in a small, self-contained, traditional culture: a suburban high school in a small Midwestern city in, say, 1960. One student decides to wear his hair down below his ear lobes, thus knowingly challenging the rules that govern being a student. The struggle that follows finds the establishment and its institutional representatives—teachers, ministers, principals, school board members, PTA officers, and sometimes parents—firmly lined up behind the rule book. This, they insist, is the set of established standards that have to be maintained for all sorts of good and obvious reasons: morals, masculinity, custom, cleanliness, safety, or plain old maintenance of discipline. The culprit, on the other hand, acting either alone or with a bare minority of support, defends his rebellious act on higher ground; personal attire, he insists, should be determined solely by individual taste, which is one aspect of the individual's freedom and therefore not bound by collective standards.

As long as the two sides stick to their positions, there is no easy way to settle the matter so that the establishment and the rebel are both satisfied. What usually happens is that the student is punished—what began as an act of rebellion is redefined as an act of criminality and appropriately treated—or else the local standards are gradually changed and the lone rebel's behavior is recognized as socially acceptable: *Mad* magazine triumphs again.

Here is my point in using this example: From the point of view of the student rebel, neither solution is particularly disturbing; that is, it does not make him anxious. Since he has already adopted his own idea of what kind of person he should be, and since he feels himself acting in accordance with it, society's punitive reaction to his behavior may be unpleasant but not anxiety-arousing. He feels no split within himself between the way he is and the way he might or should be. And of course if society swings around to his point of view, that is all the more reason for him to feel no internal split; he has been proven right in the first place. In short, the committed rebel who begins by changing his own conception of the ideal thereby eliminates the neurotic split—even though this may be at the cost of being punished by a community that maintains quite different standards.

Then there is the case that seems more extreme but in some respects is not—the true criminal, as opposed to the mere rebel. The difference between them is, on the surface, simple enough. The rebel acts asocially because he chooses to oppose society, at least in regard to his area of rebellion. The criminal, however, acts this way because it is, for him, the best means to get the goods he wants. The difference shows up clearly when success becomes possible. The criminal is just as willing to do his thing legally (and, as in the case of the Mafia, might even seek out "legal" ways to keep doing it); when acting either under cover of the law or as a reformed criminal, he tends to become stuffily and almost disgracefully respectable. The rebel, on the other hand, has to avoid this kind of success; indeed, if his acts become widely acceptable he is likely to shift to new acts of rebellion. Witness Lenny Bruce's increasingly more far-out performances as a quicksand culture softly embraced and accepted even his bitterest and most objectionable satire. The criminal may have temporarily covered over his own neurotic split, but as soon as he snatches eagerly at crumbs of respectability he is headed back toward the same anxiety that afflicts his fellows. The rebel is different; and in the pure case, such as Genet, in which he freely chooses to be both rebel and criminal, to do wrong, to know it but not to care about it, to be a traitor and a liar and a homosexual thief,[19] then he has found, at whatever cost, one of the ultimate solutions to our common neurosis. He has given up the source for any self-statement as to what he might be or should be; he has become purely and simply what he is. His anxiety is healed by the demonic.

### Fitting
A third general means of staving off the experience of the neurotic split may be the most elaborate of all. It consists of acting so that finally the rebel's dream comes true: to see the world change. When this happens, what the individual has been (wrongly) doing becomes what society (rightly) does. The split then disappears because one sustaining end of it no longer exists.

In its commonest form, the dream goes like this: What if I, the rebel outsider, begin on my own but then gradually come to be accepted as the standard by the society around me? But even this may not be necessary; there is a still simpler way. All I need to do is find a place within the existing society in which my own particular wrongness is not only accepted but is considered the right thing to do; then my actual state becomes completely synonymous with my ideal state—at least as long as I restrict myself to acting within this selected small compass. If my pleasure consists in exercising a brutal authority over my fellows, what I should do is quit my job as office manager (where I now keep those around me in constant fear), or teacher (ditto), and take a position as a prison guard. If my true vocation is the scholarly and ascetic life, I would do better as a Jesuit teacher than being a dentist or the owner of a movie theater. And this is just what many people do. They try to fit into the place, the style, the way of life, the setting in which their own inner split is minimized. What is anxiety-provoking in one setting may be acceptable and even preferred in another. In a relatively free and mobile society, the switch can usually be made.

How far do you suppose this can be pushed? How far will a society stretch to accommodate those who do not already have a comfortable niche? It used to be true (remember Sinclair Lewis's *Main Street?*) that small, local, traditional societies typically left very little room for deviants; the big city was then identified with freedom to do your own thing. What was forbidden in the small town was ignored and even sometimes accepted in the metropolis; what was odd in the town was simply different in the city. The plaint of Mary MacLane (at the opening of chapter 7) is a fine example and raises all sorts of questions about fitting in. Considering what it must have been like to live in Butte, Montana, in 1904, was her "illness" peculiar only to her hometown? Might things have been different if she had run off with a traveling man to the lively and wicked city of Chicago? In how many closed little societies of the world do lonely people agonize over their own distinctiveness and wonder vainly whether there are others like themselves? They used to tell us that masturbation leads to mental illness. Was this so in an unexpected way—that guilt and lonely doubt, unrelieved by knowledge of others who were similar, led finally to changes in personality?

When the nature of one's distinctiveness could barely be mentioned but only whispered in shame to oneself, what tortured self-recriminations these isolated individuals must have known—the homosexuals, those with a taste for individualized adventures in sex, the drinkers and dopers, sometimes even the artists and political dissidents. And then the joy and freedom that became possible if they found a home in a more open and accepting community, or among others who were like them. How many of them were "cured" in just this way? Indeed, how much of what we are pleased to call neurosis in our own day might be healed, or at least bettered, if only the world stretched a bit to make room for those whose experience is different? I mean this not only in the narrow political sense of community mores changing toward being more open and accepting, but more importantly in the sense of a politics of personal identity. I am referring to the possibility that our individual neuroses are all too often the product of restricted acceptance on the part of those with whom we come in contact. By analogy with what happens when the neurotic finds a more accepting social setting, it can be argued that his split is also healed over whenever he meets a single other person who accepts him fully and makes no demands as to what he might or should be. Neurosis might then begin to be healed in the interpersonal arena.

There may be one other method for what I have called fitting in to one's setting; it consists simply of accepting the way things are, at whatever cost to the range or richness of one's experience. The neurotic split is healed over by so restricting experience that it no longer provides, for the person himself, a ground for inner tension. An example on a very large scale can be found in the German citizenry during the Nazi era. I think in particular of those who just happened to live in a village that was located next to a concentration camp. When the wind was right and the smoke from the crematoria, laden with the thick sweet stench of burning bodies, came their way at suppertime; when neat advertisements appeared in their local newspapers asking for temporary help at the ovens; when the camp guards came into town to spend an evening drinking beer and talking about their work, about the packed trainloads of Jews, already half-dead, who had been unloaded that day and dispatched by nightfall, their piles of clothes and gold teeth and pocket watches still to be sorted out and packed for shipment[20]—how was it then to sit and listen and even to think, to be a good father, a worthy citizen, a person of decency and moral standards and human feeling? Not to act when inaction means complicity is as shameful as any deed, even the worst. How did these villagers reconcile their inactive action with their own standards? Which way could they look when reality appeared to them in the glaring flames from the pits?

But I have no right to ask these questions. Whenever I allow myself to be a true citizen of the TV age I begin to glimpse in myself the ability somehow to live with horror. Not long ago thousands, perhaps hundreds of thousands, died and were finally buried on the coast of East Pakistan after a monstrous tidal wave swept over an entire colony. I see the report on TV and I think, with some slight irritation: If they want to show it on the news, they should at least save it for the late news and not show it at dinner time. This is how one does it, I find. Just this far is where my standards of decency extend; here are the boundaries of what I am fond of calling my citizenship of the world. At some point I choose simply not to get involved. I will suffer a split in myself thus far and no more—but I claim no honor for it. If I am accused, and rightly so, the split will show most clearly when I become defensive, and then angry, and finally closed off. Is this how we all do it?

### Easing up

My definition of the neurotic split implies that to be human is to experience the gap between what I am and what I might be. The message has been told and retold since Kierkegaard that our human experience consists of necessary but absolutely vain efforts to reach beyond ourselves. Our defining characteristic, and what distinguishes us from all other animals, is that we keep constructing systems that reach beyond where we are, and we then curse our finite bodies for keeping us from reaching as far as our systems extend. None of us would choose to give up imagination, yet it is imagination that provides me with the dream of being able to do and be more than I ever can in actuality; hence the split between what I am and what I might be. As long as I choose to be completely human, I am in the midst of becoming more than I am now; I stretch time, I reach for goals, I search out possibilities, and I set my sights on that unreachable place beyond where I can go. I not only go, I also venture; and so I may make discoveries, but I may also fall flat on my face. The image is a pratfall somewhere between heaven and hell.

My own accumulated experience teaches me that the world is not set up for me and my dreams. As I live, I learn bit by bit what the world is like—its unbridgeable rivers, its mountains too tall, its buildings that no one can push over, its people who do not know of me or don't give a damn, above all the demands and constraints and tugs it imposes on me; I think I know it well. And either because of my knowing or in spite of it, and between my own impossible dreaming and the world's unlikely fulfillment, I continue on, like everyone else, astride a gap. Reaching, blaming, sensing my own inner split, and even the anxiety and guilt that go along are all the necessary adjuncts of being and remaining typically human—that is, being and remaining able to sense beyond my immediate body experience. I am not an animal, though I share a body with animals; I am, to be precise about it, a dreamer trapped in the body of an animal, an apple coiled in the heart of a worm.

I am certainly not arguing here for a state of animal innocence or for its logical alternative, the human capacity to set up a distance from my body. Rather, given the way things are, I am suggesting the inevitability of a split within a creature so curiously and miraculously jointed. If I had the chance to rewrite the biblical legend of creation, I would not have man created as a kind of angel on earth, born especially to have dominion over the animals. No, I would tell of the angels and the animals who were created first and who then fought over which group should have dominion; and I could describe the compromise that was created so as to reconcile their differences and that was then left to shift for itself in a world actually made only for either the beasts or the angels.

But it does seem to me that although the split within is itself beyond our experiencing and therefore inevitable in a human sense, some of its burdens are less than productive. There may, then, be ways to ease up our continuing pressure on the split, perhaps to make our experience more productive and even more joyous. Here are three suggestions.

1. The gap that many persons sense within themselves is between what they are and what they feel they should be. In place of a split between their actuality and an ideal state, they substitute all the whips associated with a driving conscience. They are kept going by the split, but mostly by helping themselves to be driven, driven by a scourge whose face they can never see, by a whip wielded by an unknown hand always behind them. There is, then, no way for them ever to catch up, for they have no goal ahead to sense, only an urging, accusing, punishing

Fate behind them. What might they do? The simplest way is to drop the *Should*. In its place they can substitute *Might*—and so they may end up being pulled toward a possible, even if unrealizable goal. It is really a matter of cleansing a whole set of words from the vocabulary, all the duty words connected with *Should* and *Ought*. There need be no fear that this will leave them defenseless against the inner onslaughts of their depraved instincts, for these driven people have shifted too far from *I Want* to *I Won't*. If they are frightened at the prospect of reversing this shift, if they recoil from the possibility that they may then catch themselves heading toward what they might become by doing just what they want to do, then they are in fact just the ones who most need to try this step toward inner peace.

2. A second step may now be easier. Allow yourself some sin—not sin in the traditional sense of immoral behavior, but in the sense of neurosis, of a modern fall from grace. Whatever sin now appears, whatever gap between the real and the imagined is now experienced, let it be so. Today depressed, tomorrow perhaps more cheerful; this morning angry, later today rather lighthearted and pleasant; afraid at some times but brave and confident at others—it is a matter of allowing the sin, even of literally going into it and experiencing it to the full. For after all, why not? Why compound the sin by working to add guilt and anxiety on top of it? Why insist on being overly human and thence even more anxious over the split itself? A prayer is appropriate here: No one is perfect, no one is ever cured and adjusted and free of problems forever; therefore let me have at least the chance to be alive and human and perhaps to live in sin.

3. What is true of me is true of you and of everyone; there are no exceptions among us. Sin is the only universal—so why hide it? The world needs a great deal more sharing of its collective sin, a great deal less shameful hiding of it. Everyone who knows you—some of whom even love you—is probably willing to hear you out when you confess your own private, unique, and utterly individual version of our collective original sin. If you are really lucky those who love you will not try to help you, but only listen to you and hear you out. What they will be saying is that someone is there, listening to you as one more sinner, and allowing it all to hang out in front of both of you. If you seek out these persons, and then if you stand ready to do the same for them—my goodness, what a world this might turn out to be.

## FATAL CONSEQUENCES

### The Widening Split

In some persons neither character nor rebellion serves to keep the neurotic split from widening or the inwardly felt tension from becoming less and less bearable. No permanent way of easing its effect is available. One possible consequence is that at this point some part of the person's experience begins to recede. It disappears for him, falling back behind his own awareness, until finally the significance of that aspect of his experience is hidden even from himself. Part of the experience involved in the neurotic split is now hidden, and the tension is thereby eased—the price for this being, of course, that not all of his experience is now available to him. He will appear to himself, as well as to others, as significantly impoverished.

The name that Freud gave to this phenomenon when he first encountered it in the clinical session was *repression*. He made it into a central mechanism of the working personality, as perhaps it should be if it is conceived as a major device for everyday handling of the tensions involved in the neurotic split. But even this may not work to paper over a widening inner split. What happens then? It may be that no way out can be found, short of death. In a famous vignette, the poet Edward Arlington Robinson tells us of one kind of consequence:

> *Whenever Richard Cory went down town,*
> *We people on the pavement looked at him:*
> *He was a gentleman from sole to crown,*
> *Clean favored, and imperially slim.*
>
> *And he was always quietly arrayed,*
> *And he was always human when he talked;*
> *But still he fluttered pulses when he said,*
> *"Good morning," and he glittered when he walked.*
>
> *And he was rich—yes, richer than a king—*
> *And admirably schooled in every grace:*
> *In fine, we thought that he was everything*
> *To make us wish that we were in his place.*
>
> *So on we worked, and waited for the light,*
> *And went without the meat, and cursed the bread;*
> *And Richard Cory, one calm summer night,*
> *Went home and put a bullet through his head.*[21]

In many ways we are all Richard Corys, and so his case has all sorts of things to teach us. About lying, for example. This is the necessary basis for lying—that what I, the liar, experience inwardly is different from what I, the pretender, show in my outward behavior. Sartre has offered, for this reason, that man may be defined quite simply: He is the only creature who can lie. Lying has to be learned, however, and like acting—of which it is the extemporized form— some people have a knack for it. But everyone tries and keeps trying, no matter how amateurish is his attempt—the little child, for example, who knows that he just got into the jam, who tells his parents that he didn't just get into the jam, but who forgot to wipe the jam off his face. Part of his seen behavior cancels out the other part that carries the lie. Richard Cory did better, he was all of a piece; so no one ever guessed how great the strain between what he was inside and what he displayed to others. From seeing only his outer face, observers might have guessed that his inner experience coincided perfectly with his outer behavior, that he was just what he meant to be. What they never knew and never even imagined was that he experienced a continuing gap and teetered and straddled over it; and that it became a steadily widening spread, too great to bear, until finally only a bullet could reach across the span. No need to be surprised at him; he reminds us of all of us.

### Killer Boy
With the case of Richard Cory, we have come to the most extreme conse- quence of a neurotic split that cannot be healed over by any act short of death. Because these are extreme ways out, they are also so rare as to be of use only as case studies. With this qualification in mind, then, we may consider a rather lengthy example of a man whose final surcease from an unbearably widening split could be found only in a world destroyed.

*THE FACTS.* On August 2, 1966, there occurred a mass killing, unexpected and unpredicted as all such events are. It was hardly the first of its kind, how- ever; records of such journalistic wonders may be found as far back as one chooses to search. In modern times, there was the famous case of Hauptlehrer Wagner who, in September 1913, made a valiant attempt to wipe out all the males in the German village of Mülhausen. More recently, in 1949, a model adolescent (they are always model pupils, you will note) named Howard Unruh went on a shooting spree on the streets near his home in Camden, New Jersey, and killed a dozen people before he was apprehended. The pattern repeats itself with deadly accuracy: a nearly perfect person quite suddenly and inexplicably—and thus without any warning to those around him—cracks up completely. In one terrible moment he becomes precisely the opposite of what he had always seemed to be, and so when he starts to kill everyone is taken by surprise. He may slaughter a number of friends and strangers before he is stopped. It is certainly enough to make a person shiver. Why, if it could happen to him, it could happen to anyone— to my nearest and dearest family or friends, to all the good, kindly people I know, even (gulp) to me!

Now, does all this really make sense? I have, myself, no general theory of what makes people do what they do; perhaps indeed, no comprehensive theory is even possible, given the complexity of humans or given their freedom as a first principle. But of this much I am certain, as an article of faith—that what people do makes some kind of sense and that there are no completely random, totally unpredictable human events. Nor can the significant things that an indi- vidual does run counter to the sensible. Not only must people make sense, but they must make good sense, not stupid sense. Yet, so we are told, the only way to make sense out of the newspaper stories I have cited above is to buy—lock, stock, and barrel—a theory that turns these killers from attackers into victims. According to such a theory the killer may be the victim of something physical (in the case I will describe, the villain was thought to be a pecan-sized brain tumor) but more often he is thought to be the victim of overpowering instinctual urges, formerly buried deep in his unconscious, which suddenly break through weak ego defenses and precipitate his unexpected behavior.

The facts in the case are these: On the evening of August 1, 1966, Charles Joseph Whitman, a student at the University of Texas at Austin, spent some hours making preparations for his next day's activities while his wife was at her job as a telephone operator. Friends who visited him during the evening found him much more calm and relaxed than usual, for ordinarily he was a tense, driven, angry young man. After they left him he wrote a long note, then went across town to where his mother lived, killed her, came back and picked up his wife from work, took her home and killed her too, wrote some more notes, gathered together a truckful of supplies, went out and bought some camping equipment and a couple of guns, came home again and loaded his trunk, and then took it to the 300-foot-high tower at the center of the campus. He went up to the parapet on top, taking with him his supplies and armament, and on the way up killing a receptionist and two tourists visiting the tower. For over an hour he sprayed the campus with accurately aimed shots from a variety of weapons. His total of victims, before two policemen went up the tower elevator and shot him to death, was fourteen dead and thirty-one wounded.

What kind of person was it who had done such a monstrous thing? From his photographs we can tell a little: he was a blonde, husky, pleasant-looking adolescent, with very much the typical face and air of the star tackle of the football team.[22] He came from an upper-middle-class home in Florida. He had been a newsboy and a marine, an altar boy, and the youngest Eagle Scout in the history of American scouting. Indeed, a national magazine ran a picture of him standing in front of an altar, dressed in his Eagle Scout regalia—and surely one can't get much closer to heaven, not in this life. He was a hard worker, though perhaps rather perfectionist, a scoutmaster, a faithful husband, and nearly an A student, friendly and likeable. A neighbor of his in-laws said of him, "I loved him like a son." The all-American litany goes on and on, incredibly banal, impossibly true.

Some other material may also be relevant. About five months before these events, Whitman's father and mother had separated—not under the best of circumstances, one gathers, since the father had worked "like the devil," though unsuccessfully, to get her back. In full conformity with the American style of filial devotion, this model son's statement about them was that he resented and hated his "brutal" father but deeply loved his mother. What he actually did, however, was to imitate his father (who was a "fanatic" gun lover) by collecting guns and then using one of them to kill his mother. What is fact here and what is clinical fiction?

The boy's immediate reaction to his parents' separation, after he had gone to Florida and driven his mother back to Austin, was to quit school. He resigned from school, sold his books, and even told his wife that he was leaving her. His friends could not get him to talk about his decision or explain it, but his mind was finally changed by one of his instructors, an ex-marine whose description pins him down as a more sympathetic version of the elder Whitman. The instructor simply put his foot down and ordered the son to "stay on the job." He did.

Only a few weeks before the killings, and apparently at his wife's insistence, Whitman went to see the college psychiatrist. Although the reports on this visit are not too clear, the psychiatrist did say later that the boy "oozed hostility"— a phrase so unpleasant that one can gather that the doctor was genuinely impressed. The young man talked to him about going up on the tower and shooting some people, so he was asked to come back to see the psychiatrist a week later. He never kept this appointment.

*AN ANALYSIS.* Whitman's appearance to others—rather, his deportment, for that word fits him better—was nearly that of the unflawed, all-American lad. True, he liked guns a little too much, just like his father before him, but liking guns is an American trait and in many circles is considered the mark of a real man. True, he was a little too tough, a little too mean, especially to people weaker than he—for example, a friend whom he frightened out of trying to collect a small gambling debt, or his sweet wife whom he beat on occasion—but these may well have been the rough edges to an essentially good personality. Good points and bad points seem to have added up to a nearly perfect image. He had to work hard to preserve this status, and so he was a sweating and tense perfectionist in everything he did, but preserve it he did.

But it is an unreal status; that is the point we have to keep in mind. Perfection is an ideal, not a reality; and the all-American boy is an image, not an actuality. To live in terms of an image, as Charlie Whitman did, is not the same as behaving. Rather, it is acting in terms of an abstract notion of what ought to be. A lifetime of utter devotion to an image—religious dedication is our most familiar example—necessarily removes one from the practice of everyday life in the arena of social reality. And this is what I think best describes Charlie: his everyday comportment was not normal behavior, much less realizable behavior, but rather the mimicking of an unreal state.

What about his inner experience? Here we must do some guessing. A lot of the evidence helps us, however, since it points in the same direction. He seems to have been one of those people who never really knew himself. Perhaps he had no self to know. There are such persons. In the struggle to live without anxiety, they settle for less; and they do this by giving up one of the two sides that are needed to preserve the neurotic split. They give up knowing themselves from the inside, in the way that most of us are sure that we truly know ourselves, and finally they become resigned to knowing of themselves only in terms of labels for identifiable conditions. Ask such a person about himself, or even about someone for whom he might have some feeling, and his answer takes the form of a recital of the facts that might result from clinical scrutiny. Thus:

I'm a very compulsive person.

My wife has a lot of hostility, and sometimes it gets out of control.

According to my therapist, I have a severe phobia.

My diagnosis is personality disorder, passive-dependent type.

The recital becomes painfully, horribly empty when it refers to someone else. The man who can think of no more meaningful, necessary question about his own

## A FATHER'S REQUEST

Dear Dr. Schoenfeld: While my daughter was in college she took LSD 14 times and methedrine intravenously, 2 grams weekly, average dose. She is now 23 and has paranoid schizophrenia. (It's been two years since it was diagnosed.) I can't seem to get a straight answer from anyone anywhere, so I'm writing to you in hopes you can tell me:

1. Could her psychosis have been directly drug induced?
2. It appears she probably had a hereditary predisposition to schizophrenia, although her behavior and perception were essentially normal until she was 19 and started taking the drugs. If she did indeed have this predisposition, would it have evolved during her college years anyway, drug ingestion or not?
3. Or, had she not taken the drugs, would it have remained in its initial, latent phase?
4. If, indeed, the drugs were a contributing factor (which seems irrefutable) which one was it—LSD or Speed or both?

I would certainly appreciate any straight information you could give me. [A letter to a medical column in the newspaper]

daughter than "Would the predisposition have remained in its initial, latent phase if . . . ?" is telling us that his sorrow is not the result of grief but of lack of knowledge. Supply him with a diagnosis in which he can have confidence, and he will then rest content that his daughter's life has been satisfactorily accounted for. She is not to him a person but the carrier of a label.

If you live all your life in terms of an image of what you ought to be; if you have built into your system the model of a tough, gun-toting father who is unrelenting in his pressure on those weaker than he is; and if you are lucky enough to have it all pay off in conventional rewards; then the result will be that you will live a role but not a life. What will happen is that your experience, instead of developing an independent position in dialogue with your behavior, will end up simply trailing your behavior—that is, you will end up experiencing yourself not as you really are, but entirely in terms of the image you have of yourself. You will then have no self to get in touch with; the question of who you really are stays unanswered because you did not know how to ask it.

But it may not be quite as bad as it sounds. With a few breaks, and with some marketable abilities such as intelligence and determination and good health, you may even look like everyone's idea of a success. You may live out your life within the bubble of your own dream, never knowing that this was all there was, never realizing that the applause you kept hearing was only for your audience's fantasy because there never was anyone there on stage: you were a voice, a set of gestures, a shadow of a real person—to yourself and to everyone you met. You were a street-corner imitation of a movie star, that prototypic and wholly imagined leading character of the American dream.

My guess is that something like this describes the background of Charlie Whitman. But in his case it does not last. The reflection of himself begins to get flawed in the only mirror that he knows: the eyes of the world. Something real and unavoidable begins to seep into his closed-off experience—perhaps the profound shock of his parents' permanent separation, with its consequent demand that he has to declare which side he is on. His almost reflex response would have been that he loved his mom and hated his dad; what kind of all-American boy is it who doesn't love his mom? But this might well have been followed by the much weightier notion that he couldn't bring himself to be all that much against his father. Besides, if he had any hatred in him for his father, even in a confused sense, and maybe for his mother too, in a doubly confused sense, then he wasn't any altar boy angel after all, was he? Maybe he was a hater, maybe even a killer at heart—which was exactly what he tried to say to the ex-Marine professor, his only friend, the only one (he thought) who might have understood what was happening to him. Or maybe he wasn't meant to be the good, hard-working student, the devoted husband, so why not just quit school, leave his wife, and cut out?

Now the trap began to close. He was driven back into his old pattern by the professor, who acted just like Charlie's father: C'mon, boy, let's shape up there. More desperate now, he tried to tell the psychiatrist what was happening to him— that his experience was changing and allowing some sense of self to enter, but that this meant only a widening divergence from his image of his own behavior. He permitted some of his anger to appear as the outer expression of his inner experience, and he talked of his killer fantasies—but the psychiatrist didn't really listen. (Later, he said that a lot of students come in and make general statements like wanting to go up on the tower and shoot at strangers. You can't get excited over every patient.) No one understood, no one would listen, and he himself, who might have been his own last resort, had no training or background at all in listening to the voice of his own inner self. A rank amateur in knowing himself, and dismissed by his more experienced elders who might have helped him with some first lessons in becoming a real person, he may well have sensed an unbridgeable gap developing inside. His growing experience of himself was as a dangerous killer, on the model that his father had given him, though he had never been able to experience it in himself before; and his sense of himself remained the same, as a good boy who loved his wife and his mother—although in different ways, of course, as a good boy should. When the gap became too great and the strain unbearable, it could only be spanned by a bullet; and so Charlie Whitman might well have become one of the small army of Richard Corys.

What he did, instead, was to refashion his behavior so that it fitted his new experience. It is at this point in his career that tragedy mounts beyond tragedy. For in Charlie Whitman's case there were only the most minimal resources with which to construct a sense of self, a structure of experience within which he could continue to live. He could not, for example, arrive at the solution that is acceptable to many neurotics—to behave in conformity with accepted or ideal standards, but to carry on simultaneously a divergent experience compounded of wish and fantasy. He could not be a Walter Mitty, someone ordinary or even mean in actuality but a hero and villain on a vast, swashbuckling scale in the private realms of his own experiencing. He lacked too many of the resources for building and sustaining an inner world that he could call his own. And so the self that he began painfully to build may have been true for him—all the truth he was ever able to know—but horribly enough it was still a false creation, one more image in a life riddled like buckshot with images. All the truth that was left for him in the world lay in his experience, and so he changed his behavior to act in terms of what he now saw himself to be: the all-American boy turned killer. It brought him—as his friends noted on that last evening—the only peace he had ever known.

What it also brought him was the chance to act out his last role. As though he were reading the lines of a movie script, he carefully packed a footlocker with every needed item for a camping trip. The remembered TV commercials were omnipresent, as of course they have to be in a well-written script, and so he made sure to include among his supplies a quantity of Spam and some underarm deodorant. Equipped with all the things that (as it says here in the magazine ads) are indispensable for personal fulfillment, he then polished up his guns and took the truckload of stuff up to a spot he had himself picked out as ideal. It was the perfect place in which to spend a pleasant day shooting some helpless small game.

Even in his final moment of travail, I do not think that Charlie Whitman experienced himself as much different from the average American, well equipped with supplies of all sorts, who goes off on a shooting spree. I think he died happy. Even at the climactic instant when he convulsively tried to bring together the image that was his outer side and the confused sense of self that was his inner, he was only carrying out the kind of logic that had marked his whole life. In the note that he left—it finally turned into a long, rambling confession—he carefully requested that an autopsy be performed on him so as to determine, if possible, the pressures that had driven him to kill. There you have it—even at the ultimate moment of life, before the chosen moment of his own death, the question that stood out for him was the diagnostic one: What reasons can be assigned for the behavior I am now about to manifest? Even here, at the very last, he was not much more than a role to himself, a dual role composed of a pair of images endlessly reflecting each other back and forth.

*A FUNERAL ORATION.* He died swiftly and savagely, on a tower high above the campus. His shattered body was brought down and hustled into an ambulance, and no one stayed around to see it except the newspaper photographers taking the final pictures to finish out their stories. I do not know where or when he was buried, but it must have been with a minimum of publicity and an absence of well-wishers. He probably did not get a funeral oration—that final statement addressed as much to those gathered at the graveside as to the memory of the deceased himself. But surely he deserved one.

He seems to have been an extreme case, no doubt of it—but on sober second thought, was he all that unique or special? Oh, a little unique, perhaps. In very few persons would the objectification, the absolute mechanical hardening of self, have gone this far. Most people have some solid core of selfhood, some meaningful set of relations with others, to keep them together as persons. In very few would there come together that individual combination of elements that made Charlie a mass killer. But he was no more than an exaggeration of the norm, I think, not totally different. The world is filled with overfed scoutmasters, victims of the American dream. The best clue to Charlie Whitman's essential humanity, to how close he was to the heart of us all, dearly beloved, may be in the kind of statement made by some of his victims—those who were fortunate enough to have been merely wounded by his murderous sharpshooting. All these people had been going peacefully about their affairs on a sunny summer afternoon; all of them were innocent and unsuspecting, harming no one, when the bullets began to zing down and ricochet off the buildings. Who could be doing this to them? Some madman, that was it, some maniac who didn't know them but had chosen this time, this place, to live out his personal high tragedy—at the expense of their blood. They were struck, wounded, lay bleeding.

Now, what did they all say, quite spontaneously? "I'm not angry at him," they all said. "Oh, no, I just feel sorry for the poor man—because (some of them added, incomprehensibly) he must be sick, poor man."

This is a most remarkable statement for one person to make about another under such circumstances. Yet it appeared that all his victims said something like this—that is, those who lived long enough. They may have been wounded, frightened, bleeding, but they did not feel sorry for themselves, only for their attacker. How does one explain this Christlike forgiveness? The answer, I think, is that they too, just like Charlie himself, were trapped in a set of ideas and expectations about people, trapped and mired so deeply that even in this extreme moment they, no more than Charlie himself, could imagine a way out. For Charlie, the trap consisted of living totally through images of ideal personages; for them, his victims, the trap was to understand others, not as real persons, but in terms of diagnoses. Charlie himself was right on the mark when he used his last piece of paper to request an autopsy so as to arrive at a diagnosis for himself. The peace that his soul needed, that could be achieved only by being properly diagnosed and laid to rest in some knowable category, he found at last in the innocent, victimized statements by his victims when they said, to the last man, as the blood was wiped from their wounds, "Poor man, I'm not mad at him. He was sick." It takes a lifetime of special training to educate out of a human being the natural retaliatory reaction of rage or fear on being gunned down. Who does this job—our parents? Our schools?

# part
# four
# healing
# and
# helping

# chapter 7
# rules
# and
# roles
# of
# psychotherapy

One of the marks of an organized society is that subgroups within it become marked as different from the central, dominant group. I have referred to these as deviants, and I have said that society deals with them either by making them into Strangers—who are different but still a part of the larger group—or by causing them to declare themselves as Saints—who have chosen to be different. Increasingly, in our culture, both Strangers and Saints are defined in psychological terms, and the fact of their being different is considered to be caused by some defect or abnormality in their personalities.

In earlier chapters I have discussed a variety of selected and self-chosen deviants—women, lepers, Jews, madmen, drug addicts, homosexuals, and rebels. Together, they total much more than a majority of the population. However, there is one more category of "the different" that may be the most numerous of all, and, more important for our purposes here, whose origin and development have themselves been psychological phenomena. These are the deviants, either Strangers or Saints, whose status is known first of all to themselves. Whether or not they choose their state, what is certain is that they are the first to identify it. Mary MacLane is an example—and, significantly, her tortured confession was written long before the impact of Freud on our thinking. The expression "All but thee and me" may be no jest in regard to this group of deviants. To some

MARY MacLANE

BUTTE, MONTANA,
JANUARY 13, 1901

I of womankind and of nineteen years, will now begin to set down as full and frank a Portrayal as I am able of myself, Mary MacLane, for whom the world contains not a parallel.

I am convinced of this, for I am odd.

I am distinctly original innately and in development.

I have in me a quite unusual intensity of life.

I can feel.

I have a marvelous capacity for misery and for happiness.

I am broad-minded.

I am a genius.

I am a philosopher of my own good peripatetic school.

I care neither for right nor for wrong—my conscience is nil.

My brain is a conglomeration of aggressive versatility.

I have reached a truly wonderful state of miserable morbid unhappiness.

I know myself, oh, very well.

I have attained an egotism that is rare indeed.

I have gone into the deep shadows.

All this constitutes oddity. I find, therefore, that I am quite, quite odd.

I have hunted for even the suggestion of a parallel among the several hundred persons that I call acquaintances. But in vain. . . .[1] Along some lines I have gotten to the edge of the world. A step more and I fall off. I stand on the edge, and I suffer. . . .[2]

I have no particular thing to occupy me. I write every day. . . . But mostly I take walks far away in the open country.

Butte and its immediate vicinity present as ugly an outlook as one could wish to see. It is so ugly indeed that it is near the perfection of ugliness. . . .[3]

There's but a tiny step between the great and the little, the tender and the contemptuous, the sublime and the ridiculous, the aggressive and the humble, the paradise and the perdition.

And so it is between the genius and the fool.

I am a genius.

I am not prepared to say how many times I may overstep the finely-drawn line, or how many times I have already overstepped it. 'Tis a matter of small moment.

I have entered into certain things marvelously deep. I know things. . . . It is magnificent of me to have gotten so far, at the age of nineteen, with no training other than that of the sand and the barrenness. Magnificent—do you hear? . . .[4]

My soul goes blindly seeking, seeking, asking. Nothing answers. I cry out after some unknown Thing with all the strength of my being; every nerve and fiber in my young woman's-body and my young woman's-soul reaches and strains in anguished unrest. At times as I hurry over my sand and barrenness all my life's manifold passions culminate in utter rage and woe. Waves of intense, hopeless longing rush over me and envelop me round and round. My heart, my soul, my mind go wandering—wandering; ploughing their way through darkness with never a ray of light; groping with helpless hands; asking, longing, wanting things: pursued by a Demon of Unrest.

I shall go mad—I shall go mad, I say over and over to myself.[5]

---

degree at least, nearly all of us may suffer from a state that we each identify as different, a little odd, sometimes out of control, and often markedly unpleasant.

The name that we give to this state is *neurosis*. In the preceding chapter I defined it in experiential terms; in this chapter I want to argue the proposition that neurosis is a discovery of the modern age—a period extending back no farther than a few centuries—and then I want to discuss the general structure of the activity known as *psychotherapy*, which was invented in order to deal with neurosis.

## THE DISCOVERY OF NEUROSIS

Edgar Friedenberg, in his usual lucid manner, provides the starting point for this topic.[6] He notes that it is "paradoxical" that until the beginning of the twentieth century there existed no "effective institutional form" for the function of psychotherapy. He adds: "I am not talking about technical theoretical limitations at all—that is another matter—but about the absence from earlier cultures of a conception of the *kind* of help a psychotherapist gives. . . ."

To illustrate, Friedenberg gives the following example:

*Once there were two very wealthy and influential English people—man and daughter—who were very seriously disturbed. They were given to fantasies of grandeur and persecution, during which they perpetrated acts of egregious cruelty on those who had been closest to them. . . . Their sexual lives were dreadfully impaired, although in contrasting ways. They were often miserable themselves; and before Henry and Elizabeth died, and the Tudor line with them, they had completely altered the social fabric of the world in which they lived—whether for good or ill, indubitably for neurotic reasons.*

By modern standards, then, these two monarchs were severely neurotic. Yet, as Friedenberg points out, although they surely had access to the best medical treatment available at the time their realm had no resources at all for helping them. More than that, their society had no conception, no vocabulary, no means whatever by which to state their difficulties in the terms familiar to every layman today: that they were very neurotic or emotionally disturbed, and that they should have gone to someone for help with "their problems."

In concluding his discussion of Henry VIII and his daughter Queen Elizabeth, Friedenberg has this to suggest about what was lacking in the culture and the thinking of their day:

*When Elizabeth was physically ill she could call a physician. He would come to her with virtually none of the resources available to his modern counterpart, but with an identical purpose. The conception of the physician and his function were there for her to use. Similarly, if Henry had wanted to go up to Hampton Court from Westminster, he could get in a boat and be taken there. His court could not have conceived of British Railways, but it could conceive of transportation. . . . It had no idea, however, that the things Henry felt and did were related in such a way as to require a kind of expert help if his life and theirs were to be spared; and it had no provision at all for such offices. It had provision for dealing with madmen, of course, but a man who murders his friends, his wife, destroys churches, and starts civil war is not necessarily mad. He is, however, in some kind of bad trouble; and by the time of Sigmund Freud western culture was about ready to establish an administrative basis on which such trouble could be recognized and dealt with.*[7]

Before it was possible to establish this administrative basis that we call psychotherapy today, a change was required in the collective experience of Western society. Only a few hundred years ago it would not have been possible for even the most intelligent or privileged person to say, "There is something wrong with me as a person, something about myself and my attitudes and feelings and experience that I'm not happy about. I don't like it, and I would very much like to do something to change it." Many people manage to say something like this today, either to themselves or to someone close to them. Indeed, thinking along these lines, and saying something like this, is today almost the identifying characteristic of the critical period we call adolescence.

It is difficult for us to imagine an era so different that the statement above would have, quite literally, been meaningless to adults of that time. Yet such great changes in consciousness do occur in the course of history. Our modern notion of romantic love, to take one example, goes back no farther than to the troubadours of the early Renaissance. Seeing Nature as beautiful is a recent kind of sensibility, no more than four hundred years old, as are such conceptions as national pride or a love of the sea as a source of health and good feeling. For an impressive set of examples, look at the list of concepts that Logan Pearsall Smith has traced back a few centuries through changes in the meaning and use of words.

---

### THE WORD AND THE THING

If we were given what purported to be a transcript of a medieval manuscript, and should find in it words like ENLIGHTENMENT or SCEPTICISM, we should not hesitate to pronounce it a glaring and absurd forgery; and we should reject with equal promptness a pretended Elizabethan play in which we came upon such phrases as an EXCITING EVENT, an INTERESTING PERSONALITY, or found the characters speaking of their FEELINGS. . . .[8] This curious sense of the dates of words, or rather of the ideas that they express, comes to us from our knowledge, grown half-instinctive, of the ways of thought dominant in different epochs, the "mental atmosphere," as we call it, which made certain thoughts current and possible, and others impossible at this time or that. . . .[9]

It is a commonplace to say that the dominant conception of modern times is that of science, of immutable law and order in the material universe. . . .[10] But if we study the vocabulary of science, the words by which its fundamental thoughts are expressed, we shall find that the greater part of them are not to be found in the English language a few centuries ago; or if they did exist, that they were used of religious institutions or human affairs; and that their transference to natural phenomena has been very gradual and late. ORDER is, indeed, a very old word in English, and appears in the XIIIth Century in reference to monastic orders, and the heavenly hierarchy . . . of Christian theology. It acquires some notion of fixed arrangement in the XIVth Century, but it is not till the XVIth Century that its derivatives ORDERLINESS and ORDERLY are found. ORDERED meant "in holy orders" till this period, when we also find the noun DISORDER. . . .[11] The verb to ARRANGE is an old word, and was used like ARRAY in a military sense; but it does not appear in Shakespeare or the Bible,[12] and did not acquire its present meaning until the XVIIIth Century, at which time ARRANGEMENT is also found. . . .[13]

Partly produced by this sense of law and order in nature, and probably still more the cause of it, we notice also, at this time, a great increase in the vocabulary of observation. Speaking generally, the names of the abstract reasoning processes—REASON, COGITATION, INTUITION, etc., belong to the Middle Ages, while those which describe the investigation of natural phenomena belong to the modern epoch, or only acquire, at that time, their present meaning and their popular use. To OBSERVE meant to obey a rule, or to inspect auguries for the purpose of divination, until the XVIth Century, when it acquired the meaning of examination of phenomena. . . .[14] We may also note that while words expressing belief—CERTAINTY, ASSURANCE, CREDENCE, etc., are generally old in the language, those that suggest doubt, questioning, and criticism, almost all belong to the modern period. DOUBT is, of course, an old theological word, and DOUBTFUL appears in the XIVth Century; but DOUBTFULNESS, DUBIOUS, DUBIOUSNESS, DUBITABLE, with SCEPTIC, SCEPTICAL, SCEPTICISM, are of modern formation. . . .[15]

The great pioneers of the Renaissance discovered not only the world of natural phenomena, but another world, equally vast and varied and new—the world of man. . . .[16] Probably to each of us the sense of his own personality, the knowledge that he exists and thinks and feels, is the ultimate and fundamental fact of life. But this sense of personality, of the existence of men as separate individuals, is one of the latest developments of human thought. Man in early societies is not thought of as an individual, and there are savage languages that possess no word for "I" or for the conception of "myself." . . .[17] The EGO, with EGOISM, are terms introduced by French philosophers in the XVIIth Century, and EGOTISM is another French term. These were borrowed at various periods; EGOTISM, which is used by Addison, being the first to appear in English, while EGOTISTICAL belongs to the XIXth Century. But before this the old word SELF, like a germ that finds a soil and atmosphere favourable to its multiplication, began to form compounds in enormous quantities. SELF-LIKING, SELF-LOVE, SELF-CONCEIT, SELF-ASSURANCE, SELF-REGARD, SELF-DESTRUCTION, SELF-MURDER, belong to the later part of the XVIth Century, and these are followed in the next hundred years by SELF-CONTEMPT, SELF-APPLAUSE, SELF-CONFIDENCE. . . .[18] SELFISH and SELFISHNESS are Puritan words, formed by the Presbyterians about 1640, to express a vague notion for which the older SELF-LOVE was too vague, and PHILAUTY from the Greek and SUICISM from the Latin, too pedantic for popular acceptance, though both of them were tried. . . .[19]

But the study of human nature can be pursued from two points of view; we may observe our fellow-men and their ways and characters; or we may turn within and study our own selves. "Know thyself" was an exhortation inherited from antiquity, but its complete realization has only been accomplished in modern times. Speaking generally, we may say that the men of the Renaissance devoted their minds to observing their fellow human beings; and that men did not turn to the study of themselves, the second great chapter in the book of life, until more than a century had passed. . . .[20] This can be well seen in the history of the word CONSCIOUS and its derivatives. CONSCIOUS was borrowed from the Latin poets in the time of Shakespeare, with the sense of sharing knowledge with another, and was used of inanimate things, as Milton's CONSCIOUS NIGHT. . . .[21] It was used by Locke of thoughts and feelings, and finds its full extension and definition early in the XVIIIth Century, when we read of "conscious beings." CONSCIOUSNESS, first found in 1632, attained its philosophical definition late in the XVIIth Century, when it was described by Locke as "perception of what passes in a man's own mind." To Locke also we owe the use of the compound SELF-CONSCIOUSNESS. . . .[22] SELF-KNOWLEDGE, SELF-EXAMINATION, SELF-PITY, and SELF-CONTEMPT belong to the "self" words of the XVIIth Century, and with them appear a swarm of what we may call "introspective" words—words that describe moods and feelings, as seen from within, as part of our own inner experience. The older kind of names for human passions and feelings we may call "objective," that is to say, they are observed from outside, and named by their effects and moral consequences.[23]

---

The use of words to talk about oneself and others is like the art of painting: words, like portraits, may simply record what appears—as both did until the sixteenth century—or they may describe and analyze as well, as they have done only for the past few hundred years.[24]

In no other area has the change in collective experience been greater than in how people have thought about themselves and each other. In a fascinating exercise on this theme, Bernard Rosenthal has recently speculated on what other eras, each with its own guiding "image," might have done with the modern intelligence test or with current approaches to the analysis of group behavior.[25] His conclusions point up to an almost embarrassing degree how parochial are the values of contemporary psychology, how tightly bound to a conceptual climate that has come about only within the past few centuries. Indeed, this very notion that differences in culture and in human behavior result in part from differences in environmental conditions—the seemingly self-evident notion that I need here in order to pursue the thread of my argument—itself seems to go back only as far as the eighteenth-century essayist Montesquieu.

The Middle Ages came to an end when man was able to say to God, in effect, "Well, see you around. Take care." Saying this was the first step toward the conceptual climate that determines our contemporary thinking—a climate based on the conviction that every doubt and every distress can be restated as a problem and so can be solved by man; a climate resting on a natural science framework that applies even to what people think and want to do; and, most important, a climate colored by an acute self-consciousness over the climate itself. It was a brave first step to take; man was now thrown back completely on himself. He had no choice but to build a sense of himself, one such unique sense for each individual, who in the last resort had to do it alone.

Issues unknown in previous ages now became critical for the person. Once the individual citizen gave up the confining but comforting medieval notion of himself as a pawn in God's hands, once he became engaged in building a sense of himself, he faced the choice of developing a self with which he might be comfortable, or a self with which he felt in conflict, or of denying selfhood to himself. In many ways, as the history of consciousness teaches us, the modern self is God made inner; this is the blessed and accursed position to which modern man has driven himself.

### Myself in History

The phenomenon to which I am referring here is *myself*, my own grasp of me by me. There is no way of telling whether previous centuries possessed this concept or were capable of this experience; that is, whether people thought of themselves in the same sense that we do today. But what is clear from what they wrote down is that they had no vocabulary by which to address themselves. This is the point that was implied in the excerpts from Smith quoted above. There were certainly individuals who were unhappy, and they were often so described in the literature of the day, but the description was at best a reference to the individual's behavior, perhaps to his situation, sometimes even to his state at the moment. What is not to be found in any of the literature before the eighteenth century is the direct expression of an individual's grasp of his own self. Shakespeare provides all sorts of examples; *Hamlet* is probably the most familiar.

There is no denying that Hamlet himself and the other characters in the play show an amazing sensitivity to nuances of expression in others; Hamlet says to Guildenstern, "There is a kind of confession in your looks, which your modesties have not craft enough to colour" (act 2, sc. 2), and Ophelia remarks about Hamlet, "He seem'd to find his way without his eyes" (act 2, sc. 1). Like all of Shakespeare's plays, *Hamlet* is crammed with indicators of a wonderfully subtle sense of the complexity revealed in externals. But that is just the point. On closer examination, it turns out that the target of this perceptiveness is either an external manifestation or else something internal that is described as though it were an external object. Thus, the queen: "O Hamlet, speak no more: / Thou turn'st mine eyes into my very soul; / And there I see such black and grained spots . . ." (act 3, sc. 4). Hamlet's famous line is similar: "But thou wouldst not think how ill all's here about my heart" (act 5, sc. 2).

It does not seem to have been the concept itself to which Shakespeare lacked access. That he could grasp the idea of a self is quite clear from the well-known advice given by Polonius: ". . . to thine own self be true; / And it must follow, as the night the day, / Thou canst not then be false to any man" (act 1, sc. 3). Nor is it that Shakespeare's characters were unable to refer to themselves as unique individuals and even to tell others about themselves, as Hamlet does very effectively: "I am myself indifferent honest; but yet I could accuse me of such things, that it were better my mother had not borne me . . . What should such fellows as I do crawling between earth and heaven? We are arrant knaves, all; believe none of us" (act 3, sc. 1).

If Shakespeare was able to make his characters talk about themselves; and if he was aware of a self to which someone might be true rather than false; if he could, in addition, have the king say, in reference to Hamlet's change of manner, ". . . nor th' exterior nor the inward man / Resembles that it was" (act 2, sc. 2); does all this not add up to a very contemporary sense of self? My point is that it does not; that with all his genius, Shakespeare had no true vocabulary of the self, and that he was always compelled to fall back on the words, the phrasings, the sensibility appropriate to an outsider's grasp of a sufferer's inner life. A contemporary poet, Archibald MacLeish, in the 1920s composed his own Shakespearean drama, *The Hamlet of A. MacLeish*, and his wording suggests the difference:

> *It is always the same. It is always as though some*
> *Smell of leaves had made me not quite remember;*
> *As though I had turned to look and there were no one.*
> *It has always been secret like that with me.*
> *Always something has not been said.*[26]

The suffering is there in both works, and MacLeish is not more distressed than Hamlet was—but no form was available to Shakespeare to get hold of that inner pain, as the contemporary poetic image was available to MacLeish. All that Hamlet could do was talk movingly about himself; he had no key to open himself to himself in spite of all of Shakespeare's brilliance in knowing about it. With all his seeming ability to probe into what he presents to others, the Shakespearean character is not able to assign his distress to an internal locus.

The phenomenon of *myself* took a number of centuries to develop; it is understood today in varying degrees by different groups in our culture. It was conditioned by history; now it is conditioned by group and by situation. In Melvin Kohn's recent study of middle-class families, for example, comparing them with lower-class families of the same (either Italian or northern European) background uncovered significant differences in ways of valuing oneself.[27] For middle-class persons, what is attended to and valued is what is inner; whereas for lower-class persons, what is outer, what belongs to society and its norms, is what is valued. The difference as far as the parents were concerned—a difference that was reflected in what they taught their children—is between *myself* as a source

---

A few years ago I shared a six-month experience with a black cotherapist: we were coleaders of an encounter group composed of ten black and ten white college undergraduates. Half the group was female and half male. The differences were evident at the first meeting, and in time they made it impossible for the group to fulfill the function that the leaders had envisioned. The simplest way of stating the difference which divided the blacks from the whites is that for the blacks what was important, what was to be attended to and valued, was the way the world "out there" was organized. Their interest was almost exclusively in the influence of the world, of society, on them as persons, and on what they might do to change that influence for the better. They had virtually no interest in looking into themselves, in contemplating their selves in the way that we, as therapists, would have wanted them to do.

Only the whites were ready and willing to do this; they had joined the group for just this purpose, to confront their own selves, their anxious, guilt-ridden selves. The result was six months of maneuvering over whether we should start "encountering."

---

of personal values, for middle-class persons, and *myself* as a reflection of society's values, for lower-class persons. I suspect that a very similar distinction gave rise to the difficulties I had in the black-white encounter group. As Goffman remarked in reference to differences in seeing oneself as a candidate for psychotherapy, "subcultures in American society apparently differ in the amount of ready imagery and encouragement they supply for such self-views, leading to differential rates of self-referral; the capacity to take this disintegrative view of oneself without psychiatric prompting seems to be one of the questionable cultural privileges of the upper classes."[28]

### The Shattered Self

The discovery of *myself* may be viewed in different ways. It will provide anyone who is willing the opportunity—painful, but finally rewarding—to explore the inner world that is his alone. If he wishes to get on with the guided inner struggle, the modern person need not be as incapacitated for self-improvement as were, say, Henry VIII and his daughter Elizabeth. If there are, as we all suspect, so many of us who could stand a serious self-exploration and self-improvement, then the modern discovery and naming of this fault is surely a needed first step.

But, to look at it another way, there is a price that has to be paid by each one of us in order to know the self. With all its attendant glory, the modern sense of self carries along with it a secret knowledge that harries the person from within. Perhaps it is because the self, as I am tempted to argue, can be considered

---

THE SELF AS GARBAGE

Neurosis, the self, anxiety, psychotherapy—all these appurtenances of our modern age—are merely inventions of modern man. They are not at all necessary aspects of being human. Modern man equipped with them is a curious creature: an idiot child sitting on the potty of history. His greatest achievement may well be the belated recognition of his own downfall. His self-knowledge burns inside him, for the self fits his life

in a peculiar way; it is a kind of psychic garbage.

I mean by this that man, uniquely in all the range of living creatures, seems to produce a garbage that he is not naturally equipped to live with or dispose of. In infancy and early childhood he has to be carefully taught to do what the puppy does naturally—to excrete his waste in some place over there where it is out of the way. When he grows up, he refuses to accept the fact that when all the "over theres" are filled up, there will be no place for his garbage; and so he had better change his diet and his habits so that the waste he produces can be recycled back into nature. As a cultural phenomenon, modern man has created a new source of what can only be called garbage, for it has no natural place in human experience: it is an excrescence on the biological organism; a burning sense of self that haunts him and will not let him rest until he has agonized beyond all justification.

After five thousand years, modern Adam and modern Eve can look back at Eden and say, "So that's why we were thrown out. This is what God meant when he said we had eaten of the Tree of Knowledge. And this is why we were cast out when all we did was look at our own bodies and know them as naked." Self. That was the discovery they made in the Garden of Eden. For the serpent's secret was simple: as long as you remain innocent and natural, totally unself, you may stay here forever—but the moment you reach for the knowledge that comes only in the guise of looking at Self, then you become human; then you are condemned to live in the world and in the end, to befoul the world.

---

a kind of psychic garbage. Or perhaps it is that the owner of a modern self finds that he interposes between his experience and his world an entity that is neither true experience nor true behavior, but a third category: a category of knowing about experience and behavior, becoming concerned, and then passing judgment. Thus, modern man is distinguished by his ability to be anxious; to be concerned with himself; to judge himself and very often find himself wanting. He distrusts what he himself does or thinks or feels, and he may even become convinced that he is not real but phony, not true to himself but playing a role without being able to help it. All these lapses from grace are indicators of the possibilities opened up for the owner of the modern self. No other century deserved to be called an age of anxiety—though this may be small comfort to those who might prefer a simpler time when one was merely unhappy.[29]

It has not escaped the notice of some contemporary writers that our collective condition today is in some ways the counterpart of a state known to many persons in a more religious era. Poised as he was just midway between the angels and the beasts, man might look to the one for his higher aims and to the other for his lower drives, but always in the knowledge that resolving the conflict between the two was his own responsibility as a creature endowed by God with reason. If he failed or fell short of what God intended for him, he was in Sin; he was damned and headed for hell—or this at least was what the faithful believed and therefore held as a guide for their conduct. The difference between then and now is that in our time one falls short of what the self might be; one invents one's own personal hell; one plucks the guide out of heaven and installs it in the inward being. Thus, as O. H. Mowrer puts it, "Hell is still very much with us in these states of mind and being which we call neurosis and psychosis; and I have come increasingly, at least in my own mind, to identify anything that carries toward these forms of perdition as *sin*."[30]

Mowrer draws an interesting, if somewhat extreme, practical conclusion from this line of thought. If neurotic difficulties can be equated with sin, then recovery becomes the equivalent of redemption. How does one become assured of redemption? By confessing one's sins, of course—that is, by accepting them in oneself.

*Just so long as a person lives under the shadow of real, unacknowledged, and unexpiated guilt, he cannot (if he has any character at all) "accept himself"; and all our efforts to reassure and accept him will avail nothing. He will continue to hate himself and to suffer the inevitable consequences of self-hatred. But the moment he (with or without "assistance") begins to accept his guilt and his sinfulness, the possibility of radical reformation opens up; and with this, the individual may legitimately, though not without pain and effort, pass from deep, pervasive self-rejection and self-torture to a new freedom, of self-respect and peace.*[31]

This may be perfectly apt in regard to contemporary neurotics whose concern is identified as guilt and self-hatred; here Mowrer is on solid ground. The weakness in his position is in restricting the self in neurosis to this one role, when it has many more possibilities, on many dimensions—from love to hate, from tortured self-knowledge to bland unknowing, from anxiety to all the forms of its denial. There are many paths down in the fall from grace. One of the consequences, as we shall now see, is that patience and ingenuity and concern have made it possible to point out an equal number of paths back up.

### The Invention of Psychotherapy

It is very difficult for someone born in this century to grasp the full impact on nineteenth-century thinking of the contributions of its troika of revolutionary thinkers—Darwin, Marx, and Freud. Over the course of the preceding two hundred years a groundwork had been laid in the form of the slow erosion of medieval thinking. By the beginning of the nineteenth century it was generally conceded among educated persons that the form and behavior of living organisms, whether trees or insects, fishes or even men, could not be understood as merely the working out of a divine purpose. Whatever additional explanation was needed had to be sought in the organisms themselves or in their interaction with their material environment; it was not to be sought in some force imposed on them from outside their material universe. If the world of nature consisted of a great variety of living things, each somehow developing and maintaining itself on its own unique terms in a complex pattern of survival among different types, the explanation of how this elaborate arrangement came about had to be sought within nature itself. This was the problem to which Darwin addressed himself. Similarly, if the social world of man consisted of a wide range of institutions, organizations, societies, and appropriate forms of behavior, the explanation of how all this developed had to be found not in a divinely ordered scheme that assigned every man to his place but in the very history of social institutions. Karl Marx took this problem as his life work.

On his part, Freud undertook to explain the behavior and development of the individual, his accomplishments and his troubles, all in the same naturalistic terms, without recourse to causes that were neither biological nor social. His idol was Hermann von Helmholtz, a physicist and physiologist who founded modern sensory psychology. Freud's first full-scale system was in the form of a neuro-physiological model of the psychic apparatus. His lifetime dream was to establish firm links between the basic forces of the instincts and man's biological nature. His goal, in short, was a science among the other sciences.

This was even more true, of course, for the other makers of modern psychology, from Wilhelm Wundt to B. F. Skinner—all devotedly patterning their work after the model of the natural sciences. But Freud's task was different; his material was found under different conditions and was not so easily molded into the aspect of a collection of things. Throughout the four productive decades of his career there runs the continuing compromise that he was forced to accept, between a set of data demanding a personal psychology of experience and a set of methodological principles requiring a science of facts and things. The subsequent history of psychotherapy, as we shall see, is in many ways an expression of the compromises he devised and of their fate in a changing world.

Psychotherapy was invented as a means to help individual selves accommodate to their experience: truly, once neurosis was discovered, psychotherapy had to be invented. Each of these led to the creation of its characteristic role. Neurosis was represented in the psychotherapy patient; his counterpart in the role of therapist was the Freudian psychoanalyst—and it is interesting to note in how many ways they were mirror images. The patient appeared in an astonishing variety of roles and parts, often displaying a dazzling talent at quick-change artistry within one treatment program. He was tragically human, victim of every existential fault, helpless and stumbling, and often blind to his own weaknesses. The analyst, by contrast, was far less human, less real, much more the ideal figure of a child's dreams—calm and noble and knowing, complete master of this great new engine called Self. And so the very first rules of the game arose from this mirror contrast between the roles. These were the rules that specified, in myriad forms, that only one of the two was to hold power in their exchanges. Only the therapist had a title, a position, a place in the world, an office, a schedule—to all of this the nearly anonymous patient came, fitting in his time and his schedule as best he could, to bring his troubled self to the doctor's office and there be told what he should now do. For all its claims to being a part of a science, psychotherapy was from its very beginning a specific form of human interchange. The model that it took, in part because Freud had been so strongly influenced by his visits to Jean Martin Charcot in Paris, was that of the healer face to face with his afflicted brother.

The profession that has taken over a healing role from the priesthood is, as we all know, medicine. It is this, rather than the simple fact that Freud was a physician, which made it almost inevitable that Freud's work should be modeled on medical theory and practice. Other alternatives were available and perhaps equally sensible—the model of the priesthood and its confessional; the model of the experimental laboratory with its researcher and subject; and certainly the model of the classroom or tutorial with its teacher and student. Any of these alternatives would have been as appropriate, considering the nature of Freud's material, but since medicine is the healing profession par excellence, its forms immediately became the framework for psychotherapy, and remained so for more than half a century. The results make for an interesting story.

## THE MEDICAL MODEL

I am concerned here with what might be called the sociology of medical practice. In every society there have been gifted and learned persons who could be called upon to cure their fellows of distress; the story of their successes can be found in any history of medicine. They were not always the most respected of practitioners. In classical Rome a good reader of entrails probably earned more respect, and for many centuries the difficult craft of surgery was coupled with barbering. While physicians in ancient societies were often only clever slaves, the profession of priest was reserved to the highborn or the specially appointed, for it held by far the highest status. It has, in fact, only been during the past century or so that the medical profession has come to take over from the priesthood all the marks of status and importance in society. Today's doctor is a secular priest—in white robes instead of black, fingering a stethoscope in place of his beads or cross, but still the only one professionally able to give or take life.

The first major characteristic of such a profession is that it occupies a position of superior status and that both its practitioners and their clients are aware of the gap in status between them. This is not simply a matter of social prestige—that the profession is considered a desirable one and that those in it are highly respected and usually make a lot of money. The status of the physician is even more evident in his relation to his patients. Like all professionals—and this is one of the elements of professionalization—he maintains a place to which his clients come like supplicants to an oracle, although in fact he is selling chiefly a service and therefore might just as well travel around to see them. In addition, he dresses in the clothes befitting his office; he is addressed by title rather than by name; and his decisions are neither to be questioned nor disobeyed. Long years of training and strict accreditation are requisite for acceptance into this fraternity—and where professionalization flourishes in the extreme, as in the United States, degrees of membership in the fraternity are also regulated by law. These laws are ostensibly passed to protect the client, but as anyone knows who has tried to mount a serious complaint against a professional society, the basic purpose of the laws is more probably to protect the professionals themselves, by restricting membership to those whom they approve.

These matters might be of interest only to students of the history of medicine—except for the fact that they have also influenced many aspects of psychotherapy, its theory as well as its practice. The most obvious of these aspects is the professionalization that has always marked the practice of therapy. Its practitioners have either been physicians or acted like physicians, with all the appropriate role indicators, from internships during graduate training to office arrangements on setting up a practice. Closer to the heart of the matter is the concept of *illness*, which has dominated both theory and practice in psychotherapy. The terminology is always related to illness: doctor and patient, diagnosis, symptoms, treatment, prognosis, and cure. The theory of illness, with its presuppositions in medicine, determines what goes on between the two participants. The doctor, who is free of the illness in question, receives his patient, who carries within him the illness; and by the use of appropriately timed treatment measures, given to the patient during the course of his continuous treatment, the latter is changed from a sick person to a well person; and all this without any significant change occurring in the doctor.

This concept of illness clearly belongs within a pragmatic, reason-oriented culture. Only in such a culture could there have been created and given great prestige a role so marked by its impersonality, its untouchability. The doctor is the scientist at his noble best—dealing every day with the most frightening and messiest of human dangers but remaining, in theory at least, untouched, rational, Olympian. One writer has summed up this role by contrasting it with another: "To Western man, illness is an impersonal event brought about by neutral, non-emotional, natural agents, such as germs, while for the Mexican-American, illness relates to an individual's life, his community, his interpersonal relationships, and, above all, to his God. In such a culture, illness is a social as well as a biological fact."[32] As a consequence, he adds:

*The Mexican-American, who is more fatalistic and accepting of his lot, is not initially as receptive to the goals of psychotherapy. The Mexican-American attitude has usually been one of heroic defiance or of passive resignation to fate, in contrast to the trust in reason and the mastery of nature which has characterized the Americans. The Mexican-American is often willing to accept fluctuating states of health and the vagaries of life as inevitable or as the will of God, not as a difficulty within him which requires personal change.[33]*

Other consequences of the illness concept inevitably follow. For one, the patient's state is understood as a kind of possession; he is perceived, and then dealt with, as though an alien influence had entered him and produced certain observable signs that are called symptoms. The nature of this influence has changed through the centuries as medicine became more firmly grounded in an efficacious natural science, but the principle has remained unchanged: what used to be called evil spirits, and later was called the devil, is now seen more realistically as an infectious state caused by germs. However, the inner influence itself is never seen; that is part of the guiding principle. What is seen is what the influence produces—a fever, a rash, a pain, a swelling, a coma. The logical consequence of this reasoning is that the doctor's task becomes, first, to identify the symptom; second, to relate it to an appropriate causative influence; and finally, triumphantly, to exorcise the influence. It follows, in addition, that to alter or eliminate only the symptom would be a waste of effort and a confession of professional ignorance as well, for the influence would then simply recur in another form. Thus, aspirin may provide prompt, temporary relief for the pain of headache; this the label brightly promises. But then it adds darkly, but if the pain persists, consult your physician; for this is an indication that an influence is at work causing the damage that has only been suppressed by the palliative, nonprofessional medication.

Much of the doctor's training consists of learning to reason backward from evident symptom to probable influencing cause. The process is called *diagnosis*, and it is of crucial importance for the simple reason that treatment modalities are related to types of causes rather than types of symptoms. For example, a headache might turn out to be caused on the one hand by the need for corrective glasses, or on the other hand by a brain tumor; the presenting symptom is the same in both cases, but the treatment requirements should differ if the patient is to benefit. In effect, the process of diagnosis consists of organizing the array of observable symptoms, a step that must also include ferreting out symptoms that are not immediately evident, and then using the organization of symptoms to identify an underlying cause and so assign the patient to the class of persons suffering from that cause.

Physicians used to deal primarily with physically measurable causes; when they were unable to relate a collection of symptoms to any known influence, they often dismissed the patient's complaint as "only psychological"—meaning that other, nonphysical and probably obscure causative factors were operating that were outside the true doctor's province. More recently, physicians have been taught that in the majority of complaints brought to their offices they will find that a psychological influence is usually coupled with a physical influence and that they had better be alert to both parts of this more complex set of causes. Even with this more sophisticated extension of the doctor's theory of illness, nothing of significance has changed; the basic structure of overt symptom and covert influence remains, together with the practice of diagnosis that reads out the latter from the former.

All of these essential characteristics of the medical model were carried over unchanged when psychoanalysis was developed as a theory and then gave rise to psychotherapy as a profession. Freud's patients came to him originally with problems that in no way resembled conventional illnesses; indeed, they came to him in many cases because their conditions were clearly not medical or had proved recalcitrant to medical treatment. The speculation current in the clinics of Europe during the 1880s and 1890s, in fact, revolved largely around these strange conditions for which the term *hysteria* was usually reserved; they were conditions without a demonstrable physical cause that still resulted in medical-like symptoms. Today we would call these conditions neuroses. But what I have been maintaining thus far is that the neurotic condition is a discovery of modern man and woman, and is in fact specifically a discovery on the part of citizens of the modern world who are capable of inner complexity in the form of a self. Freud's first patients were middle-class people, sophisticated, relatively liberated from conventional moral and religious restrictions. They were afflicted, in fact, with troubles that signaled their entry into the modern world, and being the kind of persons they were they could hardly take their troubles to their family ministers or priests. Physicians were the next most likely candidates to help them; and by this route some of them came finally to Freud. Because he saw himself as a physician-healer, and because his patients saw themselves as coming to a physician, their conditions were perforce translated into those that fitted a medical model. The consequences are with us yet.

For the simple truth, only now beginning to be realized, is that neurotic conditions do not conform to the medical model, or do so only by virtue of being badly twisted, Procrustes-fashion. Szasz has put it succinctly:

> *I contend that, as science, psychiatry is the study of communicative behavior, and, as therapy, the practice of dialectic and rhetoric (and of social control). The psychiatrist who wants to change people, and uses language to do so, acts as a rhetorician. His work is like that of the advertiser or legal advocate, and unlike that of the research scientist or medical practitioner.*[34]

Neurotic conditions are conflicts of experience, as I have argued in the preceding chapter, and so they are not caused in any physical sense; they are not illnesses, ought not to be diagnosed, and can be dealt with and even changed but not cured. The practice of dealing with neuroses professionally has followed the medical tradition and so has become a kind of *healing* game, but it need not be so. As we will see in later chapters, an alternative practice in the form of *helping* is possible. Our purpose at the moment, however, is to trace how the key elements of psychotherapy developed as a consequence of following the medical model. In Chapter 8 we shall see how this structure was slowly changed during a half century of practice.

*UNILATERAL ILLNESS.* In the medical tradition, illness is something contained within the patient's body that he brings to the doctor's office in hopes of alleviating his condition. By definition, the doctor does not have the illness; if he did, he would himself be off being treated by still another doctor, and so on. This makes good sense in medical practice. But what happens, now, when the concept is transferred, unchanged, to the practice of psychotherapy? The patients who came to Freud were, as he saw, deeply troubled; such terms as *anxiety*, *depression, fear,* and *inability to face their own deep feelings* were clearly applicable. But as Freud very well knew, and as any sensitive physician could have known, these troubles were not unique to patients. Doctors were also prone to their distress. What, then, differentiated the doctor from his patient?

Here was Freud's first problem. The solution he reached constituted the outlines of a theory to which he held, in one form or another, all his life. It stated that the patient's illness was not simply a current condition but the end result of a developmental history. What differentiated the doctor and the patient was that the patient carried within himself the consequences of a unique and aberrant lifetime; more precisely, the consequences of an early childhood in which natural developmental stages were not achieved in the normal manner. The patient's illness, then—that germ that was contained within his body and finally erupted in adult symptomatology—consisted of *matter preserved unchanged since child-*

*hood*. All of the consequences for Freud's theory—the unconscious, the instincts, the psychosexual stages—followed from this fundamental notion.[35]

By contrast, consider what might have happened if Freud, with all his originality, his determination, and his admitted inventive genius, had been a member of another profession—a lawyer, perhaps, or even a masseur. He might have come immediately to the insights that Wilhelm Reich gained in the 1920s, to the effect that the patient's current behavior, his manner and behavior during the present clinical hour, was itself his illness, and that there was no need to postulate psychic remnants from childhood as causes. He might then have gone on to develop ways of dealing with and changing the patient's current modes of being and behaving. And if he had been trained in another tradition—for example, education—he might not have found it necessary to have his patients come back again and again, in the manner of the clients of a physician, until they no longer felt the need to see him. Rather, he might have seen them only once, as teachers do their students when helping them with a specific problem or teaching them some specified knowledge. Many professional activities—education, law, physiotherapy, to name a few—are directed only at the problem that is presented during the current hour, and no more than that; only medicine and the psychotherapy that is modeled after it follow the tradition of treating a hidden set of problems that are presumed to antedate and to underlie the problem that is evident. Thus, if the medical model is dropped, the whole structure of psychotherapy is changed; conversely, the outlines of psychotherapy make sense when they are viewed as historic expressions of Freud's imitation of medical practice.

*DATA SEEN AND UNSEEN.*   One consequence of the notion of symptoms, which is an integral part of the whole theory of illness, is that the doctor sees only what might possibly result from known influences. In Freud's view, maintained essentially without change through four decades of controversy, the major important influences on development were all intrapsychic; that is, they consisted of forces that operated entirely within the person himself. Social relations were never causes but only results of these intrapsychic forces in collision with each other. Such a viewpoint might better be maintained as a hypothesis, but for Freud and many who followed him in the medical tradition it was rather an axiom—and so not only unargued but also unexamined.

This axiom structured not only Freud's theoretical writings—for example, his theory of the origin of the human family in *Totem and Taboo*[36]—but also the clinical observations of those who followed him in the psychoanalytic tradition. In one of his most famous cases, Ludwig Binswanger, the great Swiss founder of existential analysis, reported in great detail the life history of a patient he called Ellen West.[37] Using her diaries and poems, as well as a profusion of medical records extending over more than a decade of treatment, Binswanger reconstructed the pattern of existence that led her to a series of depressive episodes, psychosis, and finally suicide, as she struggled in vain against her one recurring symptom: a tendency to be fat, slow, and gross, when all her ideals, all her dreams and wishes, were of herself as slim, light, and graceful.

What is truly remarkable about Binswanger's book-length analysis of Ellen West is that, for all its insights, he never for a moment appears to suspect that her difficulties might have been related to influences outside her personality—for example, the changes in women's clothes and looks that were occurring about this time, immediately after World War I. Here is an instance of how an unexamined premise, though it may direct the observer to some kinds of data, at the same time hides other data from him. The illness concept, with its assumption of an underlying, invisible cause acting to produce an observable symptom, is another example. Perhaps the idea of data both seen and unseen, related in a kind of two-story structure, is applicable in matters of physical illness; I am not competent to judge. But in regard to human behavior, whether neurotic or not, this theory has come to seem sufficiently weak to justify severe attack, particularly from contemporary experimental psychologists.

Whatever may be said about its theory or lack of it, a behaviorist approach in psychology has the virtue of being empirical in its approach to data. The behaviorist is interested only in what is present and evident; his interest is in gathering only the kind of data that one might obtain in a laboratory study: an observable record, obtained under publicly stated conditions, which can if necessary be duplicated by another experimenter. His methodological bias, whatever its other limitations might be, at least leads him to accepting only overt data and ignoring hypothesized information that is presumed to be under the surface. If the patient insists that he loves his mother, the behaviorist will note merely that he states he loves his mother, not that the degree of the patient's protest makes it more likely that he really hates his mother. What is likely is simply what is given.

On this basis, a neurosis is defined entirely in terms of what is observably evident—the way the patient behaves over a period of time. The cause of the behavior is not the neurosis, nor is it the set of forces that are supposed to have led to the behavior; the neurosis is the behavior itself: "a persistent maladaptive habit that has been acquired by learning in one or a series of anxiety-generating situations. Conditioned anxiety is usually the central component of neurotic habits."[38] Since observation may be by means of instruments as well as by the clinician in his office, anxiety is then defined as "an individual organism's characteristic constellation of autonomic responses to noxious stimulation."[39]

More traditional forms of psychotherapy, on the other hand, which were heavily influenced by psychoanalysis and the practice of medicine, have tended to rely on a two-layer concept of human conduct—often with the benefit of the doubt given to what was hidden rather than what was evident. As a consequence, both the attacks on the medical model of therapy and the changes occurring in therapeutic practice have centered around the symptom—or, more precisely, around the question of what constitutes proper clinical data, and specifically around the further question of the reality of inner versus outer data. In the extreme psychoanalytic view, very little of what is immediately evident in the patient's behavior is meaningful or "true" or clinically useful; rather, what the analyst searches out is the unconscious significance of overt material. In the extreme behaviorist view, on the other hand, the only data of value are those immediately present, but even this much is restricted entirely to data called forth by experimental conditions. Thus, psychoanalysis often sees too much that is unseeable and perhaps unnecessary, while the behaviorist sees too little of what there is to see. But these are by no means the only positions—and as we shall see later in discussing the contributions of Reich, the ability to take a fresh look at the problem of seen and unseen data can lead to revolutionary changes in clinical practice.

*WHO JUDGES WHOM.* When therapist and patient meet, both of them, understandably, are somewhat anxious. Who would not be anxious in the face of a pending encounter that bodes so significantly for them? There is a universal and often effective means for allaying interpersonal anxiety so common that, though we all use it, we rarely notice that we do. If what makes me anxious about a significant interaction with a stranger is that he is a stranger and therefore relatively unpredictable, that he does not yet fit into any of the categories I am familiar with and so may stretch my own ways beyond their accustomed bounds, then my appropriate gambit is to discount this possibility in advance. What I do is define him in some limited way as soon as possible, preferably before I even get to know him well, certainly before giving him a chance to do his unique and unpredictable thing with me. For this purpose I need only use that form of interpersonal prejudging that we call *prejudice*. I note immediately that he has a beard, and so I am ready to add that fact to his apparent age and prejudge him as a middle-aged hippie. If that is a category of my own, in the sense that I already have opinions about it, I will not have to run the risk of openly interacting with him but will be able to behave in familiar ways. I will not then be involved in an encounter but only in a routine. A little narrow, you may say. Yes, but quite safe, say I.

In the therapeutic situation, however, an additional factor comes into play. Recall that an essential feature of this situation, when it is based on the medical model, is the gap in status between therapist and patient. Each of them depends upon that prejudging, categorizing action we call prejudice—but because the two occupy distinct roles, differently described in the literature and very differently evaluated in theory, their quite similar actions go by two different names.

What the therapist does is better known. He uses his clinical skill at postulating unseen causes in order to place the patient into a known category. Since he is familiar with the category, his own anxiety is alleviated and his interpersonal risks reduced to a minimum; he can now account in advance for most of the patient's significant behavior. The technical name for this categorizing maneuver is, of course, *diagnosis*. It works surprisingly well, far better than one might suppose from thinking of the maneuver as a harmless and not very useful form of classification. In the simplest case, let us say, a man "diagnoses" his partner as a woman; he is then prepared to say, in moments of stress, "Well, after all, what can you expect from a woman?" (Freud's sexism was only a little more subtle. He once said that after twenty years of studying the soul of woman, he was still puzzled by the question: "What is it that women want?") On a seemingly more professional level, the clinician who diagnoses a patient as schizophrenic has taken care of a lot of problems in advance; he will feel comfortable on hearing "crazy" talk from the patient (for isn't that what crazy people do?), and so he will not be moved to make sense out of it nor to find justification for it. To know the full clinical significance of a behavioral datum in advance is to have drained it of much of its terror, but also most of its human meaning. The therapist's position might then be characterized, bluntly and perhaps a little unfairly, with this remark: If there is to be any anxiety freely floating around here, I would prefer it be in you rather than in me; and the greater the discrepancy, the greater the imbalance of power when we two get down to business.

Now the patient takes the same route and for much the same reasons—which is just as it should be, for they are two partners in the same drama. But since he is a patient he has no professional background on which to rest his case. What he does, then, is more obvious, less refined. In the psychoanalytic paradigm, his pre-judgment of the therapist takes the form of what is technically called *transference*. He transfers to the analyst his repressed and unconscious childhood strivings—for example, attaching to the analyst the identity of his father, as the father was perceived in the patient's childhood. Then in the course of treatment he is helped to work through his unresolved wishes toward his father, using the analyst as a kind of blank screen on which to project his feelings. This, in theory, is the dynamics involved; it is also, and basically, a convenient form of prejudgment, its structure being exactly the same as that of the therapist's diagnostic efforts. Both maneuvers, diagnosis and transference, consist of prejudging the other person by assigning him in advance to a familiar and meaningful category out of one's past; and so both maneuvers make the judge, at least initially, a lot more comfortable in an anxiety-arousing situation.

The result is a situation of two protagonists who are programmed to meet each other at an angle rather than face-to-face. They are to this degree unable to see each other fully as persons. Hampered by their mutual start, they must then work at sharing an experience. If they are able to do this, therapy progresses; if they fail to do it, they will know that they are merely spending each other's time and so had best break up; but if they succeed in breaking completely through their prejudicial anxieties and can see each other simply as persons, then they know that the treatment is over, the mutual drama finished. Therapists often say that when once they know a patient well, they are unable to view him as a diagnostic entity and that this is the point at which therapy ought to end. On his part, the patient works through what is called, with the curious bias that afflicts clinicians, his *transference neurosis*; and when this happens he too is able to look at his therapist, decide that he likes and dislikes him to some sensible degree, shake his hand, and walk out. Perhaps they cure each other a little bit.

When we look in some detail at recent developments in therapeutic practice, we will see that as the status gap of the clinical session lessened, decade by decade, the concept of transference disappeared and the practice of diagnosis along with it. Both forms of clinical prejudice depended on turning the session from a human encounter—with all the risks involved—into a special form of drama, complete with roles and prepared script. At its basis, the drama was in turn an idealized version of the medical treatment program; its disappearance was further evidence that the medical model came to be replaced by some form of a psychological model.

*ON PROGRESS AND POWER.*   A simple example: A therapist begins a session by saying, "Well, how's it going?" to which the patient answers, "You know, I feel pretty good today." Ordinarily, and nontherapeutically, this would serve as nothing more than an elaborate way to pass the time or else to ease into a conversation, a key to an often creaking door. But suppose the patient's original complaint had been rather severe episodes of depression, and suppose also that the other indicators of his state—his posture, his face, the sound of his voice—were at the moment in support of his statement about feeling good. In that case both participants might feel pleased about the exchange. They would be in agreement that the patient's condition today represents a change for the better. The interchange then takes on the status of an indicator that therapeutic progress has occurred.

This is one of the two major requirements for progress in therapy. Therapist and patient must agree that things have changed for the better, and they must be able to communicate their agreement to each other. A second requirement is that each step of progress must serve either to lessen anxiety or to broaden the collective experience of patient and therapist. A second example: The patient has recently made the latest in a series of moves, from apartment to apartment, that clearly serve to keep him living at a fixed distance away from his mother's apartment. Therapist and patient together now plot these sequential moves on a map, and the picture is made graphically clear—so clear that the patient achieves an insight concerning his denied dependence on his mother. That is one way to describe what has happened. A more helpful way would be to say that the two, therapist and patient, have achieved a joint statement that has broadened their collective experience. They can now look at each other and share a great smile, knowing that they have trusted each other enough to venture together into strange territory and learn something important together, and they can lean back as one and realize what they have done, and say, "Wow! What about that?"

But it doesn't happen this way too often. There is a technique known as *interpretation* that is central to the kind of therapy based on the medical model. It consists of revealing to the patient, at an appropriate time, a piece of information that will provide the last necessary push for a repressed wish to break into consciousness, information that is presumed to be "true" at this moment for the patient. The interpretation is perhaps the clearest instance of the application of the medical model to the therapeutic situation; it is perfectly analogous to the shot that the obstetrician gives to induce labor, or to the proper dosage of anesthetic, or to the pill that causes a drop in the patient's temperature. Its use is based solidly on the assumption that this interchange is a one-way street, with all the informational input flowing from patient to doctor and all the curative output flowing back the other way. Thus, a lot of time and energy used to be spent on the training of therapists in such matters as the proper timing of interpretations, the requisite "depth" demanded by the stage of therapeutic progress, and so on. As in the case of most aspects of therapy, very little evidence has been available to assess the value of interpretive statements. The one study that was directed to this question, by Mendel, was quite clear in demonstrating that the content of an

## INTERPRETATION IN THERAPY

I set up a situation in which the same interpretation was made to four patients on the same day. All of these patients were involved in intensive, expressive psychotherapy and the content of the interpretation, though somewhat general, did not apply specifically to any one of these patients. This procedure was repeated on six occasions for these four patients, with each interpretation approximately one month following the previous one. The interpretation was made ten minutes after the beginning of the hour and the material produced in response to the interpretation was dealt with. Between these experimentally inexact interpretations, the case was carried on in the usual manner, using the material produced by the patient.

The six inexact "interpretations" used were as follows:

1) You seem to live your life as though you are apologizing all the time.
2) Much of what you say now seems to be related to the difficulties you have with men.
3) You seem hesitant in the exploration of your strong points.
4) Apparently, you have always felt that you had to take on the burdens of all the family.
5) You seem frightened of the effect your expression of feelings have on me and others.
6) Much of what you say seems to be related to the difficulties you have with women.

In twenty of the twenty-four instances, the patients responded to the interpretation by a change in the level of anxiety. . . . In only two instances were the patients so skeptical of the interpretation that they could not use it to give meaning to what they were talking about at the moment. In the other two instances, the patients completely disregarded the interpretive intervention. . . .

The change, occurring in the existence when it moves from the pre-interpreted state, is to a large extent the result of making sense out of nonsense, of assigning meaning to apparently meaningless sequences, and of explaining and calling by name those forces which push, pull, and drive us in many directions. We can not alter many of these forces, but we can master them by reflecting, understanding, and explaining. Thus, the structural change occurring in the world of the patient as a result of the interpretive intervention in itself can lead to therapeutic movement.[40]

interpretation was much less important than its function simply to organize the patient's thinking and so lessen his anxiety.

A third example will suggest how an interpretation can function so as to produce an illusion of progress in therapy. A novice therapist brings in to his supervisor some details of his current patient, a young man whose repeated, abortive attempts at setting up living arrangements with roommates rather clearly suggest strong though unacknowledged homosexual tendencies. The novice so totally ignores this possibility in his patient that it soon dawns on the supervisor that the novice himself may have a problem in this area. His own difficulties in regard to his unacknowledged wishes are effectively preventing him from an objective consideration of this problem in his own patient. At some appropriate point, then, the supervisor makes an interpretation to the novice. He suggests, in whatever manner he deems suitable, that the latter has some difficulty himself in dealing with this kind of interpersonal possibility. Suppose, too, that the novice accepts this interpretation without either breaking off the supervisory relation or angrily denying the implication; as O. Henry once put it, he neither denies the allegation nor defies the allegator.

Note that to accept an interpretation in this way need not be at all the same as achieving an insight, either alone or collectively. In this instance, in fact, the novice's experience could better be described as being persuaded of something. No new experience has been generated, only a new fact; no growth, only a proof. What has happened is that the balance of power between the two protagonists has shifted. Before this occurred their relation might have been nearly that of equals, but now the supervisor, they agree, has access to fundamental secrets about the novice. And they are secrets rather than simply items of information or knowledge, because, as the two agree, they have until now been hidden from the novice himself.[41]

If interpretation were a technique available to both parties in this encounter, it might result in some interesting opportunities for the joint production of public secrets. But by the rules of the game an interpretation can only be made by the therapist, never by his patient. In the days of orthodox analytic practice, were the patient to attempt an interpretive remark about his therapist, it would in turn have been interpreted as resistance. Since the interpretation belongs in the therapist's hands only, it can produce only facts in what amounts to a power struggle—increasing rather than decreasing the status gap, and perhaps even giving a false picture of progress.

In reviewing these topics of illness, symptoms, diagnosis, transference, and interpretation, I may seem to have painted too negative a portrait of psychotherapy. To be fair, as well as to bring the discussion more in line with my own biases, I must now correct this impression. I will not deny—I would even passionately affirm—that therapists do indeed help many of their patients. I am myself a happier person—more productive and better able to live constructively and joyfully with myself and others—because over a period of time I went to a therapist and he helped me.

There are many ways that this positive achievement can be described and its importance for human experience adequately evaluated. The therapeutic enterprise, as I have stated, at its best can be a helping function. But the other aspect—the aspect of healing game rather than helping art—must also be considered. Moreover, these two aspects, the healing and the helping, the game and the art, are not simply equivalent choices independently available to a therapist. Every enduring human relation shows this same Janus quality. We are all high-wire artists in the

Real creativeness, in my experience, is inextricably linked with the experience of mortality. . . . This is what makes out of sex, love; out of the herd, society; out of wheat and fruit, bread and wine; and out of sound, music. This is what makes life livable and—incidentally—makes therapy possible.[42]

terrible enterprise of social living. We are carefully, even dangerously, poised on a wire strung between the two poles of love and power; the best we can do is to walk straight toward the goal and not look down. Nor can we ever get off the wire that holds us tautly: we can neither live in a perpetual scream of love-for-all, nor can we live without others, having destroyed them in struggles for power. We must find our place somewhere between the two extremes in every relation with another person—and this includes those special relations we set up as either patient or therapist.

## THE RULES OF THE GAME

One of the unfortunate consequences of the split between the experimental and the clinical wings of contemporary psychology is that the incomparable data available to clinicians have rarely been made available for study by experimentalists. This is a tragic loss to general psychology, for the therapeutic situation is of value not only as the setting in which important and often positive changes take place in people, but also as a setting which is paradigmatic of all human relations.

Carl Rogers has boldly reduced the complexity of the therapeutic process to the simple consequence of six "necessary and sufficient conditions of therapeutic personality change":

1. *Two persons are in psychological contact.*
2. *The first, whom we shall term the client, is in a state of incongruence, being vulnerable or anxious.*
3. *The second person, whom we shall term the therapist, is congruent or integrated in the relationship.*
4. *The therapist experiences unconditional positive regard for the client.*
5. *The therapist experiences an empathic understanding of the client's internal frame of reference and endeavors to communicate this experience to the client.*
6. *The communication to the client of the therapist's empathic understanding and unconditional positive regard is to a minimal degree achieved.*

*No other conditions are necessary. If these six conditions exist, and continue over a period of time, this is sufficient. The process of constructive personality change will follow.*[43]

I suspect that Rogers is largely correct, at least in regard to what I would rather call the base conditions for therapeutic progress, for one person helping another. What his conditions do not tell, however, are the rules of the game itself and the course that is in large part directed by these rules. Only in his first condition, that two persons are "in psychological contact," does Rogers point to the most obvious requirement of all, the one that starts off the therapeutic encounter. Since the therapist does not advertise for clients nor ask strangers if they want to undertake therapy, it can only begin when one person makes the decision to seek out a therapist and begin treatment. This is the kind of condition that results in what I am calling the rules of the therapeutic game—that is, a general requirement to which both parties always accede, just as though each of them had read the same book of rules and agreed to abide by it. In every significant human encounter this circumstance seems to exist, that the participants act just as though they knew about a fixed set of rules to which they both must adhere. What seems to happen in psychotherapy, as in every other encounter that matters, is that all the parties concerned accept the conditions of the situation, and in so doing they buy into a game whose rules make sense to them. It is not dissimilar to an elaborate contract, except that in the case of psychotherapy very little of the contract is made explicit and none of it, of course, is committed to writing.

*RULE NO. 1.*   One person defines himself as a patient or client and presents himself to a therapist, who accepts him as such. This may seem too self-evident to need stating. No one would expect a therapist to begin treatment on just anyone who shows up at his office—for example, an encyclopedia salesman—and of course the client who comes to the office must announce that he is there for therapy. But the rule means more than this. It implies that these two persons do not meet simply as adults but in their respective roles. The client makes the initial contact, usually by telephone or, in the case of a clinic, by coming in to see the receptionist and making an appointment. He is asked certain information, and reveals certain details about himself that he would not normally divulge to others. Indeed it may be the very fact of his not having been able to divulge the information to friends or family that brings him to therapy in the first place. For example, if a young man of abnormally strict and repressive background begins to feel sexual urges that he experiences with great guilt, if he occasionally masturbates, if he fantasies about peeping in windows or accosting women on the street at night, he may then become withdrawn, preoccupied, and depressed. He may fall behind in his work or studies, he may have trouble sleeping, and during all this he may be completely unable to talk about it frankly with his father, his minister, or his friends. In his first contact with a therapist, when he is asked about his presenting problem (his symptoms), he pours out the details I have just given. The fact that they are now openly discussing a very special and private kind of material is an indication of the special relation already existing between them. Further, this kind of relation may itself play some part in changing the patient for the better.

There is some evidence, indeed, that the fact of the person declaring himself as a patient may be an important element in whatever changes come about. To do this he has had to buy into a very modern view of the self and has then had to apply this view specifically and personally to himself. He has had to declare to himself that he is not able to conduct his life completely on his own, that he needs the intercession of a competent professional, and that some significant change in himself is now demanded. Many clinics that have the practice of examining or testing prospective patients first and then putting them on a waiting list for treatment have discovered that a surprisingly large percentage of those on the list seem to improve even before their turn for treatment comes up—often they do not need to begin formal treatment after all. One explanation for this "waiting list cure," as it is called, is that the change involved in having declared oneself a patient is itself the change needed to start the patient off on a new and more constructive track. For this reason, too, the first rule of the therapeutic game is more than just a restatement of the obvious.

*RULE NO. 2.* The two participants agree that they are in a situation together and therefore that each needs the other.

What this rule implies is that therapist and client share a situation and that both know that they share it. To a surprising degree, as the clinical evidence shows, therapy is a matter of a mutuality, a shared situation, and even a commonly held set of beliefs, in spite of the often marked difference between the two participants as persons or in their degree of congruence, as Rogers calls it. An elaborate study by Hans Strupp and his colleagues of how patients experienced psychotherapy in retrospect, found "rather substantial agreement between patients and therapists in their view of each other and their assessment of the relationship and its outcome."[44] Similarly, in discussing the general presuppositions of all therapeutic methods, Kenneth Colby remarks:

> *Beliefs concerning the nature of man underlie the articulated suppositions of psychotherapy. This* Menschanschauung, *as it might be called, presupposes that man's suffering is an outcome of his experience, that mental suffering should be relieved, that man has some freedom of choice and decision, that he can control himself to some extent, that he can be changed by experience, that one man can help another to change, and so on. . . . It is of obvious importance that these beliefs are held by both therapist and patient.*[45]

When two persons are caught up in the same situation and when it is significant for both and when in addition they have agreed to continue in it, a consequence is that each will need the other in order to fill out his own role. The roles though individual are by no means separate; because the roles arise out of the same situation, they are intermeshed. No matter what the relation between them or how it changes, no matter if it seems at times that one of them is present chiefly to win out over the other, the rule of mutual need will hold. Therapist needs patient just exactly as much as patient needs therapist. If we study Genet's brilliant scene, it may appear at first that the penitent thief needs the judge for forgiveness or perhaps punishment, and that the judge is simply there to do his

ON BEING A JUDGE

THE JUDGE: (to The Executioner) . . . Are you there? You're all there, my huge arm, too heavy for me, too big, too fat for my shoulder, walking at my side all by itself! Arm, hundredweight of meat, without you I'd be nothing. . . . (To the Thief) And without you too, my child. You're my two perfect complements . . . Ah, what a fine trio we make! (To the Thief) But you, you have a privilege that he hasn't, nor I either, that of priority. My being a judge is an emanation of your being a thief. You need only refuse—but you'd better not!—need only refuse to be who you are—for me to cease to be . . . to vanish, evaporated. Burst. Volatilized. Denied. Hence: good born of . . . What then? What then? But you won't refuse, will you? You won't refuse to be a thief? That would be wicked. It would be criminal. You'd deprive me of being! (Imploringly) Say it, my child, my love, you won't refuse? . . . Look, I beseech you. Don't leave me in this position, waiting to be a judge. If there were no judge, what would become of us, but what if there were no thieves?[46]

duty when the thief comes crawling to him. But Genet's point is more profound and more telling: in the judge's realization that he needs the thief as much as she needs him, that if there were no thieves there would be no judges, resides the lesson about roles that we can learn from any situation that two persons share.

Because therapist and patient need each other, they may ring all the changes on this dance of mutual need; like two planets caught in each other's gravitational field and swinging around each other, they will continue to feed on each other, make contact, collide and dodge, until they come to the mutual decision that the game is over. When they no longer need each other, when each can walk away from the situation, it is done.

*RULE NO. 3.* Each of the participants agrees to adopt, and to stick to, specific forms of role-directed behavior.

By a tacit understanding, each of the participants as he joins the cast of two agrees to learn his role, to stick to it, and to refrain from intruding on the other's role even while learning its general requirements. This is all understandable in general, but it raises some questions. How are the roles established? Who decides what the roles shall consist of? Are the roles unchangeable?

As a corollary to this particular rule of the game, it would seem that the various approaches to psychotherapy differ chiefly in how the two actors come to state and recognize their respective roles. This can be seen most clearly in the development of a new approach or system in therapy, which appears to occur about once in every decade. New systems, we should note, are always devised by therapists, never by patients—an observation that may seem so obvious as to be trivial, until we think about it for a moment. Consider the case of behavior therapy, introduced by Joseph Wolpe, Arnold Lazarus, and very soon a number of others, during the early 1950s.

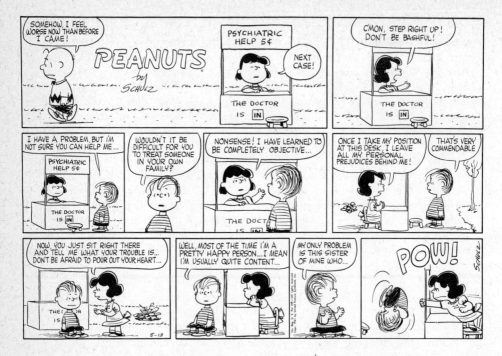

Since behavior therapy is professedly based on the principles of learning theory, and since the principles in question were already known to many psychologists, and since many of these same psychologists were undoubtedly suffering from neurotic difficulties and might even have been undergoing various other forms of therapy not based on learning principles—why, then, did it not occur to some of them to develop a form of treatment more in accordance with their own conceptions about the nature of their difficulties? Perhaps it did—although there is always such a gap between one's personal experience and one's theoretical professional views, especially among psychologists, that it is unlikely the connection would have been made by many neurotic learning theorists who were in therapy.

But even if this had happened, I am sure that those who made the connection would have then set out to become therapists. They would surely not have presented themselves as patients to some professional, or even to a sympathetic and skilled nonprofessional, and offered to teach their new system so that the latter could become their therapist. Indeed, when I put the possibility this way, the idea seems almost ludicrous. I think we can see the reason for this if we consider an alternative that in some ways resembles the therapy situation. Can a pupil ever devise a new approach to teaching and then teach it to his teacher so that the latter can in turn use it with the pupil? I think so. A pupil might suggest (to an open-minded teacher, of course): "Maybe if you'd stop being so threatening, talk a little slower, let me ask some questions, and write the hard words on the blackboard—you know, loosen up a little, then I'd be able to learn better." The pupil can do this because the teacher usually has some content to communicate or information to pass on; and in addition he has his own technique for doing so. He can then sometimes change the technique in order to do better at passing on the information. Because his essential function in this case is to convey information, a function that is not intruded upon by the pupil's suggestion, he is free to accept it.

But this is not true of the therapy situation. The therapist has no package of information to hand out; if he did, he would simply have to lecture, and therapy would then look nothing like it does. What, then, is it that he does? It is not easy to identify. Theodore Reik, a psychoanalyst who wrote extensively about his practice, said that there is really no such thing as analytic technique; there is only sincerity.[47] It seems that the therapist has only himself to offer, for good or ill—often for both. His technique, or his approach, seems to reduce to the guise in which he offers himself; a new system or approach is, then, only a new guise in which to present himself. It is for this reason that the discovery of a new approach will not help someone to construct a new patient role. All the discovery can do is to make it possible to develop a new guise in which to be a therapist.

What this point leads to is that in the normal course of events, it is the therapist who first determines his own role—whether it is a new one or one that he has been in before—and then makes it possible for the patient to assume his role. This answers the questions raised above concerning how the roles are established and whether they can be changed. The patient begins by accepting the patient role in its most general sense; he agrees to see himself as a troubled self, and he places this self in the hands of someone who in our culture is defined as a helper for this kind of problem.

A number of points should be mentioned at this juncture. The first is that it is not always the therapist professional who is so defined. The identification will differ from place to place and will change through time as well. In a comprehensive survey some years back,[48] it was found that one third of a national sample of adults had seriously considered some form of personal help for their problems at some point in their lives, but that more than half of them had first gone to their family physicians, most of the remainder to their minister, and less than 10 percent to a recognizable psychotherapist. Among the urban population, and in the middle class, and more recently, these figures have tended to change, with an increasing number choosing a psychotherapist as the person of first resort. This, in turn, has been encouraged by the increasing number of guises in which therapists are now able to present themselves, thereby greatly enlarging the range of choices open to prospective patients.

A second point is that both patient and therapist do have a great deal more freedom than I seem to have indicated thus far. The misunderstanding may arise from my use of the term *rules*, as though the participants were as restricted as players in a contest. In fact, the patient-to-be may withdraw at any point, with or without significant change in himself. He may shop from one therapist to another until he finds the one whose set of rules is most acceptable, and he may do this shopping even after having started with each therapist. He may begin one kind of therapy and manage not to adjust to this approach, thereby putting pressure on the therapist either to terminate him in some way or to alter his approach. And he may maintain his freedom all the way through a course of therapy, even to the point of never giving up his private opinion that it is a lot of nonsense or that he is not being helped at all. The therapist, on his part, may not adopt a fixed approach at all but may choose to benefit from the best aspects of a number of different approaches with which he is familiar. He may accept or reject any patient, and he may change what he does because of what happens with a particular patient. He may even help a patient to change while maintaining that he does not understand what has happened or does not believe that any significant change has occurred.

*RULE NO. 4.* The course of the therapy is determined, first, by the therapist's definitions of roles, and, second, by the nature of their shared beginning.

The therapist having declared himself, so to speak, patients will come to him, already determined to some extent in their roles. But at this point it will make a lot of difference to him how they proceed as patients. He can not be open to just anything. If a patient has been through psychoanalysis and now prepares to lie down on a couch and free associate, he will have to be gently instructed otherwise if his new therapist is a follower of Carl Rogers or Fritz Perls. More to the point, the therapist will have to make quite clear how the two are to relate to each other in regard to the usual status gap. Does the patient call the therapist by his first name? Do they sit facing each other? Does it all take place in this office? Is touching permitted? What kind of language will be allowed? How active will the therapist be, and who will do the most work? Who determines their schedule, and what will it be?

These are not simply trivial regulations or small matters of technique, but critically important determinants of their respective roles. Some major changes in approaches to psychotherapy, as we will see, have centered around precisely these points, and not by accident. In a real sense the therapist has to instruct his patient; he has to teach him how to be the kind of patient he is expected to be in this office, with this practitioner, using this approach. The teaching that follows may be more or less subtle. For example, George Devereux, like all psychoanalytically oriented therapists, has to instruct his patient in how to obtain the necessary dream material and then how to deal with it in the treatment hours; he also has to

---

TWO MODES OF
INSTRUCTION IN THERAPY

(In the psychoanalytically oriented session between an anthropologist, George Devereux, and his Plains Indian patient, the latter has said that he doesn't recall last night's dream. They then talk about the patient's experience with a girl much younger than he is.)

THERAPIST: Let us look at the way you handled this business with that young girl. You gave me what you believe to be "good" reasons for your actions. A "good" reason is something you think up to justify doing something you want to do anyhow. Sometimes you think of "good" reasons for explaining afterwards why you did something in a certain way. But the real reason why you did it may be entirely different. There may be something you may not care to admit, either to yourself, or to others. . . . Now let us examine what you did with that young girl. Maybe you had some other reasons—reasons you don't even know yourself—for not marrying her. . . .

(After a brief conversation about the patient's going back to college, they continue.)

THERAPIST: Now, what DID you dream? PATIENT: I don't recall. Does one dream even when one does not remember?

T: Yes. Let me briefly read back to you what we have talked about today. It might help you remember your dream. (The interview is summarized.)

P: I still don't recall.

T: Close your eyes and tell me the first thing you visualize.

P: It is you.

T: Did you dream of me?

P: (His face shows intense surprise.) I think I did—now—now I recall. When I was at college, one day I was waiting in the street for the bus and saw a very old car—one of the first of that kind ever made. This is what I dreamed: I dreamed you were driving this old car. Maybe I was riding with you in it. I am not sure of that. But I think I did. That is what I dreamed. . . .[49]

T: You see, this proves we are able to recover a forgotten dream, and it shows that there is a lot in a man's mind, in the back of it, that he does not really know about, but which can be gotten out.[50]

(In the session between a behavior therapist, Joseph Wolpe, and his patient, she has explained that she is afraid of being alone on Sunday mornings.)

T: How near must other people be, that you're sure of, to make you comfortable?

P: Actually they could even be far away, just so long as I have a means of getting to them or communicating with them.

T: Well suppose the nearest people were in Boston. Would that be all right?

P: No, that's too far.

T. Philadelphia?

P: (Laughs) I don't know. But usually when I first started to spend evenings alone I always had my friends alerted. . . . And it could be, you know the distance could be increased. At one time I had to have somebody close by, then the distance did increase.

T: Well look, let's try and purify the situation. Let's assume that you go to the seaside and you take a cottage on your own, but there is also a friend of yours who has another cottage. Now if that friend's cottage is a ten-minute car ride away, will you feel happy?

P: If I have the car outside.

T: Well assuming that, O.K.?

P: Yes.

T: 15 minutes?

P: Well, this car experience is comparatively new. It's just something I'm learning to do. I'm just learning to drive. I don't know how good I'll be at it, or how much distance I'll be able to cover.

T: Let's assume that the friend has a driver and can be . . .

P: That wouldn't be as good. I can't wait for someone to get to me. I have to feel that I'm going, that I'm moving there.

T: Well for purposes of this discussion let us assume, and I think we are entitled to assume, namely, that you would be able to drive just as well as anybody else, and we'll also assume that you have accomplished this. Right. If that person is fifteen minutes away, is that all right?

P: I think so.

T: 20?

P: Well actually I have progressed to the point where I don't have to be concerned about anyone being there. I've stopped calling people to find out whether they're home. . . .

T: Yes, but there is a point at which you do become anxious? I'm just trying to find where, establishing that point.

P: Yes, that's true. Um-hum.

T: So that's why we're taking a seaside cottage where there's only one person you see, and everything has to be focused on this one person who is going to be under control. On Saturday night there's a kind of a vague uncertainty about everybody. So, here instead, we're just going to have one person whom we will locate in space. Now, this, if this friend of yours were only 20 minutes away by car . . .

P. At this point I would say that I don't think I could take more than 10, possibly 15 minutes.

T: Yes, well, that's what I want to know.

P: I don't think I could take any more than that.

T: Assuming that you can drive and get there, even then 10 minutes would be about the maximum?

P: I think so. On a dark country road, yes.

T: Well, we don't have to complicate the issue. . . .

P: Ten minutes, no more.

T: All right, that's all I wanted to know.[51]

---

instruct the patient in what is to be considered important material. Wolpe, on the other hand, because his whole approach is more directive from moment to moment, has only to make clear to the patient what he is to emphasize, and the therapist will determine himself how to make use of the resulting material.[52]

A disclaimer is in order here. I am not trying to say that the course of psychotherapy consists of a set of instructions passed from therapist to patient, as though someone were being taught to embroider or to speak a foreign language. What I have described so far is only the barest beginning of the subtle confluence of roles that begins to take place from session to session. Straightforward directives concerning technique are needed at the outset—statements concerning place and time and how they address one another, plus a little about what the therapist expects they will do. Following this, more subtle instructional materials are offered regarding the kinds of content to be emphasized. Will it be feelings, as in nondirective approaches, or something closer to behavior and attitudes, as in Albert Ellis' rational-emotive method? Will the two not look at each other, as in classical psychoanalysis, or will the analyst physically manipulate the patient's body, as Wilhelm Reich did? Will the patient be responsible for "doing the dirty work," as Perls said of his system of Gestalt therapy, or will the therapist conduct a session much like an interview, as the behavior therapists tend to do?

But once all this has been established, and assuming that therapist and patient are still in agreement that they will remain together, the therapy will very soon come to its first important choice point. In some way the two participants must decide whether they are therapeutically meant for one another. In one or more of the very early sessions, having made their respective declarations of purpose and briefed each other on requirements and limitations, they have begun to test each other out. If the patient has been distressed enough to be in great need of help, and if he feels that the present arrangement is what he needs, he may play the proper role magnificently; he may even overdo it, in the phenomenon that is ironically termed *flight into health*. Or he may show a mixture of acceding and refusing, posing problems immediately for the therapist. The two may then click and, if so, things can proceed. If not, one or both will surely find a way to end it. All the studies of factors contributing to therapeutic success or failure seem to agree on this point—that if therapy breaks off it is most likely to break off within the first few sessions.[53] If patient and therapist stick together for more than a few sessions, the indications are good that they have come to a tacit agreement to work together and that they will then keep at it for as long as is warranted by the nature of the case and the skill and interest of the therapist.

Either one can terminate at this early stage—the patient more obviously by not returning for the second or third session, the therapist usually in more subtle ways but often equally directly. It is all done in terms of a complex script, although neither of them ever gets a copy. They seem to know their roles by heart (a very apt phrase) and to play them by ear (another remarkably apt expression), getting it perfectly the first time without rehearsal. This is the reason that I suspect there is a fine logic to the whole structure and that the relation between two persons in psychotherapy is one of those rare phenomena, a basic paradigm of the human encounter.

There is one more device the therapist has at his command to help assure his own satisfaction and success. If he had to depend entirely on chance to select patients with whom he could work successfully, he might have to start and then break off with a fairly high percentage of those who knock on his door. To prevent this, and also to help the patient make the same kind of choice, both participants must be fairly selective, often in covert ways, during their early meetings. They have to size each other up, make rapid judgments, and come to important decisions in a hurry. The matter is more critical for the therapist than for the patient, because patients are more variable as a group and therefore more likely to contain undesirable members. They are certainly less experienced and thus less likely to have been screened by previous contacts. One of the earliest studies of therapist characteristics showed that experienced therapists regardless of orientation resemble each other far more than experienced therapists of any one school resemble beginners of that school[54]—and so the patient stands a fairly good chance, if he goes to someone with some background, of finding a therapist who will at least be minimally acceptable to him and who will have had long experience in being acceptable to many different kinds of patients. But the therapist, on his part, cannot so easily pick and choose among prospective patients who present themselves to him. He has, however, one major move open to him; its use gives rise to a final rule.

*RULE NO. 5.* Innovations in psychotherapy can often be defined in terms of the new populations of patients for whom they are fitted.

Occasionally therapists trained and working within one tradition or approach find that they are not satisfied with their own results. Usually in writing about what led them to change they will attribute the move, in retrospect, to dissatis-faction with the approach itself, either its theory or its technique. But what seems to occur, although they do not usually speak of the change in this way, is that they develop an approach whose novelty is defined by the fact that it appeals to a hitherto untapped population of prospective patients. It would appear, from this evidence, that new approaches to psychotherapy may be recognized, not by their novelty of theory or technique, but by the type of patient with whom they are uniquely successful.

A summary of some major innovations, decade by decade, will provide sug-gestive data for this rule:

Around 1900, Freud introduced a radically different mode of treatment. It involved talking, demanded a high degree of psychological-mindedness, required time and money, and emphasized matters that only the most sophisticated and liberal persons of that day could handle unblushingly. It appealed immediately and primarily to a select population of intelligent, middle-class, liberated women, very few of whom had ever before had an opportunity to express their needs for freedom of experience in a constricting Victorian culture.[55]

By 1910, a larger group of middle-class, mostly professional, men and women had been attracted to psychoanalysis. The theoretical emphasis now began to shift to accommodate the problems they brought to the analyst's office; in place of a concern with culturally based sexual and experiential freedom, they looked to become free of the restrictions they had imposed on themselves. The issues that were dealt with were now just as often questions of guilt, of tormenting demands on the self, of disorders of reason rather than of feeling, of inability to experience feelings, and of control of aggressive impulses. What now came under attack was the full range of the Protestant work ethic as it was represented in middle-class professionals; it was this large group of patients who made psychoanalytic treatment a success.

After World War I, when psychoanalysis came to America, it changed again to accommodate a new group of artistically inclined neurotics whose central con-cern was personal independence and integrity. The emphasis now shifted from the content of the patients' productions to their manner; from concentrating on the past to an interest in the present session; and from dealing with symptoms to dealing with character. All of these changes were required in order to make treatment available to a new group of patients whose problems were not in neurotic symptoms within an otherwise normal life but in developing a total life-style to fit a culture undergoing very rapid change.[56]

By 1930, psychoanalysis had become enough of an institution for its prac-titioners to begin to look around in the general population for prospective patients. They were easy to find. Women, who had not been listened to seriously for three decades, were an obvious group, and Karen Horney offered a theory and a practice to fit their special demands.[57] Therapists trained in the field of social work took their psychoanalytic techniques out into settlement houses and markedly changed the technique to treat younger patients in groups. The influ-ence of social and cultural factors was evident on all sides, and the group of neo-

Freudians, as they came to be called, developed both a socially conscious theory and an informal, culturally relative treatment approach to take account of the newly discovered factors.[58]

Beginning about 1940, Carl Rogers, whose experience had been first with children and then with college students, discovered on the campuses a distinctively new population of patients.[59] They were relatively healthy, of high potential but blocked in achieving it, intelligent and verbal, markedly democratic in their orientation and their relations with others, unwilling to tolerate a gap in status between themselves and a therapist, and capable of tremendous growth in a short time if they had the chance to do it in the presence of a sympathetic and accepting guide. His client-centered counseling answered directly to these patient characteristics.

About 1950, two new groups of prospective patients were independently discovered. Albert Ellis, who found the first of them, developed a system of therapy to respond to their demands:[60] they were big-city dwellers, and relatively healthy, but in chronic distress over their inability to become assertive and self-fulfilling in their relations with others, particularly in sexual contacts. He answered them with what amounted to a straightforward program of re-education, of trial and trial again, of success building on success—a program emphasizing behavior but with a reasonable theory concerning habits and inappropriate messages as an underpinning to the practice. What he gave his patients was a supportive explanation, a plan of attack, and a firm basis for their attempts to try out new directions in relating to others.

The second of these new groups of patients was that discovered by the innovators in behavior therapy: primarily middle-class or lower-middle class persons, more often women than men, who were not particularly sophisticated or psychologically minded and not verbally facile enough to talk about their problems. They comprised large groups of persons, previously almost ignored, who tended to, or preferred to, see their problems in terms of symptoms that could be stated in factual terms, like a medical disease, who needed firm and re-educative guidance rather than insight or elaborations of thinking, and whose emotional lives were rather simple and barren rather than complex or subtle. The various techniques of behavior therapy answered the needs of this group by providing simple explanations in terms of habit, practical analysis, guidance, homework, clear-cut indications of value received in the form of improvement, and a minimum of elaborate theory, conceptualizing, or complex emotional involvement.

During the past decade or so, new approaches have proliferated faster than patient groups have been found, with the result that there has been some overlap in appeal between one type of therapy and another. But what most of the approaches seem to have in common is that they speak directly to the increasing number of persons who, as self-conscious members of the post-Freudian generation, now seek some way to come to terms with their own often empty lives without going back into forms of psychoanalytic treatment. The defining characteristic of these patients may be that they simply know too much, they talk too well, they are far too sophisticated for an approach that demands the naïve exploration of their own impulse life, as psychoanalysis does. All the new approaches de-emphasize merely verbal productions and emphasize the direct experience and expression of feeling, giving up game-playing, and developing honest, open, and growth-promoting contact with self and others.[61] These are the basic consumer demands of a population that may soon come to include just about every one of us.

# chapter
# 8
# changes

We saw in the last chapter that one way to look at the development of new approaches in psychotherapy was in terms of new and different populations of patients. Practitioners of therapy seem to be very enterprising, and their prospective patients appear eager to be cast in a role that in many circles is almost the mark of intellectual sophistication. One obvious consequence is that psychotherapy has become one of the most widespread of professional activities in this country—and almost universally admired as well. Nationally syndicated columnists who advise their distressed and lovelorn readers publicly and on the basis of minimal information do not hesitate to recommend what they call professional help for a startingly wide range of problems. When a number of ministers started a "telephone booth" service, called The Listening Ear, a few years ago in Pittsburgh, Pennsylvania, they were surprised at the immediate response: as many as twenty-five calls a day to a service that was known only by word-of-mouth report. At least four established professions—the ministry, medicine, psychology, and social work—now regularly train and accredit their own members for full-time work as therapists, and there are an even larger number of persons from other disciplines, as well as those with no formal background at all, who can and do set up shop, often with approaches that in no way resemble what we usually think of as psychotherapy. In an age when service occupations are coming to outnumber jobs that produce goods for consumption, psychotherapy may well be taking its place as one of the most pervasive of all the service trades.

In the light of all these changes, there may be no way to categorize the historical development of psychotherapy under any simple scheme. This is particularly true since an increasing number of therapeutic practitioners, having trained in or learned about a wide range of approaches, have tended to combine them. Today not many therapists can be identified as belonging to a school, even though rough divisions can still be made: for example, the talking therapies, ranging from those still heavily influenced by psychoanalysis to those influenced by Carl Rogers; the training therapies, including methods of behavior modification as well as Albert Ellis' rational-emotive method; the amalgam of techniques for work with groups, recently popularized as encounter approaches; the body-oriented therapies stemming from the work of Wilhelm Reich and now best known as the bioenergetic approach; and the phenomenological approach of Fritz Perls, which he called Gestalt therapy. This rough breakdown is useful mainly for purposes of an overall survey.[1] In the remainder of this chapter I refer in general to this grouping—but for purposes of exposition the material will be organized in terms of what appear to be the major kinds of changes in the rules of the game that have taken place, particularly during the exciting series of developments since about 1955.

## THEORY TAKES A SHARP TURN

In discussing the medical model of therapy and the more recent attacks on it, I have already given some indication of the theoretical developments that led to new forms of therapy based on principles of learning and reinforcement—the so-called behavior therapies. Although a case can be made for the claim that the term *learning theory* has always been a misnomer, its development under this

---

### "LEARNING" THEORY?

Whatever theory is advanced to explain, say, the behavior of a pigeon under specified conditions in a Skinner box, it ought not to be called a learning theory. It is not really a theory about the pigeon—for one adult bird of the same species will do as well as another—nor is it particularly a theory about its learning. Rather, the theory is concerned with the conditions, the operations, and the results in the experimenter's apparatus. If we assume that it is the pigeon which is the learner and the experimenter therefore the teacher, then the theory properly refers to teaching and not to learning. I would offer that learning—

in any meaningful sense of that term as referring to something more than just a change in behavior—takes place when, from the point of view of the learner, some relevant aspect of the world is restructured; that is, he now sees some relevant things in a different way. But such a definition could not appear as part of the theory of a learning theorist. He has denied himself the privilege of talking about learning.

Similarly, the behavior therapist's patient is not supposed to be learning; that is not his function. Just as one hungry rat will do as well as another of the same age and weight and species, so will one phobic person of normal I.Q. do as well as another. Like the animal subject in the Skinner box, he is present only as emitter of responses that enable the procedure to continue. As a consequence, the be-

havior therapist has denied himself the privilege of entering into the wondrous inner world of his patients.

---

name has been part of a long-term trend toward de-emphasizing the products of human experience—fantasy, imagining, wishes, awareness and self-awareness. Jay Haley sums up his contemporary critique of the original, Freudian position:

*The emphasis upon thought processes and the development of fantasy life would seem to be related to Freud's fascination with the processes of human thinking. One cannot read Freud without admiring his tenacity and skill as he traces a patient's ideas all through their symbolic ramifications. . . . [It] will be suggested [here] that the exploration of the human psyche may be irrelevant to therapeutic change. . . . Freud appeared during a period when it was assumed that man could change through self-understanding, and it seems more apparent today that the ability of a person to change because of self-knowledge is definitely limited. A description of psychoanalytic therapy which includes both analyst and patient, rather than only the subjective processes within the patient, makes apparent other possibilities besides self-understanding as the source of therapeutic change.*[2]

In this view, the patient does not need self-understanding in order to change; and changes in what goes on inside his head, so to speak, will not necessarily lead to changes in how he acts. This is a revolutionary turn for psychological theory. To understand its implications, we turn to one of the most famous examples in the psychoanalytic literature—the story of how Freud altered his own theoretical position in regard to the origins of adult hysteria. He had been told by a number of his patients that they had been sexually molested or assaulted by the father during early childhood, and so his initial view was that the adult symptoms he saw were a direct consequence of the fact of the childhood trauma. In formal terms, he began by holding to the theory that early behavior in childhood (being the victim of a sexual assault) led to later behavior in adulthood (neurotic symptoms). On rethinking the matter he became convinced that it was in fact highly improbable that so many respectable fathers had sexually molested their own children; by a stroke of insight he changed his theory to read: not the fact of the childhood trauma but the child's wish or fantasy concerning the trauma was what led to the later neurosis. He realized that the attack itself had never occurred, but that the child, wishing or fantasying its occurrence and then repressing the wish, began to develop complexes in the form of repressed material that gave rise in adulthood to neurotic symptoms. Again in formal terms, Freud's new formulation was that early wish-and-fantasy in childhood led to later behavior in adulthood, in contrast to his earlier view that behavior led to behavior.

Here, then, we have two kinds of causes: (1) those that occur inside the head, as it were, in the form of knowledge, wish, fantasy, and so on; and (2) those that occur in the world, so to speak, in the form of observable behavior. Which of these two is it that causes subsequent behavior? Or are these the only possibilities? Haley suggests some others:

*This shift also centered psychoanalysis upon the fantasy life of the patient rather than his behavior in relation to other people. If Freud had emphasized the possibility of the hysteric's parents behaving in a particular way with the patient, he would have entered the field of family study and classification. If he had emphasized the way the hysteric was manipulating him by falsely telling him about such an assault, he would have examined psychotherapy in terms of tactics between patient and therapist. Instead, he centered upon the patient's misinterpretations of his past and so entered the field of symbolic process.*[3]

This gives us two other possible modes of causation: (3) a background of learned interpersonal strategies, gained in early childhood with parents and other family members, may give rise in adulthood to neurotic behavior; or, (4) symptomatic behavior in the therapy session can be understood as the result of here-and-now purposes vis-à-vis the therapist, although these purposes might in turn be traceable to earlier causative influences. The four types of causation, then, are mental, behavioral, strategic, and symptomatic.

As a general rule, psychology has tended to emphasize the first of these four modes of causation whenever it dealt with the why of people's behavior; people do what they do because something inside them motivates them to do it. Thus, it is said that people act crazy because of something in them that we call schizophrenia or, more broadly, mental illness; people do well in school because of something in them that we call intelligence or musical ability or what have you; people continue to drink because of an inner something we call their alcoholism; people tie their ties in a certain way every day because inside of them is what we call a habit; and so on and on. The most notable example of this mode of causation is in social psychology, in regard to certain kinds of relations between people. Why do some white people act unfairly and even cruelly toward some black people, and why do they get angry or defensive or irrational when they are caught at it? The answer is that they carry around inside them something we call attitudes, specifically those special attitudes called prejudices.

It is only recently that this approach to the causation of behavior has been called into question. Increasingly, and for very good practical reasons, it has been noted that every test of this view has shown that there is no basis for it. If the immediate cause of people acting in a bigoted manner were in fact the attitudes they carry around inside them, then it would follow that if we knew their attitudes in detail, we would be able to predict their behavior. In fact, we cannot—we cannot predict behavior from a knowledge of the relevant attitudes. We can, however, predict someone's behavior quite well if we know the general situation in which the behavior occurs, or if we know how the person has behaved in the past in similar situations. For example, if our subject is a typical male college sophomore in the United States, and if we place him successively in three different situations—first, alone in a car on a dark side road at night with his girl friend; second, eating dinner at the home of his girl friend's parents; and third, with his girl friend at the climax of an important basketball game, with his team ahead by one point and eight seconds to go and the opponents in possession of the ball—I think that we could predict reasonably well, with a fair degree of confidence, and quite accurately, many of the details of his behavior. Similarly, if we know that someone has voted for conservative Republicans in the past, we would do quite well in predicting which way he will vote in the future. Behavior predicts behavior; attitudes do not predict behavior.[4]

So runs the theoretical argument, and it is a telling one. If the various aspects of experience, such as attitudes, are not the immediate causes of what a person does and if on the contrary his actions, including abnormal actions, are caused rather by his past behavior and by his general life situations, then we are well advised to try changing him either by changing his life patterns or by teaching him new ways to behave, or preferably both. Therapy then becomes a process of retraining or behavior modification, no longer understood as a treatment for disturbances, but rather as the presentation of new and more constructive options and then teaching the patient how to take advantage of them. This is just what learning theory has specialized in ever since John B. Watson began the behaviorist revolution with an all-out attack on the primacy of experiential causes and data in 1913.[5] Learning experiments in the laboratory over a forty-year period have in fact consisted of just this—presenting the subject with some options for new ways of behaving, and then studying the conditions that aid or impede the acquisition and maintaining of the learned behaviors.

The systematic application of such a learning theory to psychotherapy was delayed until the 1950s when a South African psychiatrist, Joseph Wolpe, demonstrated that many neurotic symptoms could be successfully treated in an office practice by the use of relatively simple *counterconditioning* procedures.[6] These consisted of first teaching the patient some self-induced techniques for relaxing; then instructing the patient in how to bring about relaxation, and therefore a lessening of anxiety, whenever an image or idea caused distress; then leading the patient through a planned series of fantasies, so arranged as to be progressively more anxiety-arousing because they were increasingly similar to what usually triggered off the symptom; and in this way making it possible for the patient to entertain thoughts of previously threatening stimuli. Following these office procedures, it was then feasible for the patient to attempt new modes of behavior in what were formerly anxiety-provoking situations.

Only a few years later a number of workers at Harvard, following Skinner, adopted his methods of operant conditioning to build up new behavioral patterns in disturbed adults; these methods were then greatly extended by Ogden Lindsley in work with retarded and brain-damaged children. Building on the pioneering work by Arnold Lazarus with neurotic adults and children, Nathan Azrin and Teodoro Ayllon with hospitalized mental patients, and O. Ivar Lovaas with autistic children, many hundreds of behavior therapists were soon engaged in working on a wide range of problems—specific neurotic disorders, delinquency, school behavior, classroom management, behavioral "engineering" in institutions, and marriage counseling.[7]

The range of methods used is now as wide as the variety of clients treated. The methods may be categorized as follows, using Albert Bandura's suggested classification:[8]

1. *COUNTERCONDITIONING.* New responses are conditioned that are incompatible with the behavior that is to be eliminated. In positive counterconditioning, for example, the presence of food may be coupled with the object or situation that evokes anxiety, thereby weakening the anxiety response; and in such aversive counterconditioning as the antabuse treatment for alcoholism, a noxious substance produces its effect when alcohol is ingested, thereby decreasing the probability of the drinking behavior. Neutral counterconditioning is exemplified by the Mowrers' well-known bell-and-pad device for controlling bed-wetting. Dampening of the bed pad by starting to wet the bed completes an electrical circuit that serves to ring a loud buzzer and wake up the bed-wetter; in this way, having to urinate is conditioned to waking up, so that involuntary urinating is then controlled.

2. *EXTINCTION.* The behavior to be eliminated is repeated in the absence of reinforcement, thus weakening it. This was first suggested many years ago by Knight Dunlap, who noted that the simplest way to get rid of a small, unwanted habit is to practice doing it deliberately. Behavior therapists view this method as the essential process in conventional, talking psychotherapy; that is, the patient repeats behavior that he is sure will provoke punishment, and when the therapist's response is, rather, to be permissive and accepting the effect is one of extinction of the fear, guilt, or anxiety associated with the behavior.

3. *CONDITIONING.* Aimed primarily at that class of therapy clients who lack acceptable modes of behavior, the conditioning method may consist of either operant or classical conditioning in the presence of reward. Lovaas has used this method extensively with severely disturbed children; the rewards are made contingent on such desired behavior as talking or responding positively to the therapist; in this way new behavioral repertoires are built up. Although in principle the conditioning method may also be used with punishment in order to eliminate undesirable behavior—either by operant methods, in which case the client's responses are punished, or by classical conditioning methods, in which case the stimuli leading to the incorrect behavior are paired with punishment—the results are uncertain in most cases where more than the mildest of punishments is to be used.

4. *MODELING.* The client, or subject, is allowed the opportunity to observe the behavior of some person with whom rewarding experiences are associated. This method has been exploited chiefly by Bandura himself who has presented a great deal of experimental evidence in support of it.[9] In addition, he argues convincingly that this method enters as a significant factor in the practice of most forms of psychotherapy, whatever their orientation.

---

BEHAVIOR THERAPY: A SUMMARY

What distinguishes behavior therapies from more traditional approaches? Behavior therapists tend to select specific symptoms or behaviors as targets for change, to employ concrete, planned interventions to manipulate these behaviors, and to monitor progress continuously and quantitatively. A patient's early life history is largely ignored, except as it may provide clues about such factors as currently active events which maintain symptoms, or hierarchies of reinforcers. Behavior therapists tend to concentrate on an analysis of particular symptoms. They devote far less attention than other clinicians to subjective experiences, attitudes, insights and dreams. Their tools include electronic equipment and devices which permit precise measurement of behavior. Their programs tend to give less consideration to evidence based on empathy than on observations. . . .

Behavior therapy is most distinguishable from other approaches after a program with a carefully outlined procedure has been established for treatment of a defined problematic response. Treatment in which a patient's nervous tic is conditioned by applying an aversive stimulus whenever the tic occurs is markedly different from the psychodynamic treatment of the same problem by repeated interviews attempting to ascertain conflicts of which the tic is said to be a manifestation. On the other hand, assignments to a subassertive patient to note and record his subassertive behavior or to practice assertive behaviors in planned situations,

or the use of relaxation and hypnosis in therapy during recall of embarrassing or anxiety-arousing situations are much more likely to be found among various schools of psychotherapy. The essential distinction of behavior therapy seemingly may be most vivid in its unique methods, but it actually lies in the approach of the clinician, from his very first contact with the patient. The questions asked about the patient's complaints, sources of information sought, methods of record keeping, selection of a behavior for therapeutic attack, the rationale underlying all of these, not just the actual techniques used, are the hallmarks of behavior therapy.

The differences in procedures are based on the differences between traditional and behavior therapy with regard to several important assumptions about the nature of the problem, including:

1. With regard to etiology, behavior therapies do not accept the concept of psychological problems as "diseases" due to early faulty personality development.
2. The behavior to be altered is not viewed as a superficial "symptom" or manifestation of an underlying disease process, but as the patient's problem. The target behavior is not a substitute for a conflict or an unconscious expression of a blocked desire, but is a learned response which has detrimental consequences for the patient or his environment, regardless of how it was acquired.
3. Treatment is aimed at the problem

behavior, not at the hypothesized disease, conflict, or unconscious struggle within the patient's personality.

4. Treatment techniques are tailored to the individual patient's problems, not to the diagnostic label attached to his condition or personality.[10]

The basic ideas behind behavior modification approaches are so straightforward and profound that they have often been expressed in the folk wisdom of aphorisms: Nothing succeeds like success. You can do more with a carrot than with a stick. Or, in the most general terms, living organisms learn to do what brings them satisfaction and to stop doing what hurts. This generalization, in its original form as the Law of Effect, has always constituted nearly all the general theory that can be found in behaviorist thinking, particularly that of the atheoretical school following Skinner. The major contribution of behavior therapists has consisted of the systematic use of this basic principle under controlled and repeatable conditions—that is, in planning and carrying out change in the clinic just as though the situation were a research laboratory rather than a therapist's office. This experimental emphasis seems now to be undergoing some modification, however, as behavior therapy becomes more widely known and as more and different kinds of patient problems are offered for treatment. One team of friendly critics, after spending five days observing the clinical work of Wolpe and Lazarus, had this to say:

> *From our acquaintance with the literature we know intellectually at least that behavior therapists do not work in a unitary fashion and indeed take pains to vary their approach from case to case. We were surprised to find, however, that within most cases, too, a number of manipulations were routinely employed. Even where desensitization was the primary technique, others such as assertiveness or expressiveness training, manipulation of behavior outside the treatment setting, and education in learning principles were also included. With the more complex cases the spectrum of techniques became even broader. In addition to desensitization involving a variety of hierarchies, many variants of assertion and expression, often elaborate role-playing and behavioral programs of homework were devised to correct response deficiencies. Along with these specific procedures we found also that patients were given a good deal of indoctrination, teaching, and exhortation, apparently intended to provide a rationale for the treatment and to enhance motivation.[11]*

### A Model of Two-Choice Behavior

In spite of these changes to accommodate to a more varied practice, however, the claim of the behavior therapist is that in his work with clients he hews as close as circumstances allow to the ideal of the laboratory experiment. It will not be taking an example out of context, then, if I use as the basis for the following discussion a research-like demonstration of behavior modification techniques. It was carried out by Sidney Bijou and his associates as part of a program of research with "problem" children—in this case, a little boy who was, according to his mother's complaint, overly demanding.[12]

The research was carried out in a series of steps, as follows:

1. The mother was instructed in the general nature of the procedures and was then asked to play with her child, in the observation room, just as though they were at home. Their behavior was monitored by two observers.
2. On the basis of these observations, it was determined that the boy's behavior could be classified either as demanding (e.g., "You go there and I'll stay here!") or as compliant and cooperative (e.g., "Will you help me?" or "This is fun.").
3. In the next session, the observers recorded: (a) commanding or demanding behavior on the part of the child; (b) compliant or cooperative behavior on the part of the child; and (c) the presence or absence of responsive behavior by the mother immediately following either (a) or (b). The interest here was in how often the mother responded to the two categories of the boy's behavior.
4. Two base-line curves were then plotted, one showing the frequency of demanding behavior that was followed by the mother's response to it and the other showing compliant behavior that was followed by a response. The frequency of the former far exceeded the frequency of the latter; that is, the mother tended to respond to her child when he showed demanding behavior rather than when he showed compliant behavior. (This, of course, is quite typical in such situations; the boy was in fact getting the attention he wanted.)
5. During the next two sessions of twenty minutes each, the mother was instructed to ignore her son's behavior except when a signal (in the form of a flashing red light that he could not see) alerted her to act in whatever way seemed natural at the moment. The light was then used to have her not respond to demanding behavior but to respond to compliant behavior. The former decreased, and the latter increased, during these sessions.
6. Finally, in the ensuing two sessions the light was eliminated, thus reinstating the original conditions. The mother was now instructed to act the way she would usually act, and the boy's demanding behavior (predictably) increased while compliant behavior decreased.

The design is admittedly elegant; the conclusion seems unarguable, that with the mother's attention as the carrot, the boy's behavior could be made to be either cooperative or commanding. It is to be hoped the mother went away convinced that it was she who was keeping the boy's behavior in its demanding mode, all the while she was complaining about it. The conclusion might have been hard for her to accept, but its logic was irrefutable.

But of course this is true of every carefully designed experiment; the demonstrated conclusion follows perfectly from the given conditions. To this must be added, however, that the logic of every experiment is bounded by the neatly circumscribed limits of the experimental situation. Were we to step outside these limits, it might well be that quite different alternatives would present themselves. I suggest that we do just this in regard to the research I have described and that we begin by considering the psychological situation of the boy himself. Everything depends on him in this situation; he is the bit player on whom swings the whole tragic plot.

For the truth is that this neat arrangement works purely and simply because the boy has been restricted to two, and only two, alternatives. He can either act one way and have his mother give him her attention, or he can act another and have her turn away. But is this all that might ordinarily happen between parent and child? No; we all know that this pair of possibilities is not exhaustive of interchanges between a mother and her son. How does it happen, then, that in this situation there are no other alternatives?

The answer is, I think, that this situation has been so constructed that for the boy himself no other alternatives are possible. He has been boxed in by a theory and a set of experimental conditions, in exactly the same way that subjects are always boxed in for laboratory studies. But the important difference is that when adults such as college students are restricted by a set of experimental conditions and then goaded into behaving in specified ways, they have all sorts of personal and private exits from the psychological situation, even though it may appear on the surface that they are still bound to the objective situation. A great deal of what is called experimental error, a lot of what is revealed as between-subjects variance, must be the result of just this factor—that subjects do not always conform to the imposed conditions and do exactly what they are supposed to do, but answer at random, ignore instructions, try out other possibilities, and so on.

But as we saw, the trick in the example above is that the little boy is unable to find any other alternatives. I know that I could easily offer him one. I could say to him, "For God's sake, little boy, why don't you just break up this idiot tragedy by walking out of it? Why don't you just say to your mother (and to all those eager students watching on the other side of the one-way mirror), 'Hey, the hell with all of you! I'm free to walk out of here,' and then walk out? Why not try *that* alternative?" But no, this boy could never do that. We all know the boy's public secret, the experimenters and his mother most of all—only he has no direct access to it: that the truth about his condition is that he is not free; that this in fact is his problem; that he is bound to his mother, and she to him, in a tight and mutually strangling bond; and that because of this only one of them can survive, if it ever comes (as it has) to a conflict, and that if she can help it, by God, she will be the one who survives, armed with all the tricks of the "new therapy," and he will no longer be a sometimes difficult human being who is striving for independence but her dutiful appendage, swung around at the end of a silver cord that has been blessed by a benevolent and helpful therapist. The boy is not free; that is his problem. His problem is not that he clings to his mother and is overly demanding of her attention, but that he has no other choices except either to cling to her for attention or not to cling to her for attention. And note this: to say his problem is that he is not free is very different from saying that his problem is that he and his mother don't get along. The one problem that a behavior therapy cannot handle is this one of freedom, precisely because it demands of its client, if he stays in therapy at all, that he be not free but bound by its experimental conditions.

### The Question of Freedom

At the heart of the problem of learning is the question of freedom. I would not be exaggerating very much to say that freedom, and whether it is possible, and how we may help to make it possible are what any theory in psychology is about; they are what this book is about, too.

It can be demonstrated that conditioning works. That is to say, a lot of evidence can be brought forth to show that under the proper circumstances, conditioning takes place, predictably and reliably. Understandably, theorists whose sphere of interest in psychology consists of externally observed behavior come to believe that a theory about conditioning is at the heart of a behavioral science. But it is precisely because they have restricted their concern to externals, to what I have called an outer view, that they cannot be expected to spot the restrictions under which such a theory labors. The major restriction is that conditioning can only succeed when the subject is not free.

To understand the implications of that rather blunt statement, we have to consider what it is like to be subjected to a conditioning procedure. Imagine any sort of conditioning arrangement that you like—that you are one of Pavlov's dogs, wired and strapped and restrained in a sterile and soundproof training room; or that your eyelid reflex is being conditioned to the stimulus of a puff of air; or that you are a patient in a mental hospital who is rewarded with a brass token, exchangeable for some privilege, whenever you eat a meal like a "normal" person would; or that someone is reinforcing your assertive statements in psychotherapy with a nod and an approving smile. It makes no difference what the circumstances are or even what specific conditioning method is being used on you. It is the same in every case; the conditioning will succeed with you only if you are significantly unaware of what is really going on, or if you are aware but have no control over what happens. In order for the conditioning procedure to work, it must run its course mechanically. Since you, as subject, are one element in that course, you must be reduced to the mechanical level of the rest of the elements, either by forcing you into unawareness or by taking advantage of your state of unawareness. In each of the instances that I just cited, or in any others that might be mentioned, the conditioning will fail if you, as subject, exercise your freedom as an individual. All that you need do is say something like this (to yourself, of course, for if you said it aloud you would be dismissed as an experimental subject): "Now, wait a minute. If I eat the meal quietly, I get a token. If I create a disturbance, no token, and I probably get sent back to my room. It looks like I'm trapped. But no—how about if I just sit quietly at the table but don't eat?" Or you might say to your therapist: "Whenever I say something that sounds assertive, you nod and smile at me. I admit that I sort of want you to approve of me. That's why you're doing it, isn't it?"

Of course these are improbable responses to the conditioning procedures I have described, highly improbable, indeed. They are unlikely to occur, as we know, because the subjects who are being conditioned here either cannot or will not break free of the constraints placed on them. But that is precisely the point—the conditioning procedure is absolutely limited in terms of the individual and personal freedom it can allow its subjects. In this respect it is only one other form of the conventional laboratory experiment, which is built on denying freedom to its subjects.

Now, all this is not to deny that in every one of the examples I cited the conditioning procedure often does work, and it works in many other situations as well. It works because—and this is undeniable—the subjects are, unfortunately, quite unable to break free in the way that I suggested above. But the reason for their inability to break free—that the whole procedure rests on their original or imposed lack of freedom—is not an insight to which behavior theorists could ever come. They are apparently unable to recognize and then think seriously about the pillar on which their own procedure rests: its denial of freedom to their subjects.

If we do think seriously about the matter of freedom, we will have to consider opening a door to admit the data of experience on an equal basis with the data of behavior. For that is what experience must rest on, the individual's freedom. Experience is unassailably and basically a matter of the possibility of freedom. From the point of view of the person himself, from inside his own experience, all that freedom can ever mean is that he is in touch with his own situation, that his awareness is not completely bounded nor determined, and therefore that he has within himself the sources of his next decisive act. It is precisely this state of freedom-as-experienced to which every form of psychotherapy would lead its clients, behavior therapy included. But I suggest that we will surely not be able to understand how psychotherapies, including behavior therapy, accomplish this unless we think seriously about freedom and its expression as a pillar of experience and unless we recognize that purely external approaches to theory and to therapy must on principle deny that expression.

A wise and thoughtful psychiatrist once put it this way: "Neuroses can be produced only in domesticated laboratory animals in which dependence on human beings has been developed and flight excluded."[13] Similarly, neuroses can appear in humans only when circumstances arrange it so that the continuing freedom to glory in one's experience is somehow restricted. When this has once occurred, the behavior therapies enter and, with a flourish, proceed to take advantage of the subject's built-in lack of freedom. For all their startling successes, then, they turn out to be best fitted for a specific kind of subject—the one who is helpless or far gone, the one who lacks any ways of fighting back or creating his own, individual alternatives. The history of behavior therapy is a succession of triumphs in the most retractable kinds of cases but, ironically, it is the very extremity of these cases that has made behavior therapy possible—the severely mentally retarded or brain-damaged, the inmates of total institutions such as back wards of mental hospitals, the animals, the schizophrenic children, all that range of "hopeless" cases in whom the horizon of experience can be bounded by conditions imposed by the therapist.[14] Given a situation in which the subject either cannot or will not seek out other options, behavior modification is bound to work. Equally, it will work on any person at all who is willing to agree that acceding to these limitations is, at least for the moment, preferable to continuing in his present state of distress. To many persons, clients and therapists alike, that would seem to be all that one could ask for. But is it?

### SHIFTS IN STATUS

A second major change in the rules of psychotherapy has been in the relative status assigned to therapist and patient in their encounter. As I noted, the characteristics of various kinds of therapy are always stated in the clinical literature in terms of the therapist: his theory, his technique, his method, and his innovations, his successes and his failures. This is surprising and a bit embarrassing because every one of these characteristics necessarily includes the patient as an equally active partner. As a partial corrective, I would like to consider, first, status changes in both partners in regard to the amount of knowledge that is assigned to each, and second, status changes as they have affected other aspects of method and technique.[15]

---

DR. BERGLER TALKS TO HIS PATIENTS

DOCTOR: It is obviously more flattering to yourself to admit to pity and a kind heart than to something else. How, by the way, do you overcome the feeling of unfairness in eliminating the companion of your years of struggle for success?

PATIENT: There it goes again! The everlasting refrain of having "given you the best years of my life"! Didn't I? Does a marriage certificate mean mortgaging one's WHOLE life?

DOCTOR: High-flown words, spoken with bitterness, do not change inner facts. And these inner facts indicate quite clearly in your case that you are inwardly NOT through with your wife. Everything else is self-delusion.[16]

"People of the type you refer to work on two levels," I explained. "Unconsciously, they cherish the kick; consciously, they run after what you call happiness. In the end the unconscious wins out."

"Simple as that?"

"It isn't simple at all. Unconsciously enjoyed self-damage is the most complicated, least believable of all psychic reactions."[17]

---

### The Doctor Knows Best

It is not at all difficult to find in the voluminous psychoanalytic literature in English innumerable instances of which Edmund Bergler is only a frank and outspoken example. For many years, in fact, the presumption that was central to the whole Freudian enterprise was that the doctor knew best and therefore all decisions about what was important were to be made by him. At the same time that this presumption helped to determine what went on in psychoanalytic sessions, the rationale given to patients was just the opposite—the patient and not the therapist did all the work and only the patient really knew what was going on. He knew it unconsciously, that was the point; and because he knew it in this way, rather than at the level of conscious awareness, it had to be up to the analyst to guide the patient along paths with which he, the patient, was already familiar. But in the end, no matter how it was phrased, the message came through that the doctor always knew best.

Far-reaching changes in therapeutic method came about, as we shall see, when Carl Rogers flatly contradicted this claim and based a system of therapy on an opposite view. But while one trend was progressively moving in the direction of assigning more equal knowledge to therapist and patient, two related systems, while radically altering many other aspects of therapy, were swinging back to an orthodox position in regard to who knew best. One of these was behavior therapy, particularly as it was practiced by Wolpe; he comes across as a kindly, skilled, fatherly teacher whom it would be almost heresy to oppose. The whole structure of the behavior therapies is based on the model of the highly skilled trainer, and so it is assumed from the outset that it is the therapist who possesses all the relevant knowledge. In addition, for obvious reasons there is no attempt to provide a publicly acceptable rationale in the form of the patient's presumed unconscious knowledge of what he is doing. Behavior therapy remains purely and simply a scheme in which the doctor knows whatever there is to know and will undertake to help the patient learn it.

The other, related system in which knowledge is preponderantly on the side of the therapist is Albert Ellis' creation—rational-emotive therapy. In this approach, neurotic difficulties are viewed as maladaptive habits and attitudes that are derived from and kept alive by the patient's own interpretations of his conduct. Partly because of what he is taught by an irrational culture, and partly because of his own upbringing, the patient tells himself the wrong things—statements that are self-defeating, propositions that are irrational or just plain mistaken. It is his thinking that is wrong; when he learns to think differently, to tell himself more sensible and constructive things, he will be in a position to try out new kinds of behavior. This is clearly first cousin to the behavior therapies, specifically to the method of reciprocal inhibition—a method in which the maladaptive response is inhibited by a new, positive response, such as acting in a more socially adaptive way, or, as in the example that follows, acting in a more self-assertive manner.

A young man's problem may be that he is afraid to ask a girl for a date. If he continues this behavior, he will of course never get a date and his social situation can hardly improve; his behavior is thus continuingly self-defeating. If he were to go to a rational-emotive therapist for help, he would first be given to understand, often in the strongest and most forceful of terms, the nature of the self-defeating propositions by which he keeps this negative behavior going. Then he would be strongly supported in taking a chance on asking a girl for a date. If it works and she accepts, he has gained an important first step toward the confidence he needs to keep changing his behavior. If she turns him down, the therapist is there to help him make one more try. It is, in short, a straightforward system of re-education in new habit patterns. As long as the patient will agree to go along with it, it can hardly fail, though it may not always succeed to the degree that doctor and patient hope it will.

But in order for success to occur, the patient must either be a certain type of person or in a certain state. He must be able to go along completely with what the therapist is educating him to do, just as though he had no useful knowledge himself of what was wrong or how he should change. If he rejects the general explanation or its specific application to his own case, or if he fails to follow instructions in trying out his new behavior, then he will not have given the system a chance to prove itself. Thus the system might help and cannot hurt; it may often succeed but it cannot really fail—and all because it takes the knowledge completely out of the patient's hands and puts it in the doctor's, where perhaps it ought to be if therapy is really a form of re-education.

## Power Comes to the People

Many of the changes in therapeutic technique, beginning as early as the 1920s, served to lessen the status gap between doctor and patient. The patient, in many offices, got up from the couch to face his therapist across a desk. Psychoanalysis slowly ceased to be the prerogative of specially trained physicians and began to be applied in college clinics and settlement houses, by psychologists and by social workers. As a result, by the time that World War II broke out there were flourishing professions of psychiatric social work and clinical psychology whose members were eager to bring a psychoanalytic orientation, if not its orthodox methods, directly to the people. It is true that many of the areas of applied psychology—intelligence testing was a prime example—still rested on the unquestioned assumption that the power and privilege belonged to the professional as opposed to his client. But this too, like so much of therapeutic practice, has changed, owing largely to the influence of one man, Carl Rogers.

---

### INTELLIGENCE AND THE SOCIAL NORM

As social critics now inform us at great length, ours is a culture based on the Protestant ethic of work and reward. It is essentially a materialist culture, in spite of its bows toward religious belief. It is male-dominated; it places a higher value on achieving ends than on experiencing means; it stresses thinking and doing at the expense of being and feeling; it maintains as an unexamined ideal the fiction of a free and open society. When these assumptions are put together as the basis for an educational system and its program of testing ability, the results are easily predictable; the system will always define the goals of education in terms of its assumptions, and it will devise tests that reward children who conform to the pattern thus expressed.

Since intelligence testing arose during

the twentieth century, at a time when a lower middle class gradually set its mark on all of American culture—primarily because it comprised most of the potential consumers in a product-oriented society—the ways of testing for ability, and the theory supporting the tests, came to fit a specific pattern. Thus, the model student was good and obedient. He repressed his physical impulses, except under group-approved conditions, and his sexual impulses under almost all conditions. He learned the manner of speaking and the basic skills that were necessary to function as an average citizen, and he gained a store of information that was standard to his time and place in history though it may have fitted neither his individual needs nor his unique developmental schedule. He learned how to learn by listening rather than by questioning. He was motivated to succeed in accordance with the models who were presented to him. He aimed to be above all sensible; rational rather than thoughtful; logical rather than emotional; organized rather than impulsive; and quick and efficient rather than careful. He learned how to substitute depression for sadness, pleasure for joy, and affection for love. He became familiar with that special dialect of English spoken by schoolteachers and printed in schoolbooks (such as this one).

Does this description also fit the kind of student who will do well on a standard test of general intelligence? It should, for this was precisely the job that such tests were devised to do—to pick out and arrange on a scale, from low to high, children who differed in terms of how well they fitted this ideal. If they scored high, one could (and did) predict that they would do well in school, in the college that they were sure to attend, and in the society that had constructed such a selection system in the first place. And if they scored low, they could be (and were) shunted off to lesser academic goals and thence to lower positions in life—often to the tune of scholarly discussions about the relative influences of heredity and environment.

It is in this sense that intelligence testing is a significant aspect of the total educational process—not that these tests are no more than elaborate achievement tests, as is sometimes incorrectly claimed, but that they assess in standardized fashion just those characteristics of children which it is the business of the schools to inculcate. And they do this, in part, by means of roles which are vastly different in status—with the examiner in possession of all the prejudged answers and the test subject limited to responding on demand and in predetermined ways.

The work of Carl Rogers represents a watershed in the historical development of the field of psychotherapy. In one stroke he demonstrated that almost all of the artificial structure of classical therapy could be dropped with no great loss. He showed that the therapist need not belong to any profession, least of all medicine; his own work was entirely within psychology, and his students and followers had no training other than in graduate school. In his approach, therapist and patient were remarkably equal in status—they were renamed as counselor and client; they were usually on a first-name basis; and it was assumed as a major premise, and communicated both overtly and covertly, that there was no significant difference between them in potential for growth, that it was not true that one was sick and the other well, one weak and the other strong. The bulk of Rogers' original patients, in fact, and the population that he discovered, were college students, therefore basically sound in their personalities, reasonably well adjusted in their life patterns, and potentially adults who could be expected to be above average in productivity. Even when this was not completely so—as when the client was clearly disturbed or when Rogers later began to deal with schizophrenic patients— the whole thrust of his approach was still to make contact with the positive and healthy and responsible part of the client's personality.[18]

In these respects, Rogers was in the mainstream of a development that had been taking place since the innovation brought about by the neo-Freudian group in the early 1930s—Harry Stack Sullivan, Erich Fromm, and Karen Horney, among others. They had argued for an emphasis on goals, rather than needs, as primary motivators; they had insisted that the person is as much pulled as pushed in his emotional and interpersonal life. The kind of psychotherapy they envisioned, even if they did not quite bring it off, was one that helped its clients to act on their own best strivings rather than simply to fulfill their least-satisfied wishes; to grow rather than just be cured. It was a tradition that included as one of its key figures the neurologist-philosopher Kurt Goldstein, with his message of the self-actualizing person.[19] This, in turn, was the message that A. H. Maslow heard and that inspired him to develop a version of motivational theory which was broad enough to become the foundation for a whole new direction in contemporary psychology.[20]

Most important, Rogers' approach made no assumption at all that the counselor knew more about the client than the client himself did. There was no claim to having access to some public secret that, on being appropriately triggered in the clinical session, would spring out to be revealed to them both. Rogers found no need for that pillar of Freudian thought, the unconscious. As a consequence—for these concepts and practices always come together as a package—he found no need either for the technique of interpretation. What was left after he had eliminated diagnosis, interpretation, illness, curing, and even the notion of the all-knowing therapist helping his distressed patient, was the alarmingly simple idea that in the presence of an accepting person who will serve as mirror, comfort, model, and companion, anyone who is motivated to do so will be able to find himself and may even dare to become himself. Rogers has described very well

---

### THE EXPERIENCE OF THERAPY
ROGERS: THE EXPERIENCE
OF BEING A THERAPIST

I launch myself into the therapeutic relationship having a hypothesis, or a faith, that my liking, my confidence, and my understanding of the other person's inner world, will lead to a significant process of becoming. I enter the relationship not as a scientist, not as a physician who can accurately diagnose and cure, but as a person, entering into a personal relationship. Insofar as I see him only as an object, the client will tend to become only an object. . . .

I let myself go into the immediacy of the relationship where it is my total organism which takes over and is sensitive to the relationship, not simply my consciousness. I am not consciously responding in a planful or analytic way, but simply in an unreflective way to the other individual, my reaction being based (but not consciously) on my total organismic sensitivity to this other person. I live the relationship on this basis. . . .

The client is able to experience his feeling in its complete intensity, as a "pure culture," without intellectual inhibitions or cautions, without having it bounded by knowledge of contradictory feelings; and I am able with equal freedom to experience my understanding of this feeling, without any conscious thought about it, without any apprehension or concern as to where this will lead. . . . When there is this complete unity, singleness, fullness of experiencing in the relationship, then it acquires the "out-of-this-world" quality which many therapists have remarked upon, a sort of trance-like feeling, . . . a timeless living in the experience which is BETWEEN the client and me. . . . It is the height of personal subjectivity.[21]

MAY: THE EXPERIENCE OF BEING A CLIENT

I remember walking that day under the elevated tracks in a slum area, feeling the thought, "I am an illegitimate child." I recall the sweat pouring forth in my anguish in trying to accept that fact. . . . Later on that night I woke up and it came to me this way, "I accept the fact that I am an illegitimate child." BUT "I am not a child anymore." So it is, "I am illegitimate." That is not so either: "I was born illegitimate." Then what is left? What is left is this, "I AM." This ACT of contact and acceptance with "I am," once gotten hold of, gave me (what I think was for me the first time) the experience "Since I am, I have the right to be."

What is this experience like? It is a primary feeling—it feels like receiving the deed to my house. It is the experience of my own aliveness not caring whether it turns out to be an ion or just a wave. . . . It is like going into my very own Garden of Eden where I am beyond good and evil and all other human concepts. It is like the experience of the poets of the intuitive world, the mystics, except that instead of the pure feeling of and union with God it is the finding of and the union with my own being. . . .[22]

---

the experience of the nondirective counselor in such a therapy; and Rollo May, although his own method is closer to the analytic and his orientation more existential, has accurately reported what the experience of finding oneself may be like to the client.

In actual practice, the nondirective, or client-centered approach—both terms are equally apt—seems deceptively simple. In fact, it is difficult to carry off without it being turned into a gimmick, for it requires that the counselor truly give up his tendency to take a superior position and cure the client's problems. All that the counselor is required to do is to reflect back, with understanding and empathic warmth and acceptance, the experiential core of what the client offers. It is then not a matter of repeating words but of reflecting a feeling-experience; and it must always stop short of that addition which would come across to the client as an interpretation. For example, if the client has been despondently listing a series of rejections he has just received from girls whom he has called for dates, the response by the therapist can be any one of a wide range of communications. He may convey understanding and acceptance by a nod, a smile, a look, or by murmuring "Mm-hm." He may repeat the names of the girls that the client has just mentioned, in a sympathetic summation. He may say the same thing in a summary sentence: "They all turned you down." Or he may reflect the feeling expressed in the client's voice and words, with, "It's tough being turned down so often." The essence of Rogers' method would seem to be in the prescription that in his own statement the counselor is not to add any personal meaning to what the client has said. If the client has not as yet said even the obvious statement of feeling that one would expect in this situation, then it is not the counselor's place to say it for him—for that statement might be, "I just feel like crying" or, "What's the matter with me that they do this to me?" but equally it might be, "It makes me so damn *mad*" or even, to everyone's surprise, "You know, I'm sort of glad they did." To have the counselor make this additional statement before the client has made it constitutes an interpretation; and now we can clearly see what it is that the interpretation does. Because the interpretation rests on the assumption that the doctor knows best, it therefore provides the therapist with the chance to parade his knowledge during one of the frequent times that the patient is unable to take his own step forward.

Here, if anywhere, the two approaches to therapy part company. On the one hand, there is interpretive therapy in its many guises, all of them providing methods for one person, the therapist, to teach another. On the other hand, there is non-interpretive therapy in almost as many guises, and these provide opportunities for the other one of the pair, the client, to learn.

## FURTHER CHANGES IN TECHNIQUE

A practice that models itself on the medical profession and thus sets up a particular relation to its patients—the acceptance of the patient as patient, followed by the dedicated application of skill and knowledge until a cure is effected or the patient dies or leaves—will naturally incorporate such elements as a treatment program and a schedule of appointments. In psychoanalytic practice and its training procedures as well, a great amount of attention, therefore, used to be paid to the details of the patient's treatment schedule. It was taken for granted that he was to be seen for an hour at a time—or more precisely, the fifty-minute hour, as it was called by Robert Lindner[23]—and usually at the same time of day. Sessions were held as often as possible, and the fee was set fairly high, both details being based on the reasoning that if the program were at least some strain on the patient, both financially and in terms of his weekly schedule, it would be more meaningful to him. And much psychological significance was attached to the patient's feelings and remarks about the fee schedule, his practice of making payment, and the way that he used his and the analyst's time—that is, his promptness or lack of it and his keeping or breaking of appointments.

One of the major consequences of this emphasis on a carefully arranged and long-drawn-out program of treatment was that many analyses added up to remarkably lengthy "careers on the couch." Three-year analyses consisting of four or five sessions a week were common, and other individual analyses of more than five years were not unknown. It was not until many other changes occurred in therapeutic technique that short-term therapies were also introduced, as well as once-a-week schedules. But there still persisted the treatment program, harking back to the image of a doctor curing his patient, that called for a patient to enter therapy, to remain in it, and not to leave until something significant had happened to him by way of change.

ESALEN

The Esalen Institute was founded in the early 1960s by Michael Murphy and Richard Price as "a center to explore those trends in the behavioral sciences, religion and philosophy which emphasize the potentialities of human existence." It consisted originally of a setting on the Big Sur coast of northern California, not much larger than a small motel, which had formerly housed a commercial hot springs and baths; and it has since added additional conference and living space at Big Sur as well as San Francisco facilities for meetings and seminars.[24] There are now dozens of Esalen-like centers around the country, and in other countries as well, of which some of the best known are Aureon in New York City, Kairos near San Diego, Adanta in Atlanta, Orizon in Washington, D. C., and Oasis in Chicago.

Fritz Perls has summarized the Esalen spirit: "Esalen is a spiritual colony island. Esalen is an opportunity. Esalen has become a symbol, a symbol very similar to the German Bauhaus, in which a number of different dissident artists came together, and out of this Bauhaus came a re-catalyzation of art all over the world. Esalen and Gestalt are not identical. We are living in a symbiosis, a very practical symbiosis. I live and work here in a beautiful house, but I am not Esalen and Esalen is not me. There are many people, many different forms of therapy: soul therapy, spiritual, yoga bits, massage bits. All, whoever wish to be heard, can have seminars in Esalen. Esalen is an opportunity, and has become a symbol of the humanistic revolution that's going on."[25]

The program at the Esalen centers consists of lectures, seminars, meetings—it is difficult to find old terms adequate to describe these new phenomena—lasting one day, a weekend, or a full month or more. There are a number of residency programs for those who wish to embark on serious, long-term programs of training, although Esalen emphasizes that it is not a place for therapy, not a hospital and not a school, and it does not give any formal accreditation. It has, however, pioneered in almost every significant and exciting new development in the "non-affective domains," from meditation[26] to massage,[27] from sensitivity training to psychosynthesis.[28] Recently, research has been started and training instituted on "confluent education," as George Brown calls it[29]—the application of the Esalen approach and methods to elementary and secondary education, so as to enrich it beyond the purely cognitive domain.[30]

Then during the 1960s a new phenomenon arose on the therapeutic scene— the *encounter group*. First developed at the Esalen Institute in California on the model of the T-group, or Training Group, which had been introduced at a summer workshop of the National Training Laboratories in Group Development in 1957,[31] the encounter group represented a convergence of many current influences. Its first effect was to make possible a place and a setting where nonpatients could go through a kind of therapy, in a way that was totally divorced from the medical background and assumptions of conventional therapy.[32] Perhaps because of the burgeoning success and fame of encountering, which soon became a national fad, or perhaps in part because the times were ripe, one other bastion of the medical model of therapy now fell. Approaches to treatment began to be tried out that can best be called in-and-out-therapy, in which the client is not treated for any condition at all. Rather, the counselor meets with the client at a time picked by the latter and under circumstances that the client feels constitute a temporary crisis in his life. He spends some time with the counselor; he is possibly helped to work through the crisis until he feels that he is in a better place; and then he leaves. He may or may not be back. If he is like most persons, his life will consist of many crises. Some of these he will learn to work through by himself; some of them he will get through with the help of a mate, family, friends, good books, drugs, or whatever works for him; some of them will not be completely worked through and will remain as scars, sore spots, or weaknesses; and perhaps some of them will require that he return to spend some additional time with a helper.

In this model of the helping game and its relation to life's problems, it is assumed that no one ever becomes perfect and that life is a problem if not a continuing struggle. With the help of available resources, however, it is possible for many persons to live with greater joy, with more fulfillment, and with more of a sense of productive achievement in work and in relations with others than if they continued to struggle on their own. The medical notions that were implicit in more traditional approaches to therapy—that there is an ideal personality type or level of functioning, that the difficulties seen in clinical practice represent deviations from this ideal, and that there is some best sequence of therapeutic steps that can be taken to achieve the ideal—are dropped completely. In their place is found the philosophy that people are what they are, for better or worse, and that life may often be difficult, but that most persons can, with help from good people and some fair opportunities in life, become as happy and constructive as they will allow themselves to be.

This new philosophy runs its own kind of risk—that help will be offered too easily and come too quickly, which is just the opposite of the former danger that help was too expensive and took too long. One of the leaders of the new therapies of the 1960s, Fritz Perls, has warned against what he has called "a new and more dangerous phase":

> *We are entering the phase of the turner-oners: turn on to instant cure, instant joy, instant sensory-awareness. We are entering the phase of the quacks and the con-men, who think if you get some breakthrough, you are cured—disregarding any growth requirements, disregarding any of the real potential, the inborn*

*genius in all of you. If this is becoming a faddism, it is as dangerous to psychology as the year-decade-century-long lying on the couch. At least the damage we suffered under psychoanalysis does little to the patient except for making him . deader and deader. This is not as obnoxious as this quick-quick-quick thing. The psychoanalysts at least bring good will with them. I must say I am very concerned with what's going on right now.*[33]

Here was a steadying voice in what threatened to become an overwhelming wave of enthusiasm for a cure for all our personal and social ills. Perhaps the warning was needed.

### A Consumer Revolt in Therapy

Perls was by no means the only well-known therapist to warn against some of the possible risks and dangers in the new type of activity called encountering. Nothing has so upset established practitioners as the emergence of a type of therapeutic practice without therapists, generally carried on in nontherapeutic settings such as motels, hotel rooms, college classes, beaches—indeed, anywhere that a half-dozen or more persons could gather with or without a leader or facilitator. The professed aim of the encounter group is simple: to encourage participants, who enter without any preparation or lengthy introduction, to deal openly with their feelings about themselves and each other and to get some practice in expressing these feelings directly, concretely, immediately, and honestly rather than indirectly, symbolically, impersonally, or in ways that are merely socially acceptable.

An impressively large array of techniques were soon offered, taken from every possible source in group and individual work, to help precipitate the members of a group into this direct expression of feeling. Some of the techniques are so ingenious and so powerful that most persons are unable to maintain their usual defenses or inhibitions against the frank and public evocation of strong feeling. The results have been dramatic and immediately productive in so many instances that it seems legitimate to claim that the encounter approach is indeed a new method for personal change, perhaps also for personal growth.

The difficulty, however, is that although hundreds of thousands of persons, perhaps more, have by now had experiences in such groups, there has been little systematic study of what happens in these sessions or of how lasting and significant are the results that undoubtedly occur. Thus, no one really knows whether encountering does as much good as its proponents claim or as much harm as its detractors insist. It is an argument that can probably be settled only by time, so we will bypass the details here. What does seem clear is that the experience very often precipitates rapid changes in life-style: a marriage that has been shaky for years is either quickly reorganized on a new and more solid basis or is broken apart for good, all in one dramatic weekend with a dozen strangers. Major personal decisions about school and career, about a job, about relations with one's family, are dealt with and resolved at white heat. No one can say with confidence that this is either good or bad. True, it is a far cry from the dictum in classical psychoanalysis that the patient must agree to make no important life decision during the course of treatment, but on the other hand, life has now speeded up and history proceeds at a manic pace; perhaps this approach fits our times.

In any case, it is clear that the array of techniques initially popularized at Esalen—and soon adopted at a dozen other similar centers and often developed independently by ingenious group leaders in other settings as the idea of encounter-type sessions caught on—comes from a background quite different from that of more conventional therapies. So do its major practitioners, who are likely to be ex-theologians, teachers, counselors, actors, architects—whatever field can furnish perceptive, person-oriented leaders—rather than formally trained psychotherapists. Its clients, too, seem to differ from patients who come for conventional therapies, although they are often in flight from the therapy of their former years. They are less likely to identify specific neurotic complaints in themselves, more likely to speak of general life dissatisfactions that culminate in current crises. They see themselves not as sick people needing help, but as relatively normal, troubled, potentially healthy persons who are quite sophisticated about psychiatry and therapy, who are looking for guidance and re-education, and who want only an opportunity to discover for themselves new options, avenues for growth, and development along more satisfying lines than they have known. Finally, the centers and settings in which encountering has flourished have usually been chosen to take the participants out of their normal places; in this respect Esalen served very well as the model for an out-of-this-world retreat.

For all of these reasons—the nature of its activities, the type of leader and client, the setting and the atmosphere—encounter groups represent an approach that is radically different from conventional psychotherapy, so different, in fact, that perhaps it ought not be called therapy at all. Many of the most influential innovators in encountering have therefore preferred to look on it as a form of *affective education*; they have called their settings growth centers and have emphasized not therapy, or even helping, but rather a basic human potential for development and growth in the affective, noncognitive domains.

Encountering may be, as Richard Farson has suggested, an esthetic experience and nothing more. He sees the participant's experience in an encounter group as psychologically similar to having attended a great opera, concert, or play. It is possible to sit through such an event and be profoundly moved, so much so that the experience will be remembered for years as an emotional high point, perhaps even as a turning point in one's life—but no one would refer to this kind of experience as having cured him of anything. At most, one goes to such an event and then leaves it, having experienced an emotional and esthetic involvement of the highest order, but that is all. And actually, this is more than enough. If what encountering accomplishes for many of its clients is to enable them to achieve a memorable emotional experience, that of itself is of historic significance in a culture in which the affective life is so often squeezed out of the social fabric. I would guess that at its best the encounter experience is also something more. If it were only an experience like seeing a great dramatic performance, it would linger, it might lighten memory, but it would hardly have the widespread impact on life-styles that the encounter weekend has so often had. However, there is another possibility: the encounter group might be viewed as a modern and middle-class equivalent of the old-fashioned revival meeting—once an important change agent in a more innocent era.

Consider the parallels. Within each group, the participants are very similar to each other in outlook, orientation, purpose, and aim; they come to the experience primed for it, committed to its values, and in large part convinced of the worth of its methods; they are a group before they they get there. The entire procedure, its tone as well as its structure, is aimed at removing the event from everyday life; its first trick is to take the participants as rapidly as possible out of this world. All the drama is then directed at making sure this is a moving group experience, with an atmosphere and presence that will be strongly felt. (At Esalen it was commonplace for group members to remark in amazement at the end of two days that they felt closer to these strangers than they had ever felt to their own family members.) A powerful and charismatic leader focuses the energies of the group, engages their absolute trust, and for a brief period is permitted to become the most important figure in their emotional lives. The methods themselves are highly ritualized and can often be repeated over and over with no loss in effectiveness. In both the revival meeting and the encounter group session there is a concerted attempt to revive, for each participant, what may be only a myth or a lost ideal. In the revival meeting, this is the living presence of God; in the encounter group, it is the authentic and spontaneous life of childhood. Finally, the aim in both events is for each person, at some point during the proceedings, to come to a special state, a stage of being overcome. He is momentarily and deliriously flooded with awareness of a whole new world of possibilities for himself; a sinner no more, he is admitted to the company of the saved; and each of these dazzling moments of experience, publicly achieved, is rejoiced in by all the other members of the group.

The script for the old-fashioned revival meeting was taken from Mark 16: 16-18, and it fits the encounter weekend too:

*He that believeth and is baptized shall be saved; but he that believeth not shall be damned. And these signs shall follow them that believe; In my name shall they cast out devils; they shall speak with new tongues; They shall take up serpents; and if they drink any deadly thing, it shall not hurt them; they shall lay hands on the sick, and they shall recover.*

Like the revival meeting, the encounter group might be called a method of cleansing or healing—but in this sense it is not therapy. It is not, in fact, a part of the healing game, for it is not a form of treatment and it is not remotely medical. Practitioners of the medical type really have no claim on it. But to say this is not to dismiss it as just another fad in a nation that is often overeager to be taken in by fads which promise miracles in everyday life. Although the great interest that encountering aroused between 1965 and 1969 seems to have lessened, and so in retrospect it may appear to have been just one of the many popular and short-lived movements of that decade—remember Flower Power?—it may well have served a number of important and far-reaching purposes. As a movement it established and legitimized the ground rules for wholly new forms of individual and communal growth experience. By serving as the point of confluence of energies from many directions—social psychology, group work, industrial relations, Eastern philosophy, group psychotherapy, modern dance and theater, and religion—it made possible the development of many viable alternatives to existing forms of the healing game. It was a proving ground for all sorts of methods and techniques in sensory work, in emotional expression, and in interpersonal contact, and so it introduced to the clinical scene such innovations as group activities, forms of physical contact, nudity, marathons, and a host of procedures for rapid evocation of feeling. Many therapists have had encounter experiences and found them positive and personally helpful, and they have brought back into their own more conventional practices some of the ingenious and powerful techniques of encountering. Most important of all, the encounter movement has represented a large-scale revolt of the therapeutic consumer; in one grand effort, the receivers of therapeutic help turned the tables, established a do-it-yourself movement, and demonstrated that as far as they, the recipients, were concerned, it did indeed work. Therapy would never again be the same.

## THE POLITICS OF HEALING

One of the points that I have made a number of times in discussing psychotherapy is that when it is based on the medical model it is marked by a status gap between therapist and patient and by specific uses of power. It is this sort of clinical situation that Haley has in mind when he says:

> *The intensity of the relationship between hypnotist and subject and psychotherapist and patient rests upon the fact that both relationships sharply focus upon one of the most important questions in human life: How much influence will one person permit another to have over him? . . . If this process is translated into more impersonal terms, it can be said that a patient is first persuaded that a therapist might influence him, he then participates in helping the therapist influence him, and he finally acknowledges, if only to himself, that he is not functioning entirely on his own terms.*[34]

The history of psychotherapy, as I have implied above, can be written in these terms: a closing of the status gap, a growing equality of power.

Existential therapy claims with some pride to have come to terms with this dimension of the clinical encounter, even if not to have resolved it. Laing, in particular, hints strongly at the power plays and power struggles that mark the families of so many of his schizophrenic patients; he even tries to make us believe that experience has its own politics.[35] But his chosen phrase should more properly be *the morals of experience*, for that is really his topic. Politics is, in fact, a far dirtier and messier business than one would gather from his consulting-room existentialism. Politics, or the uses of power for purposes of gaining advantage over others in a restricted market, begins to define human relationships whenever either participant is less than completely open—and there are surely very few occasions when this is not so. Politics has its own logic and momentum and so it cannot stop—short of exhaustion on the part of either or both, or short of intervention by a neutral and still more powerful third party. This is how it is deep in the emotional center of many families, especially the families that Laing describes—to be found there are the most valuable prizes, in the many forms of personal security, which are fought over bitterly and without mercy. For those who live through it, bearing scars they can never hide, it is both appropriate and ironic that the chosen method of healing should itself often be based on power plays within the benevolent dictatorship of therapy.

To some degree therapy might work on such scarred victims of the political wars of childhood—so long as they have not given up looking for a new and more effective distribution of power. In a sense, they are like political liberals. Though they have been defeated often, they still retain a faith that within the establishment—that is, within the existing set of options that society offers—they will be able to find some new arrangement of power blocs that will work more satisfactorily than the old. The neurotic is, by this definition, a kind of therapeutic liberal. He, too, accepts the absolute necessity of differences in status; he wants only to learn how to come to terms with this given, to secure a more comfortable position for himself, and to get rid of the heavier burdens and the harsher blows that are laid on him. He has no quarrel with power as such.

On the other hand, there are those we might term therapeutic revolutionaries. Their response to the power struggles of their own background takes the more radical form of psychosis or some mode of social delinquency. If they have suffered their defeats primarily because of security gaps between persons of their family, they may become psychotic if they can no longer see any possible option within the world they know. But for others—with whom we are concerned here—their conviction that no option is acceptable has come about primarily because they feel that society has scarred them forever; as they see it, they have lost out on the basic prizes because the prizes were never there to be had, not because some other family member won out over them. And these victims, revolutionaries of the therapeutic scene, cannot possibly be satisfied with a liberal solution. No new power arrangements, such as in skilled treatment by a psychotherapist, are acceptable—none at all.

One of the little-recognized developments of our time is that an increasing number of the difficult cases that confront clinicians consist of just such revolutionaries.[36] Their difficulties are precisely defined as a total opposition to those in authority, a complete disavowal of any possible power arrangements that would impose restrictions on them. In some ways they seem to resemble old-fashioned patients, and in fact they can often be defined and even treated as though they belonged to familiar diagnostic categories; but the most precise definition of their position is that they refuse utterly to take the role of patient in regard to the very problems that have brought them to a therapist's attention.

Every clinician who has some connection with an institution dealing with young people is by now familiar with this kind of case. On university campuses a common example is a pregnancy crisis, often coupled with threats of suicide. Pregnancy is now a different kind of situational problem from what it was in the days of the therapist's youth. It used to occur chiefly as a result of forces that were experienced as beyond a couple's control: they were driven uncontrollably to have sexual relations; they hoped against hope that this would not result in pregnancy, which could neither be avoided in advance nor terminated once begun; and if pregnancy did occur they faced a crisis that was as much society's making as their own. But today the locus of control has shifted. A girl who becomes, or remains, pregnant has chosen to do so—and it is this choice which leads to the situational crisis that is at the heart of her problem. The middle-class college girl who becomes pregnant, does nothing about it, and then attempts suicide when faced with an intolerable situation without exits is not a victim but a rebel against the sexual and moral standards of her parents' generation. In respect to presenting her problem, she puts herself absolutely against authority and the power that it wields over her; she enters the therapeutic situation as a revolutionary would enter a courtroom, defying the principle on which it runs by denying its authority over her.

An equally common example, even more clear in its implications, is the juvenile drug addict whose opposition is not simply in regard to specific rules of conduct but in regard to the social scene in its entirety. In defiance of conventional morality, legal conventions, work ethics, and standards of interpersonal relations, he chooses a life-style that demands criminality, immorality, joblessness, and the total absence of stable interpersonal relationships. To confront such a revolutionary pose with the suggestion that he accept some form of authority as prerequisite to being treated or even helped is to defeat the helping offer at the start.

These are generation-gap problems—and when the gap between the generations represents, as it does here, the difference between a liberal and a revolutionary stance, it is not very helpful to attempt to bridge the gap by means of liberal rhetoric. Consider, for example, the well-meant attempts by a typical social work agency that assigns its workers to ghetto families in a medium-sized city. The workers have been well trained; they are no doubt sympathetic to the situation of the families, particularly the situation of young children who are both trapped and bewildered. One of the workers is assigned to a family of six children, all well known to various agencies for acts ranging from simple vandalism to nearly felonious crimes. The mother has been doing her best to keep the family together, but most of her efforts are needed to do housework by the hour in order to supplement the welfare-type support they receive.

Under these grim circumstances, the father is expected home soon from a jail sentence—although there is some fear that he will again get drunk and repeat his act of cutting off the little finger of one of his children. The representative from the social agency, having exhausted his practical resources in getting work for the mother and some aid for the children, now devotes most of his efforts to a program of rehabilitation, that is, psychotherapy—for there is little doubt that by any kind of criteria they are a severely disturbed assortment of people.

This is not an unusual case; perhaps it is a little more dramatic than most, but it is not essentially different from the set of circumstances available in thousands of case files of agencies that try to do more than find jobs. In other words, this is a typical instance of the application of therapeutic approaches to a situation that is already beyond therapy; it is a liberal solution to a revolutionary problem. The problem of these children, insofar as a problem can be formulated within their own experience, is quite different: it is that they have nothing, although they have committed no sin that would make them deserving of being cut off in this way from the world's goods. They see the middle-class child who is their own age in possession of whatever seems valuable to them—his own TV, a car, clothes and friends and freedom—and they can find no good reason in their own experience for this discrepancy. Their solution, most often, is to condemn the social arrangements that give rise to the discrepancy and perhaps also to go out to get what has been unfairly denied them. The logical cure for what ails them, then, is to use the agency worker's salary to buy them a television set.

Leaving aside for a moment the practical details and considering only the principle involved, we may ask why we continue to interpose the agency worker between the problem and its solution. What is it that we all hope to accomplish? The intent is surely noble—to heal some psychic ills, in the best therapeutic tradition. But because the problem in this case begins with the clients setting themselves against any form of authority, psychotherapy inevitably becomes, at best, the exercise of benevolent power. With all the good will in the world, it must be basically dishonest. It compels the therapist to act in terms of such euphemisms as "I'm only here to help you" and "I'm only doing this for your own good," or even "This will hurt me more than it will hurt you." We are reminded of that organizational villain attacked so brilliantly by Szasz—institutional psychiatry; we are also reminded that one does not have to be a psychiatrist to practice it.

Now that I have posed this problem, however, I must also state the other side of the case: the problem contains its own paradoxes and is not at all easy to solve. Here is a social situation that reasonable persons have judged untenable, and if the participants in it are not going to straighten it out themselves, some intervention would seem to be required. But since the participants have not asked for the intervention—except perhaps to apply for money—how can this be accomplished without that exercise of interpersonal power that I have just so roundly condemned? How to accomplish the ends of psychotherapy without therapeutizing?

There is a tradition in the helping arts that may provide an answer to these questions. In its modern form it goes back to Carl Rogers, who was the first to offer a method of therapy based on a philosophy of helping; this was the point that I made above when I referred to his work as a watershed in the history of the clinical professions. A closely related tradition has been called self-help, and one form of it gained worldwide fame in the early 1920s, under the leadership of a charismatic healer named Emile Coué.[37] Its first application on a large scale was in Alcoholics Anonymous, and its more recent major success has been in the program of Synanon, for the rehabilitation of drug addicts. The two organizations have many characteristics in common: they insist on remaining free of the problems and crosscurrents of contemporary life, and so they are completely apolitical and independent of local power struggles; they are both financially self-sustaining; they de-emphasize personal ego trips and stress the completely democratic nature of the organization; they stay clear of the established clinical professions; and the members are made to feel keenly and directly that they share a responsibility for the success of *their* organization.

Both Alcoholics Anonymous and Synanon restrict their major activities to a specific category of person; in spite of their admitted successes with serious problems, they do not offer their programs as a general type of therapy, although very recently Synanon has begun to move in just this direction by accepting outsiders ("straights") who elect to join one of the ongoing communities. This restriction has in the past ruled out the use of professionals, and as a result the programs have been entirely self-helping. That they have succeeded—in many cases far better than professional treatment programs for alcoholism and drug addiction—is one of the strongest arguments in favor of a new kind of approach in the helping arts. Their success, in turn, has helped to spark a related development within the therapeutic professions in which persons without previous formal training are carefully selected and then trained as therapistlike counselors.[38]

Quite spontaneously, a movement in this direction is taking shape currently on dozens, perhaps hundreds, of college campuses, in store-front clinics, and in remodeled old houses in slum areas—that is, not in professional offices far removed from the real-life world but in the very center of places where actual and potential clients live. The best name for this sort of endeavor might be the one that is often used on campuses: peer counseling. The arrangement is simple: a place is available where people in crisis may come, and there they are accepted, allowed to stay, given the chance to spend time with someone if they wish, perhaps provided with some activities, and so helped through the crisis, at which point they may leave.

This may sound like an ideal of the asylum, and in a sense that is what it is—at least if we take the word *asylum* in its literal and gentler meaning. But the entire philosophy of the peer-counseling center (or crisis center, to give it another of its appropriate names) runs counter to establishing a place where people come for treatment.[39] The philosophy is based first of all on the notion that human life has its ups and downs, and therefore anyone may find himself on a "downer" of very serious proportions, far beyond his ability to cope. Second, such life crises can be dealt with in the person's own terms, with no implications that the person is sick, neurotic, or in some way deviant. Third, persons in crisis can be helped through the period if they are accepted, if no judgment is passed on them, and if they are allowed to pass through at their own speed. Last, the most appropriate guide during the crisis may be someone who has already been through it himself and who can accommodate himself to the person as a peer rather than by setting up a status gap between them.

Dealing with crises in this way appears to fit into a rather new view of some of the commonest human difficulties. As an example, on a typical college campus the most frequently reported emotional problem is something as simple and old-fashioned as loneliness. This, at least, is what students will say if they are surveyed on a large scale. However, when they show up at their campus Student Health Center, or at some similar professional establishment which is often the only place they have to turn, their difficulty is rarely diagnosed as loneliness. The reason, of course, is that no such term exists in the technical vocabulary of the healing professions. The professionals who are paid to give counsel or therapy to emotionally disturbed students therefore diagnose the student's condition in the only terms they know. Their treatment procedures, then, rest on interpreting the problem in a different way than the student himself might if he were simply allowed to talk about his problem.

Loneliness is a legitimate cause for distress, without a doubt—but it is not a condition arising from some fault within the person. It is not a kind of illness that can be treated and then will go away. Rather, it is a situational state. It is a normal response of a young person to the circumstances which define freshman life on a large university campus. Away from home for lengthy periods often for the first time in his or her life, thrown among strangers, faced with academic and social demands quite different from those of high school—in short, forced to take a sudden and rather big leap toward becoming an independent adult—the first-year student often finds no one to turn to or to lean on. Under these circumstances, his own worst characteristics may surface, so to speak; he will begin to display, sometimes in exaggerated form, the symptoms of his own individual neurosis—and, of course, we are all potentially quite neurotic, each in his own way. Counseling and therapy facilities are equipped to deal with the neurosis that has surfaced, and so they do; but in the course of this, they bypass the situational state of loneliness that began the process.

As we know, the general distress that characterizes so many students under the name of loneliness tends to disappear as soon as life circumstances change. They make some friends; they begin to live with new persons or get married; they find that they are feeling at home, enlarging their horizons, and beginning to plan for jobs and careers. Because loneliness is basically a situational state, it responds to situational changes. Therapy, then, is not really required for loneliness, although it may well be helpful or even necessary for students in general— that is another issue. The kind of help that is best suited for such situational states as loneliness is just what I described above as peer counseling: a place where the lonely person can appear on his own schedule, be accepted without judgment, and be allowed to spend some time in a sympathetic and listening atmosphere with someone who has himself been through the same mill not too long before. This does not cure loneliness, but it does do something much more effective; it takes the edge off loneliness and makes it possible for the student to get through the crisis period and to stick it out without too much distress until circumstances and the associated situation change for the better.

Viewed in this way, peer counseling would seem to be made to order for those situational states that are the commonest source of personal distress in campus life. Additionally, an interesting prospect now opens up. If peer counseling in its various forms is an effective means for coping with the most widespread and incapacitating of emotional problems among students, might not the same type of help also be effective for other segments of the population? There is a strikingly similar state that can be found, if one knows how to look for it, among blue-collar members of the middle class—those who work in large industries and live in endless suburban developments. The situational state that causes them the greatest distress—although again, this is not what is diagnosed if, and when, they show up in a therapist's office—is a vague, ongoing feeling of worthlessness, hopelessness, boredom, and lack of personal identity. The state is just as understandable in these persons as is loneliness on the part of college students; it is, again, a product of all their life circumstances, and it is not likely to change unless these circumstances change.

But perhaps it can be dealt with, in just the same way that loneliness can be helped in campus peer-counseling centers. The success of peer counseling suggests that a similar arrangement, with drop-in centers staffed by experienced peers, might be of great value in taking the edge off the situational state experienced by so many blue-collar workers. If such an arrangement were to work, it might help to prevent many of the neurotic symptoms that surface in this population— absenteeism, minor alcoholism, family problems, and difficulties in acting as an appropriate model for teenage children.

With all its potential for good, however, the peer counseling center is not that easy to set up and run. It is a complex contribution to the helping professions, and I suspect that it can succeed only if its essentially political nature is understood. What must be kept in mind is that even though its work consists mainly of the relatively brief procedures involved in crisis intervention, these do not define its mission. Such intervention can, in fact, be accomplished by many persons who are sufficiently sensitive to meet people in trouble and handle them in a nonjudgmental way. Ministers, for example, often do this well; and so do Scoutmasters, and parents, and teachers, and indeed, all the other categories of kindly uncles and aunts. But more than such goodwill is required here, for the crisis that brings a student to a peer-counseling center is most often a high point, or even an end point, in his continuing oppositional stance. He may, for example, have barely escaped arrest during a lengthy series of shoplifting episodes and finally be caught redhanded; or a period of random sexual activity may finally result in a case of venereal disease or a pregnancy; or a number of weekend trips on drugs may culminate in one very bad trip; or there may be a serious suicide attempt by someone who has been increasingly depressed and withdrawn. Very often none of these situations can be helped, and they might even be made worse, by the type of intervention favored by authority figures: to call in the family doctor, or send the person to a psychiatrist's office, or hold a family conference and decide on some appropriate punishment. Such a mode of cure is often only an extension of the disease.

The uniqueness of crisis intervention in the form of peer counseling lies in the message that the counselor manages to convey to the person who comes in. He says, "I can't help you. I can't treat you. I certainly can't cure you. But what I would like to do is offer myself. Here I am. I would like to spend some time with you while you're in the place you're at, just being with you. I've been there myself, so I think I understand a little of what it's like for you right now. If there's anything you'd like me to do, you can just tell me." The epilogue to this message, not necessarily spoken but somehow often understood, is that because someone is now there to be with the person, to hold a hand, to listen, and not to judge or blame, then it is just possible that this crisis is not the end of everything; there is something up ahead.

The model for this is clearly not the confessional, the group, or the physician-healer, but rather a model so common that we may not easily think of it: it is the situation of a parent, most often the mother, face to face with a very young child who has been hurt. Here there is no thought of judging or blaming the child, of diagnosing or curing. The message is simply, "Yes, I understand. You hurt. OK, let me hold you and stay with you. It will be better." And the memory that most of us have is that, in fact, this treatmentless treatment, this helping that does nothing but offer a presence, somehow got us through physical and emotional crises that were, at the time, experienced as world-shaking. It is both ironic and tragic that so few adults are able to consistently offer this sort of helping to strangers; that peer counselors have to be rather carefully selected out of all the applicants who, overflowing with goodwill, usually offer their services; and that even those who are selected often need to be trained not to be therapists.

Within the next few years there will probably be an extensive literature on peer counseling, particularly on its obvious applicability to the problem of rehabilitating drug addicts. It may even become a subspecialty within an established profession such as clinical psychology. This may be all to the good—but it will remain to be seen whether professional pressures will have their way and force peer counseling to slowly take on the organizational coloring of psychotherapy, or whether peer counseling will influence the profession from the inside toward a more open and less status-ridden arrangement.

# part
# five
# allowing

# chapter 9
# somatics and helping

In my opening discussion in chapter 1, I made a distinction between experience in general and my-experience, and I referred there to a possible discipline of shared experience. One form of this discipline, I noted, might be psychotherapy. Now I must add that this need not be the psychotherapy with which we are familiar. One reason is that at the level of shared experience, it is unlikely that we might find an organized discipline, much less a profession, devoted to the practice of healing.

Yet two persons might meet, and one of them might be in a state of distress or malaise, even of panic, while the other is, at the moment, much less distressed. Under these circumstances, one of the two might serve the other as a help, a guide, a crutch, an inspiration, a leader, a model, a beacon, a support, a companion the possibilities are, perhaps, more varied than in the traditional clinical situation. What then happens between them may not look like psychotherapy or the familiar forms of the healing game. How might we characterize the theme of their being together?

## TWO MODES OF ALLOWING

I suggest that the applicable term is *Allowing*, by which I mean the creating of a situation in which there can occur experiences leading toward each of the two becoming, or remaining, his own person. I assume here that every person, without exception, can be defined in terms of some unique and individual nexus of possibilities, and that differences among them come down to possibilities of experience realized and unrealized, faced or avoided, accepted or denied. Allowing is the occasioning of direct experience. It is when freedom occurs; that is its place in interpersonal encounters. In the therapylike situation, Allowing consists in making decisive the transient and changing moment. Laing says that "the really decisive moments in psychotherapy, as every patient or therapist who has ever experienced them knows, are unpredictable, unique, unforgettable, always unrepeatable, and often indescribable."[1] Precisely—and Allowing consists, then, in simply making that decisive moment quite unremarkable. The decisive moment is exceptional only if we work at encapsulating it, but if we Allow it, then it becomes ordinary: it is just as it is, and suddenly, decisively, both participants are all there.

Alan Watts spells out succinctly the link between direct experience and the process of Allowing in his discussion of the special character of the guru:

*Of course the* guru *is human like everyone else. His advantage, his liberation, lies in the fact that he is not in conflict with himself for being so; he is not in the double-bind of pretending that he is an independent agent without knowing that he is pretending, of imagining that he is an ego or subject which can somehow manage to be permanently "one up" on its correlative object—the changing panorama of experiences, sensations, feelings, emotions, and thoughts. The* guru *accepts himself; more exactly, he does not think of himself as something other than his behavior patterns, as something which performs them.*[2]

Building on this basis, anything is then possible, and the end can be (to use another, and closely related, term) what Kurt Wolff calls *surrender*, that is, "cognitive love," with its connotations of "total involvement, suspension of received notions, pertinence of everything, identification, and risk of being hurt."[3]

In this chapter and the next I will treat two general situations of Allowing. The first of these is Allowing the body, which I have called Somatics: that kind of situation in which caring, guiding, and helping can occur on the basis of body-experience. The second is Allowing myself, which I have called Theatrics, referring to the kind of shared experience of head and world in which the self can flourish. As we shall see, either of these two kinds of situations may resemble psychotherapy, but again they may not. Their significance is not only for the development of a praxis of shared experiences, but equally important, for what they can contribute as well to a more general, systematic discipline of human experience. In this way both general psychology and a personal psychology are enriched by each other.

## SOMATICS: ALLOWING THE BODY

### The Body as Center
The German language has two words for *body*: *der Leib* and *der Körper*, the first meaning, approximately, "lived body" or "body alive" and the second,

again approximately, "body as carcass." It is a useful distinction for it permits me to emphasize that in my discussion here I intend only the first of these meanings: the body, not as an object or a collection of mechanisms, but as lived and experienced; the body that I as an individual inhabit as my residence-on-earth. Our scientific disciplines—physiology, for example, or biology, or other disciplines such as biochemistry that focus on one set of processes—have no theory of this lived body, their interest being directed exclusively to the body conceived as object or organized process. This is as it should be; it should be up to psychology, or at the very least to medicine, to develop a theory of the lived body. However, the very concept, which might have entered the field through Freud's early thinking, has found no place. We have to go as far afield as some of the branches of Yoga to find, in the concept of *Chakras* ("centers of energy"), a theory of the functioning of the body in experience.[4]

Yet one lesson was at least implicit in Freud's thought, though it was a lesson that he himself hardly accepted and so taught with great hesitation—that it is the body state that really tells all that needs to be known about the person. The body cannot lie. Only the person himself can lie, both to himself and to others, about his body. Thus, in Freud's thinking—and quite properly, too— the psyche becomes essentially a mechanism for making do about the intransigent reality of the body. The body simply will not go away; and indeed, one of Freud's earliest definitions of an instinct was that it is what persists and cannot be willed away. But having secured an initial grip on this notion of the priority of body-experience, he could not stick determinedly to his own insight. Like so many other thinkers

## ON THE DENIAL OF THE BODY

Why is it that philosophers have always felt obliged to think badly of the basic biological functions? They may believe in a life-force; they may even applaud its ferocity; but they do not inquire whether it keeps its chin clean at table. It almost seems as if to come near the breathing, sweating, farting body were an unphilosophical act; and it is certainly true that although the philosopher frequently prefers to begin with some commonplace fragment of experience, ready enough to ponder the lessons of the spider or the problems of the sodden wax, as though to say: "Look, you think I deal with empty abstractions and make my thoughts fly off from daily life like a startled sparrow, but how unjust that is, for as you see I begin by considering the shape and color of this quite ordinary penny, the snowed-on blankness of this simple sheet of writing paper, the course these burning logs are taking, or even the existence of my own well-manicured hand"—he does not deceive us with these subterfuges, since we can also see how carefully he ignores the secretion of saliva, the shaping of dung in the lower intestine, the leap of sperm (indeed the whole history of that brazen nozzle), all our vague internal twinges, heart-stops and bellyaches, though distantly these things are made the subject of denigrating comparisons. . . .

In the West man's sexuality was never the object of any important or prolonged philosophical study before Freud (in Plato, in St. Augustine, and so on, there are brief sallies), yet of our fundamental occupations only something discreetly called "loving" has received much notice.

. . . The eighteenth-century version of human nature, for example, constructed with a Johnsonian sense of the decorous, was triumphantly shallow, and it is possibly for this reason that when Hume hunted through his own experience for that constant impression which might be identified as the source of the idea of the self, he never came upon his own breathing.[5]

---

of his time and since, he had to put down the body in its fundamental biological reality. He insisted on shifting the rewards of personality functioning to the ego, and much of the blame to the superego, and he progressively mythologized the id. The result has been that in psychoanalysis, as in psychology in general, what ought to be a starting point for theory has been denied: that we are resident in our bodies and that this is where our psychic lives begin and have their continuing vital source. In one writer's words, "We are but skin about a wind, with muscles clenched against mortality."[6]

The body cannot be denied forever—and so, at long last, it seems to have returned to the center of our collective experience, this time in the form of a shift in values. It has happened in personal habits: the dress and mannerisms and language of an increasing number of people, young and old, become simpler, more personal, and more natural. It has happened in preferences: relations between people, in particular sexual relations, tend to be direct, less encumbered by false modesty and formalisms, more closely tied to spontaneous feelings and urges. There is a revival of interest in folk art, in basic crafts and homelike skills, in choices of activity that are simpler, less artificial, less dependent on elaborate technology. In postures toward the natural world, there is a nearly overwhelming concern for natural products, ecologically sound practices, behavior toward nature that speaks of cooperation rather than dominance and destruction, even an upsurge in the popularity of ordinary household animals as pets. Mass movements begin to attract followers as soon as they promise to help the individual get back behind his own self-made screen of socialization and recapture the true self that he has lost—various approaches to meditation, to bodily grace and rhythm, to inner peace and centeredness. As the real world is revealed daily in new forms of ugliness, a countermovement toward returning to one's personal sources arises; and its active center seems to be those practices that help the person experience his own body most naturally and most fully.

There are at least formal intimations of this emphasis in the history of clinical practice, beginning with the psychoanalytic notion that bodily zones defined successive psychosexual stages of development. As we shall see, Wilhelm Reich exploded Freudian dogma and revolutionized its practice by taking seriously its promise of a somatic psychology. In Peter Marin's words, Reich moved past Freud, "tracing out the implications of Freudian thought, locating and localizing libido, *finding* it, moving the center down from the head into the body, making the richness of animal being the measure of health."[7] After Reich, clinicians began to know what to look for: patterns of bodily functioning that can show individual differences—and thus suggest unique experiential histories—

and patterns that appear to be influenced by social custom—and thus inform us about the elements common to different individuals. Here, for example, is how a contemporary psychiatrist, Moses Feldenkrais, sees the developmental patterning involved in the act of defecation.

*this act involves a social adjustment with attitudes, emotional and muscular patterns that have a profound influence on the whole being. In early infancy it is as purely a reflective [sic] act as we can imagine. Soon after, however, the mother will begin to withdraw the security which her presence brings to the child, and leave him in isolated privacy. Then a bargaining system begins: the mother expects and the child "gives" something which he alone can produce and which is eagerly expected from him. He soon learns to give freely and gain approval or to contain himself when he is neglected. Immature persons who are unable to dissociate parts of earlier experience without reinstating the whole situation, when faced with tasks where they have to give to themselves without being acknowledged, acting against their own will, become angry, feel like chucking the whole thing, and often impulsively do so. But when forcing themselves to proceed with the task they often develop diarrhoea. In a similar way rebelliousness against authority which is consistently checked is associated with chronic constipation.*[8]

### Sensory Awareness Training

While these developments were occurring within the confines of clinical practice, a distinctly different but equally promising trend was beginning in a quite unrelated field. It goes back to two persons, Heinrich Jacoby and Elsa Gindler, teachers and guides in an area that can only be called living in one's senses. Gindler, in particular, was not a teacher in the sense of someone who possesses some information or practices that can be passed on to those who come as students. She was not a teacher; she simply made learning possible. Nor can her area of interest be nicely circumscribed. It had to do with the way people moved and used their senses, the way they lived out their own purposes, in a bodily sense. To help people do this, she had them recapture what was natural and direct and simple in expression and movement. Now, what might be the name for this field of study? One of her pupils, Charlotte Selver, who started out in the 1920s as a

## THE WELL-TEMPERED CHILD

The parent invades every aspect of the child's development. The child is taught when and how much it is good for him to eat, when and how long he ought to sleep, what parts of him are bad or dirty, what is good social behavior (smiling), etc., etc. When he falls and cries he is taught not to allow the pain and shock to go their way but to seek instant distraction from them and to expect fuss and anxiety from the parent rather than quiet sympathy: "You good boy, that bad banana peel!" A little later he will be taught that exposure to cold or getting wet in the rain is unpleasant and dangerous, as it will actually become after the lesson has been thoroughly learned.

This evaluative education is the earliest and deepest, and of course it confuses the child's capacity for judgment. From that point on, the evidence of his own senses cannot simply be trusted . . . and he tends to judge at second hand and generally. The living context, on which all real value depends, becomes obscured.

Consider the efforts of the parents to influence the baby's very way of perceiving: exaggerated looking and listening; sniffing at flowers; smacking lips over food to make him taste it; and in speaking to him the artificiality and distortions of "baby-talk," implying that verbal communication cannot be peaceful and simple. These almost universal practices create the impression from the very beginning that something extra is necessary, that a technique of some sort is inseparable from living, so that the grown woman applies lipstick, not as a part of dressing up, but because she feels "naked" without it, and nobody can find employment in radio or television for just speaking naturally. The lily is not to be simply watered but must be gilded.

Close to this necessity for the something extra is the education towards making efforts, which is so common in our competitive society. It is not enough that the anxious mother urges her baby to make efforts to move his bowels. Think

of the ambition of so many parents for their baby to sit, to stand, to walk as early as possible—earlier than other children. The natural processes of energy development are not enough: They must be coaxed. . . .

Finally, among the factors in the young child's development, I must note the widespread practice of interrupting his play as though it were of no importance and impressing on him, often as not, that a "good" child always comes when mother calls him. Through this he comes to feel that there is no natural rhythm in things and that it is right for activities to be cut off in mid-air and for others to be begun, as though magically, without preparation—an impression that will be totally confirmed by what he sees on television, where presentations are violently interrupted by the ones that follow and the only preparations are shouts or blares. When the child has been interrupted often enough, his innate sense of rhythm becomes confused; and his sense of the social value of his own experience becomes so too.

What comes to replace the real world of perception—the living context—is a world of ideas and images created not by the child's own discoveries but, consciously to him or unconsciously, by our whole history and culture.[9] [Italics deleted.]

---

teacher of rhythmic dance and then studied for eleven years with Gindler, later gave the name *sensory awareness* to both the field of training and the results achieved by this method. She came to America and with her husband, Charles Brooks, began to teach—but again we come to that same barren word.

A major point that Selver has made in her work and in her writing is that our culture is to blame for what we are. It is an unnatural culture, she claims; and the evidence may be found in such a commonplace matter as the rearing of children. We might posit as an ideal the natural rhythms of unimpeded biological functioning—for example, the lively yet graceful interest of a kitten in a leaf that shines as it flickers in the sun. What stands out as we watch this animal in its untaught movement is its total absorption, its "delight," its spontaneous moving, the use of all its senses at once, the reasonable and sensible fit between what is there to be grasped and the kitten's response, the apprehension without strain, the smooth and unpredictable flow of reaction and interest, and of course the total unreflectiveness of everything that the animal does. Selver writes movingly of how many of these qualities we seem to rule out of our dealing with children— and as a consequence how restricted and distorted must be the average person's sensory awareness as he grows into adulthood. We exaggerate with children, we talk artificially with them, we fawn on them; yet we fail to take them seriously, we ignore most of their natural rhythms, we force their actions into adult molds of time and space and tempo and purpose. It is no wonder that even the "normal" adult finds himself sadly lacking in the full and natural appreciation of the world in which he so busily or frantically moves. Quite artificial and unnatural positions and actions take the place of movement that simply fits its immediate surround; only the barest minimum of sensory input is permitted to our overtrained eyes and ears and noses; and we effectively block out of our awareness all the input from what is in us and around us. Yet only a few simple "lessons," as Selver has shown, are needed to open up the average person, to begin to restore some of the beauty and wonder of full sensory and motor functioning. The sad thing is that there are so few inspired leaders helping in this way to open up the lives of adults.

The spirit behind the work of Gindler and Selver, and even of the closely related work of Bernard Gunther at Esalen,[10] seems far removed from the clinician's office. It is much closer to Zen than to cure. By this I mean that the work as it is done by the leader and by the student is not so much a treatment as an experience. Although I have tried to present some justification, even some explanation, for this way of helping others, it is clear that all I can really do is describe a goal, not a method. Such questions as how one does it or how it happens are irrelevant to discussion of an experience.

This is not to say that no lessons can be learned from the practice of sensory awareness approaches. Precisely because they are approaches that manage to capture and contain living experiences they have much to offer a vital clinical practice. They seem to fit into a general current of interest in capturing the experience of the lived body, an interest that can now be found wherever there is an attempt to get back to basics. Once the model of treatment and cure has been given up, there remains a different kind of venture that might well be called helping and whose theme is Allowing. Entry into it is first of all by way of the body and its sensory and motor functioning. Those who have come to sensory awareness sessions looking for an expansion of their restricted or impoverished lives may in fact be today's therapeutic clients, legitimate descendants of the Victorian patients who sought freedom from the cost of sexual restrictions in Freud's office.

They seem to be going to other places as well. One of the most fascinating of newer developments in this paraclinical domain has been the resurgence of dance as a form of personal involvement for growth. Out of this interest have come— again, as guides and leaders—such persons as Mary Whitehouse, Ann Halprin and Albert Pesso, all of them distinguished by their use of the techniques of modern dance for purposes of helping. Pesso, in particular, working with his wife whose background is also in the field of "dance therapy," has developed an elaborate form of what he calls psychomotor training in groups. Based on a detailed analysis of forms of movement in three areas—reflex, voluntary, and emotional—he describes specific exercises and training procedures, their aim being "to enlarge the range of possible behaviors and attitudes, giving each person a larger fund of skills, feelings, controls, and experiences to call forth in coping with given situations. It is the same as saying that one's personality is expanded as one's senses and potential behaviors are expanded."[11]

In a way, this sounds like the familiar claim of every psychotherapist—but it should be noted that the claim is made by a practitioner in a distinctly different field, that the emphasis is now shifted almost completely to training in body functions (although in the case of Pesso's methods, with a continuing awareness of the close interplay between feelings and movements), and, finally, that it is much more training than treatment. Here the group leader (sensory awareness "teacher," Zen master, dance therapist, psychomotor trainer) does not heal but helps.

If these approaches have the effect that is claimed for them—in expanding awareness and freeing the person for a wider and more satisfying range of experiences—then we might ask how far the logic can be carried. In all the somatic approaches mentioned thus far, the person has been helped toward Allowing through the avenue of the body—for example, to enhance appreciation by learning how to attend without concentrating; to reduce the strains of living by learning how to allow and to "receive" what the body does naturally; to enrich the use of the senses by practice in being "sensible" rather than by an effort of will; to see without looking and to hear without listening, in a paradoxical maneuver that one Zen master called Mu-mon-kan, the "gateless gate."[12] Does this suggest that directly working on the person's body, for example by realigning its structure, might result in related changes for the better in attitude, personality, behavior, and even the emotional problems that are the concern of therapists? Parents are prone to say to a child, "For goodness sake, straighten up your shoulders,"—just as though this change in muscular attitude might produce some desired but more subtle changes in attitudes toward life—although we have all been taught during the many years of dominance of the psychotherapeutic thesis that it really works best the other way around, that what the child needs is treatment for general attitudes in order to produce a change in observable posture. Today the opposite claim is being made, and it fits a current trend.

This reversal appears to be only the late discovery, or perhaps rediscovery, of what was known and practiced by many earlier groups who may have been closer to their own bodies than we are today. In the late eighteenth century, Captain James Cook, suffering mightily from rheumatism exacerbated by the wet quarters on his ship, put in at Tahiti and told a friendly chief of his affliction. The chief immediately ordered a "cure."

*So 12 large, muscular women, four of them the chief's relatives, were paddled out ceremoniously in a great canoe, descended to Cook's cabin, and spread a mattress and blankets on the deck. "Lie!" said the women.*

*Cook lay down. The 12 giantesses immediately fell upon him, pummeling and squeezing unmercifully with their plump, lively hands, until his joints cracked and all his flesh felt like misused blubber. After 15 minutes of this, the released victim got up. To his astonishment, he felt immediate relief.*

*"More?" asked the ladies, smiling.*

*"Indeed," agreed the captain. Three more treatments, he recorded, ended his pain.*[13]

## Rolfing

During almost forty years of work as a biochemist, in her writing and in work on her clients' bodies Ida Rolf has made the claim that by altering the very structure of the body it is possible to achieve structural integration and postural release. These are not just catchall terms but are meant to refer specifically to observable and measurable changes in posture, movement, grace, and feelings of ease and tension, as well as changes in the very chemistry of the body. Hers is one

---

### STRUCTURAL REINTEGRATION

An individual experiencing temporary fear, grief or anger, all too often carries his body in an attitude which the world recognizes as the outward manifestation of that particular emotion. If he persists in this dramatization or consistently re-establishes it, thus forming what is ordinarily referred to as a "habit pattern," the muscular arrangement becomes set. Materially speaking some muscles shorten and thicken, others are invaded by connective tissue, still others become immobilised by consolidation of the tissue involved. Once this has happened the physical attitude is invariable; it is involuntary; it can no longer be changed basically by taking thought, or even by mental suggestion. Such setting of a physical response also establishes an emotional pattern. Since it is not possible to express a free flow through the physical flesh, the subjective emotional tone becomes progressively more limited and tends to remain in a restricted and

closely defined area. Now, what the individual feels is no longer an emotion, a single response to an immediate situation; henceforth he lives, moves and has his being in an attitude. . . .[14]

It has long been recognized that in an erect man, certain spatial relationships are normal. The problem has been to evolve a technique through which they could be restored or evoked. Thus in an erect man it should be possible to draw a straight line through the ear (bisecting the external meatus), the shoulder (head of the humerus), hip bone (head of the femur), knee and ankle (external malleolus). If this idea of a one-dimensional line be expanded to three dimensions the body appears as an aggregate of blocks (head, thorax, pelvis, legs) which must be stacked in a stable fashion before this line can appear. The picture which emerges offers a practical approach to the creation of a more integrated man. Since the actual position in space of each of these units to its neighbours is determined by its muscular and fascial wrapping, the blocks can be shifted by altering the length and tone of these myofascial tissues. In order to accomplish a permanent change, it is usually necessary that the actual position or distribution of muscular fibers be very slightly altered. This happens spontaneously as individual fibrils stretch or as fascial sheaths again slide over each other instead of being glued on some adjacent sheath. Unless such a change is made the body reverts to its original posture and the restrictions to fluid flow and to interpersonal communication are rebuilt. . . .[15]

If the foregoing assumptions prove valid, and many years' work with unbalanced bodies have demonstrated this

claim, it is logical to ask two questions: one, can bodies be changed so that they transmit and utilise the gravitational field to better advantage; two, what definite landmarks indicate that this has been accomplished?

The answer to the first question is purely operational. It IS possible to change the alignment of the body blocks. Evidence of this can be seen in the contour (profile) photographs of hundreds of people who have experienced this technique. In an unbelievably short time the gravity line can be established in a more normal position. . . . A body altered in this fashion shows not only a modification in static contour, but moves dynamically in a very different pattern.[16]

---

of the few statements we have that approximates a theory of total bodily functioning and its consequences for practical application—that is, a detailed theoretical statement that leads logically to specific practices whose results can be assessed both in the observed behavior and in the reported experience of the clients.

The rationale has been put succinctly by Feldenkrais: "Radical changes cannot be expected without reforming muscular and postural habits. Indigestion, faulty breathing, crooked toes and feet, faulty sexual behavior, postural rigidity and muscular tension go together with emotional disorders. The whole self, diet, breathing, sex, muscular and postural habits, must be tackled directly and concurrently with the emotional re-education."[17] Rolf has, however, gone well beyond this point of view, which might be found in the literature of physiotherapy and chiropractic and among the followers of Reich. She offers in addition a theory of the functioning body—that it is a physical mechanism organized to resist the never-ending pulls of gravity. Perhaps because gravity is so omnipresent that it evades even scientific notice; perhaps because we have always lacked a systematic account of organisms in motion—for whatever reason, the surprising fact is that the notion that gravity may fundamentally affect our behavior has simply never been entertained. One exception may be the classic but generally ignored paper by Erwin Straus on the upright posture, in which he elaborates in remarkable detail the anatomical, physiological, behavioral, psychological, cultural, and ethical consequences of man being an upright animal who must learn to live in opposition to the pull of gravity.[18]

The human organism may indeed be a physical mechanism, but it is hardly the ideal that, say, an engineer would design if given the assignment of constructing an efficient robot. Structurally, the human body consists of three triangles mounted upside down on top of each other: the triangle of feet-to-thighs-to-hips, finishing off at the waist; the triangle of the torso, swelling out to the shoulders and ending at the neck; and the triangle of the head mounted on the vertebral column. Architecturally, it is an arrangement practically guaranteed to insure instability, to force the creature so designed to compensate in a thousand subtle ways. It is easy to understand why muscular pains localize so often in junction points at the small of the back or at the base of the neck. And it is also easy to see why the human body must be equipped with a highly flexible system of tissue to tie together the framework of muscles and bone; only an arrangement that is highly flexible could allow for the very large number of complex adjustments needed to coordinate muscle groups in all the actions that we perform.

It is because of this peculiar architectural design that humans can do so many things in a physical sense. But it is also for the same reason that we are prone to so many deviations, large and small. The ballerina can train her muscles to support her when she balances on tiptoe; but the same muscles and tissue that can stretch and harden to furnish this support may also accomodate on one side only to a childhood accident, and so set the person posturally off balance for life. The delicate and precise adjustments that make possible a baby's learning to walk—an incredible achievement of controlled falling, of what Straus calls "movement on credit"—just as miraculously become the means to express the stride of determination, jumping for joy, and the depressive's slow and heavy gait. It is all, Rolf says, a matter of the day-to-day accommodation to the stresses of life, to pressures from the environment, and to whatever accidents may occur—all immersed, as it were, in the constant tugging sea of gravitational influence. No wonder, then, that our adult bodies bear the living record of this lifetime of struggle and adjustment, of growth and incident. And if, as Rolf and Selver and so many others would argue, our lifetime of training has left us much less than the persons we could be, that too will be written into the very structure and arrangements of the main building blocks that make up our bodies.

## A secret place

Rolf's orientation was very much physical; she emphasized the significance of physically occasioned abnormalities, such as falls or bruises, and discounted the importance of structural and postural abnormalities being caused by the accumulation of emotional problems. Her aim, until very recently, was simply to realign the body and in this way provide the person with a structure that might be used to better advantage in everyday living. Neither she nor her son, Richard Demmerle, who has worked closely with her have made a practice of engaging their clients in therapeutic-like talk; and only in the last few years, as practitioners she has trained have begun to use her methods in their own ways, has Rolfing become a method of treatment for nonphysical complaints and the basis for an approach combining, as William Schutz puts it, "the body, the intrapsychic, and the interpersonal.[19]

Yet during all this time incidents in which the treatment produced results very much like a productive session of therapy have been surprisingly frequent. Sam Keen describes a typical occurrence:

> However, my chest wouldn't yield. Each time a hand approached it I went into panic and felt pain. The disarming of the emotional-physical defenses in this area involved both memory and manipulation. In the seventh hour of processing, pressure on a muscle in my shoulder released a memory of childhood conflict with a person I loved deeply—a memory that had become encysted in my chest. I wept. The release of the memory, and the grief it occasioned, eased the panic and tension that had made me unable to bear manipulative work on my chest. At the end of that hour I was able, for the first time, to fill my lungs in one smooth movement.[20]

This incident suggests an unsuspected gain in dealing directly with the body. The discovery of an "encysted" area, in Keen's case as well as in the case of others who have had similar experiences, is usually accompanied by a powerful emotional release. It appears that what is "bound" in this way is not just a neutral element which carries a memory, so to speak, but a complete experience which is still charged in all its personal significance. We should hardly be surprised at the suggestion that the body expresses emotional states; but a demonstration of this sort, linking emotion with structure, may embolden us to take a next step. Might incidents of this sort be evidence that the body actually serves as the locus of secrets which can be hidden for years from the person himself?

The question does not have to do with memory, except in an indirect sense. I am concerned here, not with possible processes of memory, but with an explanation for the persistence of material that is identified precisely by its not being remembered. Earlier I called it the public secret—that reverberating set of presences that each person both hides from and, in some way, shares with the rest of his world. In psychoanalytic theory, like all other psychologies that bypass the body in the urge to explain the mind, it is implied that such material resides somewhere in the psychic apparatus, like a tape that is stored away until the right button is pushed. For those who will accept this version of the relation between brain and experience, I suppose that the "tape" model will do. But I am asking for something more; though I do not as yet know what that is, I know an inadequate answer when I hear it. The locus of my own individual, buried material, I insist, cannot be in some deeply hidden brain connections or cell assemblies, or in whatever other product of neurological myth you care to propose. Where, then, is it? Or does it, indeed, have a "where?"

My question is really about the persistence of personal and presumably unconsciously determined characteristics of an adult's functioning: if his current fear of swimming, let us say, is rooted somehow in his childhood—rooted in ways of which he is not aware and has no way to become aware—then where did this continuing causative dynamic reside during all the years since childhood? In asking this question, I am looking for a suggestion about a place where an imprint could have occurred. How about some part of the cortex? But no imprints occur there, as we know. If not an imprint as such, then what about other structural changes, perhaps cellular, or intracellular, perhaps assemblies of cells? My own bias is against any form of such a theory, so long as it demands a structural change in the form of a neurological trace. But an alternative tack may be more acceptable. What of the possibility that functional though not structural alterations are some-how preserved from childhood? This opens up new avenues, particularly in regard to the complex interplay of subfunctions within the body. For the surprising fact is that in spite of half a century of speculation and theorizing on this issue, very little attention has been given to the simple possibility that the locus of personally held public secrets may be in the most obvious place of all—directly under the person's nose, so to speak, in the intricacies of his patterned bodily functions.

A hypothesis along these lines is certainly consistent with Rolf's work and with the evident results of her procedures. If any theory is implied in her work in regard to one's emotional and experiential life—in addition to her stated theory concerning how the body is structured—it might well be this: that a fully integrated inner life, one that is both productive and satisfying, comes about as the direct and natural result of a body structure that is completely balanced architecturally and therefore is subject to minimal internal strains. However, although this may be acceptable in the most general sense, it provides us with no more than an overall outline. What we need to know in a more detailed way is how emotions and experiences are related to known bodily functions and how it is that the body's structures are able to encapsulate, to distort, to weaken, or to hide some of the key events of our inner lives. Alexander Lowen describes a patient who "had passed her life in an attitude of unspoken defiance, afraid to say No, unable to say Yes." He then remarks that "this negative layer in her personality, which was *functionally identical* with the state of contraction of her muscles, paralyzed all aggressive movements."[21] Here is the problem: How are we to explain an observed functional identity between layers of the personality and states of the muscles? What links them together?

### REICH AND THE HELPING ART

Two types of answers to the above question are possible, and both may well be necessary. The first would be in the form of a theory, like Freud's broad enough to encompass both sets of phenomena, personality and muscular. Although no such theory is as yet available, there are some hints of it in the developing field known as *bioenergetics*, which will be discussed later. A second answer to our question might not be in the form of a theory at all, but rather in a kind of shared understanding of collective experiences of the lived body; here Stanley Keleman's work—also to be considered below—seems relevant. The first major steps toward either of these two aspects of Somatics were taken by Wilhelm Reich, whose life work has implications for clinical theory and practice, for a personal psychology of shared experiences, for biology, and perhaps even for philosophy and cosmology.

### Reich and Psychoanalysis

Reich joined the psychoanalytic movement in Vienna in 1918 or 1919, while he was still a medical student. He soon became both active and prominent; by the middle 1920s he had made his first major contribution, in the form of an almost startling new approach to clinical treatment. This approach seems rather obvious to today's readers, but it was a revolutionary notion when Reich introduced it in a paper on what he called "character analysis."

During this period analytic practice was lagging well behind analytic theory. Psychoanalyses were unpredictable and cures or improvements far from certain; no one really understood how change in the patient came about. There were no established methods for instructing junior analysts in technique, and very little in the way of method had been added to the clinician's armamentarium for more than a decade. The work was aimed at eliminating the patient's presenting symptoms by tracing back and reconstructing long-buried connections with infantile events—that is, the emphasis in treatment was on the content of the patient's dreams and fantasies. But the patient himself, curiously enough, was never an object of study; he was treated as though he were simply a vessel for containing certain psychic content, some of it adequately organized and some of it connected, so to speak, in the wrong ways to instinctual drives. It apparently never occurred to the analyst of that day to drop his therapist's role and simply take a naïve look at the patient and what he was doing as a person.

Reich describes the situation in terms of a patient whom he had treated for an inability to achieve an erection:

*At that time, I misjudged the general attitude of this patient. He was quiet, placid, "good," doing everything that was asked of him. He never got upset. In the course of three years' treatment, he never got angry or critical. That is, according to the concepts of that time, he was a "well integrated," thoroughly "adjusted" character, with only one serious symptom ("monosymptomatic neurosis"). I reported the case in the technical seminar, and earned praise for the correct elucidation of the traumatic primal scene. His symptom, lack of erection, was fully explained—theoretically. As the patient was industrious and "adjusted to reality," none of us was struck by the fact that just his lack of emotionality, his complete imperturbability, was the pathological characterological soil on which his erective impotence could persist. My older colleagues considered my analytic work complete and correct. But on leaving the meeting I felt dissatisfied. If everything was as it should be, why did the impotence fail to budge? Obviously, here was a gap that none of us understood. A few months later I discharged the patient, uncured. He took it as stoically as he had taken everything else all this time.[22]*

As Reich began to look in all seriousness at the patients whom he confronted (even though, as an orthodox analyst, he still did not *face* them), he became increasingly impressed with what could only be called their character—that is, their total way of presenting themselves: in behavior, in expression, in verbal and nonverbal communication, in doing as well as in not-doing, and of course in the content of what they offered. In every case, it seemed, the character appeared to form a functional unity; and more important, the nature and significance of that unity helped the analyst to understand his patients' problems, the difficulties that had brought them into treatment, and most vital of all, the course of the treatment itself. Finally, Reich came to understand the character of his patients as a kind of *armoring*, a defensive shield developed through the years as a way of presenting oneself to the world. Psychoanalytic treatment then became, for him, a procedure for penetrating and dissolving this armor by attacking the myriad ways in which it appeared in the clinical session.

What Reich had understood, in a flash of insight that antedated the central contribution of a later behaviorist approach, was that what the patient presented, how he presented himself, his every movement and act and expression—all these were not simply surface coverings for some deeper dynamics. Rather, they were in fact the reality of the patient himself. They were all he was as a person, if only the analyst could read them correctly. Based on Freud's teachings, analysts of that time firmly believed that the patient's illness consisted of some buried mis-connections and complexes, and that the way he presented himself in the analytic session was at worst a form of resistance to uncovering these hidden connections. What Reich was the first to realize was quite different: the patient's "inability to be honest is part of his illness."[23] Thus: "Why can a person not perceive his own innermost self? Since it is he himself! Gradually I began to see that it is just this 'he himself,' this character make-up, which forms the compact tough mass that stands in the way of analytic endeavors. The total personality, the character, the whole individuality resisted."[24]

Now, for the first time, it became possible to develop a theory that was true to clinical reality and not just to theoretical speculation. How was it that unresolved infantile conflicts appeared to show up in adulthood as neurotic symptoms? In Reich's new view, the answer lay in comprehending "the present-day and the infantile experience simultaneously. There was no longer an antithesis between the historical and the contemporaneous. The whole experiential world of the past was alive in the present in the form of character attitudes. The make-up of a person is the functional sum total of all his past experiences."[25] Specifically, "a conflict which has been active at a certain period of life always leaves its traces in the character, in the form of a rigidity. It functions automatically and is difficult to eliminate. The patient does not feel it as something alien to him, but often feels it as something rigid and unyielding or as a loss or diminution of spontaneity."[26] "A traumatic infantile experience can have a present-day effect only if it is anchored in a rigid armor."[27] With this statement Freud's mechanical theory of personal history was transformed into a clinically useful approach to the understanding of development and change.

Reich now began to practice therapy quite literally in the present, "taking as the point of attack not only what the patient said, but everything he presented, particularly the manner of his communications or of his silence. Patients who kept silent were also communicating, were expressing something that gradually could be understood and handled."[28] If the patient talked of his love for his wife but in a dead, mechanical way, Reich dealt first with his manner of talking and with its inappropriateness for the content; if the patient reacted to this attack by a still more lifeless expression, Reich dealt with that; and so on and on, never letting the patient escape into "talking about," always bringing the patient back into the present, living moment of his experience. "For years, patients had not heard any psychoanalytic technical terms from me. They were thus deprived of the possibility of covering up an instinctual desire behind a word. The patient no longer talked about his hatred, he felt it; he could not escape it, as long as his armor was being correctly taken apart."[29]

As he continued to work with patients in this way, Reich was also occupied with what he felt were the inadequacies of Freud's theoretical views, particularly on the problem of masochism. This in turn led him to a new development, again combining innovations in practice and theory. He began to conceive of the patient's armoring in a much more literal sense, as in fact a quite specific kind of structuring of the musculature itself. A contemporary therapist who acknowledges his indebtedness to Reich's work describes the process in this way:

*When needs and impulses arise, there tends to be a muscular response. The response tends to play itself out on the motor level, and the only way that one can inhibit the response is by contracting antagonistic muscles that prevent this impulse from expressing itself fully. The simplest example would be an impulse to swear at somebody. Let us suppose that you are very angry and yet you have to hold the impulse back. Now this "holding back" process can be seen as a strictly muscular process. There are contractions in the jaws; there are tensions in the arm that prevent, for example, shaking the fist. In the case of sadness, the normal postural responses if the need played itself out thoroughly would be dejected posture, drawn mouth, and empty face. In holding sadness back, the simplest alteration would be to push the lips upward into a smile, destroying the pattern associated with sadness and thus not expressing and discharging the emotion. In repression all sorts of impulse unawareness are maintained by chronic muscular contractions which are forgotten by the individual. They become habitual; the individual adapts to them and does not know that he is blocking something or what it is that he is blocking.[30]*

This comes amazingly close to the much-maligned paradigm of behaviorism: that the repeated response by certain effector muscles in the presence of a reward (in this case, the reduction of unpleasant tension) sets up, or makes more probable, this response as habitual; and this process can and does occur quite aside from such presumed processes as conscious awareness. Reich's insights led directly to a clinically useful behaviorism; we shall see later how this, in the form of Fritz Perls' phenomenology, led to important breakthroughs in clinical practice.

The logical next step was for Reich to develop a therapeutic technique by which he could dissolve the muscular armor itself—a step that now clearly changed the whole psychoanalytic session. This step was accomplished by the early 1930s, when Reich was in Norway, having fled from the Nazis; one of his earliest patients, who remained a lifelong friend, was A. S. Neill, of Summerhill fame. Reich gave the name *vegetotherapy* to his new method, which consisted of working directly on the expressive characteristics of the patient, his muscular tensions, and his breathing patterns. It was not totally a new direction but a logical extension of his earlier work on character resistances.

> *The vegetotherapeutic treatment of muscular attitudes is interwoven in a very definite way with the work on character attitudes. It does not by any means take the place of the character-analytic work. Instead, it supplements it, or rather: it is the same work taking place in a deeper layer of the biological organism. For, as we know, character armor and muscular armor are completely identical. Thus, vegetotherapy might rightly be called "character-analysis in the realm of biophysical functioning."*[31]

Its aim was to be the restoration of complete freedom and motility in the total biophysical organism, achieved by a combination of traditional psychoanalytic procedures and Reich's newer technique of a direct manipulation of the body musculature.[32] Its most important method was to be a "breathing technique," justified on the grounds that "there is no neurotic individual who is capable of exhaling in one breath, deeply and evenly. The patients have developed all conceivable practices that prevent *deep expiration*. They exhale 'jerkily,' or, as soon as the air is let out, they quickly bring their chest back into the inspiratory position."[33]

### Beyond Therapy

But Reich was, even at this mature stage in his career, well within the psychoanalytic tradition; until the late 1930s, he was still engaged in annotating Freud. True to this tradition, he saw as the central problem the question of sexuality—the nature of the sexual instinct or impulse, sexuality as a factor in neurosis, the place of sexuality in man's total life pattern, the relation of sexuality and culture, and the ethical and moral issues related to these topics. The theoretical developments, then, that accompanied these advances in therapeutic technique added up to the first stage in his new theory of sexuality—but because his views were significantly broader in scope than those of his predecessors, he quite properly called it a theory of genitality.[34] Taken too literally, Reich's views were narrow, and they soon furnished fuel for his many enemies within and without the clinical profession. He held that the single goal in therapy, and therefore the single criterion of adequate psychic harmony, was the achievement of a full sexual orgasm—orgasm potency, as he called it. But what he meant by this statement was something else again, for very soon his theory of genitality became his own expression of a biophysical, even a cosmological, philosophy applicable to all living things. His own summary of his thinking at this time will indicate the direction of his work:

1. *That the basic function of psychic life is of a sex-economic nature;*
2. *That the excitations of sexuality and anxiety are identical excitations with opposite direction; that they represent the basic antithesis in vegetative life which allows of no further derivation than a physical one;*
3. *That character formation results from a binding of bio-energy;*
4. *That character armor and muscular armor are functionally identical;*
5. *That the bio-energy can be re-mobilized from the character armor and muscular armor with a definite technique, and, for the time being, only with this technique.*[35]

Thus, the familiar sexual instinct of Freudian theory has now become bio-energy, and the basic direction of its flow, whether toward or away from the periphery of the organism, determines whether the process is one of expansion, pleasure, and genitality, or one of constriction, "unpleasure," and anxiety. Reich constantly pointed to the observable evidence for this thesis—in particular, the moist, warm, alive appearance of the person who is psychically expansive and in harmony with himself, as contrasted with the pale, cold, dry skin of the chronically anxious and constricted person. Evidence gathered about the same time based on high-speed motion picture studies of the startle response, but apparently not available to him, appears to support his position.

But there is more to the theory than this; it has a social and moral dimension as well.

*Psychic health depends upon orgastic potency, that is, on the capacity for surrender in the acme of sexual excitation in the natural sex act. Its basis is the un-neurotic character attitude of capacity for love. Mental illness is a result of a disturbance in the natural capacity for love. In the case of orgastic impotence, from which a vast majority of humans are suffering, biological energy is dammed up, thus becoming the source of all kinds of irrational behavior. The cure of psychic disturbances requires in the first place the establishment of the natural capacity for love. It depends as much upon social as upon psychic conditions.*[37]

With this last sentence, Reich took a major step away from Freud; he later came to identify the social conditions leading to orgastic impotence, to label them the emotional plague, to attribute them to a patriarchal family constellation and the conditions of society, and to establish clinics and schools for constructive re-education of the masses of people. It was the latter activity in Berlin that led to his being ejected from the Communist party in Germany as being too psychological for a political group; soon thereafter he was dismissed from the International Psychoanalytical Association because his work was too political for a professional group. His own words are perhaps the best answer to both these attacks:

*I believe that there will be no lasting peace on our earth, and that all attempts to socialize human beings will be in vain, as long as politicians and dictators of*

## THE NORMAL STARTLE RESPONSE

The pattern . . . includes blinking of the eyes, head movement forward, a characteristic facial expression, raising and drawing forward of the shoulders, abduction of the upper arms, bending of the elbows, pronation of the lower arms, flexion of the fingers, forward movement of the trunk, contraction of the abdomen, and bending of the knees. . . . The response is very rapid and follows sudden, intense stimulation. . . .

adults, in the primates and in certain of the lower animal forms. . . .

The first and most noticeable feature of the facial pattern is the immediate closing of the eyes. Then there is a widening of the mouth as though in a grin, although this only occasionally leads to a real baring of the teeth. The head and neck are brought forward. Sometimes as the head comes forward and down the chin is tilted up so that the features are still directed straight ahead despite the movement. The muscles in the neck stand out. . . . In milder responses this facial pattern is more noticeable than the bodily pattern. . . . In strong reactions, however, the bodily pattern is the more noticeable; the most prominent feature is the general flexion, which resembles a protective contraction or "shrinking" of the individual.

Not all elements of the pattern appear in every individual or in any one individual upon every occasion. The eye blink always occurs; never have we found a normal individual in whom it was not present.[36]

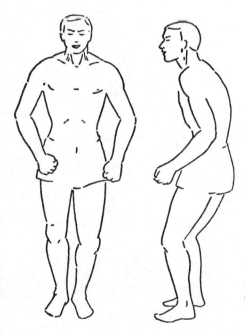

One of the most outstanding characteristics of the startle pattern is its speed. It usually comes and goes in less than one-half second. . . . It is a basic reaction, not amenable to voluntary control, is universal, and is found in Negroes as well as whites, infants as well as *one kind or another, who have not the slightest awareness of the actualities of the life process, continue to lead masses of people who are endemically neurotic and sexually sick. The natural function of the socialization of the human is that of guaranteeing work and natural fulfillment in love. These two biological activities of man have always depended upon scientific searching and thinking. Knowledge, work and natural love are the sources of life.*[38]

Implicit in this stance is a philosophy of man that rings strikingly true for our own age. Reich did not state his views in philosophic terms, preferring to identify himself as a scientist and therapist, but his position is clear enough in his repeated descriptions of what he calls the genital character: a person whom we today, heavily influenced by Maslow, might call the self-actualizing individual. What is particularly impressive about Reich's work is that it seems to contain in almost explicit form the central thought of nearly every influential worker in this

---

## THE GENITAL CHARACTER

Since the ego, as a result of sexual gratification, is under little pressure from the id as well as the super-ego, it does not have to defend itself against the id as must the ego of the neurotic character; this leaves ample energies for affective experience and realistic action in the outside world; action and experience are intensive, free-flowing; the ego is accessible to a high degree to pleasure as well as unpleasure. True, the ego of the genital character also has an armor, but it has the armor at its command instead of being at its mercy. This armor is pliable enough to allow adaptation to the various situations of life; the genital character can be very gay but also intensely angry; he reacts to an object-loss with depression but does not get lost in it; he is capable of intense love but also of intense hatred; he can, under appropriate conditions, be childlike but he will never appear infantile; his seriousness is natural and not stiff in a compensatory way because he has no tendency to show himself grown-up at all cost; his courage is not a proof of potency but directed toward a rational goal; thus he will not try to avoid the reproach of cowardice,

say, in a war which he is convinced is unjustified, but will stand up for his conviction. Since infantile wishes have lost their cathexis, his love as well as his hatred has a rational goal. The pliability as well as the solidity of his armor are shown in the fact that he can open up to the world as intensely in one case as he can shut himself off from it in another. His ability to give himself is most clearly shown in his sexual experience: In the sexual act with the loved partner the ego is practically reduced to the function of perception, the armor is temporarily dissolved almost completely, the whole personality is engulfed in the pleasurable experience, without any fear of getting lost in it, for the ego has a solid narcissistic foundation which does not serve any compensatory function. His self-confidence derives its most potent energies from the sexual experience. From the way he solves his everyday conflicts it is easy to see that these conflicts are rational, not burdened by infantile admixtures; this is again because a normal libido economy makes a cathexis of the infantile experiences and wishes impossible.

As the genital character is not stiff and rigid in any respect, we find the same thing in the forms of his sexuality. Since he is capable of gratification, he is capable of monogamy without compulsion or repression; on the other hand, if rational grounds are given, he is also capable, without suffering harm, of a change of object or of polygamy. He does not stick to his sexual object out of guilt feelings or for moralistic reasons; he maintains a sexual relationship only because the sexual partner gives him pleasure. He can overcome polygamous wishes without repression if they are in conflict with his relationship with the loved object; but he is also capable of giving in to them if they are all too disturbing. The resulting conflict he will solve in a realistic manner.

Neurotic guilt feelings are practically absent. His sociality is based not on repressed but on sublimated aggression and on his realistic orientation in life. That does not mean, however, that he always bows to external reality. On the contrary, it is precisely the genital character who—due to his structure which is at variance with the present-day moralistic and antisexual culture—is capable of criticizing and altering the social situation. His lack of fear of life guards him against concessions to the outer world which conflict with his convictions.[39]

With the ability to experience complete genital surrender, the patient's personality underwent such a thorough and rapid change that, initially, I was baffled by it. I did not understand how the tenacious neurotic process could give way so rapidly. It was not only that the neurotic anxiety symptoms disappeared—the patient's entire personality changed. I was at a loss to explain this theoretically. I interpreted the disappearance of the symptoms as the withdrawal of the sexual energy which had previously nourished them. But the character change itself eluded clinical understanding. The genital character appeared to function according to different, hitherto unknown laws. I want to cite a few examples by way of illustration.

Quite spontaneously, the patients began to experience the moralistic attitudes of the world around them as something alien and peculiar. No matter how tenaciously they might have defended premarital chastity beforehand, now they experienced this demand as grotesque. Such demands no longer had any relevancy for them; they became indifferent to them. Their attitude toward their work changed. If, until then, they had worked mechanically, had not demonstrated any real interest, had considered their work a necessary evil which one takes upon oneself without giving it much thought, now they became discriminating. If neurotic disturbances had previously prevented them from working, now they were stirred by a need to engage in some practical work in which they could take a personal interest. If the work which they performed was such that it was capable of absorbing their interests, they blossomed. If, however, their work was of a mechanical nature as, for example, that of an office employee, businessman, or middling attorney, then it became an almost intolerable burden. In such cases, I had a hard time mastering the difficulties which arose. The world was not attuned to the human aspect of work. Teachers who had been liberal, though not essentially critical of educational methods, began to sense a growing estrangement from, and intolerance of, the usual way of dealing with children. In short, the sublimation of instinctual forces in one's work took various forms, depending upon the work and the social conditions. Gradually, I was able to distinguish two trends: (1) a growing immersion in a social activity to which one was fully committed; (2) a sharp protest of the psychic organism against mechanical, stultifying work.

In other cases, there was a complete

breakdown in work when the patient became capable of genital gratification. This appeared to confirm the malicious exhortations of the world that sexuality and work were antithetical. Upon closer examination, the matter ceased to be alarming. It turned out that the latter were always patients who had, until then, performed their work on the basis of a compulsive sense of duty, at the expense of inner desires they had repudiated, desires which were by no means asocial—quite the contrary. A person who felt himself best suited to be a writer had, if employed in an attorney's office, to muster all his energy to master his rebellion and to suppress his healthy impulses. Thus, I learned the important rule that not everything unconscious is asocial, and that not everything conscious is social. On the contrary, there are highly praiseworthy, indeed culturally valuable, attributes and impulses which have to be repressed for material considerations, just as there are flagrantly asocial activities which are socially rewarded with fame

and honor. The most difficult patients were those who were studying for the priesthood. Inevitably, there was a deep conflict between sexuality and the practice of their profession. I resolved not to accept any more priests as patients.

The change in the sexual sphere was just as pronounced. Patients who had felt no qualms in going to prostitutes became incapable of going to them once they were orgastically potent. Wives who had patiently endured living with unloved husbands and had submitted to the sexual act out of "marital obligation" could no longer do so. They simply refused; they had had enough. What could I say against such behavior? It was at variance with all socially dictated views, for instance, the conventional arrangement whereby the wife must unquestioningly fulfill her husband's sexual demands as long as the marriage lasts, whether she wants to or not, whether she loves him or not, whether she is sexually aroused or not. The ocean of lies in this world is deep![40]

---

field in recent times. He anticipates Maslow and a host of existential clinicians in his description of a mature and open style of life; and his stories of how his patients reacted remind one of the reported results of encounter weekends during the early days of that movement. A description of his courage and vision in dealing directly with the sexual behavior of his patients might be the opening chapter of a treatise by Masters and Johnson. He inspired a new generation of clinicians along the direction I have called Somatics, and he invented therapeutic techniques only now beginning to come into widespread use. Every contemporary therapist is in his debt for his breakthrough toward meeting the patient as a human being with a potential for bettering himself. Reich describes his own growth as a therapist: "I learned to overcome the fear of patients' behavior and discovered an undreamed-of world. Beneath these neurotic mechanisms, behind all these dangerous, grotesque, irrational phantasies and impulses, I found a bit of simple, matter-of-fact, decent nature."[41]

# chapter 10
# theatrics: allowing the self

The new body-oriented approaches in the work of Selver, Rolf, or Reich may seem to be nothing more than recent variations within more or less traditional therapeutic practice. Indeed, this is initially what much of Somatics was, a new direction for psychoanalysis. But implicit in the work of Reich, nearly explicit in Rolfing, and often quite openly declared in sensory awareness, is something radically new. Even if, in much of this work, the doctor-patient relation has been retained, what is elicited and worked on here is clinical material very close to the client's pure experience. It is characterized by immediacy, it is inescapably tied to emotional states, and it may even be the repository of long-buried personal secrets. Once the body is allowed to become the person's organ of speech communication without language becomes possible, as we all somehow know from our own immediate experiences of other people's expressive movements; and when that happens, the mere talk that takes us out of the present moment or place is replaced by the silent expressiveness of experience here and now.

With this view of Somatics as background, we may now trace a logical development—from Lowen's extension of Reich's pioneering work, through Keleman's spiritual biology, to Perls, who brought it together in a new form of personal theatrical experience.

## BIOENERGETICS: THEORY AND PRACTICE

Lowen, a psychiatrist who trained with Reich, has taken a Reichian proposition as his guiding thesis: "If the determinants of personality and character are physically structured, must not the therapeutic endeavor equally be physically oriented?"[1] Like Reich, he may be described as a psychoanalyst, in the sense that in his work he attempts to preserve the spirit of Freudian theory as well as a practice based firmly on traditional doctor-patient roles. But he is also quite explicit as to how his approach, which he calls bioenergetic analysis, differs from that of the orthodox Freudian.

*First and foremost, the study of the patient is unitary. The bioenergetic therapist analyzes not only the psychological problem of the patient as will every analyst, but also the physical expression of that problem as it is manifested in the body structure and movement of the patient. Second, the technique involves a systematic attempt to release the physical tension which is found in chronically contracted and spastic muscles. Third, the relationship between therapist and patient has an added dimension to that found in psychoanalysis. Since the work is done on a physical level, the resulting activity involves the analyst more deeply than do the conventional techniques.*[2]

All this involves essentially a continuation of Reich's pioneering therapy, "to fill in the gaps and extend the theory and practice."[3]

The major difference between Lowen's approach and that of Reich may be in how far each sees his therapeutic work as extending. For Reich, psychotherapy was truly a means for saving civilization—an implication that may be found buried not too deeply in more conventional Freudian theory. It was therefore no accident that Reich ended by discovering the source of human problems, and the means for their alleviation, in a universal, cosmic life energy, which he called the orgone. His theory of therapy became, finally, a world philosophy and a set of explanatory principles for all living matter in the universe. Lowen's work seems quite narrow by contrast—as, indeed, might that of anyone who restricts himself to being merely an innovative clinician. On the basis of personal contact with Reich, with whom he had an analysis, and a detailed acquaintance with psychoanalytic theory, Lowen has been able to pull out of the Reichian corpus the outlines of both a useful theory and a workable method.[4] The concept that he sees as underlying the "functional identity" of character attitudes and patterns of muscular armor is, as in Reich, an energy process, but Lowen sidesteps any of the metaphysical issues involved in specifying this energy. He writes:

*If we are to avoid becoming mystical, we must regard the concept of energy as a physical phenomenon, that is, as capable of being measured. We must also follow the physical law that all energy is interchangeable and we must assume, in harmony with modern doctrines in physics, that all forms of energy can be and eventually will be reduced to a common denominator. It is not important at this point to know the final form of this basic energy. We work with the hypothesis*

*that there is one fundamental energy in the human body whether it manifests
itself in psychic phenomena or in somatic motion. This energy we call simply
"bioenergy." Psychic processes as well as somatic processes are determined by the
operation of this bioenergy. All living processes can be reduced to manifestations
of this bioenergy.*[5]

More than any contemporary approach, bioenergetics makes explicit the
concept of the body as both a living and lived thing. "Apart from the body," Lowen
says, "life is an illusion. In the body, one will encounter pain, sadness, anxiety, and
terror, but these are at least real feelings, which can be experienced and expressed."[6]
And again: "It is the body that melts with love, freezes with fear, trembles in
anger, and reaches for warmth and contact. Apart from the body these words are
poetic images."[7] I would add that it is also the body which quite literally is the
individual's unique stance in the world. "You, as *body*, are the life process."[8]
Because there is so little within each of us that is innately either masculine or
feminine (as distinct from male or female), for example, the body can easily
become the very reality of one's masculinity or femininity. Long before puberty,
boys and girls throw a ball in quite different ways, not because their bodies are
structurally so different but because the two sexes (at least in our culture) from
the earliest years occupy space in quite different ways; in other words, the body
as objective structure does not differ between the sexes, but the lived body does
differ so much that in this and in many other kinds of action boys and girls live
in different (though overlapping) realities. These realities differ as much as the
structures of animals that hunt differ from the structures of animals that are
hunted—the former having small ears, eyes at the front of the head, and good
distance vision, and the latter having larger ears, eyes set at the side of the head,
and vision capable of taking in a wide field rather than a long distance.

Lowen has taken quite literally the Reichian concept of armoring as the means
by which the person binds anxiety; the therapeutic task, then, is to free the bio-
energy locked in the tight muscles. The basic means by which binding occurs, he
has found, is in "reducing respiration through an unconscious control over the
muscles of the front of the body";[9] thus establishing completely free respiration is
a first step in treatment. In his clinical work, however, Lowen combines analytic
work on the psychic mechanisms with exercises and movements on the somatic
side. As an example, treatment of the hysterical character requires that repressed
anger be freed and the related bioenergy be allowed to flow into arms and
hands. "As the shoulders gain motility, the chest wall relaxes; respiration deepens
and energy production rises. This would result in the appearance of anxiety unless
the analytic work has prepared the way for its discharge through analysis of the
sexual function. . . . In bioenergetic therapy . . . the function of respiration is
coordinated with the total behavior of the organism and is not treated as an
isolated function."[10]

This explains why with all the goodwill in the world one cannot "cure" himself simply by trying to breathe properly, or carry his shoulders higher, or stand
in a different way. A rather elaborate technique is required, consisting of "passive

positions" as well as "active movements," forced expressions, specific exercises, and manipulation by the therapist, all embedded in a fairly conventional analytic technique. Lowen is careful to warn that the method, straightforward and harmless though it may appear, involves risks that may be beyond the power of an untrained therapist to handle. "In this technique, one deals not only with the 'derivatives of the unconscious' but with the unconscious mechanism of repression itself. In this way it is possible to bring affects to consciousness with an intensity which is impossible on the verbal level."[11] Indications to this effect were found early in the encounter group movement when exercises borrowed from bioenergetic techniques were shown to precipitate dramatic and extreme outbursts of emotion on short notice and among groups of comparative strangers. We should hardly be surprised at this, for most of us suspect, though we would hardly dare admit it publicly, that a very great pool of affective energy is contained behind the social masks of our everyday presence. Children are much freer to release this energy in many different forms—and this should warn us that it is only socialization and our armoring as adults that keeps us from the direct expression of at least as great a quantity of energy.

### The Yoga of the West

The great value of bioenergetic thought, implied in much of what Lowen has written and then made explicit in Keleman's approach, is that it provides for the first time a working vocabulary of collective experience. Here, for example, Keleman, a leading bioenergetic teacher, talks about trust—but in place of a theory of psychic functions or processes we have a statement of experience that is not meant to be believed, but to be heard; hearing his statement is itself the experience of trust to which he refers.

> *We have denied trust and dependence on life. To be in touch with your body is to trust. There is no other way. . . . Without knowing it, people will live their lives on that lack of trust: I don't know whether I can trust my own body, I don't know whether I can accept it. . . . But the minute that you begin to open up on that level and allow what your body needs to emerge, say in surrendering to sexuality or to any situation, then what emerges is new and you begin to structure that by acting on it. . . . Self-discovery experiences in my life have occurred when I have allowed myself to* surrender. *And then I have found my shyness and found my poet, and found this new part of me, and hey, that's a surprise, and this is a surprise. Different experiences bubble up like a rich fountain that never runs dry.*[12]

In the concept of energy the links between experience and action are made explicit; and this concept provides a working vocabulary for sharing and Allowing. Lowen's description of a fundamental animal action provides a fine example.

> *If one visualizes the gallop of a dog or a horse, the nature of mammalian movement is clearly evident. The alternate coming together and extension of the two*

*pairs of legs represents a process of charge and discharge which can be portrayed....
As the energy sweeps through the muscular system, which is essentially on the
back of the animal, the two ends of the animal approach each other and contact
the ground. Energy is discharged through the four legs into the ground. This
discharge of energy produces a leap in which the legs are extended. Extension
of the back opens the volar aspect of the animal and leads to the inspiration of
air. A new impulse forms which charges the front of the body first and then moves
into and charges the main muscle mass of the back. The organism is now in a
position for a new discharge and another leap.*[13]

This description rings so true that it can almost be felt. I think this is because
it isolates just those coordinate centers of energy that are experienced by humans
equally with animals. The back is the muscle center, the place where energy is
gathered for discharge and for work; the front is the center for intake and energy
renewal. Lowen has generalized this to the clinically meaningful distinction between feelings of tenderness, centered in the heart, which reside along the front
of the body, versus feelings of aggression, centered in the muscles of the back,
which reside along the dorsal aspect of the body. Two main areas, two related
kinds of feelings, two sets of activities and actions in the world, two kinds of
stances—and the energy joins the two below in the genital area and above in the
head, so that the sexual act and the psychic act, as well as every movement of
the body, represent at their best a complete fusion of the two necessary stances,
tenderness and aggression. In summary:

*One basic energy motivates all actions. When it charges and flows through the
musculature, especially the voluntary muscles, it produces spatial movement which
we equate with aggression (to move to). When it charges the soft structures such
as the blood and skin, it produces sensations which are erotic, tender or loving.
Each of these aspects of the emotional life of the individual tends to be localized
topographically: the motor component in the back and legs, the sensory component
in the front of the body and in the hands.... In un-neurotic behavior, this one
energy is distributed into the two pathways to produce an action which is rational
and appropriate to the situation. Impulses from the two pathways merge or
super-impose into an action which, seen at the surface, is a unitary expression....*

PROPOSITIONS
1. Man and his body are the same. Man does not have a body. He is a body.
2. Psychic structure and physical structure are the same.
3. To function fully man's primary identification must be grounded in bodily functions.
4. He is then in harmony with himself and nature.
5. Unity of Self, unity of energy, flow from this grounding and equal, full aliveness.
6. Psychic disease equals failure to identify with natural grounding.
7. In the development of Man, muscular contraction, a defense mechan-

ism, can become chronic, prohibiting unified energetic flow and grounding.

8. This is often manifested as fear of the bodily processes, identification with the mind processes.

9. Particular causes of contractions are contained in the contractions.

10. But the ultimate importance of the contraction is the block to grounding and unity.

11. The work is to identify the blocks, their particular causes, to remove them and demonstrate the possibility of unity.

12. When this is done, Aliveness results and a coping, a functioning, that stems from the true creative flow of nature.[15]

---

*Where complete fusion has occurred it is impossible for the observer to delineate the two components. Incomplete fusion creates ambivalence and produces irrational behavior.*[14]

It is only a short step from this to the practice of bioenergetics, the basic propositions of which are implicit in what has already been said. The methods have been summarized by Keleman:

*In working with a client, the first thing I attempt to do in understanding the blocks is to see the person as an energetic unit, and then I seek to determine the level of aliveness. For example, I look at the breathing—a depressed breathing will tell me about a depressed energy level, and this person probably cannot bear too much excitation or too much charging. This person spends a great deal of his energy keeping the energy down so that he is not experiencing himself. . . . The next thing I do in working with a client is to try to increase the energy buildup or tolerance through breathing, kicking or movement. Through the buildup more energy can be brought to them. An energy buildup occurs which then comes into contact with the block (the muscular contraction), and this will stop or repress the energetic buildup or flow. I then have the client try to work through this block. At the same time, the client as a result of the energetic buildup is experiencing his block more intensely. . . . The increase in energy carefully observed raises questions such as: Where is it blocked? Where is it directed or where does it want to go? What prevents it from getting there? What is the client's reaction to being in contact with his own energy, or energetic processes? This becomes subject to an investigation. Once a charging of energy starts moving and meeting inhibitions, contractions, the inhibition and expression of it is manifest. The client is helped to understand how the block limits his own being: the contrast between the block and the natural flow and the pleasure and unity that are possible for him.*[16]

This direction of development in the helping arts is experienced by some clients as a kind of therapy; they are, undeniably, helped in dealing with their own emotional difficulties. But although in this sense the work is treatment, it is broader than the discipline of psychotherapy. It is not restricted simply to the cure of existing neurotic difficulties; rather, "the concept of 'body' is extended to include the moral, social and imaginative realms: the person. One escapes the tyranny of the therapeutic by moving beyond the ideas of health and cure."[17] In Keleman's words, "I don't know how else to put it, but I don't like the idea of fixing which the word therapy contains in it. It's implicit in my work, certainly, but it's not really an accurate statement of the facts of what happens to a person. The words *grounding*, and *releasing*, opening and unifying seem more appropriate."[18] What is foreshadowed here is truly a "spiritual biology." "The body is the bridge between the historical past, the reality of the here and now, and the emerging tomorrow. The body is the key to time and space. Man is grounded in his body and man is a sexual being; his sexuality is him and is the link between him and the rest of the world."[19] Quite properly, Keleman refers to his developing work as "the Yoga of the West."

Perhaps most significant, Somatics in the form of a spiritual bioenergetics may have provided the second of the keys needed to unlock the full potentiality of the human biophysical organism. The first key, strange though it may seem, was, I am convinced, provided by the recent upsurge of drug usage, especially among the younger generation. Somatics needed the drug trip and might not have had its full impact if the younger generation had not gone on its collective drug trip in recent years. For what the drugs taught all of us—even those of us who refused to learn—was that there are worlds beyond worlds, some marvelous and some terrible, inside each one of us, and that these worlds are potential for every one of us because they are locked up in our bodies. That is all a drug can ever do: unlock some part of what is there, waiting, in a lived body. Once an entire generation had, for reasons both good and bad, taken advantage of modern biochemistry to unlock these doors, there was revealed another universe of worlds beyond worlds—all there in every person's body, bound into the body and waiting to be torn free or massaged loose; waiting to be sensed and breathed and felt; waiting to be finally experienced as healing.

On the basis of her study of literary figures who had tried opium and then reported on their experiences, Alethea Hayter concludes that the drug never does more than bring out what is already there. It only takes one to the "secret hiding places of their own native Earth, places whose existence they had forgotten or ignored or never observed."[20]

For every drug trip, it turns out, a bioenergetic trip is possible: the second key. The possibilities are only beginning to be glimpsed.

## THEATRICS: ALLOWING ONESELF

### Theater and Therapeutics

There is a significant contemporary movement in the arts toward breaking down existing boundaries. Painting and sculpture have almost lost their separate identities; dance and drama combine in the dance theater; and the happening turns all distinctions topsy-turvy. But more than boundaries between the traditional arts seem to be dissolving. The graphic arts can no longer be contained within museum walls as a result of contemporary techniques of reproduction and the creating of works that cannot be hung in galleries; even the frame that used to close off a picture and separate it from our space of living is often eliminated. Familiar categories that once defined a theatrical presentation—acts, a beginning and middle and end, a protagonist and antagonist and their conflict—have faded away with the death of naturalistic drama. The proscenium arch, functional cousin to the painting's frame, gives way in productions in which it is hard to tell who is audience and who are actors, what is offstage and what is on. All the neatly arranged conventions of the arts, like many social conventions in behavior, either disappear or, if they are still retained, begin to seem quaintly old-fashioned.

It is not surprising, then, that imaginative and innovative practitioners from the performing arts begin to intrude on what used to be considered sacred professional territory. The dancers in Ann Halprin's workshops have regular sessions with Gestalt therapy leaders and are trained as much in becoming aware of themselves as persons as in attending to what they do as dancers. The influence here goes back to Stanislavsky, back to the approach known as method acting in the American theater, in which one entered a dramatic part so completely that one's own self was almost lost.[21]

The implications of this fusion of theater and therapy have not yet been fully explored. It is a very large topic, and I can only touch on it here. If what is required in the performing arts is to experience becoming another person, sufficiently so to plausibly represent that person to an audience while retaining enough personal control of self to remember lines and stage business, then the phenomenon is clearly worthy of study by psychologists interested in the self.[22] Will an actor's skill be enhanced if he is helped to a deepened insight into himself through therapy? Or will this, on the other hand, stand in his way, especially since great actors have never been celebrated for the depth and insightfulness of their personalities? There are still other permutations of the factors in the fusion of theater and therapy. If, as has so often been claimed, the great neurotic illness of our time is the lack of authenticity—the role-playing and game-playing required of anyone who aims at success in competitive fields—does the art of acting have any relevance? Should people be trained to be better actors, or should they rather learn how to cut through the artificiality of their own and others' roles? It is identity that is at stake here; that essence of self we seek in different ways at every stage of growth—or so we are told.

The possibilities for therapy have been artfully exploited for many decades by J. E. Moreno, in the form of psychodrama.[23] It is a staging for purely therapeutic purposes, with audience, director, and auxiliary actors enlisted as needed to guide the patient in acting through—rather than acting-out—his problems in relation to specific other role figures in his life. Here only the most basic of the theater's tricks are used; the less stagy the result and the less literary the drama that ensues, the more successful the performance—which may then be dramatically very moving. There is a seeming paradox here, and it leads us back to some of the factors mentioned above. Psychodrama succeeds insofar as it accepts the existence of life roles and then gets the patient to play those roles to the hilt, genuinely and spontaneously. But it needs only the bare framework of theater: stage, audience, actor, director, plot situation. A consummate actor who came to a psychodrama session as a participant would do no better and might do much worse than any random member of the audience. Properly named, the procedure may not be psychodrama but a kind of dramatic psychotherapy.

But even if it is not theater, psychodrama is certainly great Theatrics—a vivid evocation of the drama that is human experience. Moreno's work has taught us that each person's experience is a drama and that whether he makes it comedy or tragedy is his own choice. A person's field of experience is a stage that he alone fills with people whom he picks from the world of persons he knows, whom he paints as he chooses, and whom he casts in roles of his own devising. It may not be too far from the truth to say that a person experiences himself in much the same way that a director sees the actor who is the star of his show: as a central figure who may or may not come up to an ideal performance, around whom the drama whirls, on whom it depends, through whom it may fall.

I am referring here, of course, to drama rather than to the contemporary entertainment that so often passes for theater. The history of what we now call the theater has moved in one direction ever since its ancient origin. Before drama as such, there were elaborate rituals carried out by the entire community on special days set aside for ceremony, but it was not long before the occasion turned into a formalized rite, carried out in public either by a cast of priests or by mummers with masks. By the fifth century B.C., in the villages of Greece, ceremonies had turned into theater; authors competed for prizes for their plays, which were presented as performances complete with chorus and actors. The direction in which the theater has moved was from an original source in community ritual to an end point in classic drama: from a participative event with great moral and religious import for every member of the group to a holiday when an audience might watch skilled actors perform on a prepared stage a drama composed by a gifted playwright.[24] Aristotle's statement about the purpose of tragedy—to stimulate the audience to feel pity and fear and then to purge the emotions thus aroused—describes very well the experience of primitive, pretheatrical drama, when it was possible for each individual to have such an experience; but a special attitude, almost a mental set, is required in order for this experience to occur in an individual member of a contemporary play audience.

With the revival of the theater as a medium for moral edification and enlightenment during the Middle Ages, every step of development involved introducing new conventions that served to increase the distance between spectator and stage.[25] What is referred to as the modern theater, dating approximately from the sixteenth century, is the heir to this development. It consists, in its traditional form, of a prepared and carefully rehearsed set of actions and speeches presented in a fixed number of segments called acts. Each portion, which may be part or all of an act, takes place in one location that is identified by some form of scenery. The same persons reappear throughout the play, each one appropriately costumed and represented by the same actor throughout the performance. The time span is realistic within each segment but not necessarily so between segments, and whatever is arranged in regard to the latter must be communicated to the audience. The performance begins at the same time of day, and the audience comes to a special building, known as a theater, where the performance takes place, and remains seated in a room next to the stage where they may watch but from which they may not enter the stage. The audience can communicate with those on the stage by some convention such as clapping hands, and may also laugh or even hiss at moments appropriate to what is being represented in the performance, but the actors may not respond or communicate to the audience or even look at the audience except under the very special convention of an aside—and so on. The canons are familiar enough; they add up to an experience for the audience that can only approximate Aristotle's description if the spectator gives himself over completely to the presentation on the stage.

To carry this line of development to its extreme, we have only to look briefly at the two forms of public entertainment that between them have almost eliminated the theater. In the first of these, the movies, the proscenium arch is replaced by the screen, and the pauses between segments almost disappear, as does the communication from audience to actors by means of applause. In exchange for this greater distance between the spectator and what he sees, however, the technology of the film makes possible a reasonable facsimile of an intimate experience. The camera is capable of taking the spectator anywhere, into any room no matter how private, and close to any person no matter who it may be. The persons represented in the drama can now be made larger than life or smaller, or whatever else is needed in order to entice the viewer into the illusion of sharing an experience. Properly used, the film may indeed accomplish this; but the truth is that the vast majority of commercial movies have been nothing but large-scale and expensive versions of the performances formerly viewed through a proscenium arch. They have rarely enabled the audience to participate in any but the most distantly vicarious manner—and the fact that generations of movie fans did in fact achieve an experience of participation, even of emotional involvement, in the face of Hollywood's fare may well demonstrate how badly most people need such an experience and how far they will strain to achieve it. Their need has been tricked still more by the purely technological achievement of the television medium, where even the cozy and intimate darkness of the movie theater as a setting has been lost, where every presentation is chopped into meaninglessly scheduled segments and the spaces between them calculated to take the viewer out of the experience of participation in the program; where, in brief, the spectator is reduced to a numb and passive sponge for the absorption of endless artificial entertainment.[26]

If television represents the tail end of a process of de-participation that began when primitive drama was changed from ritual to festival, it is understandable that both within and without the arts there is felt a great need for a return to the experience of participation in some form of Theatrics. There are many indications that the tendency toward this return is increasing today: in the examples given above of the fusion of various art forms so as to enrich the experience of each; in a new form of revolutionary politics as theater, where all the devices of contemporary public relations are utilized to turn activism into an experience involving both actors and spectators;[27] and, most far-reaching, in the development of an approach to clinical practice that combines theatrical performance with elemental and even ritualistic drama.

### Gestalt as Group Drama

The man responsible for this development on the clinical scene was, of course, Frederick S. Perls. To himself and to all those who came in contact with him over a decade he was, unforgettably, Fritz—the first major American guru. He began his career as a very respectable psychoanalyst, even acquiring during his enforced stay in South Africa a suburban home and swimming pool and an upper-middle class practice. Then he came to the United States, and moved around uncertainly while he began to fashion his own variant of psychotherapy; in the sixth decade of his life, following a severe illness and a series of crises in his personal life, both his career and his experience took a sharp turn. He embarked on a trip around the world—a kind of pilgrimage to find himself and was apparently so deeply influenced by Zen Buddhism that he came very close to settling permanently in a monastery in Kyoto, Japan. Instead, he returned to the United States and settled in Southern California. There he had a heart attack and, by his own story, his life was saved by means of a series of treatments by Ida Rolf. He moved up the West Coast to find both an atmosphere and a climate in which he could breathe more freely (and continue his habit of chain-smoking too) and in the early 1960s, by one of those miracles of historical chance, he found Esalen and Esalen found him. The marriage of a setting and a spirit produced just the foundation that Perls needed: he not only devised a distinctively new form of clinical expression; he brought together in one dramatic form all the threads of Eastern and existential thought that were then in the air, exciting but puzzling everyone. Most important of all, he charted a wholly new direction for the helping arts by reviving for our time the long-forgotten ritual of primitive drama. He made Theatrics possible.

There had been predecessors in addition to Moreno. As early as 1922, Alfred Adler, who was always as much a teacher and leader as a therapist, started what he called problem clinics, in which he interviewed children and their parents in the presence of an audience of teachers.[28] Rudolf Dreikurs, one of the leading Adlerian practitioners, later used the same setting for the counseling of alcoholics and their families.[29] Both soon became aware that, as Moreno had always emphasized, the presence and sympathetic cooperation of the audience had a therapeutic value in and of itself. Perls adopted much the same format. He dealt with group members individually in the presence of the rest of the group, either in workshops of twenty or so persons or in more public seminars with audiences of up to a hundred. In his procedure, the individual with whom he worked occupied the empty seat next to him—the "hot seat," as he called it—and was precipitated immediately into his personal drama, in the form of a statement of his problem or a recital of his dream.

The model for many aspects of traditional psychotherapy, curiously enough, may have been the Catholic confessional. The session is built around the notions of privacy and secrecy, of secrets held and given up, of a straining emphasis on what is inner and what is outer. Confidentiality is heavily stressed. At its best the analytic hour achieves an unburdening, a freeing-up of the restricted client; at its worst it reeks of shame and guilt. Yet in all this, nothing is ever really shared between therapist and patient, between penitent and confessor, except what passes through a small and carefully prepared opening between them. They do not really see each other, in any sense; both remain hidden from each other as well as from the world of other persons.

Perls changed all this in one stroke by starting with a new model: the participative and evocative community ritual. In place of privacy, secrecy, shame, and guilt, there was now an open and public presentation, group sharing of publicly evoked feelings, and at its best, the Dionysian celebration of joy.[30] Because Perls was himself an almost overwhelmingly theatrical personality, his rituals took on most of the other, more conventional trappings of theater as well: individual performances in the presence of an audience group; immediate and dramatically compelling "proof" of a thesis or an experience of change; brief and powerful sessions built toward individual climaxes; a continuing emphasis on matters of identity, role-playing, and self-consciousness. Indeed, all the techniques of Gestalt therapy, in the form of tricks and devices that can be learned, center around the fundamental problem of the actor—the problem of how to combine controlled self-awareness with an unselfconscious openness and spontaneity. Even the vocabulary of the Gestalt approach is taken from the theater; Perls referred to dialogue, script, director, and staging as the basic elements of the individual's performance. The use of the audience or groups, too, has been related to primitive drama; here, for example, is one experienced group leader's remarks on this aspect of Perlsian Theatrics:

> At some point Perls brings the group into play in a unique way which I call the "Greek chorus method." The "Greek chorus" forecasts, underlines, and cements strivings and achievements of the working patient in a way that combines conditioning with a very limited but effective form of group interaction. For example, the patient has come to a therapeutic realization: "I don't have to live up to anybody's expectations." He is now asked to "make the rounds" and say to each participant this sentence, adding individual formulations such as "I am not here to live up to your expectations. I do not have to give you my chair when I don't want to. I don't have to write a paper with you." The group members reply briefly with whatever their reactions are, such as, "You are right, you don't have to: Neither do I have to live up to yours," etc. Expressions of physical affections or rejections are permitted. . . . I have taught workshops on "Five Models of Group Interaction." . . . [and] invariably, the groups reacted with the greatest personal involvement in the Gestalt therapy workshop, in spite of the fact that they were spectators rather than interacting participants most of the time. Observing the dramatic therapeutic dialogue was of greater impact than

*personal interactional exchange. The patient's vertical plunge into previously avoided emotions seemed to touch the group of observers in the truest sense of identification and purification of a Greek drama. The members of the Greek chorus seem indeed to experience the tragic and joyful feelings of the patient's responses within themselves.*[31]

It is thus no accident that one of Perl's greatest contributions was to bring joy and excitement back into the treatment sessions—although such concepts as treatment soon seem out of place when the session turns into an expressive ritual staged with the full collaboration of a believing audience. It is a unique experience for the sophisticated adult—just as was the encounter group—to bridge the chasm of one's skin, the wall separating Me from You, and to link private and public worlds by means of a celebration in company with others who are now true peers.

As our social lives become progressively more organized and mechanized to fit the impersonal demands of a complex machine age, even familiar holidays are killed off and then revived in manufactured form: Washington's Birthday now falls, artificially, on whatever Monday is convenient for the long weekends of an affluent work force. Parades are infrequent. The sporting event is usually foregone in favor of more comfortable viewing in front of the TV set. From revival services to public hangings, all the public ceremonies we knew have disappeared, and we all now share a desperate need to learn how to ritualize and celebrate, how to discover and follow true leaders, how to become aroused in public with others, how to allow ourselves the memorable experience of feeling and fellowship in a group of which we feel a part. This is how theater started before it began to become mere entertainment; and this is what Perls brought back.

---

## PRODUCTION NOTES
## ON THE INNER DRAMA

If you understand what you can do with dreams, you can do a tremendous lot for yourself on your own. Just take any old dream or dream fragment, it doesn't matter. As long as a dream is remembered, it is still alive and available, and it still contains an unfinished, unassimilated situation. When we are working on dreams, we usually take only a small little bit from the dream, because you can get so much from even a little bit.

So if you want to work on your own, I suggest you write the dream down and make a list of all the details in the dream. Get every person, every thing, every mood, and then work on these to become each one of them. Ham it up, and really transform yourself into each of the different items. Really become that thing—whatever it is in a dream—become it. Use your magic. Turn into that ugly frog or whatever is there—the dead thing, the live thing, the demon—and stop thinking. Lose your mind and come to your senses. Every little bit is a piece of the jigsaw puzzle, which together will make up a much larger whole—a much stronger, happier, more completely real personality.

Next, take each one of these different items, characters, and parts, and let them have encounters between them. Write a script. By "write a script," I mean have a dialogue between the two opposing parts and you will find—especially if you get the correct opposites—that they always start out fighting each other. All the different parts—any part in the dream is yourself, is a projection of yourself, and if there are inconsistent sides, contradictory sides, and you use them to fight each other, you have the eternal conflict game, the self-torture game. As the process of encounter goes on, there is a mutual

learning until we come to an understanding, and an appreciation of differences, until we come to a oneness and integration of the two opposing forces. Then the civil war is finished, and your energies are ready for your struggles with the world.[32] [Italics deleted.]

Perls' advice to his listeners and followers, his patients and disciples—those who worked with him were all of these at the same time, and more—and in his instructions on how to work on your own dreams, bear a remarkable resemblance to primitive group practices. Claudio Naranjo identifies one element of the procedure as personification, that is, "an inward attempt to identify with or relive past events or, most often, a reenacting of the scenes with gestural and postural participation as well as verbal exchanges, as in psychodrama. . . . Personification is found in the history of drama, magic, and ritual, and in the enacting of dreams among some primitive people."[33] Yet at the same time that it opens up a whole new arena of experience for modern man, the method that Perls introduced as Gestalt therapy can also be termed a significant advance in both clinical theory and clinical practice.

### Toward a Theory of Helping

Unlike Freud, Perls was not a systematic thinker nor a theorist; he never considered himself a scientist. Thus, he did not try to draw his insights together into a single statement, let alone a comprehensive theory. He was always too close to the stuff of experience to fall victim to the "final word" syndrome that seems to afflict so many pioneers in the human disciplines. However, he did often express his thoughts about the human condition, usually in the form of insightful

THE LAYERED NEUROSIS

Now let me tell you something about how I see the structure of a neurosis. Of course I don't know what the theory will be next because I'm always developing and simplifying what I'm doing more and more. I now see the neurosis as consisting of five layers.

The first layer is the cliché layer. If you meet somebody you exchange clichés—"Good morning," handshake, and all of the meaningless tokens of meeting.

Now behind the clichés, you find the second layer, what I call the Eric Berne

or Sigmund Freud layer—the layer where we play games and roles—the very important person, the bully, the cry-baby, the nice little girl, the good boy—whatever roles we choose to play. So these are the superficial, social as-if layers. We pretend to be better, tougher, weaker, more polite, etc., than we really feel. This is essentially where the psychoanalysts stay. They treat playing the child as a reality and call it infantilism and try to get all the details of this child-playing. . . .

Now if we work through the role-playing layer, if we take away the roles, what do we experience then? Then we experience the anti-existence, we experience the nothingness, emptiness. This is the impasse that I talked about earlier, the feeling of being stuck and lost. The impasse is marked by a phobic attitude—avoidance. We are phobic, we avoid suffering, especially the suffering of frustration. We are spoiled, and we don't want to go through the hellgates of suffering: We stay immature, we go on manipulating the world, rather than to suffer the pains of growing up. . . . Behind the impasse lies a very interesting layer, the death layer or implosive layer. This fourth layer appears either as death or as fear of death. The death layer has nothing to do with Freud's death instinct. It only appears as death because of the paralysis of opposing forces. It is a kind of catatonic paralysis: we pull ourselves together, we contract and compress ourselves, we implode. Once we really get in contact with this deadness of the implosive layer, then something very interesting happens.

The implosion becomes explosion. The death layer comes to life, and this explosion is the link-up with the authentic person who is capable of experiencing and expressing his emotions. There are four basic kinds of explosions from the death layer. There is the explosion of genuine grief if we work through a loss or death that has not been assimilated. There is the explosion into orgasm in sexually blocked people. There is the explosion into anger, and also the explosion into joy, laughter, joie de vivre. These explosions connect with the authentic personality, with the true self. . . .

As you know, most of our role-playing is designed to use up a lot of this energy for controlling just those explosions. The death layer, the fear of death, is that if we explode, then we believe we can't survive any more—then we will die, we'll be persecuted, we'll be punished, we won't be loved any more and so on. So the whole rehearsal and self-torture game continues; we hold ourselves back and control ourselves.[34] [Italics deleted.]

---

generalizations. Typical of these theoretical contributions is his dramatic account of the layered neurosis. It is speculative in the extreme; it is tied directly to clinical data and phrased throughout in terms of experience; it is personal, usually stated as "we" rather than as "people" or "the patient"; it is partial and tentative; it is, in short, a uniquely individual guess, but an immensely learned and wise guess, about what is sensed as a mystery.

Some of Perls' separate insights deserve mention, especially since they have become part of the folklore of Fritz and Esalen and the Gestalt seminars. They are often reworkings of more familiar Freudian notions, for Perls never completely resolved his quarrel with Freud, as the running account in his autobiography shows.[35] In place of Freud's metapsychological and clinically awkward notions of id and superego, Perls substitutes the image of two opposing masters, called by him Top Dog and Under Dog; they are two parts of almost everyone's personality, two inner voices constantly tugging and pulling at each other:

*two clowns performing their weird and unnecessary plays on the stage of the tolerant and mute self. . . . Top Dog can be described as righteous, bullying, punishing, authoritarian, and primitive. Top Dog commands continually with such statements as, "You should," "You ought to" and "Why don't you?" Oddly enough, we all so strongly identify with our inner Top Dog that we no longer question its authority. We take its righteousness for granted. . . . Under Dog develops great skill in evading Top Dog's commands. Only half-heartedly intending to comply with the demands, Under Dog answers: "Yes, but . . . ," "I try so hard but next time I'll do better," and "Mañana." Under Dog usually gets the better of the conflict.*[36]

Similarly, a concept of projection derived directly from the realities of experience replaces the more mechanical process described in the Freudian literature. Basic to Perls' version of experience and the struggle to become whole is the idea that the world of each of us is very much what we make it. Projection is to overdramatize the characters on the stage of one's imaginings. "You understand," Fritz tells his group, wagging his finger at them,

*it is very difficult to bring home that all that happens here takes place in fantasy. Neurosis is a compromise between psychosis and reality. June sits on a comfortable chair. Nothing can happen to her. Yet all those things in her dream are taken for real. This is why we are far from realizing the fact that we are playing roles. There are no bombs here, there is no killing, there is no little girl, these are only images. Most of our whole striving in life is pure fantasy. We don't want to become what we are. We want to become a concept, a fantasy, what we should be like.*[37]

A conventional therapeutic approach, seeing all this as a problem that requires a cure, would have the sufferer somehow confront the problem's sources—either in the sufferer's own past as in orthodox analytic practice or in present behavior or feelings as in behavioristic or client-centered approaches. Somehow, Perls seemed to want no part of this, and so his Gestalt therapy, sophisticated and effective as it often may be, appears not to be a therapy at all but simply and vividly a way of coming to terms with one's own experience. All that he required of those who worked with him was that they undertake to be continuously aware of the living instant; he called it the Now, and he properly recognized that full understanding

---

The basic theory of Gestalt therapy is that maturation is a continuous growth process in which environmental support is transformed into self-support. In healthy development, the infant mobilizes and learns to use his own resources. A viable balance of support and frustration enables him to become independent, free to utilize his innate potential.

In contrast, a neurosis develops in an environment that does not facilitate this maturation process adequately. Development is, instead, perverted into a character formation, into a set of behavior patterns that are meant to control the environment by manipulation. The child learns, often by copying some adult, to secure environmental support by playing helpless or stupid, by bullying, by flattering, by trying to be seductive, and so on and on. Thus any helpful and too supportive therapist or member of the group who is sucked in by a patient's manipulations will only spoil that person more—by depriving him of the opportunity to discover his own strength, potential, and resources. The therapist's real tool here is skillful frustration.[38]

of the Now may be a lifetime's work. The instant is expressed in my own body, as I present myself to the world; and so part of a continuing awareness is to constantly tune in on my body and its modes of expression, and what these say about me. The instant is also the only locus of authentic temporality. By contrast, my past is where I keep my unfinished business, buried alive; my future is where I toss my dreams and fantasies; and the gaps between the Now and the Then appear in my experience as anxiety.

In my personal theater of fantasy, which Perls called the intermediate zone, there occurs that set of creative assumptions about other persons that theorists have termed projection. Perls shared this term with many other clinicians; but in place of an analysis of the projection, an attack on it, or an attempt to eliminate it, he asked that the person take the other tack: go into the projection, fully experience it, and act upon his own delusions (as the Zen master would put it). Thus:

*You never overcome anything by resisting it. You only can overcome anything by going deeper into it. If you are spiteful, be more spiteful. If you are performing, increase the performance. Whatever it is, if you go deeply enough into it, then it will disappear; it will be assimilated. Any resistance is no good. You have to go full into it—swing with it. Swing with your pain, your restlessness, whatever is there. Use your spite. Use your environment. Use all that you fight and disown.*[39]

An astounding turn of thought. This is the final, creative resolution of what in an earlier chapter I called the inner split that defines neurosis. For that split is in fact nothing but my own self judging, condemning, resisting myself, and so it is resolved, finally, if only I am able to meet and to accept—yes, to embrace—whatever it is that is mine, all the good as well as all the bad. In a word, it is to Allow; in this case, to Allow oneself.

A philosophy and a clinical doctrine underlay these precepts: to live fully in the Now; to give up games and roles and come to terms with one's own self; to accept responsibility for what is happening in one's body, as well as for the script and the characters and the personal drama that is each person's own creation. Illness, or neurosis, if such there is, consist only in a failure to live up to this responsibility; then blaming others; or being dependent on others. Therefore the goal of Perls' ritual is precisely the opposite of all therapies of the analytic school; it is not to analyze and break apart the segments of the person that have been disowned, not to get rid of what is felt by the person to be a problem or a source of distress, but rather to integrate the person, to accept oneself fully, and thus to bring together in a new harmony all the disowned and forbidden and cherished parts of the full person.

### Putting It All Together

There is more, much more in Perls' teachings than just a system filled with attractive and effective gimmicks. There is an endless sequence of memorable scenes, in a new kind of theater that has already begun to inspire artists in all the performing arts—and this in turn may lead to a new form of Gestalt theater peculiarly fitting to an era preoccupied with the drama of authenticity.[40] But whether or not a new aesthetics arises from the Gestalt experience, it is clear that Perls has already taught all therapists a great deal: that their mission is not to heal, not to traffic in sin, not to judge, not even to put lives back in order; it is to be present as a model for making ritual possible, to open the door to a temple, to set the stage for joy and celebration, to provide a temporary and fulfilling world of other people, to help in offering clues for the discovery of a seeker's true identity—to be a guide toward growth and toward becoming whole.

As Somatics needed the drug trip and might not have occurred in its present flowering without that trip, so, I think, Theatrics needed and developed out of the encounter movement. For all its promise and timeliness, I suspect that this movement would hardly have been able to have had its great impact if circumstances had not brought its early developers at Esalen into contact with Perls. He took up residence at Esalen, and during the time that encountering was being developed, in all its ramifications, he was the guru of what may have been the most turned-on and innovative community in Western history.

Perls' method and approach were uniquely fitted to be the vital center of the type of helping experience that arose at Esalen and was soon copied at many other centers. He managed to combine in practical and dramatic fashion all the elements that were then recharging the clinical scene: the concreteness and immediacy of Zen Buddhist practice; the new humanism being preached by Maslow and Rogers; the clinical effectiveness of established therapies; the drama and power of Moreno's psychodrama; and the theoretical underpinning of phenomenological and existential thought. By developing a form of individual treatment in a group setting, he gained the advantages of both methods. It was a major orchestration of trends, all of it presented in his own unique, theatrical amalgam. He deliberately frustrated his patients, made films and tapes, did demonstrations on college campuses and on television, conducted weekend seminars in which he dealt with dozens of different "patients" for fifteen or twenty minutes each before a large audience, and constantly insisted that the real work could be done by each person at home. Yet even as he provided a rationale for a widespread do-it-yourself approach, his methods were also therapeutically promising enough to inspire an entire generation of younger therapists to train under him and his associates, then to set up Gestalt institutes, and in the course of this to found a new school of legitimate psychotherapy. Most of all, Perls became in less than a decade a legend that was not diminished by his death. Perhaps this was because everyone who had contact with him, even briefly, was able to take to heart the advice he gave to so many patients:

*I, this Fritz can't go home with you. You can't have me as a permanent therapist. But you can get your own personalized Fritz and take this along with you. And he knows much more than I do because he's your creation. I can only guess or theorize or interpret what you're experiencing. I can see the scratch, but I cannot feel the itch. I'm not in you and I'm not arrogant enough to be a psychoanalyst and say that I know what you experience, what you feel. But if you understand the idea of this purely personal Fritz, you can get yourself a chair, couch or whatever you have, and whenever you're in trouble go and talk to this imaginary Fritz.*[41]

Perls died in 1970 of complications following surgery. Fittingly, his last words, to a nurse, are reported to have been: "Don't you tell me what to do!" I say "fittingly" because he left us as his personal ethic a curtain speech of which he said: "I give you the Gestalt prayer, maybe as a direction":

*I do my thing, and you do your thing.*
*I am not in this world to live up to your expectations*
*And you are not in this world to live up to mine.*
*You are you and I am I,*
*And if by chance we find each other, it's beautiful.*
*If not, it can't be helped.*[42]

# chapter 11
# a body trip

Our everyday perception is prejudiced to a degree that would shock us if we had the means to discover the fact without prejudice. We are in touch with the world as through a screen; and then, to make it worse, we usually confuse the screen with the world.

But this does not tell the whole story for we are, inescapably, two-part beings. It is true that each one of us is in touch with the world through a set of sensing processes that was once built up out of our individual histories as social creatures. Yet, at the same time, each of us is a pool of personal and unprejudiced experiencing that is centered around a core of my-self. Any account of the whole person— for example, a general and systematic psychology—will have to be concerned with the sensing processes and (even if only externally) with the pool of experiencing. The question I want to discuss in this final chapter is whether such a broad-spectrum general psychology will suffice for the study of experiencing, or whether another, different, more personal psychology may also be needed, a psychology especially concerned with an internal accounting of my-experience and experience-as-shared.

## PSYCHOLOGIES OF EXPERIENCE

A basic question about experience is whether it has, or can have, the same status in science as data with which we are more familiar. Can there be a science of experience? If not, can there be at least a discipline concerned primarily with experience—and if so, what would it be like?

According to the physical sciences, the macroscopic world is made up of things —that is, tangible objects with boundaries, that have mass, take up space, and can be apprehended by one or more of our senses. It is the first task of the physical sciences to find out as many facts as possible about these things. A fact, in this view, is the counterpart of a thing: it is an "object" of thought, a discrete datum that can also be grasped and dealt with. Just as the sum of things makes up the macroscopic real world, so the sum of facts makes up the world of information.

The information that each of us possesses about the world is, then, in the form of a collection of items of fact, and each of the items has a typical status in regard to being true. The status can be summed up thus: each item of fact can be referred to by a statement beginning, "It is true that . . ." This is what we mean by a fact—that such a statement can be made about it. Now, note that this means more than that a fact is verifiable; it also means that a fact can be denied. The central characteristic of a fact is dual in this sense—it can be both affirmed and denied. A question then arises. In general, how does a fact get affirmed or proven? How does one establish of a particular fact that it is either so or not so?

All the possible ways, I suggest, can be finally reduced to one special kind of evidence: some other set of supporting facts must be introduced that have the merit that they can be gathered independently of the fact in question. Suppose I look at a wall and want to state as a fact that it is white. How do I prove this fact? I might offer in evidence my own perception of its whiteness—but who would accept that as independent? Or I might call in my wife and ask her—but that would be equally suspect in the opinion of a hardheaded judge, especially if some valuable stake were riding on the outcome of the judgment. I could hardly offer the opinion of a friend of whom I have said that he will accept a bribe. Well, then, how about my asking a number of different people to stand where I have been standing and offer their opinions? Here the matter gets trickier. The judgments of these alternates would be more acceptable as evidence—but note the conditions that are now required. The new judges had better be strangers to me; they had better not know what judgment I made; and they should have no stake in the outcome of the judgment. What this adds up to is that the more independent are their judgments, the more they are to be trusted and the more solidly could the wall's whiteness be established as a fact.

On the other hand, an extremely strict arbiter might raise the point that all of us, I as well as my set of alternate judges, are perhaps victims of the same trick of light. To the degree that this is so, they and the "facts" they offer can no longer be considered completely independent of my own original statement of fact, for we are all in the same boat and bound, to some extent, by the same conditions. To carry the matter to a ridiculous extreme, it might even be argued—by a critic who refuses to be satisfied at all—that no human observers are to be trusted in this matter, ever; the analogy he uses is the deficiency that all human beings share in being unable to detect ultraviolet light with unaided vision. So he argues, rather convincingly, that for all we know we might be victims of a failing that is common to every living person.

My point here is that independence is a matter of degree, and therefore how you go about proving or denying that something is so is a matter that is agreed upon differently from case to case. In situations involving more than one person, the relation between them, and in particular the roles they play in the situation, will usually determine the judgments made about how independent each claim is. If the items I buy in a store total $4.87 and I give the clerk a bill in payment, and he then returns me thirteen cents in change, I may say, "No, I gave you a ten." Suppose he says, "Oh, I'm sorry, I thought it was a five." Now suppose the action is stopped at this instant to ask the question: what is the fact here—that I gave him a five-dollar bill or a ten? The usual practice among clerks, to take care of just such a contingency as this, is to leave the bill lying on the front of the cash register until the transaction has been completed—and so there are now three pieces of evidence: his statement that he thought I gave him a five, my statement that I gave him a ten, and the bill lying before us. We take for granted that the determinative evidence here is visual: what we mean when we do this is that we take for granted that the visual evidence is more objective. And that is just the point: what the two of us can see with our eyes and agree on is, by definition, more independent of the circumstances that gave rise to the disagreement than is either his statement or mine. He, of course, might be honestly lying— for reasons that are obvious to anyone who has ever engaged in such a transaction; but equally, I might be doing the same thing. His independence, and mine, are quite limited in comparison to the independence of our consensual visual evidence.

But suppose the clerk had, instead, immediately put the bill away in the cash drawer so that we had no evidence beyond our two statements. What, now, is the fact here? To tell the truth, neither of us can offer independent evidence—but what happens more often than not is that the clerk, saying "Excuse me," hands me an additional five dollars, unless he can now bring up additional, incontrovertible evidence (for example, by showing me that his cash drawer does not contain any ten-dollar bills, only fives). What happens is that the clerk, balancing his own chances of having erred against the difficulty that might arise if I were right, acts as though my statement were more independent of personal bias than his own supporting statement. The test reduces, as always, to one of relative independence.

We all spend a great deal of our time assessing facts and trying to put them in their proper order and relative positions of independence. Our experience of the world is made up of varying degrees of order (which we call information) in the form of controvertible facts. The facts we choose, the statements we make, and the specific kinds of information that we seek out are for the purpose of achieving just as much independence as is practical and needed for each occasion, and they will thus differ widely depending on the situation. Children can't be trusted at all in these matters—hence their charm, the charm of a disorderly and personal array, but also their relative uselessness in matters of import and gravity. What we as adults have managed to do is to develop cognitive capacities to help us achieve factual independence of judgment even when our view is partial or prejudicial. More important, we have collectively constructed a special community of knowledge that is on principle completely independent, and this community contains in its structure built-in methods for checking on the independent status of any of the facts in its domain.

This community we call science. The important characteristic of a science is not the content of the facts in its domain but the way in which these facts are established and known. It is for this reason that the great flowering of natural science could not have taken place until its battle had been won against that other great mode of establishing truth, the religious. The battle has been fought out during the last five centuries and has resulted in a standoff and a division of territories. Even the most dogmatically religious today will usually admit that in regard to the physical universe, what is factually so or not is to be determined by the methods of natural science. A major gain has been that the body of available facts has become enormously enlarged, now encompassing an order whose range extends from the upper limits of the universe to the lower limits of the constitution of matter. To take a common example, as human beings we have no way to offer independent evidence of whether there are categories of light energy beyond the visible spectrum. The reason for our inability is obvious enough. We are like brain-damaged patients who try to devise tests of cognitive deficiency: we have no personal means for obtaining evidence other than the restricted visual apparatus that led us to raise the question in the first place. No evidence that we might gather as individuals could ever be independent of our perception; and it is just our perception that is in question. But the logical structure of the science of optics, and the methods and tools available to it, enable scientists to postulate other kinds of energy, then to verify their existence, and thus to be able to state as a fact that the visible spectrum comprises only a small portion of the total band of electromagnetic energy. We can now say with confidence that there are other kinds of energy and that they even affect our restricted visual apparatus and the dependent facts it adduces. In theory at least, there are no limits within the physical universe to the facts that can be established by the methods of science—and established incontrovertibly, for all practical purposes.

That last sentence is so sweeping that it may appear to have no restrictions. But now we should go back to some statements with which I began this lengthy discussion. At the outset I said, "According to the physical sciences, the macroscopic world is made up of things." A fact, I then said, is the counterpart in the world of information of the thing in the real world; a fact is a cognitive thing. I mean by this that facts are on principle restricted to things; they refer only to things or to what can be handled as though they were things, in some way tangible, taking up space or using up energy, existing in the way that tables and planets and ultraviolet energy exist. But when we raise an additional question the fact takes on a new and shaky status, and so it has to go back into quotation marks: what can be said about "facts" that refer, not to things, but to experiences?

Consider two statements of "fact": (1) "My right arm is now raised above the level of my waist;" and (2) "I am happy." Both are statements about me. The first, however, concerns a part of my body, and everything I have been saying all along about controvertible facts is applicable to it. The statement is verifiable; it can be established as so or not so, at least for most conceivable practical purposes; and so it can be said that, if established as so, it is a fact that my arm is in such-and-such a position. Now, is the second statement—"I am happy"—a statement of fact in the same sense? The whole issue of what kind of psychology we develop, you should be warned, will swing on the answer to this question. I consider it the most fundamental possible question in psychology.

The question can be stated thus: can my experience of happiness be factually established as being so or not? In terms of the test I discussed above, can independent evidence regarding my experience be adduced? I will answer: No, my experience of happiness is not a fact. A statement about it does not refer to a factual datum; no significant evidence can be found regarding the experience that is independent of it. This is why I offer that in general I do not believe statements

## THE TRUTH ABOUT ME

No review of Me will ever be able to arrive at a statement of truth. All the facts that might lead to a grasp of some truth belong to that external world which is so excellently sorted out by the physical sciences—but as for me, and as for my-experience, there are no facts, only events. About people in general, or about the world, there can only be factual statements, not psychological or experiential propositions; and conversely, an experiential proposition can never be stated as being true or false. Psychological propositions are not factual but value-laden in the extreme. They sum up the individual ways in which I, or you, or anyone, twist and torture the facts of the world for our own purposes; they refer to private happenings that are never more than partially and distortedly revealed; their content is inner events that appear in public only behind special masks and in devious guises. They are lies, all lies. And as for myself, I know this about the lies that I pass off as facts—that I was capable of lying effectively, and so I am judged intelligent; and that somewhere I learned how to lie persuasively, so I seem creative. In place of the fact, my-experience spins a tissue composed of the lie, the wish, and the dream.[1] Experience is the enemy of truth.

of truth can be made about people—that is, about the experiences of people. It can be said of things, of places, of institutions, and of many propositions that each is or is not so—but no such statement in any significant sense can be said about a person. My very saying "I am happy" constitutes a distortion of my experience, a reduction to the level of the-state-of-an-object; similarly, to say of me "He is happy" freezes me for that instant as something less than a person.

I claim that in principle it is not possible to establish, or to hold as known, a significant datum in the form of a fact about any aspect of human experience. However, it most certainly and happily is possible to have and hold a significant datum about human experience—but that holding would itself be simply another experience, and so on and on, in the interwoven linkage that ties persons together.

The reason is simple, but the central concept is not easy to explicate, for we seem to have no terms by which to deal with these basic aspects of experience. I have said that the test reduces to one—whether independent evidence can be offered. Only then will a datum have the status of a fact, and if on principle no such evidence can ever be offered, then it will not. Now, in the case of my experience of being happy, where would the evidence to support or refute the statement come from? First, someone might devise some instruments to check me out at the instant that I say, "I am happy." No such instruments exist, as we know, but that is not the crucial argument. For even if we had such instruments— for example, if we could establish that each time I said, "I am happy" the needle on the instrument registered exactly five on a scale of ten—the meter reading would still not be evidence of my experience. It would, we think, refer to my experience by some unknown links, and it would, we guess, be related to my experience, but it would no more be evidence of my experience than such phenomena as room temperature, which can also be shown to covary regularly with statements about one's mood. If my shoulders drooped and my mouth were downcast, I might be lying, or I might be curiously mistaken about my own state, or I might even speak English poorly and so think that the word *happy* means *triste* in my own tongue—and what then would the meter read?

I am not trying to argue here that it is a matter of complexity; no, there is more to the matter than that. Consider a second kind of evidence that might be offered as independent: additional statements that I might make about my experience. They are not independent, of course, and I would fool no one by making them. Indeed, if I kept offering more and more such evidence, my listeners would begin to mutter to themselves the old Shakespearean saw about the extent of my protesting. But more important, my additional statements cannot be independent because they are data of exactly the same kind as my first statement: they report my experience. If we still doubt whether the first statement has to do with a fact, we will have to entertain the same doubts about my subsequent statements. So we are not yet out of the muddle.

We now come to the third and most familiar method: we ask other people to observe me and to offer confirmatory evidence, one way or another, about my experience. The question of whether judges can do this has a long history in the experimental psychology of personality.[2] The consensus has been that the average judge can in fact do significantly better than chance in identifying emotional expression in faces—but what we now have to note is that the question asked in all these experiments was heavily loaded. What was asked was whether perception of facial expression was accurate; and now we have to ask: accurate in regard to what? What is the standard? Indeed, doesn't the use of the term *accurate* presuppose that my "happy" experience is definitely, controvertibly a factual datum about which a yes or no statement can be made? Thus, haven't all these hundreds of studies proceeded on the unspoken premise that an experience is a fact which can be assessed as to its being present or not and on the further premise that an independently obtained fact (an observer's judgment) can be compared against the experience?

When the matter is put in this way perhaps we can begin to see the issue involved in trying to adduce such evidence as meters or majority judgments: admitting such evidence is equivalent to assuming that an experience, like any other fact, can be verified or disproved; the evidence will say either, "Yes, it is so that he is happy" or "No, it is not true that he is happy."

My whole point, on the contrary—but a point that I could only spell out by means of the negative route I have just traced—is that experiences belong to another realm. They exist and they are real—or at least this is my proclaimed thesis in this book and so must be accepted as axiomatic to my argument. But although experiences exist, they do not exist in the way that things exist. They are knowable, by the experiencer as well as by other persons, but they are not verifiable. They are not so, but simply are. It is proper to say of a fact or a thing—those two forms of the same phenomenon—that they occur, that they can be found in a setting of conditions or circumstances, and, further, that it is the circumstances that determine the fact or thing. In regard to experiences, the reverse is more appropriate: it is the experience that makes the situation. More precisely, to know of an experience is what helps to bring the experience into existence; knowing of the experience is itself a participant act, a part of the experience. Experience and knowing the experience (the latter is what we call reflectiveness) are two sides of the same phenomenon, each necessary to the other. An experience, plus the knowing of it, thus constitutes a full situation for the person, and so it is not appropriate to say of an experience that it is determined by a situation in the way that a fact is. Experiences are not caused; they are determinative.

To turn again to my well-worn example, if I have the experience of being happy, that is exactly the same, no more and no less, as knowing[3] that I am happy. To be purely and simply happy is the same as knowing you are happy; you could not not-know it, and you could not normally know that you are, say, sad instead of happy. Here is just the difference between experience that is pure and experience that is mediated by various forms of knowing and judging and sensing. In the case of mediated experience, it is quite possible to have one experience and yet sense something quite divergent in oneself; whereas in the case of pure experience the knowing and the being are one and the same thing. When this happens, of course, it becomes irrelevant to talk about verification by means of independent data. Similarly, when it is someone else who knows of my experience, his knowing and my-experience are part of the same shared event. One is not evidence for the other; one does not verify the existence of the other. Rather, each comes about because of and with the other. If you make a sensible contact with me and are then able to have an immediate judgment about my experience, then your contact with me helps to create just the situation that I am experiencing and that you are experiencing in judgment.

I am describing here not a realm of discrete and independent facts and things, but a realm of shared experiences. Every statement about an experience, whether made by the experiencer or by another person, is itself a new experience that links to and shares the first; and only for this reason can the statement be sensibly about the experience. In short, one of the critical points of difference between things and experiences lies in how the observing of them gets done. When it is a thing that is a target, the appropriate technique of observation is a kind of impersonal stance; whereas *the appropriate mode of observation of an experience is itself an experience*. Change the mode of observation and you change the target observed. Thus, fully experience a thing, and it tends to become more than a thing; it becomes enriched into a pure "essence of target," as evidence from meditation shows. On the other hand, sense a person distantly, factually, or impersonally, and you turn him into an object, more like a thing.

---

FROM A FOUR-THOUSAND-YEAR-OLD SANSKRIT TEACHING MANUSCRIPT: Look upon a bowl without seeing the sides or the material. In a few moments BECOME AWARE.[4]

---

An interesting consequence of this distinction is that increasing the number of observations (or observers) produces opposite results in the case of the experience versus the thing. Increase the number of observations of a thing-target, and the result will be to know the target more precisely, just as though the separate observations serve to narrow down a collective vision, to make it converge toward a more precise and narrow specification; whereas if you increase the number of observers or observations involved in experiencing another person's experience, the target broadens out and becomes richer as more about it is developed.

The net result, and in fact the very aim, of a lot of different tests of the factual whiteness of a wall is, then, to specify with greater and greater precision the exact degree of its whiteness. But it is different if the situation is one of gaining experience. If a thousand persons come in significant contact with a meaningful human experience and thus experience it themselves, their collective vision is a thousandfold richer than that of a single observer. They may come to a consensus on some factual aspect, but that is the least of their gain. Collectively— or else individually if they communicate with each other—they share in and appreciate an experience that grows with each new experiencer, as we can see every day in continuingly deepening responses to great works of art, important moments or eras of history, or even the story of a great life.

It therefore makes a great deal of difference whether the chosen targets of interest in psychology are conceived as things or as phenomena to be experienced individually or collectively.

I return now to the question with which I began this section: can there be a psychology of experience? The discussion just concluded has brought out a clear distinction between statements referring to the experience of one individual and statements about human experience in general. I have argued that the first kind of statement must itself be an experience. It will therefore have to belong in what

I would call a personal psychology—that is, a psychology of personal and individual experience. This would be a nonfactual discipline. It would not be made up of provable statements, nor would it be concerned with establishing the truth for or against any proposition. It would be a discipline, or perhaps a practice, of shared experiences, for whatever purposes the sharing might occur.

The second kind of statement, concerning human experience in general, would, however, properly belong in a discipline much like the sciences we know. It would constitute a systematic portion of a general psychology that is, perhaps, broader in its coverage and interests than academic psychology today, but not in any significant way different.

Here are two related but independent disciplines; the logic I have pursued in this chapter seem to lead inescapably to this conclusion. The one I have described as a general psychology is familiar and needs no discussion—but the other is still unclear. We know of no instance of it, unless perhaps we leave the realm of academic fields and enter that of the practicing arts. The closest example we can find, perhaps, is the craft of psychotherapy, which satisfies a number of criteria for a personal psychology. First, psychotherapy and its related clinical activities such as diagnostic testing, constitute the only practice in psychology in which the observer is limited to dealing with one person at a time. In addition, the data found in psychotherapy consist entirely of one person's experiencing of another under conditions that are recognized as significant for both of them. Finally, as the history of psychotherapy shows, theory and praxis can develop quite independently of each other[5]—just as though clinical theory might belong to a general psychology concerned with experience while clinical practice is more closely allied to a personal, and perhaps underground, psychology of shared experience.

### Existential Psychotherapy

One recent movement in the clinical field seemed to have come very close to such a personal psychology, and so it needs to be discussed here. I will briefly review the background out of which arose an existential approach to clinical practice, and then I will consider its fate in the hands of three representative writers.

The history of existentialism as a philosophic position has been told repeatedly.[6] Its recent story begins with Kierkegaard a century and a half ago, although his lessons for the situation of modern man went unheeded until he was discovered for our century by Karl Jaspers. The message which Kierkegaard had for our time concerned human subjectivity—that man is necessarily contained within a self-system which is at one and the same time his glory and his tragedy, his promise and his doom. Not man in general, not people, not that person over there, not even you individually, but I myself am the only subject of my world. I am all there is—and it is both the glory and the tragedy of my existence that, like you and like every other individual, I am constantly in process, defining myself by reaching beyond myself to construct systems which then elude me.

The existentialist view is a brand of moral lesson. It reminds me that I can easily reach beyond my animal essence—for example, in my knowledge that some day I am going to die, a knowledge that is not possible for the dog, which is trapped within its situation and has very limited ways to reach beyond it. But this very outreach that defines me as human then provides the basis for my fear of death and for all the anxieties that build on this fundamental fear. I cannot help reaching in this way; my reward for being human is also a curse, for the very glory that it permits me is at the same time my own tragic reminder of all my human limitations. For the philosopher of existence, then, systems of any sort—in philosophy, in science, or whatever—are false to our humanity unless they pay homage to their basis in human subjectivity by denying their own worth as encompassing schemes. It follows that the worst of all philosophic sins is to construct a system and then to fall victim to it by coming to believe that it encompasses all that I am.

Jaspers, in his classic psychiatric work *General Psychopathology*,[7] was the first to apply the existential dimension to psychotherapy; he emphasized that the participants were, regardless of the system under which they operated, also two very human individuals. If the situation was meaningful to them, as it ought to be in psychotherapy if anywhere, their relationship was not simply a meeting of roles but an encounter of persons; they were, he said, "partners in destiny." But the lesson was not appropriate to the times, and it was not picked up by psychotherapists of his day. Its entry into the clinical field came by a more roundabout route.

In 1927 Martin Heidegger, then the heir apparent to Edmund Husserl, the founder of modern phenomenology, published an immensely difficult work, *Being and Time*,[8] as the first of a projected series of writings in philosophy. Although his purpose in this book was to revive the study of Being, which he said had been ignored in philosophy since the time of Socrates, he included some conceptions that seemed useful to clinical theorists as well. Chief of these conceptions was *Dasein*, a term that he used to stand for the Being of Man. The Swiss psychiatrist Ludwig Binswanger, a good friend and contemporary of Freud and himself a fairly conventional psychoanalyst in his practice, was at this time dissatisfied with some aspects of clinical theory. He found in Heidegger's work just the conceptions that seemed to him useful, most important the concept of *Dasein*; he borrowed the notion and utilized it as the basis for a new approach to the understanding of psychopathology. He called his own work *Daseinsanalyse*, a term that came to be translated (not quite accurately) as existential analysis—and by this circuitous route the tortured insights of Kierkegaard first found a home in clinical theory.[9]

Although Binswanger began his studies of schizophrenia in the 1930s and over the next decade became a significant influence on European psychiatry, his thinking did not cross the Atlantic until its appearance in translation in 1958 in the book *Existence*.[10] Meanwhile, Sartre had also been published in English, with a lengthy section of his major work, *Being and Nothingness*, devoted to what he termed existential psychoanalysis.[11] American clinicians, who until this time had managed to remain quite innocent of existential thought, were now, apparently, about to be overwhelmed with expositions of this new approach. But the unfortunate and rather curious fact is that neither Binswanger's nor Sartre's purported existential analysis was the genuine product. Both were individual, and in some ways useful, contributions by their respective authors; neither could properly be called representative of existential thought. Both, also, were admittedly contributions to theory and not to practice.

More than twenty years after he had first taken over some of Heidegger's conceptions for his own use, Binswanger made the gracious admission that he had somewhat distorted the philosophical significance of these conceptions, but that in view of his own contributions, it was a "productive error." Sartre might, perhaps, appropriately make a similar admission, since he has himself provided the evidence, in the form of a point-by-point comparison, of existential and Freudian psychoanalysis. The two forms of psychoanalysis, he has said, are similar in a number of basic respects: (1) in both approaches it is assumed that the basis of the individual's character and pathology is in some preverbal and prelogical system—in Freudian analysis, the unconscious, and in Sartre's existentialism, the individual's "life-project"; (2) in both approaches what is manifest, or immediately given by the person, is assumed to symbolize the fundamental structure of the person; and (3) in neither approach is it assumed that the individual himself has any privileged position in regard to looking at what goes on with him; rather, what is needed in order to discover this are objective methods of analysis undertaken by a skilled psychoanalyst.

If these characteristics are applicable to both Freudian psychoanalysis and to Sartre's so-called existential analysis, then I think we can properly say that both approaches are much closer to what I have called healing than helping. Both conform more to a role-oriented, rule-determined profession whose origin was in medical practice than to a discipline of shared experiences. The key, as always, is in what the approach requires in regard to experience. Sartre claims that his "point of departure" is experience, but it rather appears that he simply departs from this point, never to return, for his concern is actually with consciousness, as was Freud's. Both theories—that of Freud and that of Sartre—are at best theories about experience, and in this sense they belong in what I have called a general psychology. Neither theory concerns itself directly with my-experience as such, and in fact, in the similarities between the two approaches that I have just quoted, both theories quite explicitly rule out experience as basic. Thus, to go over them again (1) the very basic data in both approaches, according to Sartre, is in some system that is preverbal and prelogical; whereas in an approach grounded solely on experience, the basic data are simply the experiences, not in anything assumed to be prior to them; (2) the immediately given, according to Sartre, merely symbolizes some underlying structure, whereas experience, if it is accepted as such, does not stand for anything else but experience itself; and (3) in Sartre's comparison, the privilege of arriving at some truth rests with either the clinician, armed with his theory, or with the person himself when he steps outside of himself; whereas, from the point of view of an experiential discipline, such privilege rests only with the person himself, insofar as he allows himself his own experience in all its forms and stays within it.

There has recently been one more attempt to ground a clinical theory on an existential approach, this time by Ernest Keen.[12] It, too, claims to take experience as its starting point, again in an effort to pose an alternative to a behaviorist or biological approach. Although it is in many ways the most useful and straightforward of such attempts, far closer to clinical actualities than either Binswanger's heavy interpretations or Sartre's conceptual insights, it too confuses healing and helping, sensing and experience. Keen builds his approach around three distinct modes of being: (1) being-in-the-world—or, in the terms that I have been using, the direct experience of myself and of the world; (2) being-for-myself—again in the terms I have used, the sensing of myself, or the awareness of myself as an object; and (3) being-for-others—a rather complex mode of being that refers to acting in terms of other persons' frames of reference. Although there is some utility in this tripartite breakdown, as Keen demonstrates in his excellent case studies, they seem to me to fail to make, and then stick to, the distinctions needed between experience and sensing and among the various possible targets of experience. The basic distinction between experience as such and that collection of ego operations that I have called sensing is lost completely in Keen's proposed organization.

Existentialism, as defined a few pages back, would seem to demand an exclusive commitment to experience. It begins and ends within human subjectivity—that is, within the bounds of what the person can experience; it claims to no more than this, because there can never be more than this, and no less, because less than this would strip the person of his humanity. Defined in this way, existentialism defines the direction for a helping art, as distinct from a healing profession: a discipline that would consist of the deliberate practice of shared experience. To the degree that such an existentialist discipline is true to its definition, its practice would most probably be a form of guiding, of collective learning, of sharing a destiny. Perhaps we might even call it a no-therapy.

The three attempts reviewed above—by Binswanger, Sartre, and Keen—have, each in its own way, tried and, I think, failed to adhere to a full commitment to experience. Perhaps this cannot be done. It may well be that by its very nature, an organized, coherent, and communicated account of the human situation demands too much that is systematic and general; and so, as it succeeds in what it claims to be, such an account pulls away from the experience to which it promises commitment. However, though it may fail again and again, I think that, for one basic reason which has not yet been mentioned, the task of constructing such a discipline is worth our collective efforts. The reason is that only on the basis of an experiential discipline, established and accepted, can we expect to take the necessary next steps toward all the other possible disciplines of experience—that immense and unknown range of disciplines which awaits our exploration of alternate states of consciousness.[13]

## A PSYCHOLOGY OF MY-EXPERIENCE

The question that haunts me, about myself and consequently about other persons in particular and finally about people in general, is: what am I (or you, or they) really like? Here, almost within my grasp, is this familiar and unknown mystery: a person. It may be I-myself, or you, or that one, or all of them. Any question that I ask comes back, and down, to this one.

### Issues and Questions

I have suggested, in the preceding pages, that two ways are open to arrive at answers. The first, in all its ramifications, is familiar as some form of a general and systematic psychology. The second is less familiar and perhaps currently non-existent, and so I have tried to introduce it in this book. Before concluding my discussion, I want now to explore some of the possible content of such an experience-centered approach. To introduce this illustrative content, some details of the approach need to be settled.

*INSIDE AND OUTSIDE DATA.* A first issue may be put as a question: Where does the truth about me (or anyone) reside? It might be inside my skin, or it might be outside. Keep in mind, however, that these are not just two different aspects of the same information; the inside view and the outside view are not mirror images of the same entity. The skin from the outside doesn't at all resemble the skin from the inside; that barrier divides two worlds.

We are by now pretty familiar with the kind of information that is gathered entirely outside the skin. I might, for example, say about myself that I am male; at the present writing, I weigh about 160 pounds; I am married; by profession, I am a university teacher of psychology; my Social Security number is 082-03-1000. We are less familiar with information gathered entirely inside the skin—for one reason, because often it cannot properly be called information. The cry of pain is an example. For another reason, it is not usually reported, and even when it is, it is not in organized form: for instance, the reverie I have as I am falling asleep. To rephrase my question, then, I might ask, does the truth about me reside in the fact that I am male, 160 pounds, etc., or in my nighttime reverie?

---

AN EXAMPLE OF TWO
KINDS OF KNOWLEDGE,
AS GIVEN BY RUSSELL JONES:
Suppose, for example, I observe my colleague grimacing, holding his jaw, and looking in the Yellow Pages under "D." I might infer that he has a toothache. The experience and knowledge of my own toothache, however, is immedi- ate and private even though its label may, in fact, have been learned through contact with the socializing community. . . . The operations by which my colleague and I arrive at the inference he has a toothache are so different as to make a comparison ludicrous. My knowledge is based on his external behavior. His, most assuredly, is not.[14] [Italics deleted.]

---

It is a question that has exercised thinkers in every field. Ask a theoretical physicist the same question in a slightly different form: How am I to know what is real? If he is of a philosophical turn of mind, he may answer, "As it happens, I have the answer for you. What is real, and I mean rock-bottom real, is a collection of forcefields, that and nothing else. In turn, these fields are best represented in the form of some mathematical equations—so that you might say, in capsule summary, that reality is at bottom a couple of equations." But if I ask the same question of a humanist, who may or may not be a psychologist, I get quite a different answer: "What is real is not an equation, in fact not any kind of abstraction at all. Reality is the everyday life-world of people and things and events, the life-sized human world in which we all conduct our lives and interact with each other and with things. That constitutes all the reality there can be."[15]

These are radically different views, in the sense that the physicist's is the logical end result of building entirely on information gathered outside the skin, while the humanist's is built entirely of information gained inside the skin. The two views may be related; indeed, I might even say that they must be related. But because they are, as they stand, so divergent as to lead to different answers for almost every question, we have to accept the fact of their difference. And given this fact, my case for a personal psychology of experience, based solely on a view from inside the skin, will necessarily refer to a different kind of reality than does the more familiar psychology based on external information.

*THE SENSE OF MY-SELF.* A second issue has to do with the self around which the data of inner reality cohere. At first sight it would seem almost an insuperable task to begin to sort out the intricate web of my-experience, that tangle of all that goes on in me and all that appears to me, especially since it is

---

How all becomes clear and simple when one opens an eye on the within, having of course previously exposed it to the without, in order to benefit by the contrast.[16]

---

my-experience that is going on all the time that I am trying to get a grip on it, and, to make matters worse, my-experience is all that I have as a means for getting this grip. The tangle cannot, and perhaps should not, be teased out into single, isolated strands—but even without doing this, I know well that there are thoughts and feelings, wishes and hopes and fears, dreams, images, acts, nonacts, doing and not-doing; the sheer complexity boggles the mind. Yet I do know, as an experiential axiom, that there is some self in there, no matter how secret, which persists. This is the conclusion, too, that comes out of the sparse experimental work in this area. Halla and John Beloff showed subjects composite pictures in a stereoscope and found that the pictures were rated more positively when the subject's own picture was part of the composite, even though there was no overt recognition of self.[17] In a very elaborate study, Werner Wolff found that subjects who wrote thumbnail personality sketches based on expressive elements such as a silhouette, the sound of a voice, or handwriting samples tended to rate their own products either more positively or more negatively, again without recognizing that they were judging products of themselves.[18] It would seem that my self is always visible to myself.

In addition, there is the curious fact that I do indeed seem to keep making some sense to myself. I am not a stranger to Me, and Me is not just a random collection of inner things to I. I could not tell you how it happens, but to me the totality of my experience hangs together in some meaningful way. Furthermore, the way that I hang together does not change sharply from day to day, although I am well aware that very great changes may have occurred through the years. The Joe Lyons discovered by Joe Lyons on awakening this morning was no surprise—or, as William James put the same point: "When Paul and Peter wake up in the same bed, and recognize that they have been asleep, each one of them mentally reaches back and makes connection with but *one* of the two streams of thought which were broken by the sleeping hours. As the current of an electrode buried in the ground uneeringly finds its way to its own buried mate, across no matter how much intervening earth; so Peter's present instantly finds out Peter's past, and never by mistake knits itself on to that of Paul."[19]

The continuity that I find within my own experience I can find just as easily in our joint experience with each other. As certain as the sense that I make to Me is the continuing sense that people make to, and with, one another. Individuals seem to get along with each other as parts of an encompassing, understandable network of interconnected relationships, and, further, they seem to do this without either bumping into one another or being utter question marks to one another. I assume that the inner processes by which this occurs are not an unknowable mystery but can be found out by looking hard enough—or perhaps, more probably, by relaxing and looking easily enough. The road to self-knowledge, I will assume, runs inward.

But because the resulting data will necessarily be in different forms from that we are accustomed to getting through controlled observation, I suggest that different tests of utility will apply. Some of the tests applicable to experiential data would be whether the report of the experience rings true; whether it leads to some increased understanding; whether it is similar to what others report in answer to the same question; and whether it is what has been said about the matter by wise and knowledgeable persons.

*PSYCHOLOGY "AS THOUGH"*   A final issue to be mentioned has to do with a characteristic quirk of a personal psychology; it is a psychology "as though." Much of what I have said in reference to such a discipline is a function of my acting as though I knew a great deal about myself and even about other persons. In this respect a report of my experience will differ in important respects from a report based on my observation. When I make a deliberate observation of another person—which is a method for obtaining outside-the-skin information— I tend to be careful, not to state something as a fact if I am uncertain about it or have no evidence to back it up. And generally I can tell you how I arrived at the observation. But when I report my own experience I am much less to be trusted. I may speak about myself with some assurance but be quite unable to tell you how I know that this is so. Sometimes, especially when reporting my experience of other people, I may not even be able to make clear what I know, let alone how I know it.

Yet in these respects I think I am in good company. Consider the following example: I place one hundred male college sophomores in a line, side by side, so that they can watch a girl walk slowly past them. She has just been chosen as Homecoming Queen, and she is dressed in a bikini. After she has walked the length of the stag line, I present to each observer a response sheet containing this multiple-choice question:

I would say that girl is pretty ———
I would say that girl is not pretty ———
I have no opinion on the matter ———

I predict that more than ninety of the hundred observers will respond "Pretty"—that is, they will act as though they know something about the girl. However, I also predict that if the observers are interviewed individually and asked, first, how they arrived at the opinion that the girl is pretty, and second, what they mean by *pretty* or how they would define the term, their answers will reveal very little consensus and very little clarity of thought. That is, by the criterion of majority vote, the experience they report in this way would seem to be real and sensible; but they themselves appear to be unable to report very much that is useful about the experience. Theirs is an effective working psychology, but a psychology "as though."

### Experiencing My Body

In Chapter 1, I introduced three possible targets of experience, my head, my world, and my body, and there I discussed the first two of these. Because it was the most fundamental, I reserved discussion of the third until the last chapter. Here, then, is the appropriate place to consider the experience of my body as the core of the content of a psychology of my-experience. Because it can be a target only for my-experience (from the independent viewpoint of another person my body would be merely an object of observation) I will have to present this content in terms that may seem a little unusual—as a diarylike account of what happens when I undertake to explore my own experience.

I sit down, then, and make myself comfortable. As I settle into the chair, my hand begins to play with the left side of my beard; a comfortable and well-established habit. I will now see what happens. I will simply drift, making no specific or directed effort except to empty my head of organized thoughts, trying only to keep the target, my body, at the center of my ongoing experience.

After a few moments, I find that I am simply here, nothing else.

Now, what can I say about this state?

The first thing that comes to me, moving in as though it had crossed an inner horizon, is that I *am here*. (It is hard to know which word to emphasize in order to capture the meaning of that phrase, and so I have emphasized both.) I am not over there somewhere; not nowhere at all; not scattered in a number of places. I am, rather, all of a piece, and I am here, now.

And I note, too, that the way that being here comes to me is that I feel it in a vague, dispersed, yet distinctly physical sense. Whatever else may be so at the moment, the very ground for my being here is, assuredly, a sense of the presence of my body.

If I now simply stay with my present state, in a kind of relaxed drifting, I can hear things, see thing, smell things, think vague thoughts, and so in this way my state changes—but behind it all, as background, my body-presence remains. Well, then, can I make it go away? I play a little I'm-not-here game. The results are clear-cut. Nothing I do will make my body go away; in fact, quite the contrary. I am reminded of the weak joke: starting right now, try to forget about elephants. The instructions guarantee that elephants will keep being thought of until they are spontaneously forgotten. For me, the same thing happens with my body. It is there, inescapably, as long as I let it be, and even more so if I work to get rid of it. It will disappear only when I spontaneously drift away to attend completely to something else—that little spot on the wall in front of me or the play that I will go to see tomorrow.

This, for the moment, is my starting point. I am here, present in my body. Now I begin to work over that notion: the *whereness* of my body. What do I mean when I think of my body-presence? It is not *at* a place. No preposition seems to fit. Then am I saying that this is all there is, that I and my body are all of a piece? No, not that; there is an experience I am trying to describe, but I don't have it yet.

Another little exercise, then: edges. I go back to the empty, pleasant relaxation. I try to block out everything except I, me, my body-presence; these become the edges of my world at the moment. Now I can come closer to the experience. Now what I can describe is an experience: that I reside in my body. Here I am, and here is how I am somehow inside, somehow situated within. And now, as I become aware of what happens, complexities begin to accumulate. Not all of my body is available to me, that's the first thing I note. There is no way I can get a feel for certain parts—the small of my back, for example, and unless I deliberately press my feet down against a surface, and even then only for a few moments, this part stays out of my wandering attention and I cannot bring it in just by willing.

Other areas come and go in still different ways. My buttocks are outside my attention, I note, and so is my entire genital area until I make an effort to bring this into focus; then I can make it stay as long as I wish. So I see that some places will adapt out while others merely shift with my changing attention. Still other parts have a tiny life of their own, I note. They carry on their brief affairs with my surroundings, but just beneath the surface level of my awareness—like a small, unnoticed nervous habit. My feet plant themselves in different ways, adjusting to the lean of the rest of me, in accordance with the shifts in my overall balance in the chair. My hands and arms and shoulders move and sway and counterbalance, each alteration slightly modifying the lift of my head, the tilt and set of my neck, the angle of my backbone and the way it sits on my haunches. How could I have thought I was merely sitting still? I bend and sway like a tree in the wind, in a silent symphony of unnoticed rhythms, and with each measure some parts of me come and go along the borders of my attention. A shifting panorama of moves and balances, of postural and tensional comings and goings, all taking place at the boundaries of my notice. How can I have been unaware of this? Where has my attention really been all this time?

I think I know the answer to that question. I have been like everyone else, particularly thinkers and scholars; we have all been unable to find our own bodies, so alive, so ever-present. Most of the time we did not think to look; and so when at last I do, what I find comes as a surprise. "How can I recognize myself who never made my acquaintance?"[20]

What if, now, I tried to change my attitude without trying to change my position or focus of attention?

There is a colleague of mine, once a fairly close friend but now, by my choice and his, no more than a nodding acquaintance. I realize that I have never really liked him; since the quarrel that broke up such relationship as we had, the mere thought of him upsets me almost to the point of anger. I bring him to mind, and to help it along I revive the thought of our quarrel. The results are immediate and surprising. I find that at once everything changes: I am no longer in my body but at its surface. A surge of energy seems to have welled out from my own center toward a charged surface. Now I let the fantasy develop. He is my victim, withering under my keen, devastating attack. All my carefully restrained feeling about him begins to enter my experience. A few moments ago I was simply a Me residing wholly within a nearly quiescent body, but now I am one with my own outer skin, stretched against it, straining through my charged arms and legs and the muscles in them.

---

### THE BODY AND THE WILL

An exercise in frustration of the will, very relevant to the situation I am describing here, is suggested by Schutz:

"Shut your eyes and imagine that you want very strongly to be somewhere else, but I am forcing you to remain right where you are. Do that for a minute before reading on. . . . Now consider where you feel this feeling in your body. Some people feel it in the face, others in the jaws, arms, chest, or legs. I usually feel it most strongly as a pull in my throat."[21]

---

That was an unplanned experiment, but it worked so well that now I think I will try another. I decide on a very fast switch. Quite suddenly I think about my daughter. In an instant, just as though I had planned to do it, I sense a collapse of what I now experience as a shell. I am still at the surface of my body, but now in a totally new and wonderfully pleased way. My surface presence is suffused with an energy that flows gently, almost pulsing. The surface feels warmed, flexible, softened. I am very content with myself.

So I have discovered, all unplanned, a game with endless variations that I can play at will. It has all the variations of which I myself am capable, and each one is unique, each one a surprise even though it seems to be a repeat. Anger, amusement, nostalgia, sadness, longing, fear, love, regret, and hope—each producing its very sensible changes in my body-experience; a wondrous complexity that I never knew existed for me in this calm and unnoticed structure. All that is needed, as I soon find out, is that I let the experiences simply happen—but this too is an important discovery. If I let them happen, they will happen, as simply as that—if I simply accept them as they occur, if I don't comment, don't pass judgment on their coming or going; if I do nothing but admit that they are there as experiences, sensing them with a kind of pleased interest, nothing more. This is all that is required. And even if, as I also discover right away, the experience is not what I might normally want—if I discover negative feelings and might want them to go away, or if there are sexual fantasies and associated feelings that I both want and don't want—even then, and especally then, I need only accept it all as it happens.

Now I am concerned with some elementary mapping operations. I want to survey the different parts of my body, so as to see how they play a part within the constant inner play of the whole. As yet I have no notion of a hierarchy of parts or functions, and in fact such a notion strikes me as running counter to what I am trying to describe. But we shall see about that.

What I find, first of all, are areas or occasionally spots of tension in many different places—some of them unexpected. One at least is quite familiar—that line across the nape of my neck and extending toward my shoulders, mostly on the left side, sometimes even spreading up over the back of my head. It is deep in the muscles there, not a mere surface tension. It is, as I am aware, a rather familiar accompaniment to any strain or continued period of worry and effort; it goes along with trying and, in my case, with the vague sense that I am either trying too hard or will not be able to make it. A related tension, for me, is what I feel across my chest as a kind of band, as though it were constraining some pressure deep within. I can dispel this deliberately, but only for the moment, by taking a deep breath.

These two are rather familiar, now that I take the trouble to notice how well I know them. But other places allow new discoveries. I never knew that it was so difficult for me to completely relax my left hand, particularly my left thumb; when I attend to it, it springs to a kind of feverish little twitching action, all on its own. Nor did I know so clearly the way that little knots, little cold spots, areas of sinking feeling in my lower abdomen, come and go with different trains of thought, especially thoughts that have to do with people.

Other discoveries are just as easy to make—in particular, sensations of all kinds patterned over and in my body: my pulse and heart beats, with a rhythm that is discoverable, if I but concentrate, at almost any soft place in my body; the inner pressures exerted outward, like the distension out from my eyeballs; the changing wetness inside my mouth; an occasional skin flash that may turn into an itch or a moment's feeling; a little flow, as of energy relaxedly moving, when I ease up on one part or shift to a more comfortable position; in short, another busy community of happenings going on all the time, just below my skin and just beneath the surface of my awareness.

There is a less clear but more pervasive happening that I now discover. This is much harder to describe, and so I suspect that it may be an aspect of my body-experience more personal, more unique to me. It is a continuing sense of my own skin, an experience of a skin stretched over my body, and with it the experience of a skin surface turned outward to the air. It would be worth sharing this in a group, and then trying to find out if each person also has some body-experience that is unique and personal in this way. I wonder; are there any completely unique body-experiences?

The most obvious aspect that I discover in the course of my mapping operations is my breathing. Again, how strange that it should never come to my awareness unless an emergency occurs—being choked, drowning, feeling short of breath, for example—or else when I deliberately go looking, as I am now. Now that I look, however, there it is, absolutely central to the ongoingness of my body and thus of my whole body-experience. It is even more strange, and wonderful as well, how marvellously complex is my ordinary breathing. Even my attending to it, though that disturbs its rhythm a little, can't hide the fact of its delicate balance, its minute and subtle attuning to everything that goes on with me and around me. It is no wonder that many systems of treatment or techniques of self-growth, from Raja Yoga to Reich's vegetotherapy, are based on allowing oneself to concentrate closely and fully on one's breathing. To be lost in one's breathing, to reduce the awareness to this and nothing else, to zero in toward breathing as to one's very center—this is what has always been sought in meditation and also what may be the quickest path to the most central and basic life processes in therapy. My own breathing pattern, I note, is to emphasize the in at the expense of the out—and surely the connection is more than accidental with the fact that my natural pattern of getting along in the world consists of holding back, absorbing, listening, learning, observing, at the expense of going out, entering, giving. Do I mean here that in a crude sense my habitual breathing patterns are the cause of my patterns of behavior? Hardly. Putting the matter in this way would trap us into the necessity for some untenable, mechanical theory. What else, then? How might this fundamental relationship that seems so evident to me be understood? I am not yet sure, but what I would offer as a preliminary statement is this: that I, as a person, am an energy field, its products represented at one time as overt actions vis-à-vis others, at other times as the taking in and giving out of materials for my physiological functioning; and the basic ways in which I-as-person-as-field function will thus show up similarly in my breathing, my behavior, my dealings with other people, or my life-style. I am all of a piece, and it not reasonable to expect one fundamental aspect of me to run counter to another, equally fundamental aspect.

Nothing in me is inert. Though I may deny some parts and ignore some pieces, hide or turn away from some aspects and not permit myself to participate fully in others, nothing is ever still. My body rings the changes on all the processes of my living. Running through the feelings, the sensations, the tensions, and most of all through the breathing, the changes go on and on. This body that I live in, then, is never still—but it is even more clear that it cannot be described as a complex, busily moving piece of machinery. Rather, it is, by my own unarguable experience of it, a shimmering and sensitive touchstone of where and what I am at every moment. In the most real sense of the term, my body is Me. And so, as I have now learned, the very first answer to what I am really like is that at the basis I am what my body is; I am all that I experience of my body.

This is not an answer to any question; rather, it only begins to raise questions. It sets the stage for whole sets of problems whose chief advantage is that they are not the topics of an impersonal science but vital issues tied closely to my own real experience. Consider the kind of question, for example, that is the mirror image, or obverse, of what I have been saying thus far. I have been speaking only of my experience of my body. What if we turn the phenomenon around and try to think of it in other terms? Thus, what is the message that my body gives to me? And equally, what kind of messages does my body give out, so to speak, to the world?

What I mean by this sort of question can be summarized under the heading of *Expression*. I have been saying thus far that my body, as I experience it, is not— cannot be—merely an elaborate mechanism. I experience it as my own lived body— and that is a very curious kind of phenomenon, one for which we have no adequate vocabulary. Certainly no vocabulary exists for such a phenomenon in contemporary science, no way to conceive of it, no way at all to describe it or deal with it. Science can deal only with objects, things, bounded and determinate entities, facts, machines—in short, with what is cut off from ongoing experience. But my own body, as I experience it, is not a thing, not a fact nor a set of facts, not an object, above all not a machine. It is—and at the moment I have no other terms to use—a vital, lived field whose function is to provide a residence for me; not a house, you note, but a home—and there is a world of difference between the two. Only because of this, only as this is so, can I have a body-experience as distinct, let us say, from sensing it—that is, knowing about it or being aware of it.

I am affirming here that my own body is, to me, a lived body, a part of me. But now consider: if this is a consequence of my own body experience, what consequences, if any, follow from my experiencing of your body (or of you experiencing mine)? Bear in mind here that I am not referring to being aware of someone's body, my own or yours. I am referring to the fact that I can have a body-experience of myself that is quite different from being aware, and so I should be able to have a similar experience of you that is not the same as being aware of you or your body.

Am I at all correct in this assumption? Do I, or can I, experience your body as distinct from sensing it, knowing about it, being aware of it? Can you do this about my body? I think so. I think that this is exactly what we mean when we talk about expression. We mean by this term something observable that occurs in a person, something that cannot be summed up simply as behavior, something that cannot conceivably occur in an object or a machine, something that seems to serve as an outward sign of an inner state, and therefore is the very basis of shared experience.

An example will help us out here. Take the lowly alarm clock, and consider its built-in capacity for communicating to us the message that some preset waking time has now arrived. Having been properly programmed, the alarm clock can say, "Hey! Your wake-up time is here!" Well, not really. I give the clock too much credit. All it really says is "R-r-r-ring!" and I then contribute the rest of the message by virtue of my knowing that this is the time I had planned to get up. But whatever its message, the one fact about the clock is that it has no inner life as distinct from its outer life. True, there is a clock face on the outside, and a casing, and some works on the inside—but these separate parts are not different in principle. They have different functions and so are put in different places in the clock's structure. The works might just as well be exposed, or even situated in different cities and connected by an electrical circuit, and these changes would not change the nature of the clock.

Contrast the clock with a person. The difference is partly one of complexity, but what is really fundamental is the qualitative difference between the clock and the person. We always seem to be able to distinguish, in the person, between what he shows on the outside and what might be going on inside. As soon as we are old enough to begin to have a legitimate experience of the other person as person, we are able to make this distinction; and the simplest, commonest way we state the distinction is to talk about the other person's motives. We say, "He did it because he wanted to do it"—and in speaking in this way, we of course clearly distinguish between his wanting, which is what goes on inside of him, and his doing, which is what we see on the outside. The distinction between the two is so basic, so necessary, that even a behavioristic psychology has to maintain it; so colleges give psychology courses on various kinds of behavior, such as learning, but they also give separate courses on motivation.

In a person, the inner and the outer seem to coexist, but never in any simple cause-effect relation. In the alarm clock, to return to it for a moment, a definable mechanical connection exists between the inner works and the outer alarm bell— a connection so fixed that if the clock is in working order certain happenings in the former must give rise to specified happenings in the latter. Not so in the person. We are still trying to discover and pin down even the simplest relations between inner phenomena (such as wishes, fears, hopes, thoughts, attitudes) and the outer phenomena of action. But again, the difference between clock and person is far more than one of complexity. Persons appear to observers as somehow comprising both inner and outer. If you think this is not so, look at another person and try to see that person as nothing more than a mechanical doll, or as a merely two-dimensional, cardboard figure. I think it cannot be done; to do it,

I would have to give up all sense of the other person as a living, experiencing creature like me.

A further point: not only do people appear as a composite of inner and outer, but we can hardly avoid at least a glimpse of the inner aspect of other persons. What I mean here is that when I see another person, I cannot help seeing some inner meaning or motivation in what he does. If I were asked, I could without any difficulty tell you my impression of his inner state at any time. I do not mean, of course, that I am always accurate or even confident when I make such a statement about another person. What I do mean is that it always seems natural to me to make such a statement. I can say, "He's upset today," or I can be made angry or grateful or fearful by him—and when this happens, I am not simply describing or reacting to his overt behavior. In fact, most of the time I would be hard put to it to pin down just what it is in his behavior that leads me to my conclusion. What I am describing is his expression, that is, something observable in him that does not coincide with his outer behavior but seems to reflect some inner state in him.

The observing of expression, or of expressive characteristics, in another person is so basic as to be almost the defining character of higher organisms. Yet it is a topic almost completely ignored in psychological writings. That this should be so is all the more disheartening for purposes of clinical theory, for surely it is the apprehension of these inner-outer states in patients and clients that makes up the clinician's work. I think that a major reason for the absence of any treatment of the topic is that expression can only be understood as a consequence of understanding and sharing experience; if the latter has not been systematically dealt with, the former is bound to be ignored.

Here is the reason for my discussing the topic of expression at this point—that expressive phenomena are one natural consequence of the more fundamental phenomenon of experience. The proposition that I would offer is this: Expression is what I grasp in another person when I experience him rather than am simply aware of him. I said earlier that I can experience another person's body as distinct from knowing him, sensing him, or being aware of him, and that I can do this in the same way that I experience my own body. When my experiencing is directed toward another body rather than my own, and when that target is, like my own body, experienced as lived, as belonging with a person, then what appears to me will depend on what I choose to attend to. If my choice is toward the external, more mechanical aspects of his total conduct, I will perceive his behavior and no more. But if I choose to grasp him as a living person to whom I am, for the moment at least, related in some meaningful way, then I will experience both inner and outer aspects of him at once. What will appear to me, inescapably and so naturally that I will not question it, is the way he expresses some inner state that is his alone.

An alarm clock cannot be expressive; a person cannot help being expressive. But that this is so is not entirely a consequence of the difference between alarm clocks and persons; it is also partly a consequence of the perceiver of clocks and persons being himself a person.

## THE PARADOX OF EXPERIENCE

Even a limited survey of my-experience of my body such as I have just attempted indicates some of the richness and the untapped possibilities for a wide-ranging discipline. At various places in this book I have touched on this issue; now, looking back at my scattered attempts to deal with the content of my-experience, I conclude, as I should have known at the beginning, that experiencing is both concretely at hand and almost despairingly indescribable. It turns out to be saturated with feeling, whirling around the ecstatic point of my Now, and pointed out toward a world peopled with my body and the persons of others. Its sheerest possibility, I now discover, is to be pure—but this occurs only in rare moments and at considerable cost. They are moments that I can discover only on thinking back about them; when I dissolve the ordinary and useful distinction that I always maintain between I, the experiencer, and that which is being experienced; between subject and object; between the doer and what is done; between the knower and what he knows. All the diverse accounts from many different sources seem to agree on this as at least one central characteristic of what I have called pure experience. Thus:

I grope my way down a dark hallway, trying to find the exit door that I have been told is at the end of the hall. I reach the door, feel around for the handle to open it, and pull open the door. Suddenly, unexpectedly, I am overwhelmed; I have opened a door into a huge lighted room that is ablaze with lights and people and noise and talk and excitement. I stand in the doorway, totally captured, and try to recover my poise before entering.

This, I think, is a moment of pure experience. Now, whatever else might be said about it, it seems to me that at this moment there is no I over here who is looking at that over there. I and that are, for the moment, all one; in the words I used above, I am totally captured.

If this, then, is one of the characteristic marks of pure and unmediated experience, we might infer that a characteristic of what I have called sensing would be, by contrast, an emphasis on the target and on the distinction between me and what I sense. In fact, I think we might say that this is what sensing consists of—trying to define as adequately as possible the current target, whether it is seen or heard or simply thought about. Thus, to continue with my example:

I stand in the doorway, blinking and taken aback and not in my usual state of calm control of my faculties. Before moving, I take a few moments to adjust myself. I take a deep breath, wait for the feeling of near-shock to die down, and then attune myself deliberately to the scene before me. A fairly large room, I note, something like a ballroom. The glare and glitter, I see, come from huge crystal chandeliers. The room is perhaps half-full, but the noise level is quite high, probably because of the poor acoustics. Everyone is well-dressed, and so I feel a little embarrassed stepping into such a gathering in my street clothes.

You can see what I am doing here. Automatically, as a matter of sheer habit, I am bringing myself sharply back to my normal state of sensing. I use all my faculties to place the target out there where I think it really belongs and to specify it in a dozen different ways—the sensory qualities, their relation to me, some possible explanations of the elements of the scene, and even my own relation to it as a social participant. My sensing survey completed to my own satisfaction (and of course it would differ depending on my personality and my anxiety level, among many other things), I am prepared to enter the room and take part in it. What I could not even imagine myself doing is plunging in without pausing to take stock, without shifting over to sensing; what I am incapable of doing is going about my affairs in the state of pure experiencing. Instead, I take the time to separate myself from what is out there; I work very fast, though automatically, to turn some of the aspects of my experience into a target of my sensing, into a series of objects that I can specify to my own satisfaction.

A wise man once said: "When the pickpocket meets a saint, he sees only pockets." This is what sensing—or, to be honest, my sensing—helps to do. For sensing means to work at the world; to construct it; to remold it nearer to the heart's desire; to make objects out of what simply is. Sensing is an occupation in the world. In sensing, joy comes very hard; sweat and guilt, shame, and pride, and achievement come much easier.

And experience? Experience comes closer to being in the world as it is; accepting, when accepting is possible; joining the world. Experience is a love affair with the world. No wonder it can lead to joy. But on the other hand, for the very reason that experience does not mold but joins, its pure state can never be had for the asking, much less for the trying. Trying to attain a state of pure experience will get one nowhere. If I do not try, then sometimes it will happen, surprisingly and even miraculously—but then there is the catch that follows: the moment that I begin to work on the fact that this has happened, the pure experience as such is gone.

I have used the term *Allowing* in this book to refer to the occasioning of experience. To Allow is to make experience possible. But Allowing is also the paradox of experience. I mean by this that I cannot ever tell anyone to Allow—least of all myself. I cannot suggest that one work at having an experience. The paradox is this, that only I can do it, yet doing is the one thing that I cannot try to bring about. I have to not-try; I must let go in order to hold on to my own center. In the words of the Beatles' song, I must simply let it be.

---

THE DARK SIDE OF ALLOWING

Like every other dimension of experience, Allowing has at least two possibilities. The following excerpts, from a paper written by a college student and entitled "On Me," suggest other, and darker, ways of letting it be.

I have my ups and downs; along with various other items of medicinal value. Maybe that's my "problem." Who knows; not me anyways. I know very little. I doubt the value of my own conclusions especially those concerning my own head. Deciphering is only half the problem. Establishing the truth is also involved. But then the lies are important too, aren't they? Or are they? Or does it really matter? Like I say, I don't know much.

I don't seem to produce much; hardly the constructive type. But I do flash a lot. Tendency toward frequent spells of bizarre mental activity, mostly uncontrollable. I'm an animal, I exist, I do take some kind of form. But why, for what purpose, at whose bidding, through what forces? Lately, though, the whole thing matters less and less, and sometimes it doesn't at all. Because I don't care.

And then, how about the way I blow my mind at least once a day? The times when I sit and "experience" the changes in my own head; the changes that I'm going through. It's an evolutionary flash, to say the least, and it's getting so more and more. I mean this feeling is getting stronger and stronger. And I mean to say that I, my own self, I have no control of any tangible sort over the flash. It's as if the thought itself takes a particular and certain position in the theme of "natural history."

Everybody has their perversions. Everybody wants. Everybody needs. Everybody wishes. Everybody dreams (or do they?)

And so do I. Speaking is difficult for me. Music is much easier to communicate with. And so is writing. Definitions are a bummer. Everyone's insane. And me. And me? It really doesn't matter. It's hard for me to love the people that I love the most. Or maybe it's just hard for me to love Aquarians. I don't know if I love some people or not.

"Heaven is in your mind." Steve Winwood sang that. Maybe even heaven is your mind. It warrants exploration either way. So let's see, where's my mind. Well, shit, I really couldn't tell you. "Really." For that matter, what is and what isn't. Mental vibrations are. And physical sensations definitely are. And sometimes they go together. Or does it always happen that way. I can't remember. I don't care. To me, it doesn't matter. Lately, one thing I know: I will do no more than what happens; I will take it as it comes; I must let it be. I want to let it be.

---

There is, finally, no way to assure myself of any reward in experience by stepping out of experience. Only staying within it will do. It is a place that Fritz Perls called the Now, a signpost whose message he kept bringing to his patients so that they might learn what it meant to trust themselves and to risk the world, to accept the world without taking it, to take by surrendering. A Hindu teacher, when he was asked for a bit of advice, answered: "Whatever anyone does is all right."

To get through the paradox of Allowing, to get to my-experience, I must begin by getting out from behind my own ego: a miraculous freakout. But note that this is not a prescription for an impossible high that is beyond the life of every day. It refers simply to the little ways of living, where it all begins and where the miracle will happen, if it happens at all. At this point, if I give up trying to see the world, I may find out how to look at it. And then, once outside of my ego, I am free to join the world. Then, but not before, there becomes possible that fullness of experience which is the body trip—the turning to my own center, the finding of my-self, and loving myself unreservedly.

All this has been said in a thousand ways before, by wise men who came to repeat the same message—but even that does not mean that what I say here is to be taken as advice. There is nothing to take, nothing to use; it will crumble to dust in your hands, or mine, if we try to carry it out. Shunryu Suzuki, a Zen master, tells his students: "When my talk is over, your listening is over. There is no need to remember what I say; there is no need to understand what I say. You understand; you have full understanding within yourself. There is no problem."[22]

The experience of trust may, after all, be the most natural of human experiences, though it is usually the one that we lose the earliest and so have to risk the most to regain. In the end, it comes down to trust in my body and thus in me. As my friend Bob Hall would say—

Follow Your Star.

# notes

## CHAPTER 1

1. Rogers (1959), p. 197.
2. McKellar (1968).
3. Singer (1966) provides an excellent introduction to the systematic study of experience; cf. especially pp. 28-35.
4. Gendlin (1962), p. 3.
5. Gendlin (1962), pp. 11-15.
6. Berenson (1963), p. 85.
7. Buber (1958), p. 27.
8. Schachtel (1959), p. 125.
9. Byrd (1938), pp. 138-39.
10. Shattock (1960), pp. 68-69.
11. Keleman (1970).
12. Carmichael (1967), p. 53.
13. James (1950), vol. 1, p. 297.
14. James (1950), vol. 1, p. 299.
15. James (1950), vol. 1, p. 300.
16. Enright (1970), p. 264.
17. Köhler (1947).
18. The phrase is from Freire (1970), who uses it in analyzing the process of gaining freedom through education.

19. Elias (1971), p. 1192.
20. The discrepancy can be stated in another way: between neural properties—that is, properties of the object which measurably affect neural response mechanisms—and stimulus properties—that is, those which can be attributed to the object by non-personal instruments. The situation I describe here is one in which the person's spontaneous report cannot be predicted from knowledge of the stimulus properties alone.
21. Nabokov (1959), p. 136.
22. I leave out of account here the question of somatic delusions in schizophrenia.
23. Some valuable, firsthand evidence is presented in Moustakas (1961).
24. Bataille (1962).
25. Cf. Young (1964), chap. 2; Sagarin (1962), chap. 22.
26. Cf. Lyons (1963), pp. 173-92; Lyons (1965), pp. 246-62.
27. Stewart (1969).
28. A new experience is, of course, a phenomenon quite different from experiencing something new. Carlos Castaneda, in the course of his account of Indian sorcery, deals with the latter: "Obviously that event or any event that occurred within this alien system of sensible interpretation could be explained or understood only in terms of the units of meaning proper to that system. This work is, therefore, a reportage and should be read as a reportage. The system I recorded was incomprehensible to me, thus the pretense to anything other than reporting about it would be misleading and impertinent" (1971, p. 25).
29. Dyson (1958), p. 80.
30. The historical development of this "principle" of intentionality is discussed in Spiegelberg (1960), vol. 1, pp. 39-42 and 107-11. Cf. also Wilshire (1968) for a thorough discussion of intentionality in the thought of William James.
31. This point was once brilliantly made by John Dewey (1896) in a paper that has not been properly appreciated.
32. Sechehaye (1951), p. 77.
33. Sechehaye (1951), p. 80.
34. These regions are analogous to what has been termed in the phenomenological-existential literature the *Eigenwelt* ("own-world"), the *Mitwelt* ("with-world"), and the *Umwelt* ("surround-world").
35. I discuss the historical background of this contemporary experience in chapter 2.
36. Sartre (1956) has used a similar term: "a mystery in broad daylight."
37. Lee Meyerson. From a personal communication.
38. Laing (1967), p. 26.
39. Merleau-Ponty (1963), p. 221.

## CHAPTER 2

1. Foucault (1965).
2. Eliàde (1964).
3. Although contemporary medical technology has made it possible to shift anatomically from either sex to the other, there are approximately three times as many procedures performed to change men into women as the reverse.
4. Greenberg (1966), p. 13.
5. Limpus (1969), p. 66.

6. Schmidt (1928), pp. 86-87.
7. Mailer (1971), p. 20.
8. Freud (1961, vol. 21), p. 103.
9. Ariès (1962).
10. For a most curious rendering of this phenomenon, cf. Réage (1965), pp. 193-99.
11. This is well documented in Kraditor (1968), and in Bird (1970).
12. Cf. Sartre (1948).
13. Ellenberger (1960), p. 138.
14. *Hamlet*, Act 1, sc. 5. Three full chapters of Leviticus (13, 14, 15) are devoted to information concerning recognizing and "treating" leprosy; and the movie *Ben Hur* has a very graphic portrayal of the "treatment" of lepers, by abandonment, in Roman times.
15. Penzer (1936).
16. This turn of events is fully described in Foucault (1965), chap. 1.
17. Deutsch (1949), p. 19.
18. Balikci (1970) reports two instances, among the Netsilik Eskimos, when the close relatives of someone who had become crazy and dangerous selected a family member to shoot the madman (pp. 189-92). A closely related theme is implied in Shirley Jackson's (1968) story *The Lottery*.
19. Edward Everett Hale's (1868) famous story, written in 1863.
20. For a recent and continuing example of extreme "Strangerhood," see De Vos and Wagatsuma (1966).
21. Reed (1952), pp. 27-28.
22. Reed (1952), p. 25.
23. Reed (1952), p. 32.
24. Fletcher, *The Mad Lover*, Act 4, sc. 1, in Waller (1908), vol. 3, p. 186.
25. Grob (1966), p. 510.
26. Deutsch (1949).
27. Grob (1965), p. 17.
28. The phrase is J. C. Whitehorn's, quoted in Vail (1964), p. 343.
29. Sharma (1970), p. 249.
30. Szasz (1960), p. 114.
31. Szasz (1960), p. 115.
32. Hurley (1969) argues that a very similar set of attitudes is held toward poor people, although perhaps more subtly; we "allow" them to become diseased or mentally retarded.
33. A good history of this development may be found in Rosen (1968).
34. Szasz (1970), p. 278. A very similar argument is advanced in Laing (1967), pp. 100-101, and in Leifer (1969).
35. Szasz (1970), p. 13.
36. Szasz (1970), p. 26.
37. Szasz (1970), p. 32.
38. Szasz (1970), p. 81.
39. Szasz (1970), p. 157.
40. Szasz (1970), p. 190.
41. Szasz (1970), p. 204.
42. As an instance of such "misinterpretation," see Baker and Wagner (1965).
43. Szasz (1970), pp. 27-28.

44. Szasz (1960).
45. Szasz (1968), pp. 28-29.
46. Szasz (1968), pp. 29-30.
47. Szasz (1968), p. 33.
48. Szasz (1968), pp. 33-34.
49. Szasz (1968), p. 34.
50. Szasz (1968), p. 35.
51. Szasz (1970), p. 241.
52. Pasamanick, Scarpitti, and Dinitz (1967).
53. Mendel (1966).
54. Mendel (1966), p. 312.
55. Mendel (1966), p. 315.
56. Deiter et al. (1965).
57. Gove (1965).
58. Gove and Lubach (1969).
59. The philosophy underlying the program is discussed at length in Hanford (1965, 1967).

## CHAPTER 3

1. See Rosen (1968).
2. American Schizophrenia Association (1970).
3. Freese (1971), p. 22.
4. Rakusin and Fierman (1963), p. 140.
5. For a comprehensive historical survey, see Rosenbaum (1970).
6. This is, of course, an Aristotelian conception; see Lewin (1935).
7. Selye (1956). His concept of the General Adaptation Syndrome is an example of the natural history that I refer to here.
8. Barber (1970).
9. Baynes (1971), p. 495.
10. Mendel and Rapport (1969), p. 328.
11. From the song "Mrs. Robinson," by Paul Simon and Art Garfunkel © 1967, 1968 by Paul Simon. Used with the permission of the publishers, Charing Cross Music (BMI).
12. What is known as recidivism is in fact the repetition of the symptoms belonging to this phase of schizophrenia.
13. This has been well described by Straus (1962).
14. An example is the widespread acceptance of the Halfway House concept; see Raush and Raush (1968).
15. Festinger (1957); Brehm and Cohen (1962).
16. Goffman (1961), pp. 61-64.
17. For a recent, and thorough, discussion of determinants in mental illness, see Plog and Edgerton (1969).
18. Kallmann (1953). For contrary evidence, see Kringlen (1966).
19. Galton (1914).
20. Rosenthal (1970).
21. Taken from Rosenthal (1963).
22. Rosenthal (1963), p. 192.

23. Rosenthal (1963), p. 148.
24. Rosenthal (1963), p. 149.
25. Laing and Esterson (1970).
26. Haley (1963), pp. 108-9.
27. Haley (1963), p. 109.
28. Haley (1963), pp. 109-10.
29. Haley (1963), p. 110.
30. Lidz, Fleck, and Cornelison (1965).
31. Mishler and Waxler (1968).
32. Hunt (1964), p. 34.
33. Calhoun (1962).
34. Spitz (1954).
35. Described in Ellenberger (1960), p. 137.
36. Hollingshead and Redlich (1958).
37. The data here are in terms of *prevalence* (the total number of cases in treatment at any one time) rather than *incidence* (the total number of new cases entering treatment during a given period of time). The two are not equivalent kinds of information.
38. Similar results were found in a follow-up study ten years later by Myers, Bean, and Pepper (1965). The general findings appear to apply as well to children, although with a greater frequency among boys than girls (Baker and Wagner, 1965).
39. Hollingshead and Redlich (1958), pp. 172-73.
40. These findings were replicated in Myers and Roberts (1959).
41. Srole et al. (1962).
42. Opler (1967).
43. Carothers (1953).
44. Straus (1951), p. 439.
45. Sartre (1956), p. 568.
46. Sartre (1956), pp. 568-69. The discussion starting on page 600 is worth examining in detail, in particular his treatment of *the slimy*, pp. 604-14.
47. Leighton (1959).
48. Dohrenwend (1957), p. 78.
49. Stanton and Schwartz (1954).
50. Ayllon and Michael (1959).
51. Ayllon and Azrin (1968).
52. Cf. Siirala (1963).
53. Simon (1965).
54. Towbin (1969).
55. Towbin (1969), p. 562.
56. Towbin (1969), p. 566.
57. Holzberg (1969), p. 7.
58. Braginsky, Braginsky, and Ring (1969).
59. Braginsky, Braginsky, and Ring (1969), p. 73.
60. Braginsky, Braginsky, and Ring (1969), p. 112.
61. Laing (1967).
62. Laing (1967), p. 118.
63. Laing (1967), p. 104.
64. Laing (1967), p. 106.

## CHAPTER 4

1. Cf. Tart (1969); Castaneda (1968).
2. Laing (1967), p. 95.
3. MacLeish (1933), from the sonnet "The end of the world," p. 93.
4. Cf. Rimland (1964).
5. Quoted in Lyons (1963), pp. 249-50.
6. Quoted in Haley (1963), p. 100.
7. Madame Romola Nijinsky, the dancer's widow, has been kind enough to review the following material for accuracy.
8. Karsavina (1961), p. 151.
9. Nijinsky (1941), p. 235. This biography has just been reissued in paperback, sporting the original cover with the legend, "Soon to be a major motion picture."
10. Nijinsky (1941), p. 236.
11. Nijinsky (1941), p. 251.
12. Nijinsky (1941), p. 261.
13. Nijinsky (1941), p. 273.
14. Curiously, this system is referred to by Anatole Bourman, who had been a classmate of Nijinsky in the Imperial School and later published his own biography. Although he could not have seen the material, he referred to it as "a curious system." Bourman (1936), p. 274.
15. Bourman (1936), pp. 265-66, p. 274. Madame Nijinsky has pointed out that the letters written by Nijinsky during this period indicate that he was still "perfectly sane" and that the rumors of his impending breakdown as early as 1916 were spread after 1920 by some of Diaghilev's associates.
16. Haskell (1935).
17. E.g., in a recent work by Diaghilev's last secretary (Kochno, 1970) Nijinsky is treated casually at best, and at one place (p. 63) is gratuitously insulted.
18. Nijinsky (1968).
19. Nijinsky (1941), p. 417. Friedrich Nietzsche, the German philosopher and author, lived in Basel for many years. In January, 1889, he suffered a breakdown—which may or may not have been schizophrenia—from which he never recovered. He died in 1900.
20. Nijinsky (1941), p. 418.
21. Nijinsky (1941), p. 421. Nijinsky's "explanation" was: "You see, I am an artist. . . . I thought it would be rather an interesting experiment to see how well I could act, and so for six weeks I played the part of a lunatic."
22. Nijinsky (1941), pp. 425-26.
23. Nijinsky (1941), pp. 428-29.
24. Nijinsky (1941), p. 431.
25. Nijinsky (1941), p. 431.
26. Nijinsky (1952). In this later work, written after her husband's death, she admits that he should never have been kept locked up and isolated from the world.
27. N. Nabokov (1949), p. 45.
28. Karsavina (1961), p. 243.
29. N. Nabokov (1949), p. 45.
30. She may have had some difficulty understanding the book since she could not speak English.

31. Lifar (1939), pp. 542-43.
32. Nijinsky (1941), forward, p. xvi.
33. Quoted by Karsavina (1961).
34. Nijinsky (1941), p. 251.
35. Cocteau (1959), p. 157.
36. Bourman (1936), p. 28.
37. R. E. Jones (1946), pp. 46-47.
38. However, the authors of the *Guinness Book of World Records* state: "This is not believed by physical education experts, since no high jumper can stay off the ground for more than one second, and no analyzable film exists" (McWhirter and McWhirter, 1971, p. 408).
39. Beaumont (1943), p. 26.
40. Beaumont (1943), p. 25.
41. Magriel (1946), preface.
42. Nijinsky (1941), p. 128.
43. Nijinsky (1941), p. 113.
44. Denby (1946), p. 17.
45. Nijinsky (1941), p. 401.
46. Nijinsky (1968), p. 88.
47. Nijinsky (1968), p. 49.
48. Nijinsky (1968), pp. 155-56.
49. It should be noted that from 1919 until his death Nijinsky showed no homosexual interests at all.
50. Haskell (1935), p. 250.
51. Haskell (1935), p. 32.
52. Nijinsky (1941), p. 71.
53. Nijinsky (1941), p. 71.
54. Nijinsky (1941), p. 71.
55. Nijinsky (1968), pp. 70-72.
56. Nijinsky (1941), p. 383.
57. Nijinsky (1941), p. 399.
58. de Weerth (1961), p. 28.
59. Quoted in Haskell (1935), pp. 270-72.
60. Nijinsky (1968), p. 103.
61. Nijinsky (1968), p. 18.
62. Nijinsky (1968), p. 30.
63. Nijinsky (1968), pp. 87-88.
64. Nijinsky (1968), p. 99.
65. Nijinsky (1968), p. 30.
66. Nijinsky (1968), pp. 50-51.
67. Menninger (1963).
68. Nijinsky (1968), p. 32.
69. Stephen (1970), n. p.
70. Heinlein (1969), pp. 139-40.
71. Whitman (1938), p. 18.
72. Whitman (1938), pp. 49-50.
73. Salinger (1952), p. 298.
74. Nijinsky (1968), pp. 186-87.

## CHAPTER 5

1. Gusfield (1963, 1968).
2. Broun and Leech (1927). For a partisan view of Comstock's career, see Trumbull (1913).
3. Jeremy Bentham put it well: "Every law is an infraction of liberty."
4. Nicholas Von Hoffman, in the *San Francisco Chronicle*, September 26, 1971.
5. My usage of the terms *Stranger* and *Saint* is quite different from that in Wilson's (1965) well-known study of the Pilgrims.
6. Sartre (1956).
7. Sartre (1963) devotes an entire book to a discussion of this phenomenon. The name he chooses, *Saint Genet*, alludes to the third century Roman martyr St. Genestus (*Genêt* in French), the patron saint of actors. Sartre sees Jean Genet as an actor because he "enacts" his existential life-choice, and as a martyr because the world misunderstands him. In the terminology I am using in this book, he is also, of course, a Saint.
8. Genet (1954), p. 185.
9. Genet (1954), p. 10.
10. Genet (1954), pp. 29-30.
11. Genet (1954), p. 30.
12. Genet (1954), p. 49.
13. Genet (1954), p. 92.
14. Genet (1954), p. 190.
15. Genet (1954), pp. 277-78.
16. Genet (1954), p. 278.
17. Hazelton (1970) describes a similar sort of idealistic, semireligious, and long-hair protest movement among German youth immediately after World War I, who were called *Wandervogel*.
18. Illich (1970), Lecture No. 8, p. 2.
19. Keniston (1968).
20. As reported in the *Davis* (Calif.) *Enterprise*, June 30, 1971.
21. Eisenberg (1970), p. 1692.
22. Park and Burgess (1924).
23. Bogardus (1925).
24. Bogardus (1933).
25. Lyons (1966), p. 23.
26. Alcoholics Anonymous (1957).
27. Endore (1968, p. 215) quotes a physician of long experience with addicts, who remarked that for a period following withdrawal they may panic at such commonplace, yet to them forgotten, sensations as that of urine passing through the urethral canal.
28. Weil, Zinberg, and Nelsen (1968) provide evidence that marijuana is safe to use in reasonable quantities and to study in the laboratory. Similarly, Dishotsky et al. (1971) find no contraindication, on the grounds of biochemical consequences, to the use of LSD-25 in pure form. For an "official" view, that the use of these substances leads to "a cancerous invasion of the moral structures," see Harney and Cross (1961).
29. Barnes (1963), p. 131.
30. The thesis I offer here has also been presented by a number of other writers, e.g.

De Ropp (1957), Lindesmith (1965), and Carey (1971). For a full discussion, see Fort (1969) and Kaplan (1970).

31. Kolb (1939).
32. Chein and Rosenfeld (1957); Chein (1964).
33. Taken from Winick (1961).
34. See Endore (1968).
35. See Alcoholics Anonymous (1957).
36. Supportive evidence may be found in Casriel (1963), who describes Synanon as "a pleasant, paternalistic, tribelike family environment" (p. 10), and in Walsh (1970).
37. Kinsey, Pomeroy, and Martin (1948), fig. 157, p. 627.
38. Smith (1956), pp. 313-16. The passages quoted are from the Loeb translation of Plato's *Symposium*.
39. As quoted in the *San Francisco Chronicle*, January 25, 1971, and January 26, 1971.
40. Cf. Fromm (1959), p. 34.
41. E.g., Noyes (1934); Henderson and Gillespie (1927).
42. See Bergler (1958).
43. Hoffman (1968).
44. See de Becker (1969), chap. 3.
45. The king had a court jester for his various sexual pleasures, but no such functionary was ever available to the queen.

## CHAPTER 6

1. This is spelled out in detail in Rank (1945), based in part on his earlier work on creativity (Rank, 1932); see Karpf (1953) for a study of Rank's contributions to the theory and practice of psychotherapy. For an excellent summary of Rank's views and an account of their value in research on creativity in architects, see MacKinnon (1965).
2. Horney (1950).
3. Laing (1969).
4. This possibility rests, in turn, on the existence of *myself* as known to me, which will be discussed in chapter 7.
5. Skinner (1971) says that this is not so, that the threat of punishment is effective only in regard to the immediate situation.
6. Fischer (1970) provides a recent summary of major theoretical views of anxiety.
7. Greenberg (1966).
8. Ram Dass (1971), "From Bindu to Ojas," p. 57. In this connection, see also the title of Stevens's (1969) book, *Don't Push the River*.
9. Reich (1969).
10. Davidoff (1952), pp. 96-101.
11. Goldstein and Scheerer (1941), p. 1.
12. Goldstein and Scheerer (1941), pp. 4-7.
13. "Coming Down" in Ram Dass (1971).
14. E. Keen (1970), p. 315.
15. E. Keen (1970), p. 308.
16. E. Keen (1970), p. 311.
17. E. Keen (1970), p. 312.
18. E. Keen (1970), p. 314.

19. See the passages from Genet (1954) in chapter 5.
20. An excellent description can be found in the stories by Borowski (1967).
21. "Richard Cory" in Robinson (1937).
22. In the words of the Beatles' song "Bungalow Bill," "the All-American bullet-headed Saxon mother's son."

## CHAPTER 7

1. Kaplan (1964), pp. 264-65. Her complete "story" is given in MacLane (1902).
2. Kaplan (1964), p. 265.
3. Kaplan (1964), p. 267.
4. Kaplan (1964), p. 269.
5. Kaplan (1964), p. 270.
6. Friedenberg (1966).
7. Friedenberg (1966), pp. 55-56.
8. Smith (1912), p. 214.
9. Smith (1912), p. 215.
10. Smith (1912), p. 218.
11. Smith (1912), pp. 218-19.
12. The King James version of the Bible was first published in 1611.
13. Smith (1912), p. 219.
14. Smith (1912), pp. 220-21.
15. Smith (1912), pp. 221-22.
16. Smith (1912), p. 233.
17. Smith (1912), pp. 233-34.
18. Smith (1912), p. 236.
19. Smith (1912), p. 237.
20. Smith (1912), pp. 242-43.
21. Smith (1912), p. 244.
22. Smith (1912), pp. 244-45.
23. Smith (1912), p. 245.
24. See Pope-Hennessy (1963).
25. B. G. Rosenthal (1970).
26. MacLeish (1933), pp. 12-13.
27. Kohn (1969).
28. Goffman (1961), p. 132.
29. One irony deserves mention—Anthony Comstock, the nineteenth-century reformer and scourge of pornographers, deserves to be called a true child of the modern age. His position may, indeed, properly be considered as the other face of Freudianism, for his concern was not with behavior (he never prosecuted prostitutes) but only with thoughts. To Comstock, sin was equated with the fantasies that accompanied knowledge; sin was in the very wish. His attack on pornographers was founded on his horror at not finding them overcome with guilt.
30. Mowrer (1960), p. 301.
31. Mowrer (1960), p. 304.
32. Kiev (1968), p. 177.
33. Kiev (1968), p. 180.
34. Szasz (1964), p. 527.
35. One other consequence also followed, but I will not deal with it here, since it is

concerned primarily with the professional issue of training. It is that if the psychoanalyst-physician was, on principle, not different from his patient, he had better change himself so as to be assured that for purposes of treatment he was different. Freud therefore found it necessary to psychoanalyze himself (by means of an analysis of his own dreams), and since Freud's day the would-be analyst has been required to undergo his own training analysis.

36. Freud (1955), pp. 1-162.
37. Binswanger (1958).
38. Wolpe (1971), p. 341.
39. Wolpe (1971), p. 341. For a more elaborate statement and review, see Wolpe (1969), and Ullmann and Krasner (1965), pp. 1-63.
40. Mendel (1964), pp. 188-89.
41. I have discussed this matter at length; see Lyons (1963), pp. 284-88.
42. Perls (1970), p. 129.
43. Rogers (1957), p. 96.
44. Strupp, Wallach, and Wogan (1964), p. 36.
45. Colby (1968), p. 173.
46. Genet (1962), p. 19.
47. Reik (1949).
48. Gurin, Veroff, and Feld (1960).
49. Devereux (1969), p. 134.
50. Devereux (1969), p. 135.
51. Wolpe (n. d.), pp. 8-10 of mimeographed transcript.
52. I do not mean to imply that the patient submissively accepts an order from his therapist; see Devereux (1969), p. 251, for an example of a patient arguing with the therapist and then rejecting the interpretation offered, and Frank (1961), chap. 7, for a discussion of how influence is channeled in the psychotherapeutic situation.
53. This was demonstrated in some of the earliest studies of the therapeutic process; see Rubenstein and Parloff (1959).
54. Fiedler (1950).
55. It is perhaps ironic that Freud, an inhibited and puritanical man with rather traditional notions concerning women's place, should have served as a major instrument for their liberation.
56. See F. J. Hoffman (1957).
57. Horney (1950).
58. There is a fine account of this development in Thompson (1950).
59. Rogers (1951).
60. Ellis (1962); Ellis and Harper (1961).
61. For perceptive accounts, see Gustaitis (1969) and Howard (1970).

## CHAPTER 8

1. For a discussion of factor analytic methods of categorizing approaches in psychotherapy, see Weissman, Goldschmid, and Stein (1971).
2. Haley (1963), p. 69.
3. Haley (1963), p. 70.
4. This position has been very well argued by Barker (1963, 1965).
5. Watson (1913).

6. See Wolpe and Lazarus (1966). Pioneer work using relaxation methods was done by Jacobsen (1938). One of Freud's early disciples, Sandor Ferenczi, wrote: "I have since then learnt that it is sometimes useful to advise *relaxation exercises*, and that with this kind of relaxation one can overcome the psychical inhibitions and resistances to association" (1953, p. 226).

7. Cf. Krasner and Ullmann (1965); Wenrich (1970).

8. Bandura (1961).

9. See Bandura (1969).

10. Kanfer and Phillips (1970), pp. 17-19.

11. Klein et al. (1969), pp. 260-61.

12. See Bijou (1965), pp. 59-60.

13. Feldenkrais (1966), p. 162. Hediger (1964) describes a similar approach to training the flight instinct out of animals in zoos.

14. Goffman (1961, p. 51) has made a similar point: "Whatever their severity, punishments are largely known in the inmate's home world as something applied to animals and children; this conditioning, behavioristic model is not widely applied to adults, since failure to maintain required standards typically leads to indirect disadvantageous consequences and not to specific immediate punishment at all."

15. Haley (1963, p. 11) makes a useful distinction between symmetrical relationships, in which two persons "exchange the same type of behavior," and complementary relationships, in which they exchange different types of behaviors—e.g., one giving and the other receiving.

16. Bergler (1954), pp. 10-11.

17. Bergler (1954), p. 135.

18. See Rogers (1951, 1959).

19. Goldstein (1940).

20. Maslow (1954). According to Maslow's own advice (1962, p. 206), the best introduction to his approach is in Moustakas (1956), and the best general texts are Jourard (1958) and Coleman (1960)—to which I would add Allport (1955).

21. Rogers (1955), pp. 267-68.

22. May (1958), p. 43.

23. Lindner (1955).

24. For a lighthearted history, see Miller (1971).

25. Perls (1969a), p. 214.

26. Trungpa (1969).

27. Downing (1972).

28. Assagioli (1971).

29. Brown (1971).

30. Leonard (1968).

31. Bradford, Gibb, and Benne (1964).

32. Schutz (1967, 1971) presents encountering as a way of life that is based on a new kind of openness and self-awareness; see also Burton (1969), for varied descriptions of experiences with encounter groups, and Rogers (1970).

33. Perls (1969a), p. 1.

34. Haley (1963), p. 51.

35. Laing (1967).

36. I should emphasize that I mean the term *revolutionary* here in a general and almost metaphorical sense, rather than in its narrow meaning of a specific stance in regard to political activism.

37. Coué (1922); Coué and Brooks (1960).
38. Guerney (1969). Recent developments are reviewed by Matarazzo (1971).
39. Since very little has yet been published on this trend, I am taking some liberties in describing its philosophy.

## CHAPTER 9

1. Laing (1967), p. 47.
2. Watts (1970), p. 71.
3. Wolff (1963).
4. In this theory, there are seven *Chakras* ("wheels"), six in the spine and one in the brain; the wheel is conceived as an "astral lotus" whose petals contain rays of the life force, or *prana*. See Schutz (1971), pp. 64-69.
5. Gass (1971), p. 33.
6. Barnes (1963), p. 122.
7. Marin (1971), p. 11.
8. Feldenkrais (1966), p. 150.
9. Selver (1966), pp. 490-92. Some consequences on a large scale are suggested by Boorstin (1962): we do not read books, only best sellers, a best seller being "a book which sells well because it sells well;" we do not take trips, but tours; there are no heroes, only celebrities; and so on.
10. Gunther (1968, 1971).
11. Pesso (1969), p. 68.
12. Quoted in Reps (n. d.).
13. Villiers (1971), pp. 341-42.
14. Rolf (1963), pp. 9-10.
15. Rolf (1963), p. 13.
16. Rolf (1963), p. 15.
17. Feldenkrais (1966), p. 163.
18. Straus (1952).
19. Schutz (1971), p. 4.
20. S. Keen (1970), p. 60. For an additional description see Lilly (1972).
21. Lowen (1967), p. 252. Italics added.
22. Reich (1967), p. 47. This book, a kind of scientific autobiography, is the best single introduction to Reich's thought.
23. Reich (1967), p. 111.
24. Reich (1967), p. 94.
25. Reich (1967), p. 91.
26. Reich (1967), p. 93.
27. Reich (1969), p. 385.
28. Reich (1967), p. 111.
29. Reich (1967), p. 112.
30. Wallen (1970), pp. 11-12.
31. Reich (1967), p. 226.
32. A detailed case history describing the method is presented by Reich (1967, pp. 213-16) and should be consulted as the best account available of his innovations in clinical practice.
33. Reich (1967), p. 229.

34. His famous statement on the sexual basis of human morality was, "To touch the truth is to touch your genitals." Some of the political and personal consequences of this stand are spelled out in Dusan Makavejev's remarkable motion picture, *WR—Mysteries of the Organism.*
35. Reich (1969), pp. 353-54.
36. Reich (1967), pp. xxiii-xxiv. A pioneer figure in literature, who said much the same thing about the body, sexuality, and energy, and about their relation to the life force, was D. H. Lawrence; see, especially, his novels, *Sons and Lovers* (1913) and *Lady Chatterley's Lover* (1928).
37. Landis and Hunt (1939), pp. 21-23.
38. Reich (1967), p. xxix.
39. Reich (1969), pp. 168-70.
40. Reich (1973), pp. 175-177.
41. Reich (1967), p. 114.

## CHAPTER 10

1. Lowen (1971), p. xii. This book is a reissue, with a more attractive title, of Lowen's basic work, *Physical Dynamics of Character Structure*, first published in 1957.
2. Lowen (1971), pp. xii-xiii.
3. Lowen (1971), p. 15.
4. Marin puts it this way: "He modulates Reich's absolutism to a more restrained approach to 'pleasure.' Common sense returns. The principles of reality and adjustment reassert themselves. Lowen accepts the tension between involuntary animal needs and half-voluntary social bonds. There is a pragmatic reasonableness to it all, a necessary reaction to Reich's driven excess" (1971, p. 12).
5. Lowen (1971), p. 18. Admittedly, a serious theoretical and methodological problem arises when energy is introduced as an explanatory concept. I leave open the question of whether the term can ever be more than an attractive, but scientifically useless, metaphor. In any case, as Lowen shows, it is extremely useful on a descriptive level.
6. Lowen (1967), p. 258.
7. Lowen (1967), p. 6.
8. Keleman (1971), p. 23.
9. Lowen (1971), p. 259.
10. Lowen (1971), pp. 258-59.
11. Lowen (1971), p. 16. Recall, for example, the intensity of affective release claimed by Janov (1970) for his "primal scream therapy," as well as the dramatic release described in the closing passage of *Portnoy's Complaint* (Roth, 1969) or in *The Painted Bird* (Kosinski, 1966).
12. Keleman (1971), pp. 65-66.
13. Lowen (1971), pp. 76-77.
14. Lowen (1971), p. 91.
15. Keleman (1970).
16. Keleman (1970), p. 4.
17. Marin (1971), p. 15.

18. Keleman (1971), p. 31.
19. Keleman (1971), p. 109.
20. Hayter (1970), p. 334.
21. Many contemporary theater groups—for example, the members of the company of San Francisco's Committee Theatre, and the various casts of *Hair* or *Oh! Calcutta!*— have required that the actors be continuing members of ongoing encounterlike groups. Rip Torn, one of the better-known method actors, has described this approach to the craft as closely related to Gestalt therapy.
22. The issue is raised in acute and dramatic form in such films as Allan King's *A Married Couple*, in which the protagonists are, in fact, not acting but acting-out their own marital difficulties.
23. The primary source for materials on psychodrama is Beacon House (P. O. Box 311, Beacon, N. Y. 12508), and the journal *Group Psychotherapy*. Moreno (1959) has written a good introductory text, as has Corsini (1966).
24. Cf. Brown (1928); Bellinger (1927).
25. Brody (1970) has traced this development in detail in the history of ritual mystery plays performed by English mummers.
26. In order to see a film I must prepare myself, go out in public at some prearranged time, join other people whom I do not know, find a seat among them in a strange place, adjust my senses to an artificially enhanced level of sight and sound and the presence and noise of others—in short, I must put myself out to take part in a public event. When I view a presentation on TV, on the other hand, I can sit or sprawl where I want, wander in and out, or even treat the little screen as background to my other activities, as children often do; for the stimulus is really no-stimulus, and the scene is nothing that holds me. Only those who are very easily entranced (such as very young children and very old people) can manage to approximate, by means of TV's empty attractions, that experience of a dramatic capture which can often be attained through the viewing of even a poor film in a theater.
27. See Brustein (1971).
28. Ansbacher and Ansbacher (1956).
29. Dreikurs (1968).
30. See Cheney (1935), p. viii.
31. Cohn (1970), pp. 137-38.
32. Perls (1969a), p. 69.
33. Naranjo (1970), p. 53.
34. Perls (1969a), pp. 55-57.
35. Perls (1966), chapter 35.
36. Perls (1969b).
37. Perls (1969a), p. 224.
38. Perls (1967), pp. 309-10.
39. Perls (1969b), p. 212.
40. This may already have started. A recent news item (*San Francisco Chronicle*, June 14, 1971) announced a public "entertainment" by a Gestalt therapist, to include "audience participation theatre games, interaction games, and techniques for self-awareness."
41. Perls (1969a), p. 112.
42. Perls (1969b), p. 4.

## CHAPTER 11

1. I take this expression from the title of Koch's (1970) book about children's poetry.
2. The area has been surveyed repeatedly—up to 1930, by Allport and Vernon (1933); then up to 1950, by Bruner and Tagiuri (1954); and most recently by Davitz (1964).
3. In using the term *knowing* here, I do not mean some kind of assessment of oneself. Rather, I have in mind a kind of penumbra of self-reflection that is a natural part of everyday experiencing and so is coterminous with each experience.
4. Quoted in Reps (n. d.), p. 165.
5. Freud was quite aware of this divergence between theory and practice, and once confessed that he would be willing to give up his metapsychological theory in favor of the "truth" to be discovered in the actual therapeutic situation.
6. Cf. Barrett (1958); Blackham (1952); Collins (1952).
7. Jaspers (1963). This work was first published in German in 1913.
8. Heidegger (1962).
9. See Lyons (1961), and the essays by Rollo May in May, Angel, and Ellenberger (1958).
10. May, Angel, and Ellenberger (1958).
11. Sartre (1956), pp. 557-75.
12. E. Keen (1970).
13. If an experiential discipline should finally turn out to be feasible, we would be entitled to consider it a new paradigm, in the sense used by Kuhn (1962), pp. 10-11. Laing (1967), p. 16, has suggested that the discipline be called social phenomenology.
14. Jones (1970), p. 742.
15. Erwin Straus is perhaps the thinker who has most clearly emphasized this humanist truth. He insists that the domain where our data are to be found, where our attention as psychologists ought to be directed, the only domain with which we can ever deal, is *the human world* (1960).
16. Beckett (1958), p. 77.
17. Beloff and Beloff (1959).
18. Wolff (1943).
19. James (1950), vol. 1, p. 238.
20. Beckett (1958), p. 156.
21. Schutz (1971), p. 2.
22. Suzuki (1970), p. 51.

# bibliography

Alcoholics Anonymous. *Alcoholics Anonymous comes of age.* New York: Harper, 1957.

Allport, G. W. *Becoming.* New Haven: Yale University Press, 1955.

Allport, G. W., and Vernon, P. E. *Studies in expressive movement.* New York: Macmillan, 1933.

American Schizophrenia Association (56 West 45th Street, New York, N. Y. 10036). Brochure dated September, 1970.

Ansbacher, H. L., and Ansbacher, R. R. *The individual psychology of Alfred Adler.* New York: Basic Books, 1956.

Ariès, P. *Centuries of childhood. A social history of family life.* New York: Vintage Books, 1962.

Assagioli, R. *Psychosynthesis: A manual of principles and techniques.* New York: Viking, 1971.

Ayllon, T., and Michael, J. The psychiatric nurse as a behavioral engineer. *Journal for the Experimental Analysis of Behavior* 2 (1959): 323-34.

Ayllon, T., and Azrin, N. H. *The token economy.* New York: Appleton-Century-Crofts, 1968.

Baker, J. Q., and Wagner, N. N. Social class and mental illness in children. *Teachers College Record* 66 (1965): 522-36.

Balicki, A. *The Netsilik Eskimo.* New York: Natural History Press, 1970.

Bandura, A. Psychotherapy as a learning process. *Psychological Bulletin* 58 (1961): 143-59.

Bandura, A. *Principles of behavior modification.* New York: Holt, Rinehart and Winston, 1969.

Barber, T. X. *LSD, marijuana, yoga, and hypnosis.* Chicago: Aldine, 1970.

Barker, R. G. On the nature of the environment. *Journal of Social Issues* 19 (1963): 17-38.

Barker, R. G. Explorations in ecological psychology. *American Psychologist* 20 (1965): 1-14.

Barnes, D. C. *Nightwood.* London: Faber and Faber, 1963.

Barrett, W. *Irrational man: a study in existential philosophy.* New York: Doubleday, 1958.

Bataille, G. *Death and sensuality. A study of eroticism and the taboo.* New York: Ballantine, 1962.

Baynes, T. E., Jr. Continuing conjectural concepts concerning civil commitment criteria. *American Psychologist* 26 (1971): 489-95.

Beaumont, C. W. *Vaslav Nijinsky.* London: C. W. Beaumont, 1943.

Beckett, S. *The unnamable.* New York: Grove Press, 1958.

Bellinger, M. F. *A short history of the drama.* New York: Holt, 1927.

Beloff, H., and Beloff, J. Unconscious self-evaluation using a stereoscope. *Journal of Abnormal and Social Psychology* 59 (1959): 275-78.

Berenson, B. *Sunset and twilight. From the diaries of 1947-1958.* New York: Harcourt, Brace and World, 1963.

Bergler, E. *The revolt of the middle-aged man.* New York: A. A. Wyn, 1954.

Bergler, E. *Counterfeit-sex; homosexuality, impotence, frigidity.* 2nd edition. New York: Grune and Stratton, 1958.

Bijou, S. W. Experimental studies of child behavior, normal and deviant. In Krasner, L., and Ullmann, L. P. (eds.), *Research in behavior modification*, pp. 56-81. New York: Holt, Rinehart and Winston, 1965.

Binswanger, L. The case of Ellen West. In May, R., Angel, E., and Ellenberger, H. F. (eds.), *Existence*, pp. 237-364. New York: Basic Books, 1958.

Bird, C., with Briller, S. W. *Born female.* New York: McKay, 1970.

Blackham, H. J. *Six existentialist thinkers.* New York: Macmillan, 1952.

Bogardus, E. S. Measuring social distance. *Journal of Applied Sociology* 9 (1925): 299-308.

Bogardus, E. S. A social distance scale. *Sociology and Social Research* 17 (1933): 265-70.

Boorstin, D. J. *The image, or what happened to the American dream.* New York: Atheneum, 1962.

Borowski, T. *This way to the gas, ladies and gentlemen.* New York: Viking, 1967.

Bourman, A. (in collaboration with Lyman, D.) *The tragedy of Nijinsky.* New York: Whittlesey House, 1936.

Bradford, L., Gibb, J., and Benne, K. *T-group theory and laboratory method.* New York: Wiley, 1964.

Braginsky, B. M., Braginsky, D. D., and Ring, K. *Methods of madness. The mental hospital as a last resort.* New York: Holt, Rinehart, and Winston, 1969.

Brehm, J. W., and Cohen, A. R. *Explorations in cognitive dissonance.* New York: Wiley, 1962.

Brody, A. *The English mummers and their plays.* Philadelphia: University of Pennsylvania Press, 1970.

Broun, H., and Leech, M. *Anthony Comstock, roundsman of the Lord.* New York: Boni, 1927.

Brown, G. I. *Human teaching for human learning.* New York: Viking, 1971.

Brown, I. J. C. *First player; the origin of drama.* New York: Morrow, 1928.

Bruner, J., and Tagiuri, R. The perception of people. In G. Lindzey (ed.), *Handbook of social psychology. Vol. 2. Special fields and applications*, pp. 634-54. Cambridge, Mass.: Addison-Wesley, 1954.

Brustein, R. *Revolution as theatre. Notes on the new radical style.* New York: Liveright, 1971.

Buber, M. *I and thou* (2nd edition). New York: Scribner's, 1958.

Burton, A. (ed.) *Encounter.* San Francisco: Jossey-Bass, 1969.

Byrd, R. E. *Alone.* New York: G. P. Putnam's Sons, 1938.

Calhoun, J. B. A "behavioral sink." In Bliss, E. L. (ed.), *Roots of behavior*, chap. 22. New York: Hoeber, 1962.

Carey, J. T. Doctor as policeman. *Contemporary Psychology* 16 (1971): 201-202.

Carmichael, L. Autobiography. In E. G. Boring and G. Lindzey (eds.), *A history of psychology in autobiography*, vol. 5, pp. 29-56. New York: Appleton-Century-Crofts, 1967.

Carothers, J. C. *The African mind in health and disease. A study in ethno-psychiatry.* Geneva: World Health Organization, 1953.

Casriel, D. *So fair a house: the story of Synanon.* Englewood Cliffs, N. J.: Prentice-Hall, 1963.

Castaneda, C. *The teachings of Don Juan: a Yaqui way of knowledge.* Berkeley: University of California Press, 1968.

Castaneda, C. *A separate reality. Further conversations with Don Juan.* New York: Simon and Schuster, 1971.

Chein, I. H. *The road to H: narcotics, delinquency, and social policy.* New York: Basic Books, 1964.

Chein, I., and Rosenfeld, E. Juvenile narcotics use. *Law and Contemporary Problems* 22 (1957): 52-68.

Cheney, S. *The theatre. Three thousand years of drama, acting and stagecraft.* New York: Tudor, 1935.

Cocteau, J. A memory of Diaghilev and Nijinsky. *Vogue* 133 (February 15, 1959): 156-57, 162.

Cohn, R. C. Therapy in groups: psychoanalytic, experiential, and Gestalt. In Fagan, J., and Shepherd, I. L. (eds.), *Gestalt therapy now; theory, techniques, applications,* pp. 130-39. Palo Alto, Calif.: Science and Behavior Books, 1970.

Colby, K. M. Treatment of mental disorders. I. Psychological treatment. In *International encyclopedia of the social sciences,* vol. 10, pp. 172-78. New York: Macmillan, 1968.

Coleman, J. *Personality dynamics and effective behavior.* New York: Scott, Foresman, 1960.

Collins, J. D. *The existentialists: A critical study.* Chicago: Regnery, 1952.

Corsini, R. J. *Roleplaying in psychotherapy; a manual.* Chicago: Aldine, 1966.

Coué, E. *Self mastery through conscious autosuggestion.* New York: American Library Service, 1922.

Coué, E., and Brooks, C. H. *Better and better every day.* London: Unwin, 1960.

Davidoff, L. M. Migraine. In Pinner, M., and Miller, B. F. (eds.), *When doctors are patients,* pp. 96-101. New York: Norton, 1952.

Davitz, J. R. A review of research concerned with facial and vocal expressions of emotion. *The communication of emotional meaning,* pp. 13-29. New York: McGraw-Hill, 1964.

de Becker, R. *The other face of love.* New York: Grove, 1969.

Deiter, J. B., Hanford, D. B., Hummel, R. T., and Lubach, J. E. Brief inpatient treatment—a pilot study. *Mental Hospitals* 16 (February 1965): 95-98.

Denby, E. Notes on Nijinsky photographs. In Magriel, P. (ed.), *Nijinsky: An illustrated monograph,* pp. 15-43. New York: Holt, 1946.

De Ropp, R. S. *Drugs and the mind.* New York: Grove, 1957.

Deutsch, A. *The mentally ill in America: A history of their care and treatment from Colonial times* (2nd ed.) New York: Columbia University Press, 1949.

Devereux, G. *Reality and dream. Psychotherapy of a Plains Indian.* New York: New York University Press, 1969.

De Vos, G., and Wagatsuma, H. *Japan's invisible race; caste in culture and personality.* Berkeley: University of California Press, 1966.

de Weerth, E. Scenes from an enchanted life: 13. Nijinsky on Mount Desert. *Opera News* 25 (March 25, 1961): 28-29.

Dewey, J. The reflex arc concept in psychology. *Psychological Review* 3 (1896): 357-70.

Dishotsky, N. I., Loughman, W. D., Mogar, R. E., and Lipscomb, W. R. LSD and genetic damage. *Science* 172 (April 30, 1971): 431-39.

Dohrenwend, B. P. The Stirling County study. A research program on relations between sociocultural factors and mental illness. *American Psychologist* 12 (1957): 78-85.

Downing, G. *The massage book*. New York: Random House, 1972; and Berkeley, Calif.: The Bookworks, 1972.

Dreikurs, R. *Logical consequences: a handbook of discipline*. New York: Meredith, 1968.

Dyson, F. J. Innovation in physics. *Scientific American* 199 (1958): 74-82.

Eisenberg, L. Student unrest: Sources and consequences. *Science* 167 (March 27, 1970): 1688-92.

Eliàde, M. *Shamanism: Archaic techniques of ecstasy*. Princeton: Princeton University Press (Bollingen Foundation), 1964.

Elias, H. Letter, in *Science* 173 (September 24, 1971): 1192.

Ellenberger, H. F. Zoological garden and mental hospital. *Canadian Psychiatric Association Journal* 5 (1960): 136-49.

Ellis, A. *Reason and emotion in psychotherapy*. New York: Lyle Stuart, 1962.

Ellis, A., and Harper, R. A. *A guide to rational living*. Englewood Cliffs, N. J.: Prentice-Hall, 1961.

Endore, G. *Synanon*. New York: Doubleday, 1968.

Enright, J. B. Awareness training in the mental health professions. In Fagan, J., and Shepherd, I. L. (eds.), *Gestalt therapy now; theory, techniques, applications,* pp. 263-73. Palo Alto, Calif.: Science and Behavior Books, 1970.

Fagan, J., and Shepherd, I. L. (eds.) *Gestalt therapy now; theory, techniques, applications*. Palo Alto, Calif.: Science and Behavior Books, 1970.

Feldenkrais, M. *Body and mature behavior. A study of anxiety, sex, gravitation and learning*. New York: International Universities Press, 1966.

Ferenczi, S. *The theory and technique of psychoanalysis*. 2. New York: Basic Books, 1953.

Festinger, L. *A theory of cognitive dissonance*. Evanston, Ill.: Row, Peterson, 1957.

Fiedler, F. E. A comparison of therapeutic relationships in psychoanalytic, nondirective and Adlerian therapy. *Journal of Consulting Psychology* 14 (1950): 436-45.

Fischer, W. F. *Theories of anxiety*. New York: Harper & Row, 1970.

Fort, J. *The pleasure seekers; the drug crisis, youth and society*. Indianapolis, Ind.: Bobbs-Merrill, 1969.

Foucault, M. *Madness and civilization*. New York: Mentor Books, 1965.

Frank, J. D. *Persuasion and healing: a comparative study of psychotherapy*. Baltimore: Johns Hopkins Press, 1961.

Freese, A. S. The millions who are schizophrenic: Can drugs help them? *Family Weekly*, March 4, 1971, 22-23.

Freire, P. *Pedagogy of the oppressed*. New York: Herder and Herder, 1970.

Freud, S. *Civilization and its discontents*. Vol. 21, pp. 64-145. (Standard edition of the complete psychological works of Sigmund Freud, James Strachey, ed.) London: Hogarth Press, 1961.

Freud, S. *Totem and taboo*. Vol. 13, pp. 1-162. (Standard edition of the complete psychological works of Sigmund Freud, James Strachey, ed.) London: Hogarth Press, 1955.

Friedenberg, E. Z. Society and the therapeutic function, in *The dignity of youth and other atavisms*, pp. 53-65. Boston: Beacon Press, 1966.

Fromm, E. *Sigmund Freud's mission. An analysis of his personality and his influence*. New York: Grove, 1959.

Galton, F. *Hereditary genius: an inquiry into its laws and consequences*. London: Macmillan, 1914.

Gass, W. H. The stylization of desire. *New York Review of Books* (February 25, 1971): 33-37.

Gendlin, E. T. *Experiencing and the creation of meaning. A philosophical and psychological approach to the subjective*. New York: Free Press, 1962.

Genet, J. *The thief's journal*. Paris: Olympia Press, 1954.

Genet, J. *The balcony*. rev. ed. London: Faber and Faber, 1962.

Goffman, E. *Asylums. Essays on the social situation of mental patients and other inmates*. New York: Doubleday, 1961. Doubleday Anchor Original A 277.

Goldstein, K. *Human nature in the light of psychopathology*. Cambridge, Mass.: Harvard University Press, 1940.

Goldstein, K., and Scheerer, M. Abstract and concrete behavior. An experimental study with special tests. *Psychological Monographs*, vol. 53, no. 2, 1941. (Whole No. 239) p. 155.

Gove, W. Post hospital adjustment of Northwest Washington Hospital-Community Pilot program patients. *The Bulletin* 9 (1965): 140-45. Division of Mental Health, State of Washington.

Gove, W., and Lubach, J. E. An intensive treatment program for psychiatric inpatients: a description and evaluation. *Journal of Health and Social Behavior* 10 (1969): 225-36.

Greenberg, D. *How to be a Jewish mother*. Los Angeles: Price, Stern, Sloan, 1966.

Grob, G. N. Origins of the state mental hospital: A case study. *Bulletin of the Menninger Clinic* 29 (1965): 1-19.

Grob, G. N. The state mental hospital in mid-nineteenth century America. *American Psychologist* 21 (1966): 510-23.

Guerney, B. J., Jr. *Psychotherapeutic agents: New roles for nonprofessionals, parents and teachers*. New York: Holt, Rinehart, and Winston, 1969.

Gunther, B. *Sense relaxation. Below your mind*. New York: Collier, 1968.

Gunther, B. *What to do till the Messiah comes*. New York: Collier, 1971.

Gurin, G., Veroff, J., and Feld, S. *Americans view their mental health*. New York: Basic Books, 1960.

Gusfield, J. R. *Symbolic crusade: Status politics and the American temperance movement*. Urbana, Ill.: University of Illinois Press, 1963.

Gusfield, J. R. On legislating morals: the symbolic process of designating deviance. *California Law Review* 56 (1968): 54-73.

Gustaitis, R. *Turning on*. New York: New American Library, 1969.

Hale, E. E. *If, yes, and perhaps*. Boston: Ticknor and Fields, 1868.

Haley, J. *Strategies of psychotherapy*. New York: Grune and Stratton, 1963.

Hanford, D. B. Life crisis viewed as opportunity. *The Bulletin* 9 (1965): 87-91. Division of Mental Health, State of Washington.

Hanford, D. B. Ecological psychology and treatment. *The Bulletin* 11 (1967): 1-11. Division of Mental Health, State of Washington.

Harney, M. L., and Cross, J. C. *The narcotic officer's handbook*. Springfield, Ill.: C. C. Thomas, 1961.

Haskell, A., In collaboration with Nouvel, W. *Diaghileff. His artistic and private life*. London: Victor Gollancz, 1935.

Hayter, A. *Opium and the Romantic imagination*. Berkeley: University of California Press, 1970.

Hazelton, P. Trailing the founders, part 1. On being a second-generation Bruder. *This Magazine is about Schools* 42 (1970): 11-41.

Hediger, H. *Wild animals in captivity.* New York: Dover, 1964.

Heidegger, M. *Being and time.* New York: Harper & Row, 1962.

Heinlein, R. A. *Stranger in a strange land.* New York: Berkeley Publishing Corp., 1969.

Henderson, D. K., and Gillespie, R. D. *Textbook of psychiatry.* London: Oxford University Press, 1927.

Hoffman, F. J. *Freudianism and the literary mind.* 2nd ed. Baton Rouge, La.: Louisiana State University Press, 1957.

Hoffman, M. *The gay world; male homosexuality and the social creation of evil.* New York: Basic Books, 1968.

Hollingshead, A. B., and Redlich, F. C. *Social class and mental illness.* New York: Wiley, 1958.

Holzberg, J. Introduction. In Braginsky, B. M., Braginsky, D. D., and Ring, K., *Methods of madness. The mental hospital as a last resort,* pp. 1-12. New York: Holt, Rinehart, and Winston, 1969.

Horney, K. *Neurosis and human growth: The struggle toward self-realization.* New York: Norton, 1950.

Howard, J. *Please touch: a guided tour of the human potential movement.* New York: McGraw-Hill, 1970.

Hunt, H. F. Problems in the interpretation of "experimental neurosis." *Psychological Reports* 15 (1964): 27-35.

Hurley, R. *Poverty and mental retardation: a causal relationship.* New York: Random House, 1969.

Illich, I. CICLO Lectures, Summer, 1970. CIDOC Cuaderno no. 1007. Cuernavaca, Mexico: CIDOC, 1970.

Jackson, S. The lottery. In Hyman, S. E., (ed.), *Come along with me,* pp. 225-33. New York: Viking, 1968.

Jacobsen, E. *Progressive relaxation.* Chicago: University of Chicago Press, 1938.

James, W. *The principles of psychology.* 2 vols. New York: Dover, 1950.

Janov, A. *The primal scream; primal therapy: the cure for neurosis.* New York: Putnam, 1970.

Jaspers, K. *General psychopathology.* Chicago: University of Chicago Press, 1963.

Jones, R. E. Nijinsky and Til Eulenspiegel. In Magriel, P. (ed.) *Nijinsky: An illustrated monograph,* pp. 45-60. New York: Holt, 1946.

Jones, R. Beyond behaviorism. Review of *Personal causation* by Richard de Charms. *Contemporary Psychology* 15 (1970): 741-42.

Jourard, S. M. *Personal adjustment.* New York: Macmillan, 1958.

Kallmann, F. J. *Heredity in health and mental disorder; principles of psychiatric genetics in the light of comparative twin studies.* New York: Norton, 1953.

Kanfer, F. H., and Phillips, J. S. *Learning foundations of behavior therapy.* New York: Wiley, 1970.

Kaplan, B. *The inner world of mental illness.* New York: Harper & Row, 1964.

Kaplan, J. *Marijuana: the new Prohibition.* New York: World, 1970.

Karpf, F. B. *The psychology and psychotherapy of Otto Rank.* New York: Philosophical Library, 1953.

Karsavina, T. *Theatre Street.* rev. ed. New York: Dutton, 1961.

Keen, E. *Three faces of being: toward an existential clinical psychology.* New York: Appleton-Century-Crofts, 1970.

Keen, S. My new carnality. *Psychology Today* 4 (1970): 59-61.

Keleman, S. The body, Eros and consciousness. Mimeographed. 1970, n. p.

Keleman, S. *Sexuality, self and survival. A bio-energetic perspective.* San Francisco: Lodestar Press, 1971.

Keniston, K. *Young radicals; notes on committed youth.* New York: Harcourt, Brace and World, 1968.

Kiev, A. *Curanderismo. Mexican-American folk psychiatry.* New York: Free Press, 1968.

Kinsey, A. C., Pomeroy, W. B., and Martin, C. E. *Sexual behavior in the human male.* Philadelphia: Saunders, 1948.

Klein, M. H., Dittmann, A. T., Parloff, M. B., and Gill, M. B. Behavior therapy: Observations and reflections. *Journal of Consulting and Clinical Psychology* 33 (1969): 259-66.

Koch, K. *Wishes, lies, and dreams; teaching children to write poetry.* New York: Chelsea House, 1970.

Kochno, B. *Diaghilev and the Ballets Russes.* New York: Harper & Row, 1970.

Köhler, W. *Gestalt psychology.* New York: Liveright, 1947.

Kohn, M. L. *Class and conformity: a study in values.* Homewood, Ill.: Dorsey, 1969.

Kolb, L. Drug addiction as a public health problem. *The Scientific Monthly* 48 (1939): 391-400.

Kosinski, J. N. *The painted bird.* New York: Pocket Books, 1966.

Kraditor, A. S. *Up from the pedestal.* Chicago: Quadrangle, 1968.

Krasner, L., and Ullmann, L. P. (eds.) *Research in behavior modification.* New York: Holt, Rinehart, and Winston, 1965.

Kringlen, E. Schizophrenia in twins: an epidemiological-clinical study. *Psychiatry* 29 (1966): 172-84.

Kuhn, T. S. *The structure of scientific revolutions.* Chicago: University of Chicago Press, 1962.

Laing, R. D. *The politics of experience and the bird of paradise.* London: Penguin, 1967.

Laing, R. D., *The divided self.* New York: Pantheon, 1969.

Laing, R. D., and Esterson, A. *Sanity, madness and the family.* 2nd ed. London: Tavistock Publications, 1970.

Landis, C., and Hunt, W. A. *The startle pattern.* New York: Farrar and Rinehart, 1939.

Leifer, R. *In the name of mental health.* New York: Science House, 1969.

Leighton, A. H. *My name is legion; foundations for a theory of man in relation to culture.* New York: Basic Books, 1959.

Leonard, G. B. *Education and ecstasy.* New York: Dell, 1968.

Lewin, K. The conflict between Aristotelian and Galileian modes of thought in contemporary psychology, in *A dynamic theory of personality: selected papers,* pp. 1-42. New York: McGraw-Hill, 1935.

Lidz, T., Fleck, S., and Cornelison, A. R. *Schizophrenia and the family.* New York: International Universities Press, 1965.

Lifar, S. Nijinsky revisited. *Living Age* 356 (1939): 540-43.

Lilly, J. C. *Center of the cyclone: an autobiography of inner space.* New York: Julian, 1972.

Limpus, L. The liberation of women. *This Magazine is about Schools* 3 (1969): 60-74.

Lindesmith, A. R. *The addict and the law.* Bloomington: Indiana University Press, 1965.

Lindner, R. M. *The fifty-minute hour: a collection of true psychoanalytic tales.* New York: Rinehart, 1955.

Lowen, A. *The betrayal of the body.* New York: Macmillan, 1967.

Lowen, A. *The language of the body.* New York: Collier, 1971.

Lyons, J. Existential therapy: fact, hope, fiction. *Journal of Abnormal and Social Psychology* 62 (1961): 242-49.

Lyons, J. *Psychology and the measure of man.* New York: Free Press, 1963.

Lyons, J. *A primer of experimental psychology.* New York: Harper & Row, 1965.

Lyons, J. Prejudice in social science. *Midstream* 12 (May 1966): 21-34.

Lyons, J. Paleolithic aesthetics: the psychology of cave art. *Journal of Aesthetics and Art Criticism* 26 (1967): 107-14.

MacKinnon, D. W. Personality and the realization of creative potential. *American Psychologist* 20 (1965): 273-81.

MacLane, M. *The story of Mary MacLane.* Milwaukee: Herbert S. Stone Co., 1902.

MacLeish, A. *Collected Poems 1917-1952.* Boston: Houghton, Mifflin Co., 1933.

Magriel, P. (ed.) *Nijinsky: an illustrated monograph.* New York: Holt, 1946.

Mailer, N. *The prisoner of sex.* Boston: Little, Brown, 1971.

Marin, P. Introduction. In Keleman, S., *Sexuality, self and survival,* pp. 7-20. San Francisco: Lodestar Press, 1971.

Maslow, A. H. *Motivation and personality.* New York: Harper, 1954.

Maslow, A. H. *Toward a psychology of being.* Princeton, N. J.: Van Nostrand, 1962.

Matarazzo, J. D. Some national developments in the utilization of nontraditional mental health manpower. *American Psychologist* 26 (1971): 363-72.

May, R. Contributions of existential psychotherapy. In May, R., Angel, E., and Ellenberger, H. F. (eds.), *Existence,* pp. 37-91. New York: Basic Books, 1958.

May, R., Angel, E., and Ellenberger, H. F. (eds.) *Existence.* New York: Basic Books, 1958.

McKellar, P. *Experience and behaviour.* Harmondsworth, England: Penguin, 1968.

McWhirter, N., and McWhirter, R. *Guinness book of world records.* New York: Bantam, 1971.

Mendel, W. M. The phenomenon of interpretation. *American Journal of Psychoanalysis* 24 (1964): 184-89.

Mendel, W. M. Brief hospitalization techniques. *Current psychiatric therapies* 6 (1966): 310-16.

Mendel, W. M., and Rapport, S. Determinants of the decision for psychiatric hospitalization *Archives of General Psychiatry* 20 (1969): 321-28.

Menninger, K., with Mayman, M., and Pruyser, P. *The vital balance; the life process in mental health and illness.* New York: Viking, 1963.

Merleau-Ponty, M. *The structure of behavior.* Boston: Beacon Press, 1963.

Miller, S. *Hot Springs, or the true adventures of the first New York Jewish literary intellectual in the Human Potential movement.* New York: Viking, 1971.

Mishler, E. G., and Waxler, N. E. *Interaction in families: An experimental study of family processes and schizophrenia.* New York: Wiley, 1968.

Moreno, J. L. Psychodrama. In Arieti, S. (ed.), *American handbook of psychiatry.* vol. 3, pp. 1375-96. New York: Basic Books, 1959.

Moustakas, C. (ed.) *The self.* New York: Harper, 1956.

Moustakas, C. *Loneliness.* Englewood Cliffs, N. J.: Prentice-Hall, 1961.

Mowrer, O. H. "Sin," the lesser of two evils. *American Psychologist* 15 (1960): 301-4.

Myers, J. K., Bean, L. L., and Pepper, M. P. Social class and psychiatric disorders: a ten year follow-up. *Journal of Health and Human Behavior* 6 (1965): 74-79.

Myers, J. K., and Roberts, B. H. *Family and class dynamics in mental illness*. New York: Wiley, 1959.

Nabokov, N. The specter of Nijinsky. *Atlantic Monthly* 184, (August 1949): 43-45.

Nabokov, V. *Invitation to a beheading*. New York: Putnam, 1959.

Naranjo, C. Present-centeredness: technique, prescription, and ideal. In Fagan, J., and Shepherd, I. L. (eds.), *Gestalt therapy now; theory, techniques, applications*. Palo Alto, Calif.: Science and Behavior Books, 1970.

Nijinsky, R. *Nijinsky*. New York: Garden City Publishing Co., 1941.

Nijinsky, R. *The last years of Nijinsky*. New York: Simon and Schuster, 1952.

Nijinsky, R. (ed.) *The diary of Waslaw Nijinsky*. Berkeley: University of California Press, 1968.

Noyes, A. P. *Modern clinical psychiatry*. Philadelphia: Saunders, 1934.

Opler, M. K. *Culture and social psychiatry*. New York: Atherton Press, 1967.

Park, R. E., and Burgess, E. W. *Introduction to the science of sociology*. Chicago: University of Chicago Press, 1924.

Pasamanick, B., Scarpitti, F. R., and Dinitz, S. *Schizophrenics in the community: an experimental study in the prevention of hospitalization*. New York: Appleton-Century-Crofts, 1967.

Penzer, N. M. *The harem*. Philadelphia: Lippincott, 1936.

Perls, F. S. Gestalt therapy. In Otto, H. A. (ed.), *Explorations in human potentialities*, chap. 35. Springfield, Ill.: Chas. C. Thomas, 1966.

Perls, F. S. Group vs. individual therapy. *ETC.: A Review of General Semantics* 24 (1967): 306-12.

Perls, F. S. *Gestalt therapy verbatim* (Stevens, J. O., ed.) Lafayette, Calif.: Real People Press, 1969 (a).

Perls, F. S. *In and out the garbage pail*. Lafayette, Calif.: Real People Press, 1969(b).

Perls, L. One Gestalt therapist's approach. In Fagan, J., and Shepherd, I. L. (eds.), *Gestalt therapy now; theory, techniques, applications*, pp. 125-29. Palo Alto, Calif.: Science and Behavior Books, 1970.

Pesso, A. *Movement in psychotherapy. Psychomotor techniques and training*. New York: New York University Press, 1969.

Plog, S. C., and Edgerton, R. B. (eds.) *Changing perspectives in mental illness*. New York: Holt, Rinehart, and Winston, 1969.

Pope-Hennessy, J. *The portrait in the Renaissance*. Princeton: Princeton University Press, 1963. Bollingen Series xxxv, No. 12.

Rakusin, J., and Fierman, L. Five assumptions for treating chronic psychotics. *Mental Hospitals* 14 (1963): 140-48.

Ram Dass, B. *Be here now*. San Cristobal, N. M.: Lama Foundation, 1971. Distributed by Crown Publishing Co., New York.

Rank, O. *Art and artist: Creative urge and personality development*. New York: Knopf, 1932.

Rank, O. *Will therapy and truth and reality*. New York: Knopf, 1945.

Raush, H. L., and Raush, C. L. *The Halfway House movement: A search for sanity*. New York: Appleton-Century-Crofts, 1968.

Réage, P. *Story of O*. New York: Grove, 1965.

Reed, R. R., Jr. *Bedlam on the Jacobean stage*. Cambridge, Mass.: Harvard University Press, 1952.

Reich, W. *The function of the orgasm*. New York: Bantam, 1967, Noonday, 1973.

Reich, W. *Character-analysis*. 3rd ed. New York: Noonday Press, 1969.

Reik, T. *Listening with the third ear. The inner experience of a psychoanalyst*. New York: Farrar, Straus, 1949.

Reps, P. (comp.) *Zen flesh, Zen bones*. Garden City, N. Y.: Doubleday (n.d.)

Rimland, B. *Infantile autism*. New York: Appleton-Century-Crofts, 1964.

Robinson, E. A. *Collected poems*. New York: Macmillan, 1937.

Rogers, C. R. *Client-centered therapy: its current practice, implications and theory*. Boston: Houghton-Mifflin, 1951.

Rogers, C. R. Persons or science? a philosophical question. *American Psychologist* 10 (1955): 267-78.

Rogers, C. R. The necessary and sufficient conditions of therapeutic personality change. *Journal of Consulting Psychology* 21 (1957): 95-103.

Rogers, C. R. A theory of therapy, personality, and interpersonal relations as developed in client-centered framework. In Koch, S. (ed.), *Psychology: A study of a science. vol. 3*. New York: McGraw-Hill, 1959.

Rogers, C. R. *Carl Rogers on encounter groups*. New York: Harper & Row, 1970.

Rolf, I. P. Structural integration. Gravity, an unexplored factor in a more human use of human beings. *The Journal of the Institute for the Comparative Study of History, Philosophy and the Sciences* 1 (1963): 3-20.

Rosen, G. *Madness in society. Chapters in the historical sociology of mental illness*. Chicago: University of Chicago Press, 1968.

Rosenbaum, C. P. *The meaning of madness: Symptomatology, sociology, biology and therapy of the schizophrenias*. New York: Science House, 1970.

Rosenthal, B. G. *Images of man*. New York: Basic Books, 1970.

Rosenthal D. (ed.) *The Genain quadruplets. A case study and theoretical analysis of heredity and environment in schizophrenia*. New York: Basic Books, 1963.

Rosenthal, D. *Genetic theory and abnormal behavior*. New York: McGraw-Hill, 1970.

Roth, P. *Portnoy's complaint*. New York: Random House, 1969.

Rubenstein, E. A., and Parloff, M. B. (eds.) *Research in psychotherapy*. Washington, D. C.: American Psychological Association, 1959.

Sagarin, E. *The anatomy of dirty words*. New York: Lyle Stuart, 1962.

Salinger, J. D. Teddy, in *Nine stories*, pp. 253-302. Boston: Little Brown, 1952.

Sartre, J-P. *Anti-semite and Jew*. New York: Schocken, 1948.

Sartre, J-P. *Being and nothingness. An essay on phenomenological ontology*. New York: Philosophical Library, 1956.

Sartre, J-P. *Saint Genet: Actor and martyr*. New York: George Braziller, 1963.

Schachtel, E. *Metamorphosis*. New York: Basic Books, 1959.

Schmidt, (Master) Franz. *A hangman's diary*. Keller, A. (ed.) London: Phillip Allan, 1928.

Schutz, W. C. *Joy. Expanding human awareness*. New York: Grove, 1967.

Schutz, W. C. *Here comes everybody: body-mind and encounter culture*. New York: Harper & Row, 1971.

Sechehaye, M. *Autobiography of a schizophrenic girl*. New York: Grune and Stratton, 1951.

Selver, C. Report on work in sensory awareness and total functioning. In Otto, H. A., (ed.), *Explorations in human potentialities*, pp. 487-504. Springfield, Ill.: C. C. Thomas, 1966.

Selye, H. *The stress of life*. New York: McGraw-Hill, 1956.

Sharma, S. L. A historical background of the development of nosology in psychiatry and psychology. *American Psychologist* 25 (1970): 248-53.

Shattock, E. H. *An experiment in mindfulness. An English admiral's experiences in a Buddhist monastery.* New York: Dutton, 1960.

Siirala, M. Schizophrenia: a human situation. *American Journal of Psychoanalysis* 23 (1963): 39-58.

Simon, W. B. On reluctance to leave the public mental hospital. *Psychiatry* 28 (1965): 145-56.

Singer, J. L. *Daydreaming; an introduction to the experimental study of inner experience.* New York: Random House, 1966.

Skinner, B. F. *Beyond freedom and dignity.* New York: Knopf, 1971.

Smith, L. P. *The English language.* New York: Holt, 1912.

Smith, T. V. (ed.) *From Thales to Plato.* 2nd ed. Chicago: University of Chicago Press, 1956.

Spiegelberg, H. *The phenomenological movement. A historical introduction.* 2 vols. The Hague: Martinus Nijhoff, 1960.

Spitz, R. A. Unhappy and fatal outcomes of emotional deprivation and stress in infancy. In Galdston, I. (ed.), *Beyond the germ theory*, pp. 120-32. New York: Health Education Council, 1954.

Srole, L., Langner, T. S., Michael, S. T., Opler, M. K., and Rennie, T. A. C. *Mental health in the metropolis. vol. 1.* New York: McGraw-Hill, 1962.

Stanton, A., and Schwartz, M. *The mental hospital.* New York: Basic Books, 1954.

Stephen [Stephen Gaskins]. *Monday night class.* Santa Rosa, Calif.: Book Farm, 1970.

Stevens, B. *Don't push the river.* Lafayette, Calif.: Real People Press, 1969.

Stewart, K. Dream theory in Malaya. In Tart, C. T. (ed.), *Altered states of consciousness*, pp. 159-67. New York: Wiley, 1969.

Straus, E. W. Rheoscopic studies of expression. Methodology of approach. *American Journal of Psychiatry* 108 (1951): 439-43.

Straus, E. W. The upright posture. *Psychiatric Quarterly* 26 (1952): 529-61.

Straus, E. W. *Psychologie der menschlichen Welt.* Berlin: Springer-Verlag, 1960.

Straus, E. W. Phenomenology of hallucinations. In West, L. J. (ed.), *Hallucinations*, pp. 220-32. New York: Grune and Stratton, 1962.

Strupp, H. H., Wallace, M. S., and Wogan, M. Psychotherapy experience in retrospect: questionnaire survey of former patients and their therapists. *Psychological Monographs: General and Applied* 78 (1964): 45.

Suzuki, S. *Zen mind, beginner's mind.* New York: Walker-Weatherhill, 1970.

Szasz, T. S. The myth of mental illness. *American Psychologist* 15 (1960): 113-18.

Szasz, T. S. The moral dilemma of psychiatry: autonomy or heteronomy. *American Journal of Psychiatry* 121 (1964): 521-28.

Szasz, T. S. Science and public policy: the crime of involuntary mental hospitalization. *Medical Opinion and Review* 4 (May 1968): 25-35.

Szasz, T. S. *The manufacture of madness. A comparative study of the Inquisition and the mental health movement.* New York: Harper & Row, 1970.

Tart, C. T. (ed.) *Altered states of consciousness.* New York: Wiley, 1969.

Thompson, C. *Psychoanalysis: Evolution and development.* New York: Hermitage House, 1950.

Towbin, A. P. Self-care unit: some lessons in institutional power. *Journal of Consulting and Clinical Psychology* 33 (1969): 561-70.

Trumbull, C. G. *Anthony Comstock, fighter*. New York: Revell, 1913.

Trungpa, C. *Meditation in action*. Berkeley, Calif.: Shambala, 1969.

Ullmann, L. P., and Krasner, L. (eds.) *Case studies in behavior modification*. New York: Holt, Rinehart, and Winston, 1965.

Vail, D. J. The mental hospital in a free society. *Psychiatric Quarterly* 38 (1964): 341-47.

Villiers, A. The man who mapped the Pacific. *National Geographic* 140 (September 1971): 297-344.

Wallen, R. Gestalt theory and Gestalt psychology. In Fagan, J., and Shepherd, I. L. (eds.), *Gestalt therapy now; theory, techniques, applications*. Palo Alto, Calif.: Science and Behavior Books, 1970.

Waller, A. R. (ed.) *The works of Francis Beaumont and John Fletcher*. vol. 3. Cambridge: University Press, 1908.

Walsh, J. Methadone and heroin addiction: Rehabilitation without a "cure." *Science* 168 (May 8, 1970): 684-86.

Watson, J. B. Psychology as the behaviorist views it. *Psychological Review* 20 (1913): 158-77.

Watts, A. W. *Psychotherapy East and West*. New York: Ballantine, 1970.

Weil, A. T., Zinberg, N. E., and Nelsen, J. M. Clinical and psychological effects of marihuana in man. *Science* 162 (December 13, 1968): 1234-42.

Weissman, H. N., Goldschmid, M. L., and Stein, D. D. Psychotherapeutic orientation and training: their relation to the practices of clinical psychologists. *Journal of Consulting and Clinical Psychology* 37 (1971): 31-37.

Wenrich, W. W. *A primer of behavior modification*. Belmont, Calif.: Brooks/Cole, 1970.

Whitman, W. Leaves of grass. In Holloway, E. (ed.), *Complete poetry and selected prose and letters of Walt Whitman*. New York: Random House, 1938.

Wilshire, G. *William James and phenomenology: a study of the "Principles of Psychology."* Bloomington, Ind.: Indiana University Press, 1968.

Wilson, G. F. *Saints and strangers*. New York: Ballantine, 1965.

Winick, C. Physician narcotic addicts. *Social Problems* 9 (1961): 174-86.

Wolff, K. H. Surrender and aesthetic experience. *Review of Existential Psychology and Psychiatry* 3 (1963): 209-26.

Wolff, W. *The expression of personality*. New York: Harper, 1943.

Wolpe, J. Desensitization for phobia. tape, n.d. *American Academy of Psychotherapists Tape Library. vol. 30*. Drs. Irwin and Francis Rothman, 6420 City Line Ave., Philadelphia, Penn. 19151.

Wolpe, J. *The practice of behavior therapy*. New York: Pergamon Press, 1969.

Wolpe, J. Desensitization for phobia. Tape, n.d. *American Academy of Psychotherapists Review* 78 (1971): 341-43.

Wolpe, J., and Lazarus, A. A. *Behavior therapy techniques*. New York: Pergamon Press, 1966.

Young, W. *Eros denied. Sex in Western society*. New York: Grove, 1964.

# index

73  74  75  7  6  5  4  3  2  1